OUTDOORS

D0092644

101 GREAT HIKES
OF THE SAN FRANCISCO BAY AREA

ANN MARIE BROWN

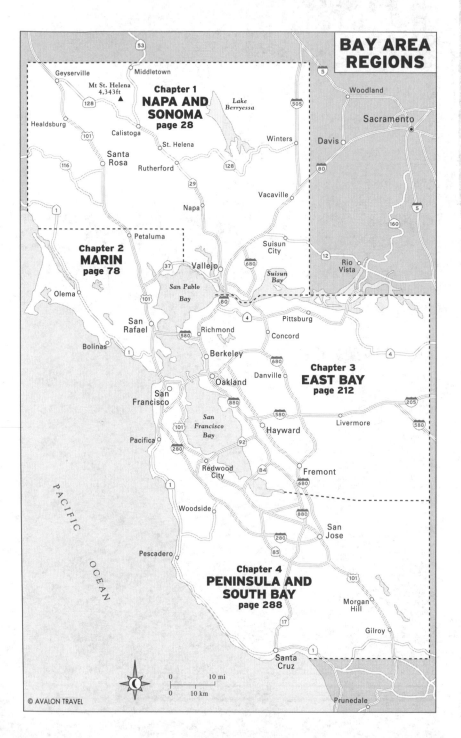

BAY AREA REGIONS

Chapter 1
NAPA AND SONOMA
page 28

Chapter 2
MARIN
page 78

Chapter 3
EAST BAY
page 212

Chapter 4
PENINSULA AND SOUTH BAY
page 288

Geyserville
Middletown
Mt St. Helena 4,343ft
Healdsburg
Calistoga
Santa Rosa
St. Helena
Rutherford
Napa
Petaluma
Olema
Vallejo
San Rafael
Bolinas
Richmond
Berkeley
Oakland
San Francisco
San Francisco Bay
Pacifica
Redwood City
Woodside
Pescadero

Lake Berryessa
Winters
Vacaville
Suisun City
Suisun Bay
San Pablo Bay
Pittsburg
Concord
Danville
Hayward
Fremont
Livermore
San Jose
Morgan Hill
Gilroy
Santa Cruz
Prunedale

Woodland
Sacramento
Davis
Rio Vista

PACIFIC OCEAN

0   10 mi
0   10 km

© AVALON TRAVEL

Contents

How to Use This Book

ABOUT THE MAPS

This book is divided into chapters based on regions that are within close reach of the city; an overview map of these regions precedes the table of contents. Each chapter begins with a region map that shows the locations and numbers of the trails listed in that chapter.

Each trail profile is also accompanied by a detailed trail map that shows the hike route.

Map Symbols

-------	Featured Trail	80	Interstate Freeway	○	City/Town
--------	Other Trail	101	U.S. Highway	✗✗	Airfield/Airport
:::::::::::::::	Expressway	21	State Highway	⚲	Golf Course
:::::::::::::::	Primary Road	66	County Highway	⟲	Waterfall
════════	Secondary Road	★	Point of Interest		Swamp
=========	Unpaved Road	℗	Parking Area	▲	Mountain
....	Ferry	❶	Trailhead	▲	Park
─ · ──── ·	National Border	▲	Campground	)(	Pass
───── ──	State Border	▪	Other Location	✦	Unique Natural Feature

ABOUT THE TRAIL PROFILES

Each profile includes a narrative description of the trail's setting and terrain. This description also typically includes mile-by-mile hiking directions, as well as information about the trail's highlights and unique attributes.

The trails marked by the **BEST** ◖ symbol are highlighted in the author's Best Hikes list.

Options

If alternative routes are available, this section is used to provide information on side trips or note how to shorten or lengthen the hike.

Directions

This section provides detailed driving directions to the trailhead from the city center or from the intersection of major highways. When public transportation is available, instructions will be noted here.

Information and Contact

This section provides information on fees, facilities, and access restrictions for the trail. It also includes the name of the land management agency or organization that oversees the trail, as well as an address, phone number, and website if available.

ABOUT THE ICONS

The icons in this book are designed to provide at-a-glance information on special features for each trail.

- The trail climbs to a high overlook with wide views.
- The trail offers an opportunity for wildlife watching.
- The trail offers an opportunity for bird-watching
- The trail features wildflower displays in spring.
- The trail visits a beach.

- The trail travels to a waterfall.
- The trail visits a historic site.
- The trail is open to snowshoers in winter.
- Dogs are allowed.
- The trail is appropriate for children.
- The trail is wheelchair accessible.
- The trailhead can be accessed via public transportation.

ABOUT THE DIFFICULTY RATING

Each profile includes a difficulty rating, from Easy to Butt-Kicker. The ratings are defined below. Remember that the difficulty level for any trail can change considerably due to weather or trail conditions, so always phone ahead to check the current state of any trail.

Easy: Easy hikes are typically less than 5 miles long and have less than 500 feet of elevation change (nearly level). They are generally suitable for families with small children or hikers seeking a mellow stroll.

Easy/Moderate: Easy/Moderate hikes are 3–8 miles round-trip and have 400–800 feet of elevation gain. They are generally suitable for families with active children (age 6 and older) and reasonably fit hikers.

Moderate: Moderate hikes are 6–9 miles round-trip and have 700–1,500 feet of elevation change. They are generally suitable for fit adults and children.

Strenuous: Strenuous hikes are 7–13 miles round-trip and have an elevation change of more than 1,500 feet. They are suitable for very fit hikers who are seeking a workout.

Butt-Kicker: Butt-Kicker hikes are 10–12 miles round-trip and have an elevation change of 3,000 feet or more. They are suitable only for advanced hikers who are very physically fit.

INTRODUCTION

Author's Note

I'm a nature lover, a wildlife-watcher, a committed hiker, and a card-carrying member of the Sierra Club and Audubon Society. I run my life's appointment calendar by the timing of the wildflower bloom, the flow of waterfalls, and the show of autumn colors. I spend my work days and play days doing basically the same thing—exploring the natural world.

This being the case, it may seem odd that I chose to write a book about a large urban area packed with nearly seven million people. But the San Francisco Bay Area is the wildest metropolitan area in the United States, with precious swaths of open space surrounding and interspersed amid its urban and suburban core. Although grizzly bears no longer roam the Bay Area as they did 150 years ago, coyotes still gallop across the grasslands, herds of tule elk wander the coastal hills, badgers build their underground dens, and mountain lions and bobcats stalk their prey. Elephant seals still breed on the Bay Area's beaches, river otters ply the waterways, and peregrine falcons, American kestrels, and golden and bald eagles soar overhead.

In the course of hiking the 101 trails in this book, I saw all of these creatures and more.

If you hike much in the Bay Area, you will be awed by the beauty and grace of centuries-old virgin redwoods. You'll wonder at the sight of rare and precious wild-flowers, some of which grow here and nowhere else in the world. Your ears will be filled with the sound of crashing surf against miles of jagged coastal bluffs. You'll gaze at waterfalls coursing down basalt cliffs, pouring over sandstone precipices, and even dashing to the sea. You'll stand on summits and look down thousands of feet to the valleys below. In autumn, you'll watch black oaks and big-leaf maples turn bright gold, and in winter, you'll see a dusting of snow fall on the Bay Area's high peaks and ridges.

Quite possibly, you'll wind up spending some of the best days of your life on Bay Area trails. I know I have.

Speaking of hiking, take a look out the window. Chances are good that it's a nice day for a walk. See you out there.

—Ann Marie Brown

Best Hikes

Can't decide where to hike this weekend? I've grouped these unique Bay Area hikes into some of my favorite categories.

◖ Best for Bird-Watching

Lake Ilsanjo Loop, Annadel State Park, Napa and Sonoma, page 40

Marsh and South Pasture Loop, Rush Ranch, Solano Land Trust, Napa and Sonoma, page 72

Abbotts Lagoon, Point Reyes National Seashore, Marin, page 90

Estero Trail to Sunset Beach, Point Reyes National Seashore, Marin, page 100

Kent, Griffin, and Zumie Loop Trails, Audubon Canyon Ranch/Bolinas Lagoon Preserve, Marin, page 132

Lagoon Trail, Golden Gate National Recreation Area, Marin, page 187

Rock City and Wall Point Summit, Mount Diablo State Park, East Bay, page 251

Bayview and Red Hill Loop, Coyote Hills Regional Park, East Bay, page 266

Sunol Loop Tour, Sunol Regional Wilderness, East Bay, page 273

Alcatraz Island's Agave Trail, Golden Gate National Recreation Area, Peninsula and South Bay, page 294

Sequoia Audubon Trail, Pescadero Marsh Natural Preserve, Peninsula and South Bay, page 353

◖ Best Peak Vistas

Bald Mountain Loop, Sugarloaf Ridge State Park, Napa and Sonoma, page 43

Mount St. Helena, Robert Louis Stevenson State Park, Napa and Sonoma, page 59

Table Rock, Robert Louis Stevenson State Park, Napa and Sonoma, page 63

Barnabe Peak Loop, Samuel P. Taylor State Park, Marin, page 121

Verna Dunshee Trail and Gardner Lookout, Mount Tamalpais State Park, Marin, page 152

Coastal Trail and Hill 88 Loop, Golden Gate National Recreation Area, Marin, page 190

North Ridge and Sunset Trail Loop, Angel Island State Park, Marin, page 204

Wildcat Peak and Laurel Canyon Loop, Tilden Regional Park, East Bay, page 224

Mount Diablo Grand Loop, Mount Diablo State Park, East Bay, page 247

Mission Peak, Mission Peak Regional Preserve, East Bay, page 269

Montara Mountain Summit, McNee Ranch State Park/Montara State Beach, Peninsula and South Bay, page 309

【 Best Redwood Forests

Matt Davis and Steep Ravine Loop, Mount Tamalpais State Park, Marin, page 156

Bootjack, Ben Johnson, and Hillside Trail Loop, Muir Woods National Monument and Mount Tamalpais State Park, Marin, page 176

Stream, Fern, and West Ridge Trail Loop, Redwood Regional Park, East Bay, page 234

Purisima Grand Loop, Purisima Creek Redwoods Open Space Preserve, Peninsula and South Bay, page 316

Heritage Grove and Hiker's Hut Loop, Sam McDonald County Park, Peninsula and South Bay, page 339

Peters Creek Grove, Portola Redwoods State Park, Peninsula and South Bay, page 342

Berry Creek, Silver, and Golden Falls, Big Basin Redwoods State Park, Peninsula and South Bay, page 349

【 Best Short Backpacking Trips

Sky Trail and Woodward Valley Loop, Point Reyes National Seashore, Marin, page 108

Coast, Fire Lane, and Laguna Loop, Point Reyes National Seashore, Marin, page 111

North Ridge and Sunset Trail Loop, Angel Island State Park, Marin, page 204

Stewartville and Ridge Trail Loop, Black Diamond Mines Regional Preserve, East Bay, page 243

Black Mountain and Stevens Creek Loop, Monte Bello Open Space Preserve, Peninsula and South Bay, page 333

Peters Creek Grove, Portola Redwoods State Park, Peninsula and South Bay, page 342

Saratoga Gap and Ridge Trail Loop, Castle Rock State Park, Peninsula and South Bay, page 345

Berry Creek, Silver, and Golden Falls, Big Basin Redwoods State Park, Peninsula and South Bay, page 349

Butano Grand Loop, Butano State Park, Peninsula and South Bay, page 356

Flat Frog, Middle Ridge, and Fish Trail Loop, Henry W. Coe State Park, Peninsula and South Bay, page 370

◖ Best Waterfalls

Zim Zim Falls, Knoxville Wildlife Area, Napa and Sonoma, page 66

Barnabe Peak Loop, Samuel P. Taylor State Park, Marin, page 121

Bass Lake, Double Point, and Alamere Falls, Point Reyes National Seashore, Marin, page 129

Cascade Canyon, Marin County Open Space District, Marin, page 135

Carson Falls, Marin Municipal Water District, Marin, page 142

Cataract Trail to Cataract Falls, Marin Municipal Water District, Marin, page 145

Back and Donner Canyon Loop, Mount Diablo State Park, East Bay, page 254

Murietta Falls, Ohlone Regional Wilderness, East Bay, page 280

Brooks Falls Loop, San Pedro Valley County Park, Peninsula and South Bay, page 306

Saratoga Gap and Ridge Trail Loop, Castle Rock State Park, Peninsula and South Bay, page 345

Berry Creek, Silver, and Golden Falls, Big Basin Redwoods State Park, Peninsula and South Bay, page 349

Waterfall Loop Trail, Uvas Canyon County Park, Peninsula and South Bay, page 374

Loma Prieta Grade and Bridge Creek Loop, The Forest of Nisene Marks State Park, Peninsula and South Bay, page 391

◖ Best Wildflower Displays

Pomo Canyon Trail, Sonoma Coast State Park, Napa and Sonoma, page 30

Goodspeed Trail to Gunsight Rock, Sugarloaf Ridge State Park and Hood Mountain Regional Park, Napa and Sonoma, page 46

Chimney Rock, Point Reyes National Seashore, Marin, page 104

Coastal, Cataract, and Old Mine Loop, Mount Tamalpais State Park, Marin, page 164

Phyllis Ellman Trail, Ring Mountain Open Space Preserve, Marin, page 197

Morgan Territory Loop, Morgan Territory Regional Preserve, East Bay, page 260

Sunol Loop Tour, Sunol Regional Wilderness, East Bay, page 273

Summit Loop Trail, San Bruno Mountain State and County Park, Peninsula and South Bay, page 298

Russian Ridge Loop, Russian Ridge Open Space Preserve, Peninsula and South Bay, page 330

◖ Best Wildlife-Watching

Marsh and South Pasture Loop (river otters), Rush Ranch, Solano Land Trust, Napa and Sonoma, page 72

Tomales Point Trail (tule elk), Point Reyes National Seashore, Marin, page 81

Chimney Rock (whales and elephant seals), Point Reyes National Seashore, Marin, page 104

Round Valley Loop (San Joaquin kit fox), Round Valley Regional Preserve, East Bay, page 257

Tidepool Walk (tidepool creatures), Fitzgerald Marine Reserve, Peninsula and South Bay, page 313

Año Nuevo Point Trail (elephant seals), Año Nuevo State Reserve, Peninsula and South Bay, page 359

Antler Point Loop (wild pigs), Joseph D. Grant County Park, Peninsula and South Bay, page 363

Old Landing Cove Trail (sea lions and whales), Wilder Ranch State Park, Peninsula and South Bay, page 388

Hiking Tips

HIKING ESSENTIALS

Food and Water

There's nothing like being hungry or thirsty to spoil a good time, or to make you anxious about getting back to the car. Even if you aren't the least bit hungry or thirsty when you park at the trailhead, you may feel completely different after 45 minutes or more of walking. A small day pack or fanny pack can keep you happily supplied with a couple quarts of water and a few snacks. Always carry more than you think you'll need. If you don't bring your own water, make sure you carry a water filter or purifier so you can obtain water from a natural source, such as a stream or lake. Never, ever drink water from a natural source without first filtering or boiling it. The risk to your health (from *Giardia lamblia* and other microorganisms) is too great. And remember, in the Mediterranean climate of the San Francisco Bay Area, it's unwise to depend on finding natural water sources. A spring or creek that flows with fervor in March may be completely dry by July.

Trail Map

Get a current map of the park or public land where you plan to hike. Maps are available from a variety of resources, including excellent private companies such

© ANN MARIE BROWN

A brief stop along the trail to examine a map can save you time and frustration.

as Tom Harrison Maps or Pease Press, as well as the managing agencies of most parks. Today most park maps are available online, so you can download a free map before starting your hike.

Extra Clothing

On the trail, conditions can change at any time. Not only can the weather suddenly turn windy, foggy, or rainy, but your own body conditions also change: You'll perspire as you hike up a sunny hill and then get chilled at the top of a windy ridge or when you head into shade. Because of this, cotton fabrics don't function well in the outdoors. Once cotton gets wet, it stays wet. Generally, polyester- or silk-blend fabrics dry faster. Some high-tech fabrics will actually wick moisture away from your skin. Invest in a few items of clothing made from these fabrics, and you'll be more comfortable when you hike.

Additionally, always carry a lightweight jacket with you, preferably one that is waterproof and also wind resistant. Put it in your day pack or tie it around your waist. If your jacket isn't waterproof, pack one of the $2, single-use rain ponchos that come in a package the size of a deck of cards (available at most drugstores and outdoor retailers).

It never hurts to carry a pair of lightweight gloves and a hat as well. You never know when you might need them, especially if that notorious Bay Area fog rolls in.

Sunglasses and Sunscreen

The dangers of the sun are well known. Always wear sunglasses and sunscreen, and/or a hat with a wide brim. Put on your sunscreen 30 minutes before you go outdoors so it has time to take effect, and don't forget about your lips. Coat them with lip balm with a high SPF to protect them.

Flashlight

Just in case your hike takes a little longer than you planned and darkness falls, bring at least one flashlight. Mini-flashlights are available everywhere, weigh almost nothing, and can save the day—or night. My favorite is the tiny squeeze flashlights, about the shape and size of a quarter, which you can clip on to any key ring (the Photon Micro-Light is a popular brand). Since these flashlights are so small, carry two or three. That way you never have to worry about the batteries running out of juice.

First-Aid Kit

Unless you're trained in first aid, nothing major is required here, but a few large and small adhesive bandages and moleskin for blisters, antibiotic ointment, ibu-profen, and an Ace bandage can be valuable tools. Also, if you or anyone in your party is allergic to bee stings or anything else in the outdoors, carry the appropriate medication. If you are hiking in an area where you might be bothered by mosquitoes, bring a small bottle of insect repellent.

Emergency Supplies

Many hikers think that if they are just going for a day hike, they don't need to carry anything for emergencies. Think again. Ask yourself this question, "What would I need to have with me if I broke my ankle and had to spend the night outdoors?" Aside from food, water, and other items previously listed, always carry a few basic supplies that will get you through an unplanned night outdoors. Of great use is a Swiss Army–style pocketknife—one with several blades, a can opener, scissors, and tweezers on it. Matches in a waterproof container and a candle will ensure you can always build a fire if you need to. A lightweight space blanket or sleeping bag made of foil-like Mylar film will keep you warm (these can be purchased at outdoors stores, weigh next to nothing, and come in a package about the size of a deck of cards). A whistle and small signal mirror can help you get found if you ever get lost. And if you know how to use a compass, carry one.

ON THE TRAIL
Mountain Lions, Ticks, and Rattlesnakes

All three of these creatures deserve your respect, and it's good to know a little bit about them. Chances are high you will never see a mountain lion, but you just might run into a tick or a snake somewhere.

Mountain lions are almost everywhere in California, but they are very shy and secretive animals, and as a result, are rarely seen. When they do show themselves, they get a lot of media attention. If you're hiking in an area where mountain lions or their tracks have been spotted, remember to keep your children close to you on the trail and your dog leashed. If you see a mountain lion, it will most likely vanish into the landscape as soon as it notices you. If it doesn't, make yourself appear as large and aggressive as possible. Raise your arms, open your jacket, wave a big stick, and speak loudly and firmly or shout. If you have children with you, pick them up off the ground, but try to do so without crouching down or leaning over. (Crouching makes you appear smaller and more submissive, like prey.) Don't turn your back on the cat or run from it, but rather back away slowly and deliberately, always retaining your aggressive pose and continuing to speak loudly.

Ticks are a common problem in the San Francisco Bay Area, especially in the spring months. The easiest way to stay clear of ticks is to wear long pants and long sleeves when you hike, and tuck your pant legs into your socks. But this system isn't foolproof. The darn things sometimes find their way onto your skin no matter what you do. Always check yourself thoroughly when you leave the trail, looking carefully for anything that might be crawling on you. Check your clothes and also your skin underneath. A good friend can be a useful assistant in this endeavor.

Of 850 tick species in the world, 49 are found in California. A very small percentage of the ticks found in the Bay Area carry Lyme disease. Most tick bites cause a sharp sting that will get your attention. But rarely, ticks will bite you without your noticing. If you've been in the outdoors, and then a few days or a week later start to experience flulike symptoms such as headaches, fever, muscle soreness, neck stiffness, or nausea, see a doctor immediately. Tell the doctor you are concerned about possible exposure to ticks and Lyme disease. Another early telltale symptom is a slowly expanding red rash near the tick bite, which appears a week to a month after the bite. Caught in its early stages, Lyme disease is easily treated with antibiotics, but left untreated, it can be severely debilitating.

Eight rattlesnake species are found in California. These members of the pit viper family have wide triangular heads, narrow necks, and rattles on their tails. Rattlesnakes live where it's warm, usually at elevations below 6,000 feet. They are commonly seen in the East Bay hills, but can also be found in cooler places such as western Marin and the San Mateo coast. If you see one, give it plenty of space to get away without feeling threatened. If you're hiking on a nice day, when rattlesnakes are often out sunning themselves on trails and rocks, keep your eyes open for them so you don't step on one or place your hand on one. Be especially on the lookout for rattlesnakes in the spring, when they leave their winter burrows and come out in the sun. Morning is the most common time to see them, as the midday sun is usually too hot for them.

Although rattlesnake bites are painful, they are very rarely fatal. Each year, more than 100 people in California are bitten by rattlesnakes with only one or two fatalities on average. About 25 percent of rattlesnake bites are dry, with no venom injected. Symptoms of bites that do contain venom usually include tingling around the mouth, nausea and vomiting, dizziness, weakness, sweating, and/or chills. If you get bitten by a rattlesnake, your car key—and the nearest telephone—are your best first aid. Call 911 as soon as you can, or have someone drive you to the nearest hospital. Don't panic or run, which can speed the circulation of venom through your system.

Except for a handful of rattlesnake species, no other California snakes are poisonous. Just give them room to slither by.

LONG DISTANCE TRAILS

The Bay Area Ridge Trail: The grand-daddy of Bay Area long distance trails and a 550-mile trail-in-progress, the Bay Area Ridge Trail will eventually circle the entire Bay Area, connecting all nine Bay Area counties. It is designed as a multiuse path for hikers, horseback riders, and mountain bikers. So far, more than 325 miles of trail have been designated. The Bay Area Ridge Trail Council is the volunteer organization putting it all together (www.ridgetrail.org).

Coastal Trail: Running through Point Reyes National Seashore, Mount Tamalpais State Park, and Golden Gate National Recreation Area, the Coastal Trail is a spectacular oceanside route. The only downer is that it isn't contiguous. But no matter; enough of the trail is connected so that you could easily put together a three- or four-day backpacking trip. Also called the Pacific Coast Trail or just the Coast Trail, the Coastal Trail begins in the Marin Headlands near Sausalito and runs continuously to Muir Beach. It then breaks off and begins again near Muir Beach Overlook and Slide Ranch, then runs through Mount Tamalpais State Park.

The most popular section for backpacking is the 15-mile Point Reyes stretch that runs from the Palomarin Trailhead near Bolinas to the Point Reyes Youth Hostel near Limantour Beach. Most people hike it from north to south, ending up at Palomarin. For more information on hiking this stretch of the Coastal Trail, contact Point Reyes National Seashore (415/464-5100, www.nps.gov/pore).

East Bay Skyline National Trail: This 31-mile ridge trail in the East Bay begins near Castro Valley and ends in Richmond. The downside? There are no trail camps, so don't think about making this a backpacking trip. You can make several nice day hikes out of it, though. (The only camping available is at Anthony Chabot Family Campground, near the southern terminus of the trail.) For a free brochure on the East Bay Skyline National Trail, contact the East Bay Regional Park District (888/327-2757, www.ebparks.org).

Ohlone Wilderness Trail: This 29-mile trail runs from Del Valle Regional Park in Livermore to Mission Peak Regional Park in Fremont. Trail camps are located in Sunol Regional Wilderness and Ohlone Regional Wilderness. Highlights of the trail include Rose Peak (3,817 feet) and Murietta Falls. The East Bay Regional Park District (888/327-2757, www.ebparks.org) is the best source of information.

Skyline-to-the-Sea Trail: This book details a short section of the Skyline-to-the-Sea Trail leading to Berry Creek Falls in Big Basin Redwoods State Park, but the trail in its entirety is a 38-mile one-way trek from Saratoga Gap at the junction of Highways 9 and 35 to Waddell Beach at Highway 1 near Davenport. Aside from the beautiful Santa Cruz Mountains scenery, a major plus on this trail is that most of it is downhill. It makes an ideal three- or four-day backpacking trip. Trail camps are conveniently spaced along the route in Castle Rock State Park and Big Basin Redwoods State Park. For more information, contact Big Basin Redwoods State Park (831/338-8860, www.bigbasin.org or www.parks.ca.gov).

Poison Oak

Poison oak is the bane of hikers everywhere, but you can avoid it with a little common sense. Learn to recognize and avoid *Toxicodendron diversilobum,* which produces an itching rash that can last for weeks. If you can't readily identify poison oak, at least remember the old Boy Scout motto: Leaves of three, let them be. But be wary: Poison oak disguises itself in different seasons. In spring and summer when in full leaf, it looks somewhat like wild blackberry bushes. In late summer, its leaves turn bright red. But in winter, the plant loses all or most of its leaves and resembles clusters of bare sticks. Poison oak is poisonous year-round.

Remember the Boy Scout motto: "Leaves of three, let them be."

To avoid poison oak, stay on the trail and watch what you brush up against. If you know you have a bad reaction to poison oak, wear long pants and long sleeves, and remove and wash your clothes immediately after hiking. If you have been exposed to poison oak, you can often prevent a rash from developing by washing thoroughly with soap and water, or with a product like Tecnu, as soon as possible. If you do develop poison oak rash, a relatively new product on the market can help you get rid of it. The product is called Zanfel, and although it costs a small fortune (about $30–40 a bottle), it is available at pharmacies without a prescription. You simply pour it on the rash and the rash vanishes, or at least greatly diminishes. A less expensive product called Biji also works well. Many hikers consider these medications to be the greatest inventions since lightweight hiking boots.

Getting Lost and Getting Found

If you're hiking with a family or group, make sure everybody knows to stay together. If anyone decides to split off from the group for any reason, make sure they have a trail map with them and know how to read it. Also, be sure that everyone in your group knows the key rules about what to do if they get lost:
• Whistle or shout loudly at regular intervals.
• "Hug" a tree or a big rock or bush. Find a noticeable landmark, sit down next

to it, and don't move. Continue to whistle or shout loudly. Lost individuals are easier to find if they stay in one place.

Hiking with Dogs

Dogs are wonderful friends and great companions. But dogs and nature don't always mix well. Bless their furry little hearts, most dogs can't help but disturb wildlife, given half a chance. Even if they don't chase or bark at wildlife, dogs leave droppings that may intimidate other mammals into altering their normal routines. But if kept on a leash, and picked up after, a dog can be the best hiking companion you could ask for.

Dogs are allowed on some trails in the Bay Area and not on others. For many dog owners, it's confusing. When using this book, check the information listing

TRAIL ETIQUETTE

Hiking is a great way to get out of the concrete jungle and into the woods and the wild, to places of natural beauty. Unfortunately, this manner of thinking is shared by millions of people. Following some basic rules of etiquette will ensure that we all get along and keep the outdoors as a place we can enjoy... together.

1. **Enjoy the silence and let nature's sounds prevail.** Keep your voice low and avoid making loud noises. This will increase your chance of encountering wildlife, plus help others enjoy their quiet time in the outdoors.

2. **Be aware of other trail users and yield appropriately.** If you hear someone coming up behind you who clearly is hiking faster than you, stand aside and let them pass. On narrow trails, hikers going downhill should always yield to hikers going uphill. Get out of their way so uphill hikers can keep their momentum as they climb. Also, large groups of hikers should always yield to smaller groups or solo travelers.

3. **Be friendly and polite to other trail users.** A smile or a "hello" as you pass others on the trail is always a good idea. And it may seem obvious, but if someone steps aside to allow you to pass, say "thank you."

4. **Obey all posted signs and trail closures.** Only hike where it's legal. Do not invent "shortcuts" or hike across private property without the express permission of the owner.

5. **Hike only on established trails.** As soon as you walk off a trail, you trample vegetation. Never cut switchbacks; hillside trails are built with switchbacks to keep the slope from eroding. Just a few people cutting switchbacks can destroy a hillside.

6. **Yield to equestrians.** Horses can be badly spooked by just about anything. Always give them plenty of room. If horses are approaching you, stop alongside the trail until they pass. If horses are traveling in your direction and you need to pass them, call out politely to the rider and ask permission. If the horse and rider move off the trail and the rider tells you it's okay, then pass.

under each trail write-up to see whether or not dogs are permitted on a specific trail. Always call the park or public land in advance if you are traveling some distance with your dog. Following are some general guidelines about Bay Area parks and dogs:

In most state parks around the Bay, dogs are not allowed at all on hiking trails, although they are permitted in campgrounds and at some picnic areas. That means no canine hiking fun at almost any place with "State Park" or "State Reserve" in the title. Unfortunately, that eliminates many of the trails in Sonoma and Napa counties. Luckily the Sonoma County Park system takes up the slack with several dog-friendly parks, including Hood Mountain Regional Park.

In Marin County, the federally managed Golden Gate National Recreation Area (GGNRA) allows leashed dogs on most, but not all, trails. Most of the wonderful GGNRA trails in the Marin Headlands are open to dogs, but a few are not, including the popular Tennessee Valley Trail. At Point Reyes National Seashore, another federal park unit, dog-friendly trails are the exception, not the rule. Only a few Point Reyes trails are open to dogs, most notably the lovely Kehoe Beach Trail. Limantour Beach is another popular spot for dogs and their owners.

Other parks in Marin County are more welcoming to dogs, including the lands

of the Marin County Open Space District and Marin Municipal Water District. But be careful on trails that travel from one jurisdiction to another, such as those that start out in Marin Water District lands and lead into Mount Tamalpais State Park. As soon as the trail enters the state park, dogs are forbidden.

East Bay dogs and dog owners can bark for joy because the East Bay Regional Park District is remarkably dog lenient, even allowing canines off-leash in many parks. But this comes with a small price: At most East Bay parks, you have to pay an entrance fee for your dog (usually $2). A few East Bay parks are still off-limits to dogs, though, including Tilden, Huckleberry, and Round Valley, but in general, the East Bay Regional Park system is doggy heaven. Keep in mind that if your dog is off-leash, he or she should

Of course your dog wants to hike with you, but before setting out, check to make sure he or she is allowed on your chosen trail.

© ANN MARIE BROWN

VOLUNTEER OPPORTUNITIES: HELPING OUR PARKS

These days, closures and cutbacks are the norm. Staffing at Bay Area parks is at an all-time low and our parks need your help. The following list includes land trusts, conservation groups, park friends associations, and trail maintenance groups. All of them need volunteers, whether the work is stuffing envelopes, removing invasive weeds, building and repairing trails, improving websites, cleaning up beaches and watersheds, leading hikes, writing letters to government officials, or educating the public as a park naturalist. Helping out for only a few hours a month – or even one day a year – can make a difference.

Angel Island Association (www.angelisland.org)

Bay Area Open Space Council (www.openspacecouncil.org)

Bay Area Ridge Trail Council (www.ridgetrail.org)

Berkeley Path Wanderers Association (www.berkeleypaths.org)

California State Parks Foundation (www.calparks.org)

California Wild Heritage Campaign (www.californiawild.org)

Coastwalk (www.coastwalk.org)

East Bay Regional Park District (www.ebparks.org)

Friends of Edgewood (www.friendsofedgewood.org)

Friends of Santa Cruz State Parks (www.thatsmypark.org)

Golden Gate National Parks Conservancy (www.parksconservancy.org)

Greenbelt Alliance (www.greenbelt.org)

Marin Agricultural Land Trust (www.malt.org)

Midpeninsula Regional Open Space District (www.openspace.org)

Mount Diablo Interpretive Association (www.mdia.org)

Mount Tamalpais Interpretive Association (www.mttam.net)

Mountain Parks Foundation (www.mountainparks.org)

Muir Heritage Land Trust (www.muirheritagelandtrust.org)

Napa County Land Trust (www.napalandtrust.org)

The Nature Conservancy (www.tnccalifornia.org)

Pacifica Land Trust (www.pacifica-land-trust.org)

Peninsula Open Space Trust (www.openspacetrust.org)

San Bruno Mountain Watch (www.mountainwatch.org)

San Mateo County Parks Foundation (www.supportparks.org)

Santa Cruz Mountains Trail Association (www.scmta-trails.org)

Save Mount Diablo (www.savemountdiablo.org)

Sempervirens Fund (www.sempervirens.org)

Sierra Club (www.sierraclub.org)

Solano Land Trust (www.solanolandtrust.org)

Sonoma Mountain Preservation Group (www.sonomamountain.org)

Tamalpais Conservation Club (www.tamalpais.org)

Trail Center (www.trailcenter.org)

Trail Workers (www.trailworkers.com)

The Trust for Public Land (www.tpl.org)

still be under voice control, if for no other reason than for his or her safety. The great outdoors presents many hazards for dogs, including mountain lions, rattlesnakes, ticks, and a host of other potential problems. Dogs can get lost after running off to chase a deer or other wildlife. Keep your dog near your side and both of you can have a safe, enjoyable hike.

South of San Francisco, dog lovers have to look harder to find places for Fido to roam. Luckily McNee Ranch State Park (Montara Mountain), just south of Pacifica and north of Half Moon Bay, is one of the few Bay Area state parks that allows dogs. Although it may be tempting to bring your dog to the beautiful shores of the San Mateo County coast, canines are off-limits on the beaches to protect nesting snowy plovers. Dogs are also prohibited in all San Mateo County parks, but they are permitted at some (but not most) of the Midpeninsula Regional Open Space District parklands off Skyline Boulevard. And, if you head farther south, you'll find that the Santa Clara County park system is remarkably dog friendly.

To restate the obvious, always follow each park's specific rules about dogs. Trails where dogs are prohibited are almost always signed as such at the trailhead, so obey the signs and you'll stay out of trouble. If the rules state that your dog must be leashed, that usually means he or she must be on a six-foot or shorter leash. Don't try to get away with carrying the leash in your hand while your dog runs free; rangers are not fooled by this and may give you a ticket.

Protecting the Outdoors

Take good care of this beautiful land you're hiking on. The basics are simple: Leave no trace of your visit. Pack out all your trash. Do your best not to disturb animal or plant life. Don't collect specimens of plants, wildlife, or even pinecones. Never, ever carve anything into the trunks of trees. If you're following a trail, don't cut the switchbacks. Leave everything in nature exactly as you found it, because each tiny piece has its place in the great scheme of things.

You can go the extra mile, too. Pick up any litter that you see on the trail. Teach your children to do this as well. Carry an extra bag to hold the litter until you get to a trash receptacle, or just keep an empty pocket for that purpose in your day pack or fanny pack.

If you have the extra time or energy, join a trail organization in your area or spend some time volunteering in your local park. Anything you do to help this beautiful planet will be repaid to you, many times over. For more information, please visit Leave No Trace at www.lnt.org or call 303/442-8222 or 800/332-4100.

NAPA AND SONOMA

© ANN MARIE BROWN

BEST HIKES

The Napa and Sonoma region encompasses a

vast and diverse landscape that runs the gamut from fog- and wave-swept beaches, rugged sea cliffs, and rolling sand dunes to neatly tended, vineyard-covered hills and valleys. Despite being famous the world over for wine-related tourism, world-class spas, and gourmet restaurants, the two side-by-side counties have managed to retain their pastoral character, which continues to charm both first-time visitors and long-time locals.

To the west, Highway 1 winds up the rocky Pacific coast past small villages with population counts lower than their elevation — which is near sea level. In these tiny hamlets, you're likely to encounter more sheep or cows than local residents. Conversation revolves around the crab harvest, or how many head of cattle are grazing in what plot of land, or whether or not grapes can grow in the fog-shrouded coastal hills. A string of beaches and headlands along this coast are protected under the umbrella of Sonoma Coast State Park. These state-managed parklands, located between Bodega Bay and Jenner, offer hiking trails that travel across flower-strewn coastal bluffs, providing breathtaking panoramas of rocky sea stacks, crashing waves, and the dramatic meeting place of the Russian River and the Pacific Ocean.

To the east of the coast lies the drier inland valleys of Sonoma and Napa, where the wine grape rules supreme. Fortunately, hiking and wine-tasting go together like a bold merlot and French bread slathered in Brie. The parks of the Wine Country provide ample opportunities for a hearty walk capped off with a gourmet picnic, whether the occasion is a romantic date or a relaxed family outing. Although the Wine Country is known for its dry and warm climate, the landscape offers a surprising amount of variation. Perennial streams can be found at Skyline Wilderness Park (Marie Creek), Sugarloaf Ridge State Park (Sonoma Creek), and Bothe-

Napa Valley State Park (Ritchey Creek). Dense, shady coastal redwoods grow in the cool canyon of Bothe-Napa Valley State Park. Grassland- and wildflower-covered hills comprise the main acreage of Sugarloaf Ridge State Park and Hood Mountain Regional Park. And on the far eastern edge of this region, immense marshes and wetlands are formed where rivers and creeks meet up with San Francisco Bay tidal waters.

Perhaps the best way to take in all that the Sonoma and Napa region has to offer is to climb a summit and get some perspective from on high. The area has several peaks worthy of climbing, including mighty Mount St. Helena (4,342 feet) in Robert Louis Stevenson State Park, scenic Sonoma Mountain (2,463 feet) in Jack London State Historic Park, aptly named Bald Mountain (2,729 feet) in Sugarloaf Ridge State Park, and the double summits of Sugarloaf Peak (1,630 feet) in Skyline Wilderness Park.

Easier jaunts are also in plentiful supply, from the mellow loop around Lake Ilsanjo in Annadel State Park, where lucky anglers will often hook a bass or bluegill, to the Lake and Fallen Bridge Loop at Jack London State Historic Park, where history buffs, aspiring writers, and those who are just plain curious can tour novelist Jack London's homestead. Indeed, literary types can find ample inspiration in the Wine Country, not only at London's beloved ranch but also at Robert Louis Stevenson State Park, where one of the West's greatest writers honeymooned with his wife on the slopes of Mount St. Helena. The mountain served as London's inspiration for Spyglass Hill in his novel *Treasure Island*.

In short, if you've always thought of the Wine Country as a place only to sample vintages or soak in a spa, it's time to reconsider. An abundance of beautiful parks are waiting to be explored. Why not pack a picnic in your day pack and hit the trails?

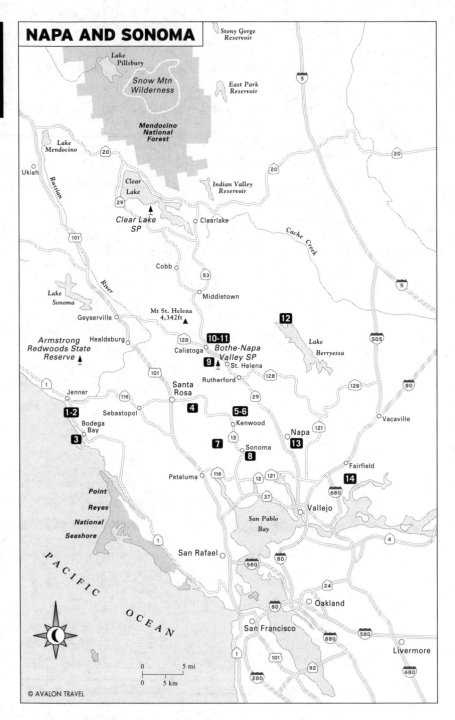

NAPA AND SONOMA

Stony Gorge Reservoir

Lake Pillsbury

Snow Mtn Wilderness

East Park Reservoir

Mendocino National Forest

Lake Mendocino

Ukiah

Russian

Clear Lake

Indian Valley Reservoir

Clear Lake SP

Clearlake

Cache Creek

Cobb

Lake Sonoma

River

Middletown

Geyserville

Mt St. Helena 4,342ft

Lake Berryessa

12

Armstrong Redwoods State Reserve

Healdsburg

Calistoga

10-11

Bothe-Napa Valley SP

9 St. Helena

Jenner

Santa Rosa

Rutherford

1-2

Sebastopol

4

5-6

Kenwood

Napa

13

3

Bodega Bay

7

Sonoma

8

Vacaville

Fairfield

14

Point Reyes National Seashore

Petaluma

Vallejo

San Pablo Bay

San Rafael

P A C I F I C

O C E A N

Oakland

San Francisco

Livermore

0   5 mi

0   5 km

© AVALON TRAVEL

TRAIL NAME	LEVEL	DISTANCE	TIME	ELEVATION	FEATURES	PAGE
1 Pomo Canyon Trail	Moderate	6.2 mi rt	3 hr	1,000 ft		30
2 Kortum Trail	Easy/Moderate	4.6 mi rt	2 hr	500 ft		33
3 Bodega Head Trail	Easy	2.0 mi rt	1 hr	400 ft		36
4 Lake Ilsanjo Loop	Easy/Moderate	5.3 mi rt	3 hr	500 ft		40
5 Bald Mountain Loop	Moderate	6.8 mi rt	4 hr	1,500 ft		43
6 Goodspeed Trail to Gunsight Rock	Strenuous	7.0 mi rt	4 hr	1,900 ft		46
7 Lake and Fallen Bridge Loop	Easy/Moderate	4.2 mi rt	2 hr	600 ft		49
8 Sonoma Overlook Trail	Easy	2.6 mi rt	1 hr	400 ft		53
9 Ritchey Canyon and Coyote Peak	Easy/Moderate	4.6 mi rt	3 hr	850 ft		56
10 Mount St. Helena	Strenuous	10.6 mi rt	6 hr	2,100 ft		59
11 Table Rock	Moderate	4.6 mi rt	2.5 hr	1,000 ft		63
12 Zim Zim Falls	Moderate	7.4 mi rt	3.5 hr	750 ft		66
13 Sugarloaf Peak Loop	Moderate	7.4 mi rt	4 hr	1,500 ft		69
14 Marsh and South Pasture Loop	Easy	4.6 mi rt	2 hr	Negligible		72

1 POMO CANYON TRAIL

BEST **C**

Sonoma Coast State Park

Level: Moderate

Total Distance: 6.2 miles round-trip

Hiking Time: 3 hours

Elevation Change: 1,000 feet

Summary: A relatively easy climb over wildflower-laden hills leads to sweeping views of the Russian River and Sonoma Coast.

If the wind is howling on the Sonoma Coast or the fog has smothered the beaches in a cool, white-gray blanket, you don't have to pack up your car and head inland. A first-rate hike can be had on the Pomo Canyon Trail from Shell Beach, where wind and fog can't ruin the trip.

Pomo Canyon Trail heads northeast from the coast, meanders over coastal grasslands covered with spring wildflowers, then visits a secluded grove of second-growth redwoods in a wind-protected canyon. Although the trail presents great views of the ocean and the Russian River when the weather is clear, it also leads to a destination that doesn't need sunshine to be enjoyable. In fact, a hike to Pomo Canyon's redwood grove in dense fog or light rain may be one of the most romantic walks you've ever taken.

© ANN MARIE BROWN

Pomo Canyon Trail harbors some dense redwood groves in addition to grasslands and wildflowers.

Wildflower lovers take note: The coastal hills and grasslands along Pomo Canyon Trail are well known for erupting in blooms during late April, May, and early June. During the peak of the bloom, more than 100 different species may flower at one time. Although the grasslands don't exhibit vast, showy carpets of individual species, the great diversity of blossoms draws flower worshippers every year.

Start your trip at the Shell Beach parking lot north of Bodega Bay. You'll have to walk across Highway 1 to access the Pomo Canyon trailhead; do so with care. The trail begins on an old paved road that has eroded into part gravel, part pavement, and part grasses. It makes

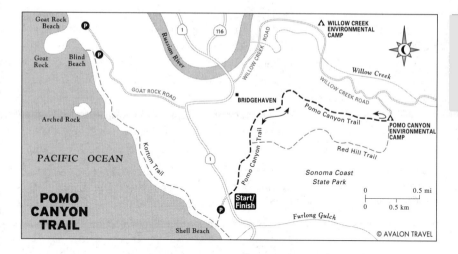

easy walking as you head uphill away from the coast. Although the noise of the highway stays with you for the first 0.5 mile, it soon disappears. Sadly, along with it goes the expansive ocean views. While you still can, turn around occasionally to gaze at the wide blue Pacific.

At a junction at 0.7 mile, where the path reaches a grassy plateau punctuated by a few large rock formations, bear right, then bear left shortly afterward. You'll leave the worn pavement behind and follow grassy double-track, which soon narrows to single-track. Bright blue and pale white Douglas iris dot the grasslands in early spring; blue gentian and tarweed follow later in summer.

The path rolls along the ridge top, traveling generally downhill toward Willow Creek's canyon. Heading north, you'll gain fine views of the Russian River's graceful curves and Goat Rock Beach beyond. Watch for a short spur trail on the left, about one mile from the start, which leads to a grassy knoll topped with a picnic table. There you gain a wider view of the 110-mile-long river at its junction with the sea.

The trail continues past dense blackberry vines and coastal chaparral that is sometimes taller than you are. It crosses several seeps and springs that provide year-round water for the lichen-covered Douglas firs and Monterey pines, passes a signed turnoff for the Red Hill Trail (see *Options,* in this listing), then enters the first grouping of redwoods at about two miles. These trees may surprise you: Their bark is not the usual reddish brown color typical of redwoods. Instead, their trunks are completely covered with a gray-green lichen, making the trees appear almost ghostlike. You might expect a leprechaun to pop out of this mysterious forest at any moment.

Pomo Canyon Trail wanders along the edge of the grove, then opens out to more grasslands with wide views of the deep green Willow Creek drainage and Russian River canyon. In another 0.5 mile, the trail enters a second stand of redwoods and begins a steep descent to the end. The narrow second- and third-growth trees have laid a soft carpet of needles under your feet. Ferns of many varieties line the woodland floor.

The path ends anticlimactically at Pomo Canyon Environmental Camp, a walk-in/environmental camp. Twenty sites are scattered among the redwood trees; campers must walk in a few hundred feet from the parking lot. If the campground is empty, you might choose a picnic table for a rest stop. Otherwise, just turn around and head back over the ridge. The beauty of this trail is worth seeing all over again.

Options

It is possible to make a semi-loop out of this trail by connecting to the Red Hill Trail at Pomo Canyon Environmental Camp, then following it for 1.25 miles until it reconnects with Pomo Canyon Trail. Finish out the trip by heading back to the Shell Beach parking lot on Pomo Canyon Trail. Red Hill Trail is more open and exposed than much of the Pomo Canyon Trail; it offers views up the Russian River Valley as far east as Geyser Peak. The summit of Red Hill can be climbed via a short spur trail; the top is marked by a circle of rocks on the ground.

Alternatively, hiking Pomo Canyon Trail also works well in reverse, starting from the Pomo Canyon Environmental Camp and hiking to Shell Beach and back. However, in the winter months the road into the campground is gated. If you park at the gate and walk in to the campground and trailhead, it will add 0.5 mile each way to your hike.

Directions

From Highway 1 in Bodega Bay, drive north for seven miles to the Shell Beach parking lot on the west side of the road. Park in the lot, then walk across Highway 1 to access the trail on its east side, signed as Dr. David Joseph Memorial Pomo Canyon Trail.

Information and Contact

There is no fee. Dogs and bikes are not allowed. A trail map is available for $1 at park headquarters at Salmon Creek, the visitors center in Jenner, or at the kiosk at Wright's Beach. It is also available free by download at www.parks.ca.gov. For more information, contact Sonoma Coast State Park, 3095 Hwy. 1, Bodega Bay, CA 94923, 707/875-3483 or 707/865-2391, www.parks.sonoma.net or www.parks.ca.gov.

2 KORTUM TRAIL
Sonoma Coast State Park

Level: Easy/Moderate

Total Distance: 4.6 miles round-trip

Hiking Time: 2 hours

Elevation Change: 500 feet

Summary: A gentle hike over coastal bluffs travels to a landlocked sea stack, Blind Beach, and Goat Rock.

Sonoma Coast State Park encompasses 13 miles of shoreline stretching from Bodega Bay to the Russian River. Located north of Marin County's coastline and west of the Sonoma County towns of Petaluma and Santa Rosa, the Sonoma Coast is on the road to few other places. This is one of many factors that make the shoreline here so appealing.

The best way to get to know this coast is to take a walk on the Kortum Trail, which skirts grassland bluffs from Blind Beach to Wright's Beach over a distance of 3.8 miles one-way. By starting in the middle of the trail at Shell Beach, you can follow the scenic northern length of trail for a 4.6-mile, out-and-back round-trip.

The path is named for environmentalist and veterinarian Bill Kortum, who volunteered for 30 years to protect this stretch of coast. Numerous issues threatened the region, including the planned building of a nuclear power plant at Bodega Bay and the closure of public access to the coast at Sea Ranch. Thanks to the efforts of Kortum and others like him, thousands of acres of Sonoma coastline have remained unspoiled and open for enjoyment.

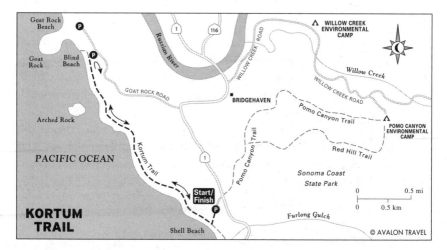

Heading north from the Shell Beach parking lot, you'll immediately notice two parallel trails: The wider, more obvious path is routed slightly inland and runs a straighter course, while a narrower spur-trail meanders along the jagged edge of the bluffs. Take your pick; the paths soon converge.

Kortum Trail leads across classic California coastal bluff terrain, with open grasslands intersected by brushy drainages and ravines. Views of offshore outcrops and spring wildflowers are a feast for the eyes. Douglas iris, lupine, and Indian paintbrush gild the grasslands April–June. To the south is Bodega Head and the northern tip of Point Reyes, visible on clear days. To the west, the shimmering Pacific extends as far as your gaze can follow.

A highlight of the trip is a massive rock outcrop rising from the grasslands at 1.3 miles, which invites a climb to its summit. Coastal views are superb from the top of the lichen-covered, fern-dotted Pleistocene sea stack, which was buried undersea eons ago, before this marine terrace was uncovered. Beyond the rock, Kortum Trail leads away from the ocean and ascends a coastal hill (take the short spur to its summit for more views), then drops back down the other side, exposing views of the wave-pounded tunnel at Arched Rock. The path ends about 100 feet from Blind Beach's parking lot; follow the short trail from the lot down to the beach. From there, it's a 0.5-mile stroll north to Goat Rock Beach. Goat Rock, a massive offshore outcrop, is connected to the mainland by a paved road.

Bird-watchers will not want to forget their binoculars on this hike. Raptors are commonly seen hunting in the grasslands; watch for harriers, red-shouldered hawks, black-shouldered kites, and even great horned owls. Don't be surprised if you see a human bird soar overhead as well. The coastal skies are the playground of local hang gliders.

Options

To extend your hike, follow the southern length of Kortum Trail from Shell Beach to Wright's Beach, adding three miles to your round-trip. The trail drops steeply into Furlong Gulch at 0.5 mile out, then switchbacks uphill on wooden steps. Thereafter the route curves inland, parallels Highway 1, and reaches popular Wright's Beach in 1.5 miles.

For even more Pacific Ocean eye candy, drive north through Jenner for about seven miles to the Vista Trail and Overlook on the west side of the highway. This short, wheelchair-accessible pathway doesn't offer much in the way of distance, but its coastal views more than compensate.

Directions

From Highway 1 in Bodega Bay, drive north for seven miles to the Shell Beach

© ANN MARIE BROWN

Pleistocene sea stacks are left high and dry on the coastal bluffs along the Kortum Trail.

parking lot on the west side of the road. The trail begins on the northwest side of the parking lot (a separate trail section begins on the southwest side).

Information and Contact

There is no fee. Dogs and bikes are not allowed. A trail map is available for $1 at park headquarters at Salmon Creek, the visitors center in Jenner, or at the kiosk at Wright's Beach. It is also available free by download at www.parks.ca.gov. For more information, contact Sonoma Coast State Park, 3095 Hwy. 1, Bodega Bay, CA 94923, 707/875-3483 or 707/865-2391, www.parks.sonoma.net or www.parks.ca.gov.

3 BODEGA HEAD TRAIL
Sonoma Coast State Park

🚶 ⛵ 🚻

Level: Easy   **Total Distance:** 2.0 miles round-trip

Hiking Time: 1 hour   **Elevation Change:** 400 feet

Summary: Crashing surf, offshore outcrops, secluded coves, and a sheltered harbor are revealed from the tip-top of Bodega Head.

Say "Bodega Bay" and most people's thoughts turn to Alfred Hitchcock movies and birds gone crazy. Better they should think of hiking instead, and wildflowers, whale-watching, and coastal vistas.

Bodega Head is the tip of the curving peninsula of land that juts out from the coast west of Santa Rosa and Sebastopol. The headlands of the Head extend toward the ocean, then curve back in toward the mainland, like the fingers of a hand bending inward. From a high point on Bodega Head you can wave to a wide audience that includes the expansive Pacific, the sheltered harbor at Bodega Bay, the northern tip of Point Reyes, and the rolling hills and farms of western Sonoma. On a clear day, the view is unparalleled.

The clear day is the tricky part. Bodega Bay is almost as famous for fog as it is for the Hitchcock thriller *The Birds*. When the fog finally clears from Bodega Bay, the coastal wind is often daunting. But there's a way to beat the system: Plan your trip for autumn or winter, and arrive in the morning, not the afternoon. This gives you the best chance for a sunny, windless hike.

Start your trip at Bodega Head's west parking lot (bear right at the fork as you drive in). The view from this lot is mesmerizing enough. The sea crashes against dark sandy beaches, rugged bluffs, and rock outcrops. Tenacious sea palms grip the offshore rocks, holding on for dear life as each passing breaker explodes into spray. The moment the wave dissipates, the plants spring back to an upright position, as if made of rubber.

Take the signed Bodega Head Trail from the north (right) side of the lot. It climbs uphill on grassy bluffs to the highest point on Bodega Head, where a 360-degree vista is yours for viewing. An optional left fork at the start of the trail leads a short distance to the sandstone bluffs' eroded edges. This colorful miniature badlands looks like something straight out of Death Valley.

Follow the main path uphill to a signed junction. Take the left trail for Horseshoe Cove Overlook; the right fork continues to Salmon Creek Beach and Bodega Dunes Campground. The overlook trail dead-ends at a high, rock-covered point, which looks down at rightfully named Horseshoe Cove and the University of California Marine Laboratory alongside it. To the east is the town of Bodega Bay and a cavalcade of RVs lined up along Doran Park, on the sand spit protecting Bodega Harbor. It's fascinating to watch the fishing boats slowly putter through the harbor, squeeze through the narrow channel between Doran Park and Bodega Head, then motor out to freedom in Bodega Bay.

When you've soaked in the view, retrace your steps to the parking lot. Follow the trail that begins on the other side of the parking lot, to the left of the restrooms. This footpath circles around the "closed fist" shape that is Bodega Head. It climbs initially to a memorial site for Bodega Bay's commercial fishermen, then hugs the bluff edges as it curves around the Head's south side. On windy days, hikers can take refuge in a stand of cypress trees.

At the southern tip of the Head, what looks like an island rises from the sea. It's Tomales Point, the northern tip of the Point Reyes peninsula. On the clearest days, tiny Bird Rock island is also visible, just off Tomales Point's coast. Geographically speaking, Point Reyes is directly south of Bodega Head. The two peninsulas are separated by only five miles of sea, although Point Reyes' peninsula is immense in comparison to tiny Bodega Head. If you have visited the tule elk preserve at the

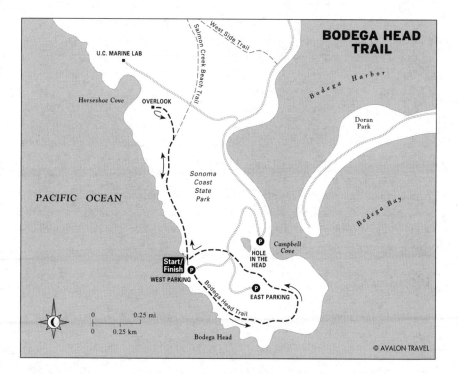

Small pocket beaches can be found below the bluffs on Bodega Head.

northern tip of Point Reyes or hiked the Tomales Point Trail, you were standing just opposite here looking north at Bodega Head.

As your trail turns away from the sea, you have a choice: Continue on a loop past the east parking lot and back to your car, or simply turn around and retrace your steps. The latter option is the most scenic. You'll enjoy Bodega Head's crashing surf, offshore outcrops, and secluded coves all over again.

Options

After visiting Horseshoe Cove Overlook, follow the fork in the trail that is signed for Salmon Creek Beach and Bodega Dunes Campground. After crossing over the access road to the U.C. Marine Laboratory, you'll drop down to the start of a loop trail that traverses the dunes of South Salmon Creek Beach. Take the right fork, Upper Dunes Trail, and head northward. Several cutoff trails allow you to turn left and join the Lower Dunes Trail at different points, so just hike as far as you wish, then return on Lower Dunes. You can add on up to four miles on the Dunes loop. The loop can also be accessed from West Side Trail off West Shore Road, or from Bodega Dunes Campground.

Directions

From Highway 1 in Bodega Bay, turn west on Eastshore Road. (The turnoff is signed for Bodega Head.) Drive 0.5 mile, then turn right on Bay Flat Road, which becomes Westshore Road. Drive 3.5 miles to Bodega Head; take the right fork in the road and head to the west parking lot. The trailhead is on the north (right) side of the lot.

Information and Contact

There is no fee. Dogs and bikes are not allowed. A trail map is available for $1 at park headquarters at Salmon Creek, the visitors center in Jenner, or at the kiosk at Wright's Beach. It is also available free by download at www.parks.ca.gov. For more information, contact Sonoma Coast State Park, 3095 Hwy. 1, Bodega Bay, CA 94923, 707/875-3483 or 707/865-2391, www.parks.sonoma.net or www.parks.ca.gov.

4 LAKE ILSANJO LOOP   BEST (

Annadel State Park

Level: Easy/Moderate   Total Distance: 5.3 miles round-trip

Hiking Time: 3 hours   Elevation Change: 500 feet

Summary: A casual meander through Santa Rosa's favorite park is the ideal outing for wildflower admirers and hikers who like to fish.

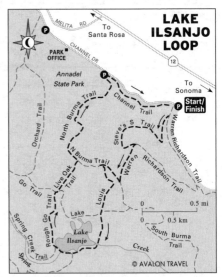

Annadel State Park is a horsy kind of place. If you count the horse trailers in the parking lot, the hoofprints all over the place, and the horse droppings along the trail, you might think more horses visit here than people.

Then again, Annadel is also a mountain biker's kind of place. Almost all of the trails at Annadel are open to bikes, and not just the usual wide fire roads. Mountain bikers and equestrians share the trails with great equanimity, and trail conflicts are rare to nonexistent.

Considering all this, it's surprising that Annadel is also a hiker's kind of place, but it is. Annadel's 5,000 acres are filled with woodlands, meadows, seasonal creeks, wildflowers, and even a 26-acre lake, all of which are worth seeing on foot. One particularly pleasant trail, Steve's S, is designated for hikers only. If you are a flower aficionado, don't miss a visit to Annadel in April or May. Among many other species, lupine, poppies, mule's ears, redwood orchids, sticky monkeyflower, checkerbloom, and scarlet fritillary make an appearance here.

With dozens of trail junctions in this large park, a good map is essential. Pick one up at the ranger station when you drive in or download a map from the park website before you visit. Start your hike at the Warren Richardson trailhead at the end of Channel Drive. On one trip, we got out of our car and heard a loud ruckus. Two-dozen male turkeys, divided into two groups, were battling over a flock of hens alongside the parking lot. It was like *West Side Story* with feathers.

Take the hikers-only Warren Richardson Trail from the far end of the parking lot or the wide fire road from its center; both meet up in a few hundred feet. At that junction, head uphill on narrow Steve's S Trail, leaving the road to the cyclists and horses. The trail makes a good climb over nearly a mile with just enough of a pitch to get your heart rate up. It weaves through a dense and shady Douglas fir forest interspersed with occasional bay laurel and coast redwood trees. The woodland floor is lined with sword ferns. In early spring, look for rare redwood orchids among them.

If you are wondering what the "S" in Steve's S Trail stands for, it's a secret. Literally. This was one of the "secret" trails built by Steve Hutchison, the grandson of the family who once owned this land.

After gaining a ridge, Steve's S Trail meets back up with Warren Richardson Trail. Go right (south) and then in 0.4 mile, go right again on North Burma Trail. In 0.3 mile, turn left on Louis Trail. You'll walk through an open meadow peppered with bright yellow mule's ears, goldfields, and golden fairy lanterns in the spring. Bordering the meadow is a mixed variety of oaks—coast live, black, and Oregon—which attract a wide variety of birds, especially woodpeckers. Many birders come to Annadel specifically to spot the pileated woodpecker, a resident in this park. Continue on Louis Trail for 0.7 mile to the northern edge of Lake Ilsanjo. You'll head back into the forest again, but this time into an oak and madrone woodland. The black oaks turn bright colors in the fall.

Go left to circle the lake clockwise. You'll gain the best views of blue water, tules, and paddling waterbirds as you walk across Lake Ilsanjo's earthen dam. The natural-looking reservoir is a refreshing contrast to the xeric chaparral surrounding

the tule-lined shores of Lake Ilsanjo

it. The origin of the lake's name, Ilsanjo, is a combination of Ilsa and Joe, the first names of the land's former owners, who built the lake's dam.

Ilsanjo's tule-lined shores are popular with bikers, hikers, picnickers, swimmers, and anglers. More than a few visitors make this a combination hiking/fishing trip, stalking Ilsanjo's shoreline to cast for large black bass and plentiful bluegill.

About two-thirds of the way around the lake, you'll see a left fork for Rough Go Trail. Follow it away from the lake for 0.5 mile, then bear right on Live Oak Trail. Continue north for almost a mile until you reconnect with North Burma Trail. Turn left on North Burma; it will lead you in 0.7 mile to Channel Trail, where you will turn right to finish out your loop back at the parking lot.

Options

To add on a few more miles to this hike, take Spring Creek Trail from the west end of Lake Ilsanjo's dam. The trail follows Spring Creek for 1.7 miles to Rough Go Trail and eventually rejoins the loop described earlier. This option will add just under three miles to your loop. Or, if you've visited Lake Ilsanjo before, you might want to try one of Annadel's other special trails. Bring your binoculars and bird identification book for a hike to Ledson Marsh, accessed via Warren Richardson Trail, Two Quarry Trail, and Marsh Trail (3.5 miles one-way). Make your trip early in the year, as Ledson Marsh often dries up by August. For a bit of history, don't miss the 0.5-mile Rhyolite Trail spur off Marsh Trail, which leads to the site of the Gordenker Quarry.

Directions

From U.S. 101 in Santa Rosa, take the Fairgrounds/Highway 12 exit. Highway 12 becomes Farmers Lane. Turn right on Montgomery Drive and follow it for 2.7 miles (veering to the right), then turn right on Channel Drive. Follow Channel Drive into the park, stop at the ranger station for information and maps, then drive to the end of the road and park in the lot (it's a total of 2.2 miles on Channel Drive).

Information and Contact

A $6 day-use fee is charged per vehicle. Dogs are not allowed. Bikes are allowed on all trails except Steve's S and Rhyolite Trails. Park maps are available at the ranger station or can be downloaded for free at www.parks.ca.gov. For more information, contact Annadel State Park, 6201 Channel Drive, Santa Rosa, CA 95409, 707/539-3911, www.parks.sonoma.net or www.parks.ca.gov.

5 BALD MOUNTAIN LOOP

Sugarloaf Ridge State Park

BEST ℂ

Level: Moderate

Total Distance: 6.8 miles round-trip

Hiking Time: 4 hours

Elevation Change: 1,500 feet

Summary: A climb along serpentine-dotted slopes leads to the grass-covered summit of Bald Mountain, Sonoma County's answer to Marin's Mount Tamalpais.

While the grassy summit of Bald Mountain is the crowning glory of this loop trip in Sugarloaf Ridge State Park, each leg of the route bestows its own rewards. Take the most direct path to the summit, then loop back downhill on a series of trails for a roundabout tour of the park's varied terrain.

Start your trip on Lower Bald Mountain Trail from the parking lot just past the entrance kiosk. At its start, the well-graded path climbs a grassy slope. Deer frequently graze in the open meadow, which is covered with wildflowers in the spring, especially Douglas iris, California poppies, brodiaea, and blue-eyed grass.

Tunneling through a hardwood forest, the path meets up with Bald Mountain Trail, a paved service road. The pavement makes less pleasant hiking, but this 1.4-mile stretch ascends quickly through slopes covered with ceanothus, manzanita, chemise, and toyon. The blooming, scented chaparral will take your attention away from the asphalt.

At 2.3 miles from the start, reach the pavement's end at a saddle and trail junction. The left fork leads to microwave tower–covered Red Mountain at 2,548 feet.

© ANN MARIE BROWN

Equestrians share the trails of Sugarloaf Ridge State Park.

You'll go right for Bald Mountain, now following a dirt fire road. The final 0.5 mile ascends grassy slopes with occasional outcrops of green serpentine. The dirt road curves around the north side of the peak to a junction with Gray Pine Trail. Take the short spur on the right to reach the 2,729-foot summit of Bald Mountain. It's bald indeed; not a single tree obstructs the sweeping panoramic view.

Two signs at the top identify all the neighboring landmarks, including Mount St. Helena, Mount Diablo, Bodega Bay, Mount Wittenberg in Point Reyes, Snow Mountain, Mount Tamalpais, the Golden Gate Bridge towers, Angel Island, and the Bay Bridge. Most impressive is a rarely seen glimpse of the Sierra Nevada, 130 miles away. A quote from author Robert Louis Stevenson sums up the scene: "There are days in a life when thus to climb out of the lowlands seems like scaling heaven."

From Bald Mountain's summit, take wide Gray Pine Trail east, descending along a ridge. In 0.8 mile, turn right on single-track Red Mountain Trail. The trail dips and climbs through chaparral for nearly a mile. Watch for the left turnoff for Headwaters Trail; take it and enjoy a nice downhill stretch along the headwaters of Sonoma Creek. After 0.5 mile, bear right on Vista Trail. The path skirts lovely meadows with fine views of the Sonoma Creek canyon and Sugarloaf Ridge, then ends at paved Bald Mountain Trail. Follow the pavement downhill for only 0.25 mile to the left turnoff for Lower Bald Mountain Trail. The final mile is an easy descent back to your car.

Options

An alternative and slightly shorter route downhill from Bald Mountain's summit stays on Gray Pine Trail for a rollicking descent along the ridgeline. Gray Pine Trail rolls along and then descends for 2.5 miles to Meadow Trail, where you turn right for a mile-long stretch along Sonoma Creek to the site of the park's Ferguson Observatory (707/833-6979, www.rfo.org), which is open to the public for stargazing on certain weekends throughout the year. Beyond it lies the last 0.25 mile of Lower Bald Mountain Trail, which leads back to your car.

If you'd rather extend your trip instead of shortening it, take Gray Pine Trail east for 1.1 miles from Bald Mountain's summit to Brushy Peaks Trail. This pathway leads southeast for another 1.1 miles to the summit of Brushy Peaks, elevation 2,243 feet. The trail continues past the peaks for two miles and then eventually joins with Hillside, Meadow, and Gray Pine Trails. Meadow Trail is the shortest route back to your car. The combined Bald Mountain and Brushy Peaks loop makes an eight-mile day.

Directions

From U.S. 101 in Santa Rosa, take the Fairgrounds/Highway 12 exit. Highway

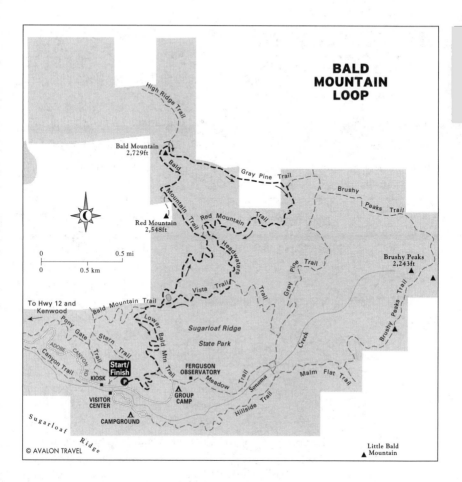

12 becomes Farmers Lane as it heads through downtown Santa Rosa. Continue on Highway 12 for 11 miles to Adobe Canyon Road in Kenwood and turn left. (Or, from Highway 12 in Sonoma, drive 11 miles north to Adobe Canyon Road, then turn right.) Drive 3.5 miles to the park entrance kiosk. Park in the lot about 100 yards past the kiosk, on the left. Take the trail signed as Lower Bald Mountain Trail.

Information and Contact

An $8 day-use fee is charged per vehicle. Dogs are not allowed. Bikes are allowed only on fire roads. A trail map is available at the entrance kiosk for $1 or can be downloaded for free at www.parks.ca.gov. For more information, contact Sugarloaf Ridge State Park, 2605 Adobe Canyon Road, Kenwood, CA 95452, 707/833-5712, www.parks.sonoma.net or www.parks.ca.gov.

6 GOODSPEED TRAIL TO GUNSIGHT ROCK

BEST ☾

Sugarloaf Ridge State Park and Hood Mountain Regional Park

Level: Strenuous

Total Distance: 7.0 miles round-trip

Hiking Time: 4 hours

Elevation Change: 1,900 feet

Summary: A half-day hike leads to a precipitous perch with an unforgettable view of Sonoma, Napa, and Marin County landmarks.

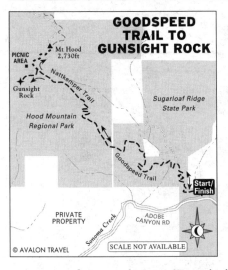

Hood Mountain is a 2,730-foot peak in Sonoma County located just outside the border of Sugarloaf Ridge State Park. Despite its respectable size, Hood Mountain has one drawback—its summit view is a big disappointment. Manzanita and pine trees cover its wide, rounded top. You can't see a darn thing from up there.

Fortunately, Hood Mountain has Gunsight Rock, a distinct promontory located 0.25 mile and 300 feet below its summit. From lofty Gunsight Rock, just about everything in Sonoma County comes into view, plus the big mountains of Napa and Marin. Not only that, but Gunsight Rock's boulder-lined outcrop is perched so dramatically on the steep slope of Hood Mountain that its precarious drop-off makes the vista even more impressive.

Getting to Gunsight Rock is as enjoyable as being there. The route to the rock on Goodspeed Trail is a study in diversity. It passes by redwoods, bay laurel, manzanita, oaks, grasslands, wildflowers, serpentine, and wildlife. You get a sampling of much of the North Bay's natural history on the seven-mile round-trip. For the best experience, pick a clear, cool day, preferably in spring when the wildflowers are in bloom.

Goodspeed Trail's trailhead and first two miles are located in Sugarloaf Ridge State Park. The trail's final 1.5 miles are located in Hood Mountain Regional Park, managed by Sonoma County. From the trailhead at the bridge on Adobe Canyon Road, you enter a shady redwood forest and take a mellow stroll through the big trees. Two footbridges carry you across Sonoma Creek and Bear Creek.

The first 0.25 mile of redwood forest is so captivating that you may be tempted not to press onward, but do so and you quickly exit the shady stream canyon and enter drier, rockier terrain. The trail begins its moderate but steady ascent on sunny slopes. Blue and white Douglas iris line the path in April.

At nearly one mile out, you'll cross a dirt road, then pick up the single-track trail on the far side. The trail drops down to a stream crossing that is dry in summer but a wide, coursing flow in winter and spring. Huge boulders line the stream.

Goodspeed Trail climbs out of the canyon, then continues through an alternating progression of sunshine and shade, grasslands and forest. The exposed areas are dotted with serpentine and wildflowers, including red paintbrush, California poppies, brodiaea, blue-eyed grass, and red thistles. The forested slopes are covered by a mix of bay laurel, oak, manzanita, and pine, plus woodland flowers like hound's tongue and shooting stars.

The trail gets progressively steeper as you go, and without any fanfare suddenly changes its name to Nattkemper Trail. Two conical-shaped peaks come into view at two miles. One looks very green and grassy, the other is covered with chaparral and woodland, but neither is Hood Mountain. Goodspeed/Nattkemper Trail ascends along the southwest shoulder of the unnamed grassy summit, elevation 2,350 feet, then makes a series of short, steep switchbacks to rise above it. Look for plentiful poppies and lupine in these grasslands in springtime.

You're given a brief respite at a small saddle, then—surprise—the trail drops downhill on the northeast side of the forested summit. Soon it soon climbs again, but fortunately this final ascent is shaded. You come out to a broad saddle between the two small summits and Hood Mountain itself. Very shortly thereafter is the left turnoff for Gunsight Rock, where you leave the main trail and walk 200 yards to your destination.

A cluster of boulders with a wide notch in the middle, aptly named Gunsight Rock presents sweeping views to the south, west, and north. Mount St. Helena in Napa, Mount Tamalpais in Marin, and the Golden Gate Bridge are easy landmarks. The whole of Sonoma Valley can be seen in one glance. The

© ANN MARIE BROWN

Goodspeed Trail begins in a streamside redwood grove, then opens out to grass-covered hillsides.

rapidly growing metropolis of Santa Rosa lies to the west. The drop-off is extreme from this rocky promontory, so exercise caution as you clamber around for the best view. Be on the lookout for peregrine falcons, which nest in these cliffs in spring and summer.

Should you choose to hike the final 0.25 mile to the summit of Hood Mountain, just follow the main trail uphill. Its grade steepens as it enters a dry, brittle forest of manzanita and knobcone pines. The summit consists of a wide dirt clearing, most likely a turnaround for fire engines, encircled by tall chaparral. A visit to this disappointing spot will probably inspire you to head back down to the drama of Gunsight Rock.

Options

Those looking for an easy hike in the neighborhood of the Goodspeed Trailhead should drive uphill on Adobe Canyon Road to the main entrance to Sugarloaf Ridge State Park. A few yards west of the entrance kiosk is the trailhead for Canyon Trail, which descends a short 0.5 mile to a fetching waterfall on Sonoma Creek. The cataract makes a fine destination by itself, or can serve as a cool, refreshing finale to the Gunsight Rock hike.

Hikers coming from the Santa Rosa area may prefer to access Gunsight Rock and Hood Mountain from the Sonoma County Parks trailhead at the end of Los Alamos Road, just southeast of Santa Rosa. A wide fire road named Hood Mountain Trail leads to the summit, but most hikers opt to branch off on the narrower Summit Trail, which passes through a pygmy Sargent cypress forest. Leashed dogs are permitted if you start your hike at Los Alamos Road.

Directions

From U.S. 101 in Santa Rosa, take the Fairgrounds/Highway 12 exit. Highway 12 becomes Farmers Lane as it heads through downtown Santa Rosa. Continue on Highway 12 for 11 miles to Adobe Canyon Road in Kenwood and turn left. (Or, from Highway 12 in Sonoma, drive 11 miles north to Adobe Canyon Road, then turn right.) Drive 2.2 miles to the small parking area on the left at a bridge over Sonoma Creek (it's 1.3 miles before the entrance kiosk for Sugarloaf Ridge State Park).

Information and Contact

An $8 day-use fee is charged per vehicle. Dogs and bikes are not allowed. A trail map is available free by download at www.sonoma-county.org. For more information, contact Sonoma County Regional Parks, 2300 County Circle Drive, Santa Rosa, CA 95403, 707/565-2041, www.sonoma-county.org or www.parks. sonoma.net.

7 LAKE AND FALLEN BRIDGE LOOP
Jack London State Historic Park

Level: Easy/Moderate

Hiking Time: 2 hours

Total Distance: 4.2 miles round-trip

Elevation Change: 600 feet

Summary: Tour novelist Jack London's beloved ranch, vineyard, and swimming lake in the scenic Valley of the Moon.

Author Jack London wanted beauty, and so he "bought beauty, and was content with beauty for awhile." Those were his words to describe his love affair with his Sonoma ranch and its surrounding hills, which are now part of Jack London State Historic Park.

London, famous for his novels *Call of the Wild* and *The Sea Wolf,* which made him one of the most popular and highest-paid fiction writers of the early 1900s, wanted to build his home in Glen Ellen to escape city life. After two years of construction, his ranch dream house caught fire and burned to the ground just days before he and his wife were to move in. It was a devastating loss, both personally and financially, for the Londons. The couple lived on the ranch in a small wood-frame house until Jack London's death in 1916.

London's vision of beauty is the setting for this easy loop hike that begins at the

Crumbling buildings and thriving grapevines can be seen near Jack London's home.

ranch vineyards, then leads through a scenic woodland to a small lake and high vistas. Be sure to begin or end your trip with a visit to the Jack London Museum (10 A.M.–5 P.M. daily) at the visitors center, which features interesting exhibits and photographs from the author's life.

Take the paved trail from the parking lot to the picnic area, then pick up the dirt fire road signed as Lake Trail. Head right, past the barns and winery buildings. Turn right at the sign for Pig Palace—the extravagant pigsty enjoyed by London's beloved pigs. Check out this elaborate stone structure, then return to the Lake Trail. Skirting past carefully tended vineyards, the road forks at a gate; hikers take the right turnoff on single-track Lake Trail. You'll climb for 0.5 mile

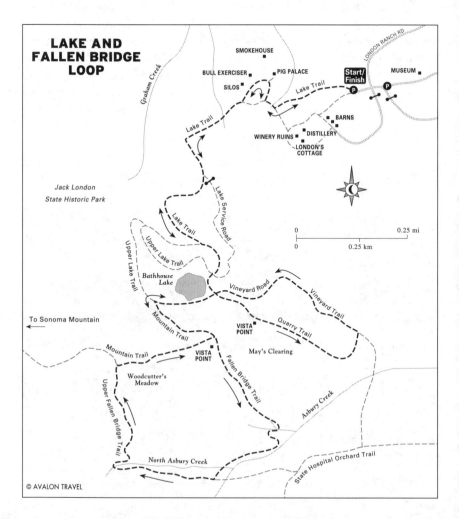

LAKE AND FALLEN BRIDGE LOOP

SMOKEHOUSE

BULL EXERCISER   PIG PALACE

SILOS

Lake Trail

Start/Finish   MUSEUM

P   P

BARNS

WINERY RUINS   DISTILLERY

LONDON'S COTTAGE

Graham Creek

LONDON RANCH RD

Lake Trail

Jack London State Historic Park

Lake Trail

Lake Service Road

Upper Lake Trail

Upper Lake Trail

Bathhouse Lake

Vineyard Road

Vineyard Trail

0   0.25 mi
0   0.25 km

To Sonoma Mountain

Mountain Trail

VISTA POINT

Quarry Trail

May's Clearing

Mountain Trail

VISTA POINT

Woodcutter's Meadow

Fallen Bridge Trail

Asbury Creek

Upper Fallen Bridge Trail

North Asbury Creek

State Hospital Orchard Trail

© AVALON TRAVEL

through mixed hardwoods and Douglas firs to the edge of Bathhouse Lake. (Several paths join with Lake Trail; all lead to the lake.)

London's prized lake is more of a pond nowadays. With sediment continually encroaching upon it, it has shrunk to half its original size. A redwood log cabin that was used as a bathhouse still stands. The Londons swam, fished, and entertained guests at the lake.

Beyond the lake lie the park's "real" hiking trails, which consist of two separate loops. From the ranch road on the southeast edge of the lake, take single-track Quarry Trail east. A 0.25-mile walk leads you to a bench and a vista point that overlooks the bucolic Valley of the Moon and green ridges behind it. Enjoy this spot, then continue on Quarry Trail, turn left and loop back on Vineyard Trail and Vineyard Road.

Back near the lake again, follow the wide ranch road uphill through a few switchbacks. (The road is now called Mountain Trail.) At a large clearing and second vista point, you gain another wide view of Sonoma Valley. This is also the intersection with Fallen Bridge Trail, where you'll head south to make a 1.3-mile loop. Take the left fork first, crunching through the leaves lining the path. The route tunnels through madrones and oaks, then meets up with Asbury Creek and parallels it. Bear right to loop back on Upper Fallen Bridge Trail, now climbing steeply through the redwood-lined creek canyon. At a junction with Mountain Trail, turn right and follow the dirt road back to the clearing, then continue downhill through the switchbacks to the lake.

Options

If you're feeling more ambitious, the Sonoma Ridge Trail allows for an 11-mile round-trip hike to a ridge-top overlook just below the summit of 2,463-foot Sonoma Mountain (the summit itself is on private property). To access the trail, instead of following the meandering route around the ranch property described earlier in this listing, head straight uphill on Lake Trail and Mountain Trail. Watch for Sonoma Ridge Trail, a hard left turn off Mountain Trail, 2.2 miles from the parking lot. The single-track path climbs moderately but steadily for 3.3 miles through a lovely mixed forest until it finally tops out at a wide overlook of the Valley of the Moon, Napa River, San Pablo Bay, and far-off Mount Diablo.

Alternatively, if you prefer a shorter, steeper path to the high ridge of Sonoma Mountain, simply stay on Mountain Trail, a wide fire road, and follow it all the way to the park border (a 6.6-mile round-trip). A short spur trail at its end leads to an overlook on an eastern ridge of Sonoma Mountain, about 100 feet lower than the summit. This vantage point provides broad views of Mount St. Helena, San Pablo Bay, and Mount Tamalpais.

Directions

From Sonoma on Highway 12, drive north for 4.5 miles to Madrone Road and turn left. At the end of Madrone Road, turn right on Arnold Drive and follow it for three miles into Glen Ellen, then turn left on London Ranch Road. Follow London Ranch Road for one mile to the park entrance kiosk. Park in the day-use area on the right (not in the visitors center lot on the left). The trail leads from the parking area.

Information and Contact

An $8 day-use fee is charged per vehicle. Dogs are allowed only on the short trails around Beauty Ranch and Wolf House. Bikes are allowed only on fire roads. A park map is available at the visitors center for $1 or free by download at www.parks.ca.gov. For more information, contact Jack London State Historic Park, 2400 London Ranch Road, Glen Ellen, CA 95442, 707/938-5216, www.jacklondonpark.com or www.parks.ca.gov.

8 SONOMA OVERLOOK TRAIL

City of Sonoma

Level: Easy   **Total Distance:** 2.6 miles round-trip

Hiking Time: 1 hour   **Elevation Change:** 400 feet

Summary: An easy walk to a high ridge rewards Sonoma hikers with views, exercise, and wildflowers in spring.

Even the most dedicated gourmands must occasionally take a break from sipping cappuccinos, nibbling on croissants, and noshing exotic cheeses in Sonoma's historic downtown plaza. When your practical sense of "all-things-in-moderation" kicks in, drag yourself away from Sonoma Plaza's indulgent food and tempting shopping opportunities and walk off some of that self-induced guilt on the Sonoma Overlook Trail.

A joint project of the City of Sonoma and the Sonoma Ecology Center, this 1.3-mile walking path starts at the entrance to Mountain Cemetery, just four blocks north of the plaza (off First Street West). Being so close to town, this is not a wilderness trail by any means, but it offers lovely views of the town of Sonoma and surrounding Valley of the Moon. Docent-led hikes are free to the public on many weekends, or you can walk this trail any time by yourself.

The route meanders gently uphill, traveling north mostly through a woodland of bay laurel and coast live oak. Along the way you'll also pass buckeyes, madrone,

© ANN MARIE BROWN

A bench at the top of the Sonoma Overlook Trail provides an inspiring view of the valley below.

toyon, and a variety of manzanitas. The trail skirts past two meadows then switchbacks left to depart the tree canopy once and for all as it nears the ridge top. Spring wildflower season brings a colorful mix of angiosperms, including yellow mariposa lilies, clarkia, soaproot, and blue-eyed grass. As the trail gradually climbs, you'll pass by occasional hand-built stone benches with plaques commemorating Sonoma nature lovers.

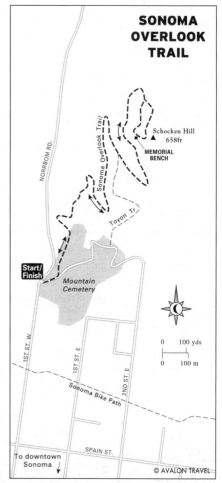

After an ascent that's so mellow you will hardly notice that you are climbing, Sonoma Overlook Trail tops out below the summit of 658-foot Schocken Hill. The hill was named for Solomon Schocken, who operated a quarry here in the 1890s. Schocken's stones were used for cobblestones on streets throughout the Bay Area. Long before its use as a quarry, this hillside was used as hunting grounds by the Native Americans living and working at the Sonoma Mission.

A short path loops around the meadow, leading to a memorial bench and views of the City of Sonoma, Sonoma Mountain, and stretching as far as San Pablo Bay. On the clearest day, you can easily pick out the tall buildings of San Francisco.

As you enjoy this lovely trail, consider that in 2002 the city planned to lease this land to a resort. Sonoma Valley citizens worked with the Sonoma Overlook Trail Task Force to save the land for public use. One of the most persistent rabble-rousers was Ditty Vella, who formerly ran the Cheesemaker's Daughter in downtown Sonoma.

Options

Once you've topped the ascent, take the alternative Toyon Trail for your return trip downhill. This trail leads to the upper trailhead in the cemetery, then travels through the cemetery and back to the starting point of your hike for a fascinating look at some of Sonoma's historic, moss-covered gravesites.

Directions

From Highway 12 at Sonoma Plaza, head north on First Street West for four blocks. The trailhead is on the right just past Mountain Cemetery (90 First Street West, 8 A.M.–5 P.M. daily). There is also an upper trailhead off Toyon Road within the cemetery.

Information and Contact

There is no fee. Dogs and bikes are not allowed. A trail map/brochure is available at the trailhead or can be downloaded for free at www.sonomaecologycenter.org. For more information, contact Sonoma Ecology Center, P.O. Box 533, Sonoma, CA 95476, 707/933-8128, www.sonomaecologycenter.org.

9 RITCHEY CANYON AND COYOTE PEAK
Bothe-Napa Valley State Park

Level: Easy/Moderate

Hiking Time: 3 hours

Total Distance: 4.6 miles round-trip

Elevation Change: 850 feet

Summary: This trail follows a perennial stream and visits one of the easternmost groves of coastal redwoods in California.

Even the most devoted and enthusiastic Napa Valley wine tasters eventually tire of their task. If it's a hot summer day, perhaps they start to daydream of a shady redwood forest where they could walk for a while or sit by a stream. Such musing might seem preposterous: Where in the midst of the sun-baked vineyards could a redwood tree possibly grow?

At Bothe-Napa Valley State Park, that's where. Ritchey Canyon and Redwood Trails take you through a delightful stand of them, one of the most eastern groves of coastal redwoods in the state. Paired with a visit to the summit of Coyote Peak, this loop trip will leave you even more intoxicated with Napa Valley's wine country.

Joining the redwoods are plenty of Douglas firs, buckeyes, and big-leaf maples, plus ferns galore. Look carefully among the branches of the trees: Five different kinds of woodpeckers dwell within the park's borders. I spotted the largest of these, the pileated woodpecker, on a tree right by the picnic area. He was working his way up and down a big Douglas fir like a telephone lineman on triple overtime.

Spring is the best season to hike at Bothe-Napa. In April and May, the buckeyes are in fragrant bloom and the creek is running strong. Wildflowers, including Solomon's seal and redwood orchids, bloom in the cool shade in February and March. Park volunteers manage a small Native American plant garden near the

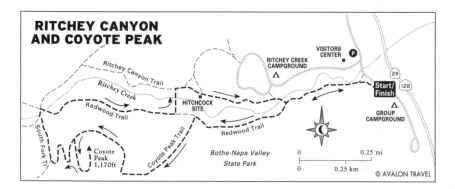

© ANN MARIE BROWN

view from Coyote Peak

visitors center, with signs that interpret local native flora and how it was used by the people who once lived here.

Start your hike by heading up Ritchey Canyon Trail from the horse trailer parking lot. (You can also start by the small bridge near the visitors center, or access the trail from the park campground if you are camping there.) The first 0.5 mile is somewhat noisy due to the proximity of the highway and campground, but soon you leave those distractions behind. Ferns, wild grape, and spice bush line the path. Second-growth redwoods are mixed in with Douglas firs. Black oaks and big-leaf maples form a canopy over the trail as well as Ritchey Creek, which runs dependably year-round. (The oaks and maples wear bright yellow coats in autumn.) Keep the creek on your right; the trail narrows and meets up with Redwood Trail, which you then follow. Ritchey Canyon Trail crosses to the north side of the stream.

Three-quarters of a mile from the start, reach a junction with Coyote Peak Trail and bear left. The trail doles out a fair climb but remains shaded most of the way. Soon you leave the conifers and enter drier slopes and a bay and live oak forest. In short order the oaks give way to low-growing chaparral and scattered rock outcrops. Wide views open up on your right of conifer-covered Ritchey Canyon below.

Near the top of the climb you reach a junction; the right fork will be your return. Bear left and make a short but steep ascent to a knoll just below Coyote Peak's summit. You're rewarded with a pastoral view of the vineyards and valley far below—the best view of the day. The summit is a short distance farther, but its vista is somewhat obstructed by trees. Peering through the branches, you can make out Mount St. Helena to the northwest.

Return to the junction with the western leg of Coyote Peak Trail and follow it steeply down the opposite side of the mountain. You'll soon leave toyon, chemise, and ceanothus in favor of shady redwoods. At a junction with South Fork Trail, turn right. Follow a concrete apron across Ritchey Creek, then turn right on Redwood Trail and cross the creek again. The next 0.5 mile on Redwood Trail is the loveliest of the trip, featuring the densest redwoods and ferns.

If Ritchey Creek isn't running too full and wide, turn left to cross it at an obvious (but unbridged) spur, then follow Ritchey Canyon Trail east for part of your return. On the opposite bank of Ritchey Creek, Ritchey Canyon Trail passes the old Hitchcock homesite, where Lillie Hitchcock Coit and her parents spent their summers in the 1870s. Lillie Coit is best known for lending her name and money to Coit Tower on Telegraph Hill in San Francisco. Ritchey Canyon Trail eventually meets up again with Redwood Trail to return you to your starting point.

Options

Another rewarding path at Bothe-Napa Valley State Park is the History Trail, which leads from the picnic area beyond the group campground. This trail runs 1.2 miles to neighboring Bale Grist Mill State Park (10 A.M.–5 P.M. Sat.–Sun.), passing a pioneer cemetery along the way. At the trail's end, you have an up-close look at the 36-foot waterwheel, still in operating condition, which ran Edward Bale's flour mill in the 1840s and 1850s. Perennially flowing Mill Creek powered the wheel.

Directions

From Highway 29/128 in St. Helena, drive north on Highway 29/128 for five miles to the entrance to Bothe-Napa Valley State Park on the left side of the highway. (It's 3.5 miles south of Calistoga.) Turn left and drive 0.25 mile to the entrance kiosk, then continue past the visitors center to the horse trailer parking lot on the right. The trail begins on the right side of the horse trailer parking lot.

Information and Contact

An $8 day-use fee is charged per vehicle. Dogs and bikes are not allowed. Trail maps are available at the entrance kiosk or visitors center for $1. For more information, contact Bothe-Napa Valley State Park, 3801 St. Helena Highway North, Calistoga, CA 94515, 707/942-4575, www.parks.ca.gov.

🔟 MOUNT ST. HELENA   BEST ◖

Robert Louis Stevenson State Park

Level: Strenuous   **Total Distance:** 10.6 miles round-trip

Hiking Time: 6 hours   **Elevation Change:** 2,100 feet

Summary: Pick a crystal clear day for this epic trek to the highest summit in the Wine Country, where the vista can expand to more than 100 miles.

Normally a trail that is 80 percent fire road would not interest me in the slightest. But the spectacular view from the top of Mount St. Helena makes the climb on its wide, exposed road completely worthwhile. And unlike other Bay Area peaks bearing world-class vistas, like Mount Diablo and Mount Tamalpais, Mount St. Helena has no public automobile access to its summit—although an occasional service vehicle may pass by on the trail/road. This is one summit view that must be earned with some effort.

For the best possible trip, pick a cool, clear day in late autumn, winter, or spring—forget the hot days of summer. Then pack along the finest picnic lunch you can put together, drive to the trailhead, and start climbing.

At its start, the trail is called the Stevenson Memorial Trail, named for author

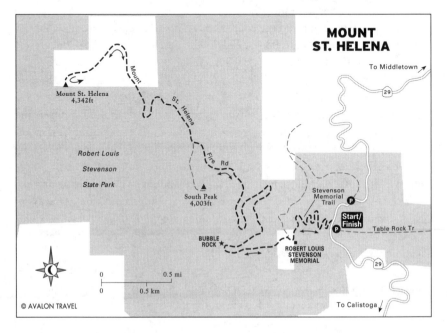

Robert Louis Stevenson. He and his wife honeymooned at an abandoned mine site along this trail in the summer of 1880. The first mile consists of well-graded single-track through a densely wooded canyon. Except for some road noise from the highway below, this stretch is a delightful stroll past giant madrones, bay laurels, Douglas firs, and black oaks. The switchbacks are plentiful, making the ascent easy. Enjoy the good trail and the shade, because both will come to an end in short order.

Three-quarters of a mile from the start is a stone monument marking the spot where the Stevensons honeymooned. Lacking the finances for a fancier vacation, the Stevensons camped here for a month in an old cabin, using hay for bedding. During their rustic holiday, Stevenson took extensive notes on both the mountain landscape and the couple's camping experience. These scribblings later became the basis for his book *The Silverado Squatters*. Mount St. Helena was the model for Spyglass Hill in *Treasure Island*.

© ANN MARIE BROWN

Columnar basalt covers the summit of Mount St. Helena.

At the monument site, hikers say farewell to the shade and single-track. Shortly beyond it, the trail joins Mount St. Helena Fire Road. Turn left on the dirt road (one of only two junctions on the entire route). Take a look around and note the terrain change. You're surrounded by big knobcone pines and manzanita now, on a wide, exposed track with views of the Napa Valley.

Keep climbing. At a major switchback at 1.6 miles, you reach Bubble Rock, where rock climbers strut their stuff. The grade is surprisingly moderate, and the miles go by quickly (provided you aren't hiking on a hot day). Visual rewards are doled out long before you reach the summit; you gain open vistas of Napa Valley, the Vaca Mountains, Lake Berryessa, and the volcanic rock of the Palisades at several points along the road.

The route's second major junction shows up at 3.1 miles, along the ridgeline of Mount St. Helena. The road to the left leads to South Peak, a lesser summit at 4,003 feet. Continue straight for the mountain's higher summit, but not without first oohing and aahing over the vista from this saddle. This is your most expansive view so far.

Save some space on your camera's memory card, because now it's less than two miles to Mount St. Helena's summit at 4,342 feet. When you reach the top, pay no attention to the buildings and all-too-numerous cell phone towers. Instead stroll around and take in the amazing 360-degree scenery. There's Lake Berryessa and the Sierra Nevada to the east. To the southeast lies Mount Diablo, 60 miles away. Most impressive of all—and this is the part that gives the whole trip an A-plus grade—is the clear-day view of Mount Shasta to the north, nearly 200 miles distant. Often Mount Lassen is visible as well, with 7,056-foot Snow Mountain in the northern foreground. Pull out a map of Northern California, a pair of binoculars, and your picnic lunch.

You may notice some odd-shaped rocks under your feet on the northwest side of the wide summit. If you have visited Devils Postpile National Monument in the Eastern Sierra, you'll recognize them—they're the five-sided tops of lava columns. Although Mount St. Helena is composed of volcanic rock, it's not a volcano. It's part of a large, ancient lava flow.

One more tip on climbing Mount St. Helena: Every winter, usually during the coldest days in December or January, the peak receives a thorough dusting of snow. If you can keep your eye on the winter weather and take off on a moment's notice, you could have the exhilarating experience of climbing mighty Mount St. Helena when its peak is covered in snow.

Options

Another favorite trail at Robert Louis Stevenson State Park begins at this same trailhead and explores the nearby volcanic tablelands. Take the Table Rock Trail from the opposite side of the parking lot. You'll climb through a series of switchbacks and then cross Garnett Creek. At 2.2 miles you reach Table Rock, a 200-foot-high, sheer volcanic cliff. Turn around here for a 4.4-mile round-trip, or take the Palisades Trail fork that you passed 100 yards before Table Rock. This rugged trail skirts the base of the fascinating volcanic formation known as the Palisades. Hike as far as you please, then retrace your steps. Some hikers follow Palisades Trail 3.9 miles to Oat Hill Mine Trail, then take that trail 4.5 miles downhill to the town of Calistoga, where they have a car shuttle waiting. Even with a shuttle, this is a long, 11-mile trip with some gruelingly steep downhill sections. Your knees may not appreciate it.

Directions

From Highway 29/128 in Calistoga, turn north on Highway 29 and drive eight miles (through the town of Calistoga) to the signed trailhead. Park in the pullouts on either side of the road. The trail begins on the left side of the road.

Information and Contact

There is no fee. Dogs are not allowed. Bikes are allowed only on fire roads. Trail maps are available at the visitors center in Bothe-Napa Valley State Park. For more information, contact Robert Louis Stevenson State Park c/o Bothe-Napa Valley State Park, 3801 St. Helena Highway North, Calistoga, CA 94515, 707/942-4575, www.parks.ca.gov.

11 TABLE ROCK

BEST ◖

Robert Louis Stevenson State Park

Level: Moderate | **Total Distance:** 4.6 miles round-trip
Hiking Time: 2.5 hours | **Elevation Change:** 1,000 feet

Summary: Take a walk on the "other side" of Robert Louis Stevenson State Park, where a single-track trail leads to a rock outcrop with a superlative view.

If you're not feeling ambitious enough to tackle the 10-mile round-trip to mighty Mount St. Helena, there's another worthwhile reason to drive the winding eight miles on Highway 29 from Calistoga to Robert Louis Stevenson State Park. It's the Table Rock Trail, a much easier hike that offers some of the Wine Country's best views. A mere 4.6 miles round-trip, with only a moderate amount of up-and-down, leads you to the craggy summit of Table Rock, a large block of igneous rock with sheer drop-offs on three sides. This moonscape-like rock outcrop with its crags, gullies, and pockmarks is fascinating enough from a geological perspective, but it's the view from the top—a postcard panorama of the Napa Valley—that you will long remember.

The trailhead lies on Highway 29 directly across from the trailhead for Mount St. Helena. If possible, park on the southeast or right side of the road, and not the

© ANN MARIE BROWN

Along the path to Table Rock, a labyrinth made of volcanic rocks entices hikers to walk and meditate.

Mount St. Helena side, so you don't have to cross Highway 29 on foot. Drivers tend to speed up this mountain road as if it were the Autobahn, so be extra cautious.

The hike begins with a climb up a small hill through a canopy of tanoaks, madrones, and Douglas firs, topping out at a boulder-studded vista point 0.7 mile from the trailhead. From here and other points along the trail, Mount St. Helena is visible to the west, looming 2,000 feet above while green hills and vineyards line the valley below. Snow Mountain to the north is usually snow-covered in winter and easy to spot.

This brief climb is followed by a rocky descent down to a small valley, where someone has gone to the effort to build a small labyrinth of stones suitable for a short walking meditation. After a few minutes of easy strolling, you'll reach a signpost for Table Rock Overlook; bear right and you'll arrive at the overlook in less than 100 yards. The rock, perched at 2,465 feet elevation, offers outstanding views of Calistoga and its environs, plus Mount St. Helena and Snow Mountain.

Table Rock's sheer cliffs attract a nesting pair of peregrine falcons; you can often hear them squawking and might even be lucky enough to see one in flight. Peregrines, with their blue-gray backs and white undersides, are famous for reaching speeds of 200 miles per hour.

Options

A short distance to the east of Table Rock are the magnificent Palisades. Most people recognize them as a looming band of volcanic rock visible when driving Highway 29 or while visiting Calistoga-area wineries. To see this rock formation close-up, continue east on the obvious trail from Table Rock. You're now following the Palisades Trail. You'll descend about 300 feet to Garrett Creek, cross over it, and then continue onward to Lasky Point, named for Moses Lasky, a lifelong rock climber who helped to create this trail. Soon the trail rounds a shoulder and you get your first view of the sheer volcanic cliffs of the Palisades. Continuing onward, the trail passes right along the base of the Palisades cliffs. In the wet season, numerous small waterfalls pour down the cliffs, adding even more drama to the scenery.

The round-trip tally from the Table Rock trailhead to the Palisades is about 5 miles, or 10 miles out-and-back from the trailhead on Highway 29. You can also make this a one-way shuttle hike, covering 11 miles from the Table Rock Trailhead to the Oat Hill Mine Trailhead located on Silverado Trail near its junction with Highway 29. You'll need to leave a car at each trailhead. Follow the trail from Table Rock to the Palisades, then continue eastward, descending to an intersection with Oat Hill Mine Road. The 4.5-mile Oat Hill Mine Road will deposit you at your shuttle car on Silverado Trail.

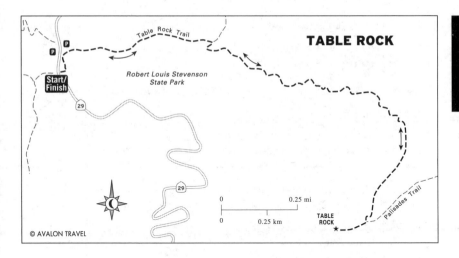

Directions

From Highway 29/128 in Calistoga, turn north on Highway 29 and drive eight miles (through the town of Calistoga) to the signed trailhead. Park in the pullouts on either side of the road. The trail begins on the right side of the road.

Information and Contact

There is no fee. Dogs and bikes are not allowed. Trail maps are available at the visitors center in Bothe-Napa Valley State Park. For more information, contact Robert Louis Stevenson State Park c/o Bothe-Napa Valley State Park, 3801 St. Helena Highway North, Calistoga, CA 94515, 707/942-4575, www.parks.ca.gov.

12 ZIM ZIM FALLS

BEST ☾

Knoxville Wildlife Area

Level: Moderate

Total Distance: 7.4 miles round-trip

Hiking Time: 3.5 hours

Elevation Change: 750 feet

Summary: One of the Bay Area's most spectacular and little-known waterfalls drops in a remote canyon north of Lake Berryessa.

For most people in the Bay Area, this waterfall is pretty far *out there,* and that's why few Bay Area hikers have seen it. Unless you happen to live in or near the town of Napa, this trip is best for a "plan-ahead" day, when you've gotten out of bed early enough that you don't mind making the long drive to Knoxville Wildlife Area, 10 miles north of Lake Berryessa. The drive is long, slow, and somewhat tedious, but hikers who go to this extra effort during or just after a period of substantial rain will be well rewarded.

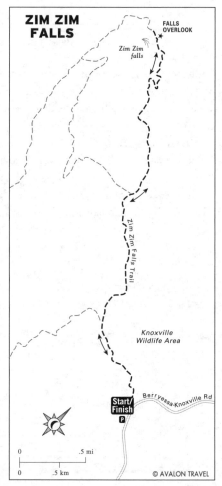

Knoxville Wildlife Area is the home of Zim Zim Falls, quite possibly the tallest waterfall in the greater Bay Area—even taller than Murietta Falls, which is much harder to get to and flows on even fewer days of the year. Cascading just over 100 feet, Zim Zim Falls is an impressive sight to behold during the winter and early spring months. By the first of June, however, the show is usually over, or severely diminished.

The waterfall is just one of the highlights of this wildlife preserve managed by the California Department of Fish and Game. Popular with hunters in the autumn, and far too hot to be popular with anyone in the summer,

Knoxville Wildlife Area is a land of rugged hills and canyons, with elevations ranging from 1,000 to 2,000 feet. Think of Mount Diablo or the Ohlone Wilderness—right down to the blue oaks and the gray pines—and you get an idea of what this landscape is like.

It's more special than it may appear at first glance. Knoxville is one of only a handful of sites in California that protects serpentine habitats. Most plant species are intolerant of serpentine soil, so only highly unusual types of plants can tolerate them—often rare and endemic species. The wildlife area provides important breeding grounds and feeding areas for black-tailed deer, Rio Grande wild turkeys, California quail, hawks, harriers, falcons, and owls.

© ANDREW SAWADISAVI

Zim Zim Falls tumbles more than 100 feet.

The trail to Zim Zim Falls starts at a green gate and follows an old dirt road along the Zim Zim Creek canyon. It is mostly level for the entire route and fairly easy to follow, as long as you remember to stay close to the creek. (Ignore all the side trails that spur off the main road.) You'll cross the creek nearly a dozen times before you reach the falls. If you don't get your feet wet, then there won't be a strong flow at the falls. Hope for wet feet.

For most of the hike, it's hard to believe you are approaching a waterfall. There's nothing about these rolling, oak-studded, chaparral-clad hills that says "sudden vertical drop of falling water." Just have faith and keep walking.

Shortly after the last stream crossing, as you near the end of the valley, there will be a trail fork near a prominent, pink-colored boulder. Go right and head up the hill, then at a second junction, go left. The trail cuts back to a high viewpoint of Zim Zim Falls from about 150 yards away. This lovely overlook makes a great spot for lunch.

Many hikers aren't content with the long-distance view and insist on scrambling down the steep, chaparral-covered slopes to the base of the falls, but a somewhat easier way to get there is to simply backtrack to the boulder-marked fork and head straight up the creek.

If you're wondering about this waterfall's name, Zim Zim is actually a misspelling of Zem Zem, which was the name given to a sulphur spring and hotel located near here in the 1860s. The story goes that a visitor to the spring tasted the water and exclaimed, "This water taste like it's from the sacred well of Zem Zem!" He was referring to a term from the Islam religion. Zem Zem is a sacred stop along the way for pilgrims traveling to Mecca; a goal of all pilgrims is to drink the water of Zem Zem.

Unless you've brought a filter or purifier with you, you probably shouldn't taste the water of Zim Zim, but you might want to hang out for a while and soak in its surprising beauty. When done, retrace your steps and return to the trailhead.

Options

After viewing the falls from on high, continue on the trail up and behind the falls, ascending to the western ridge above Zim Zim Valley. From this ridge, you can look down onto both Zim Zim and Nevada canyons, plus gain an impressive view of Lake Berryessa and Blue Ridge.

Directions

From Napa, take Highway 128 east through Rutherford to Berryessa-Knoxville Road, a distance of about 25 miles. Turn north on Berryessa Knoxville Road and drive about 22 miles to the signed trailhead on the left. During the wet season, you will have to drive through the shallow waters of Eticuera Creek numerous times to get to the trailhead, so a high-clearance vehicle is a good idea.

Information and Contact

There is no fee. Dogs and bikes are allowed. Maps are available by contacting the Department of Fish and Game Bay-Delta Regional Office, 7329 Silverado Trail, Napa, CA 94599, 707/944-5531 or 707/944-5537, www.dfg.ca.gov.

13 SUGARLOAF PEAK LOOP
Skyline Wilderness Park

Level: Moderate

Total Distance: 7.4 miles round-trip

Hiking Time: 4 hours

Elevation Change: 1,500 feet

Summary: A hike to a lesser-known peak just a few miles from busy downtown Napa, where oaks, buckeyes, and fern-covered rock walls line the path.

Napa Valley hikers speak of Skyline Wilderness Park in hushed tones. Several Napa friends told me repeatedly that Skyline Park had the best hiking in the region. So imagine my surprise when I drove up and discovered that the trailhead for this "wilderness park" is located in an RV camp packed with trailers, lawn chairs, and plastic flowers and flamingos.

That's the way it is, but don't be discouraged by your first glimpse. To reach the park's excellent trail system, you must walk by the RVs, past the park's social hall and picnic areas, and through a 150-yard corridor of chain-link fencing. (The latter passes by neighboring state hospital property.) Finally, after about 10 minutes of this strange meandering, you leave it all behind and enter the quiet, steep-walled canyon of Marie Creek.

Trail choices are plentiful. The park isn't large, so by connecting a series of paths you can see a good portion of it. This 7.4-mile loop tours both high walls of Marie Creek canyon, visits the summit of Sugarloaf Peak, then finishes out alongside babbling Marie Creek.

After passing through a maze of well-marked paths to reach the actual trailhead, make your first trail choice based on the day's weather. If visibility is good, take Skyline Trail for the first leg of the loop. Skyline Trail, a part of the Bay Area Ridge Trail that is open to horses and bikes as well as hikers, climbs to the top of the park's southwest

descending Sugarloaf Peak's grassy slopes

© ANN MARIE BROWN

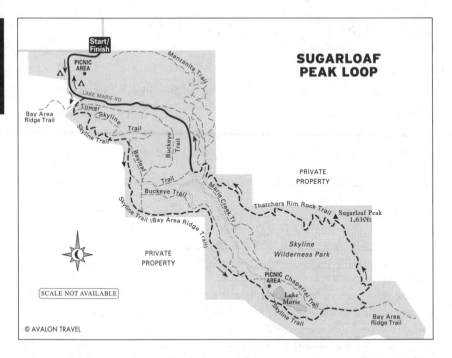

ridge and follows it four miles. The trail features good views of Napa Valley and San Pablo Bay.

If it's cloudy, take Buckeye Trail for the loop's first leg. Buckeye Trail is narrow single-track and open to hikers only. It climbs halfway up the southwest canyon wall, then contours along this steep slope for its entire three-mile distance. The path wanders through a series of oak and buckeye groves, grasslands, and fern-covered rock walls. This area is beautiful after a period of rain, when all the tiny ferns come to life.

Buckeye Trail and Skyline Trail meet up just before Lake Marie, a long, narrow reservoir on Marie Creek. The lake is popular with bass anglers, most of whom access it by hiking on wide, level Lake Marie Road. If you wish, take the spur trail from Skyline Trail down to the lake's edge. Then follow Skyline Trail as it curves around the lake and crosses Marie Creek. You'll hike a pleasant stretch along the stream, then turn left on Thatchers Rim Rock Trail. Prepare for a healthy climb up Sugarloaf Peak.

Thatchers Rim Rock Trail traverses open, grassy slopes, an ideal environment for spring wildflowers. Lichen-covered outcrops of volcanic rock are scattered among the grasses. The trail makes a steep climb through oaks and manzanitas to the mountain summit. As you ascend, turn around occasionally to check out the gorgeous views of the canyon below you. Mount Diablo peeks out above the hills to the south.

Sugarloaf Peak has two summits—the west peak at 1,630 feet, which you're hiking on, and the east peak at 1,686 feet, which is covered with microwave towers. Your summit is broad and dotted with coast live oaks, so you must wander around to locate the best views. (Head downhill to the west to reach an open clearing.) Although the peak's perspective on the Napa Valley, Napa River, and the northern tip of San Pablo Bay is interesting, the long-distance vista south is the real draw. You can clearly make out the looming outline of Mount Tamalpais in Marin County, as well as the towers of the Golden Gate Bridge and the San Francisco skyline. Nowhere is it more obvious than from this perspective that Mount Tamalpais is a ridge, not a single peak. Looking west and northwest, you can see Mount Veeder and Mount St. Helena as well.

Continue along Thatchers Rim Rock Trail, now descending the west side of Sugarloaf Peak. The trail makes a steep drop through several switchbacks to the canyon bottom. Remarkably tall manzanita shrubs border the trail. Cross Marie Creek on a footbridge, then continue straight to a junction with Lake Marie Road. A right turn will lead you on a final level mile back to the edge of the RV park and eventually to your car.

Options

Hikers looking for an easier stroll will enjoy an out-and-back walk on Lake Marie Road. The wide fire road leads uphill alongside Marie Creek for two miles to Lake Marie. The canyon walls on both side of the road are marked by striking cliff formations and small caves set amid a dense forest of oaks, madrones, and bay laurel. Watch for a 100-year-old fig tree on the left at 1.3 miles, near the junction with Bayleaf Trail. The enormous old tree still produces edible fruit.

Directions

From Highway 29 in the city of Napa, turn east on Imola Avenue. Follow Imola Avenue four miles to where it dead-ends at Fourth Avenue. Turn right into the park entrance.

Information and Contact

A $5 day-use fee is charged per vehicle. Dogs are not allowed. Bikes are allowed only on designated roads and trails. A free park map is available at the entrance kiosk. For more information, contact Skyline Wilderness Park, 2201 Imola Avenue, Napa, CA 94510, 707/252-0481, www.skylinepark.org.

14 MARSH AND SOUTH PASTURE LOOP

Rush Ranch, Solano Land Trust   **BEST**

Level: Easy   **Total Distance:** 4.6 miles round-trip

Hiking Time: 2 hours   **Elevation Change:** Negligible

Summary: A ramble along the farthest northeast edge of San Francisco Bay, where marshes, wetlands, and a seasonal pond are a haven for birds and wildlife.

It takes more than an hour's drive from the Golden Gate to reach the northeast edge of immense San Francisco Bay. Although in this region it bears a different name, the final stretch of bay water lies some 40 miles distant from the Golden Gate. Here it makes its fluid transition to the narrow waterways of the Sacramento Delta—the long and slender fingers of the hand that is San Francisco Bay.

Located at this meeting place is Suisun Marsh, an important and distinct component of the San Francisco Bay ecosystem. Unlike in most of the East Bay and South Bay, where diking and filling have destroyed the bay's natural wetland edges, the North Bay's Suisun Marsh remains relatively untouched. Such tidal wetland areas have become so rare in today's world that Suisun is considered to be the largest contiguous estuarine marsh in the United States.

Although much of Suisun Marsh is run by the California Department of Fish

© ANN MARIE BROWN

Rusting farm equipment is a part of the landscape at Rush Ranch.

and Game as a wildlife management area, one section is operated by the Solano Land Trust specifically as a nature preserve. That's Rush Ranch, a former sheep and cattle ranch that is now a 2,070-acre open space area, including more than 1,000 acres of wetlands. At least 12 rare or endangered species can be found at Rush Ranch, including the salt marsh harvest mouse, the Suisun shrew, the Suisun Marsh song sparrow, the black rail, and the clapper rail. Many rare marsh plants may also be seen.

Rush Ranch offers educational programs, a top-notch nature center, and three trails for hikers. Visiting the ranch feels like a trip to the country: Except for the spiffy new nature center (built in 2007), most of the picturesque ranch buildings look much as they did when the Rush family lived here in the early 1900s. Despite the proximity of bustling Fairfield and Suisun City, the ranch feels remote and peaceful. A variety of farm animals—goats, horses, pigs, and sheep—stare curiously at visitors. The ranch's acreage on Suisun Marsh is mostly flat as a pancake, punctuated by the rounded Potrero Hills and bordered by two distant mountains—Mount Diablo to the south at 3,849 feet and Mount Vaca to the north at 2,819 feet.

Bring your binoculars along for this walk—wildlife sightings are nearly guaranteed. More than 230 species of birds reside in or pass through the 80-acre marsh. By combining two trails that begin at the ranch buildings, you can make a figure-eight loop of 4.6 miles. Start your trip by picking up an interpretive brochure at the visitors center, then head out its back side on Marsh Trail. The path leads around a managed freshwater marsh and along Suisun Slough, an unaltered salt marsh. Be sure to climb to the top of the small hill near interpretive post number 3. Here you are high enough to gain some perspective on this wide, flat, marshy plain and its waterways. Small boats sometimes cruise up the slough.

Much of this walk follows levees just a few feet from the water's edge. Although tall cattails and blackberry vines sometimes block the view, there are openings in the foliage where you can see the waterway. It's not uncommon to glimpse a river otter swim by.

Amid all this nature, one sight may surprise you. Every now and then a huge, gray military plane from nearby Travis Air Force Base will cruise slowly and almost silently overhead. The strange, slow-motion maneuverability of these planes allows them to take off and land on short runways.

Marsh Trail's final stretch crosses the grasslands to return by the barn and parking area. Head to your right to set out on the second half of the figure eight on South Pasture Cut-off Trail. The trail begins near the water tower and windmill on the south side of the ranch.

South Pasture Cut-Off Trail circles a restored seasonal pond and affords more views of Suisun Marsh. Don't miss the Native American grinding rock site, where the Patwin Indians, also known as Southern Wintun Indians, ground acorns and nuts into meal. Bird-watching is very satisfying along this path. Red-tailed hawks are commonly seen flying over the grasslands and tidal marsh, searching for prey. Other common raptors are northern harriers, osprey, barn owls, American kestrels, and golden eagles. Butterfly-watching is rewarding, too, especially when the spring wildflowers bloom. South Pasture Cut-Off Trail connects to the main South Pasture Trail, which winds its way through a cattle pasture that offers a great view of Mount Diablo.

Options

Another good choice for visitors looking to add a few miles is the Suisun Hill Trail, which begins across the road from Rush Ranch's main entrance. The trail climbs into the grassland-covered hills just east of Grizzly Island Road. The small elevation gain allows a much wider perspective on Suisun Marsh and the surrounding hills and mountains, and provides an ideal spot for watching the sunset. Dogs are permitted on Suisun Hill Trail, but not on the preserve's other trails.

Directions

From I-80 near Fairfield, take Highway 12 east. Drive four miles on Highway 12 to Grizzly Island Road. Turn right and drive 2.2 miles to the sign for Rush Ranch on the right. Turn right and drive to the parking area.

Information and Contact

There is no fee. Dogs are permitted on Suisun Hill Trail only. Bikes are not allowed. Free trail maps and brochures are available at the visitors center. For more information, contact Rush Ranch, c/o Solano Land Trust, 1001 Texas Street, Fairfield, CA 94533, 707/432-0150, www.solanolandtrust.org.

MARIN

© KEVIN GONG

BEST HIKES

Marin County is known for sky-high real estate

prices, million-dollar views of the Bay, hot tubs in every backyard, and horrendous traffic on its one and only freeway, U.S. 101. It is one of the most coveted places to live in the entire Bay Area, largely due to the fact that nearly half of the county's total acreage is public parkland. The scattered pockets of remaining private property consistently sell for a premium. And it's no surprise – who wouldn't want to live amid such a vast patchwork of scenic public lands?

Stretching from the middle span of the Golden Gate Bridge to the northernmost tip of the Point Reyes peninsula, Marin County has all the right ingredients for hiking nirvana: mild weather with plenty of sun but not too much heat, a jaw-dropping stretch of rugged Pacific coast, massive groves of coastal redwoods, warm inland valleys highlighted by five sparkling lakes, and world-famous landmarks like Muir Woods and the Point Reyes Lighthouse. From many of the county's high points, the tall buildings of San Francisco can easily be spotted, yet when viewed from one of Marin's immense swaths of uninhabited parkland, the city seems a world away. By any standard, Marin County's scenery qualifies as sublime.

Parks in the region are managed by a passel of federal, state, and regional agencies. Three national park units grace the county: Point Reyes National Seashore, Muir Woods National Monument, and the Golden Gate National Recreation Area. These are joined by a half-dozen state parks, including Mount Tamalpais, Tomales Bay, Samuel P. Taylor, Olompali, China Camp, and Angel Island; and several regional parks, including the lands of Marin Municipal Water District and Marin County Open Space District. It's important to pay attention to posted regulations and know whose jurisdiction you are hiking in, because each managing agency has different rules directing public use. In some areas, you can hike with your dog; in other areas, you can't. At some trailheads, parking is free; at others, it's not. In some lakes, you can swim or fish; in others, you can't.

The parklands of Marin have vastly different personalities as well. If you like solitude and a sense of remoteness, the parks of western Marin are most likely to appeal to you. It's possible to hike all day on some trails in Point Reyes National Seashore and see no one at all. If you'd rather be close to the city, the spectacular Marin Headlands, including Rodeo Beach and Tennessee Valley, are just a few minutes' drive beyond the Golden Gate Bridge. Solitude is more unlikely there, but the classic views of bridge, bay, and ocean are fine compensation. And in close proximity to Marin's suburban towns are a surprising wealth of parks that somehow manage to *feel* like they are a world away, such as Ring Mountain Open Space Preserve in Tiburon, Cascade Canyon in Fairfax, and China Camp State Park in San Rafael.

Perhaps the best part about exploring the parks of Marin is that they have so much to offer besides just miles of trails to walk. Watch for whale spouts or gape at massive sea lions along the shores of Drakes Bay. Step back in time at a 19th-century Chinese shrimp fishing village at China Camp, tour one of two historic lighthouses perched along the precipitous Marin coast, or visit an immigrant detention center on an island in the middle of San Francisco Bay. Visit a coastal waterfall, a black-sand beach, or a dwarf grove of cypress trees. In this hiker's paradise, an amazing array of side trips and activities await.

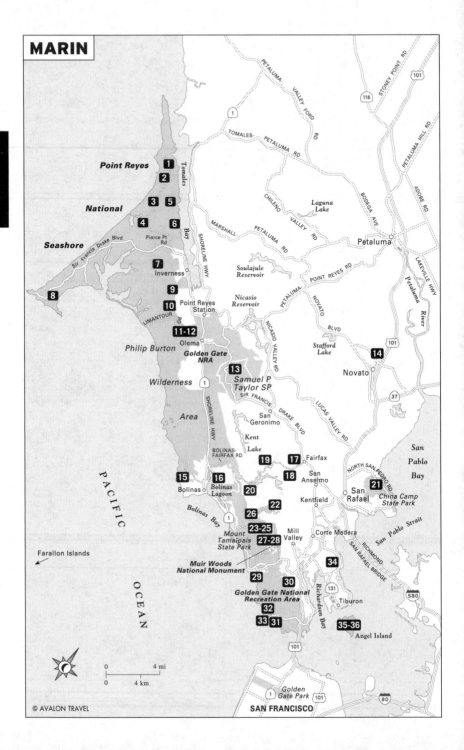

MARIN

	TRAIL NAME	LEVEL	DISTANCE	TIME	ELEVATION	FEATURES	PAGE
1	Tomales Point Trail	Moderate	9.4 mi rt	5 hr	900 ft		81
2	McClures Beach	Easy	1.0 mile rt	1 hr	250 ft		85
3	Kehoe Beach	Easy	1.0–3.0 mi rt	1–2 hr	Negligible		87
4	Abbotts Lagoon	Easy	2.4–6.0 mi rt	1–3 hr	Negligible		90
5	Marshall Beach	Easy	2.4 mi rt	1.5 hr	300 ft		93
6	Jepson, Johnstone, and Beaches Loop	Easy/Moderate	4.2 mi rt	2.0 hr	500 ft		96
7	Estero Trail to Sunset Beach	Moderate	7.8 mi rt	4 hr	720 ft		100
8	Chimney Rock	Easy	1.4 mi rt	1 hr	Negligible		104
9	Sky Trail and Woodward Valley Loop	Strenuous	13.6 mi rt	7 hr	1,600 ft		108
10	Coast, Fire Lane, and Laguna Loop	Easy/Moderate	5.0 mi rt	2.5 hr	450 ft		111
11	Bear Valley Trail to Arch Rock	Easy/Moderate	8.2 mi rt	4 hr	400 ft		114
12	Bear Valley, Old Pine, Woodward Valley, and Coast Loop	Strenuous	13.0 mi rt	7 hr	1,700 ft		117
13	Barnabe Peak Loop	Moderate	6.0 mi rt	3 hr	1,300 ft		121
14	Mount Burdell	Moderate	7.8 mi rt	4 hr	1,500 ft		125
15	Bass Lake, Double Point, and Alamere Falls	Moderate	8.4 mi rt	4 hr	550 ft		129
16	Kent, Griffin, and Zumie Loop Trails	Easy/Moderate	3.0 mi rt	1.5 hr	800 ft		132
17	Cascade Canyon	Easy	1.5 mi rt	1 hr	100 ft		135
18	Bon Tempe and Lagunitas Lake Loop	Easy	5.0 mi rt	2.5 hr	200 ft		138
19	Carson Falls	Easy/Moderate	3.4 mi rt	1.5 hr	800 ft		142
20	Cataract Trail to Cataract Falls	Easy/Moderate	3.2 mi rt	1.5 hr	800 ft		145

TRAIL NAME	LEVEL	DISTANCE	TIME	ELEVATION	FEATURES	PAGE
21 Shoreline Trail	Easy/Moderate	7.0 mi rt	3 hr	100 ft		148
22 Verna Dunshee Trail and Gardner Lookout	Easy	1.4 mi rt	1 hr	170 ft		152
23 Matt Davis and Steep Ravine Loop	Moderate	7.8 mi rt	4 hr	1,500 ft		156
24 Mountain Theater and West Point Inn Loop	Easy/Moderate	5.0 mi rt	2.5 hr	500 ft or 1,300 ft		160
25 Coastal, Cataract, and Old Mine Loop	Moderate	6.8 mi rt	3 hr	700 ft		164
26 Benstein, Mickey O'Brien, and Cataract Loop	Easy/Moderate	4.0 mi rt	2 hr	500 ft		168
27 Ocean View, Lost Trail, and Fern Creek Loop	Easy/Moderate	3.4 mi rt	1.5 hr	800 ft		172
28 Bootjack, Ben Johnson, and Hillside Trail Loop	Moderate	6.4 mi rt	3 hr	1,100 ft		176
29 Muir Beach/Coastal Trail	Strenuous	7.0 mi rt	4 hr	1,800 ft		180
30 Tennessee Valley Trail	Easy	4.0 mi rt	2 hr	150 ft		184
31 Lagoon Trail	Easy	1.75 mi rt	1 hr	Negligible		187
32 Coastal Trail and Hill 88 Loop	Moderate	5.5 mi rt	3 hr	1,000 ft		190
33 Point Bonita Lighthouse	Easy	1.0 mile rt	1 hr	100 ft		194
34 Phyllis Ellman Trail	Easy/Moderate	3.0 mi rt	1.5 hr	600 ft		197
35 Perimeter Trail	Easy	5.5 mi rt	2.5 hr	200 ft		200
36 North Ridge and Sunset Trail Loop	Easy/Moderate	4.5 mi rt	2 hr	780 ft		204

1 TOMALES POINT TRAIL   BEST ◖

Point Reyes National Seashore

Level: Moderate   **Total Distance:** 9.4 miles round-trip

Hiking Time: 5 hours   **Elevation Change:** 900 feet

Summary: A long but mostly level walk along the northern tip of the Point Reyes peninsula, with a near guarantee of spotting herds of tule elk.

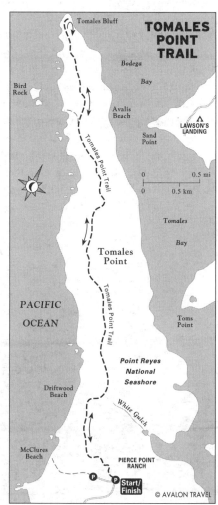

If viewing wildlife is one of the reasons you enjoy hiking, the Tomales Point Trail is sure to satisfy. You'll have a good chance at spotting big, furry animals before you even get out of your car (and not just the usual Point Reyes bovines).

The wildlife is abundant because Tomales Point Trail is located in Point Reyes National Seashore's tule elk preserve. Before 1860, thousands of native tule elk roamed Tomales Point, but in the late 19th century the animals were hunted out of existence. The creation of the preserve was the National Park Service's attempt to reestablish the elk in their native habitat. Their efforts have succeeded; as of 2009, the Point Reyes herd numbered 440 and was going strong.

Seeing the magnificent tule elk is almost a given. Frequently they're hanging out in large numbers near the trailhead parking lot. Often you spot them as you drive in on Pierce Point Road. From July through September, when the bull elks are in their "rut" and trying to round up a harem of females, you can often hear the elk bugling and may even see a couple of males sparring with a magnificent clash of antlers. On weekends during this period, volunteer docents are stationed at the trailhead and at Windy Gap, one mile out along the trail, with spotting scopes and binoculars for visitors to peer through.

Once you're out on the trail, there is often plenty of other wildlife to see. If you hike early in the morning, before many other people have traipsed down the trail, check the dirt path for footprints. I've seen mountain lion tracks as well as more common raccoon and elk prints. While hiking, I've encountered large jackrabbits, various harmless snakes, big fuzzy caterpillars, and a variety of birds. Once I had to make a wide circle off the path to avoid a big skunk who was sauntering down the trail ahead of me. He was just moseying along, indifferent to my presence.

It's 4.7 miles to the trail's end at the tip of Tomales Point, but you don't have to walk that far to have a great trip. Only a mile or two of hiking will allow splendid coastal and Tomales Bay views, plus a probable wildlife encounter. Set your own trail distance and turn around when you please. Just make sure you pick a clear day for this trip; although you may still see tule elk in the fog, you'll miss out on the trail's blue-water vistas. And be sure to carry a few extra layers. If the weather is clear, it's almost guaranteed to be windy.

The Tomales Point Trail begins at Pierce Point Ranch, one of the oldest dairies in Point Reyes. The ranch manufactured milk and butter for San Francisco dinner tables in the 1850s. Begin hiking around the western perimeter of the ranch, or

bull tule elk show off their racks at Tomales Point

© ANN MARIE BROWN

take a few minutes to inspect its buildings. Interpretive signs describe the history of Pierce Point's dairy business.

The trail curves uphill around the ranch, then heads northwest along the bluff tops toward Tomales Point, the northernmost tip of Point Reyes. The path is wide, smooth, and easy to hike from beginning to end. Wildflowers bloom profusely in the spring, typically April to June, particularly poppies, gold fields, tidy tips, and bush lupine.

At 0.5 mile out, you reach the first short climb, in which you gain about 100 feet. Turn around and look behind you as you ascend: This thin peninsula of land is bracketed by the ocean on one side and Tomales Bay on the other. On clear days, the water views are exquisite. Look for forested Hog Island in Tomales Bay, a popular pull-up spot for kayakers.

At 1.8 miles, the path starts to descend, supplying a good view of Bird Rock jutting upward from the sea and the town and campground at Lawson's Landing across Tomales Bay. At 2.5 miles, the trail reaches its highest point. Views of Bodega Bay and the Sonoma Coast to the north are a standout. Continuing onward, you'll descend to the site of an outpost of Pierce Point Ranch, then pass by windswept Bird Rock, often covered with pelicans and cormorants.

In the final 0.75 mile past Bird Rock, the trail becomes a bit sketchy. Masses of yellow bush lupine carpet the sandy soil in April and May. Amid a series of low dunes, the trail peters out, then vanishes. But the route is obvious; just keep hiking until the land runs out. You'll be rewarded with breathtaking views of Bodega Head to the north, Tomales Bay to the east, and the Pacific Ocean to the west. Look closely and you can discern tiny boats departing the harbor at Bodega Bay.

Options

Many hikers abbreviate this trip by making the high knoll at 2.5 miles their turn-around point. After completing a five-mile round-trip, there is usually enough time left in the day to pay a visit to neighboring McClures Beach (see *McClures Beach* listing in this chapter).

Directions

From San Francisco, cross the Golden Gate Bridge and drive north on U.S. 101 for 7.5 miles. Take the Sir Francis Drake Boulevard exit west toward San Anselmo, and drive 20 miles to the town of Olema. At Olema, turn right (north) on Highway 1 for about 150 yards, then turn left on Bear Valley Road. Drive 2.2 miles on Bear Valley Road until it joins with Sir Francis Drake Boulevard. Bear left on Sir

Francis Drake Boulevard and drive 5.6 miles, then take the right fork onto Pierce Point Road. Drive nine miles to the Pierce Point Ranch parking area.

Information and Contact

There is no fee. Dogs and bikes are not allowed. A free park map is available at the Bear Valley Visitor Center on Bear Valley Road. A more detailed Point Reyes map is available from Tom Harrison Maps, 415/456-7940, www.tomharrison-maps.com. For more information, contact Point Reyes National Seashore, Point Reyes, CA 94956, 415/464-5100, www.nps.gov/pore.

2 McCLURES BEACH

Point Reyes National Seashore

Level: Easy

Hiking Time: 1 hour

Total Distance: 1.0 mile round-trip

Elevation Change: 250 feet

Summary: One of the most dramatic beaches of Point Reyes, complete with tan sands and rocky tidepools, is accessible via an easy, short walk.

Most people don't make the long drive out to the northern tip of Point Reyes just to hike to McClures Beach. The majority of visitors show up because they are hoping to spot Tomales Point's tule elk herd, visit the historic buildings at Pierce Point Ranch, or hike the Tomales Point Trail (see *Tomales Point Trail* listing in this chapter). But Mc-

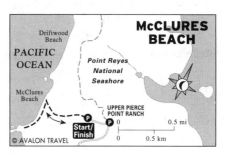

Clures Beach is worth a trip all by itself, especially during periods of low tides when its most precious secrets are revealed. In addition, because of its remote location and relatively small size, McClures Beach often presents a chance for solitude along its rocky stretch of sand, especially in the winter months.

The trail from the parking lot leads steeply downhill to the beach in 0.5 mile. This same stretch will get you huffing and puffing on the way back up, but it's short enough so that almost anybody can handle it. Buckwheat, ice plant, and morning glories border the path. The trail runs parallel to the eroding streambed of a steep ravine, which can roar with water during winter storms but is usually just a trickle in summer. Near the end of the trail, on the left, is a fascinating stretch of sculpted sandstone and mudstone.

The south end of McClures' reef-lined beach is a prime area for tidepools, especially if you are fortunate enough to show up during a minus tide. Even during more common, above-zero low tides, a narrow passageway on the beach's south end is revealed. By passing through this rock-lined gap, you'll gain access to another sandy beach, which is connected to McClures by a narrow peninsula of rock extending from the coastal bluffs.

Even at high tide, when sand and water have closed off the passageway and covered many of McClures' tidepools, you'll find shards of abalone shells, mussels, and assorted body parts of crabs as you walk along the sand. After one winter storm, we found the beach littered with dozens of starfish, which had been torn from their holds on the reef by the battering surf. You won't have to walk far to see all there is to see—McClures Beach is only about 0.75 mile long, and bounded by granite cliffs.

Swimming is definitely not recommended, although some hardy surfers attempt to claim the winter waves here. Because of its rocky shores and crashing breakers, McClures Beach is considered to be one of the most dangerous beaches in Point Reyes.

A short walk to McClures Beach reveals a magical stretch of rock and sand.

Options

Beach lovers who enjoy McClures should pay a visit to North Beach and South Beach off Sir Francis Drake Boulevard near Chimney Rock and the Point Reyes Lighthouse. If the wind is howling at these scenic stretches of sand, head to Drakes Beach on the opposite side of the highway, which faces the calmer waters of Drakes Bay. Although Drakes Beach is often popular and crowded, it is easy enough to get away from everybody by simply hiking eastward (left) from the parking lot.

Directions

From San Francisco, cross the Golden Gate Bridge and drive north on U.S. 101 for 7.5 miles. Take the Sir Francis Drake Boulevard exit west toward San Anselmo, and drive 20 miles to the town of Olema. At Olema, turn right (north) on Highway 1 for about 150 yards, then turn left on Bear Valley Road. Drive 2.2 miles on Bear Valley Road until it joins with Sir Francis Drake Boulevard. Bear left on Sir Francis Drake Boulevard and drive 5.6 miles, then take the right fork onto Pierce Point Road. Drive 8.9 miles to the left turnoff for McClures Beach, just before you reach Pierce Point Ranch. Turn left and park in the lot.

Information and Contact

There is no fee. Dogs and bikes are not allowed. A free park map is available at the Bear Valley Visitor Center on Bear Valley Road. A more detailed Point Reyes map is available from Tom Harrison Maps, 415/456-7940, www.tomharrison-maps.com. For more information, contact Point Reyes National Seashore, Point Reyes, CA 94956, 415/464-5100, www.nps.gov/pore.

3 KEHOE BEACH
Point Reyes National Seashore

🦌 🥾 🌿 🏊 🐕 👫

Level: Easy

Total Distance: 1.0-3.0 miles round-trip

Hiking Time: 1-2 hours

Elevation Change: Negligible

Summary: An easy, dog-friendly trail alongside a freshwater marsh travels to the inviting sands of Kehoe Beach.

At most beaches in California, you just drive up, park your car in the paved parking lot, walk a few feet, and plop down in the sand. Kehoe Beach beats that by a mile. Exactly a mile, in fact, because that's how far it is to hike there (round-trip). The distance is just long enough for a pleasant, level walk, and it can be combined with another mile or so of sauntering along Kehoe's wide strip of sandy beach.

The trail proves that the journey can be as good as the destination. The fun starts right where you park your car. In late summer you'll find a huge patch of blackberries across the road from the trailhead. If you're wearing long sleeves and long pants, you can pick enough berries to sustain you as you hike. You'll also find that many of your trail companions are of the canine persuasion, as this is one of the few trails in Point Reyes where dogs are permitted.

The trail is gravel, almost completely level, and wide enough for holding hands with your hiking partner. It runs alongside Kehoe Marsh, a freshwater marsh that provides habitat for birds and bird-watchers. Songbirds are nearly as abundant as the

© ANN MARIE BROWN

Wildflowers carpet the bluffs above Kehoe Beach.

nonnative ice plant that weaves thick cushions of matted foliage alongside the trail. Grasses and vines grow in profusion, encouraged by the proximity of the marshy creek and its underground spring. Colorful mustard weed grows waist-high during the spring wildflower season. As you near the ocean, the wet, marshy land transforms to sandy dunes, where you may see big jackrabbits hopping among the grasses.

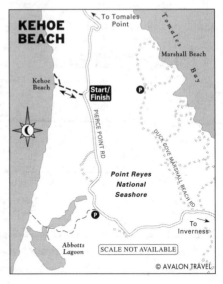

Before you sprint down to Kehoe's brayed, tan sands, take the spur trail that cuts off to the right (near a wooden bench) and climb up on the bluffs above the beach. In springtime, the slope is painted bright blue and gold with prolific yellow tidy tips, blue lupine, and orange poppies. It's a glorious sight to behold. Once you've admired the flowers, head to the beach to hike farther or have a picnic lunch. You'll return on the same trail.

Hikers visiting with their dogs should keep in mind that while they are welcome on the trail and on the beach to the north of the trail, *dogs are not permitted on the beach to the south of the trail.* This rule is designed to protect the habitat of nesting snowy plovers.

Options

If you can arrange a shuttle car, you can hike from Kehoe Beach's trailhead to Abbotts Lagoon's trailhead, a five-mile stretch that includes two miles on the beach. (If you can't arrange a shuttle, you could always hike back on the road—it's only a two-mile leg.) In spring, you will be treated to a fantastic wildflower display, and in fall, you have your best shot at clear, warm weather. For more information, see *Abbotts Lagoon* listing in this chapter.

Directions

From San Francisco, cross the Golden Gate Bridge and drive north on U.S. 101 for 7.5 miles. Take the Sir Francis Drake Boulevard exit west toward San Anselmo, and drive 20 miles to the town of Olema. At Olema, turn right (north) on Highway 1 for about 150 yards, then turn left on Bear Valley Road. Drive 2.2 miles on Bear Valley Road until it joins with Sir Francis Drake Boulevard. Bear left on Sir Francis Drake Boulevard and drive 5.6 miles, then take the right fork onto Pierce Point Road. Drive 5.5 miles to the Kehoe Beach Trailhead on your left. Park along either side of the road in the pullouts.

Information and Contact

There is no fee. Leashed dogs are allowed. Bikes are not allowed. A free park map is available at the Bear Valley Visitor Center on Bear Valley Road. A more detailed Point Reyes map is available from Tom Harrison Maps, 415/456-7940, www.tomharrisonmaps.com. For more information, contact Point Reyes National Seashore, Point Reyes, CA 94956, 415/464-5100, www.nps.gov/pore.

4 ABBOTTS LAGOON

BEST ◖

Point Reyes National Seashore

![icons]

Level: Easy

Total Distance: 2.4-6.0 miles round-trip

Hiking Time: 1-3 hours

Elevation Change: Negligible

Summary: Bring along your bird identification book for this nearly level stroll alongside a brackish lagoon.

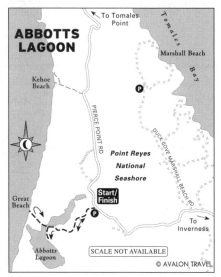

If the wind is howling and you've been blown off the path on other Point Reyes trails, drive over to Abbotts Lagoon for a trip through a sheltered watery paradise. The trail itself isn't long, but it leads to the Great Beach, where you can extend your hike for miles along the sand. The result is a memorable two-part trip: first, an easy 1.2-mile stroll through protected lagoons teeming with birdlife; second, a windswept walk to the north or south along wide-open coastline.

Abbotts Lagoon is huge—more than 200 acres—and joined by a spillway to two freshwater ponds. The lagoon is only rarely influenced by tides, specifically during the few times a year when harsh winter storms break through its low sandbar, allowing seawater to rush in. Soon thereafter sand will accumulate and seal off the lagoon, but these brief openings result in water that is continually brackish—a mix of saltwater and freshwater— and a haven for many species of birds, mammals, and plants.

The trail is a favorite with both beach lovers and bird-watchers. The latter are thrilled by the amount and diversity of bird habitat in a relatively small area; the former enjoy the level trail and easy access to the Great Beach, also known as Ten-Mile Beach or Point Reyes Beach. If you're a birding novice and want to give the sport a try, look for these easy-to-spot species: western grebes (large, gray-and-white diving birds with a long, swanlike neck and yellow bill); pie-billed grebes (similar to western grebes but with a short, rounded bill and no white patch); coots (dark grey or black henlike birds that skitter across the water when they fly, dragging their feet); and Caspian terns (like seagulls but more angular and elegant, with large red bills). The autumn migration season is the best time for bird-watching, although birds are present at the lagoon year-round.

The first 0.5 mile of trail is level and hard-packed for wheelchair use, and the rest of the route is wide, flat, and sandy. The landscape is composed of coastal scrub and open grasslands that are gilded with wildflowers in the spring. A bucolic-looking white farmhouse, perched on a distant hillside, keeps watch over the scene.

At one mile out, just before you cross a small footbridge that separates the two parts of the lagoon, you'll notice a spur trail that leads up the hillside to the left. Take this spur and climb to the top of the bluff. High on this grassy knoll is the best spot to gain perspective on the immense size of Abbotts Lagoon and its distinctive two-part shape. It's also an idyllic spot to bird-watch, picnic, or just admire the beauty of the place. West of the lagoon, bright white ocean waves crash on the sandy beach. To the north, the lagoon is edged by a series of sand dunes.

If you want to hike along the Great Beach, walk back downhill to the footbridge and follow the trail that leads west from the lagoon to the ocean, only 0.25 mile away. Or you can just trek across the sand dunes, but watch your step amid the many fragile dune plants—yellow bush lupines, beach strawberry, morning glories, and yellow sand verbena.

Beach explorers should bundle up in an extra layer of clothing, as the coast is much windier than the protected lagoon, then head north or south and walk as

© ANN MARIE BROWN

A footbridge across Abbotts Lagoon leads hikers to the sand dunes and beyond to the Pacific Ocean.

long and far as desired. Harbor seals and sea lions often haul out on the Great Beach's sand.

The April and May wildflower season brings colorful shows of poppies and lupine along the Abbotts Lagoon Trail. Also look for cobweb thistle, a native thistle that is brilliant red, and prolific Douglas irises. If you miss the bloom, another good time to visit Abbotts Lagoon is on a late fall or winter day, when the fog has vanished and the rich, primary colors of water, sky, and grasslands are thoroughly saturated by the low light of the season.

Options

Another superior bird-watching trail is found nearby at Bull Point. Backtrack on Pierce Point Road to Sir Francis Drake Boulevard, then turn right (southwest, toward the lighthouse) and drive five miles to the Bull Point Trailhead. The 1.9-mile, level trail cuts across the coastal bluffs to a high overlook above Drakes Estero.

Directions

From San Francisco, cross the Golden Gate Bridge and drive north on U.S. 101 for 7.5 miles. Take the Sir Francis Drake Boulevard exit west toward San Anselmo, and drive 20 miles to the town of Olema. At Olema, turn right (north) on Highway 1 for about 150 yards, then turn left on Bear Valley Road. Drive 2.2 miles on Bear Valley Road until it joins with Sir Francis Drake Boulevard. Bear left on Sir Francis Drake Boulevard and drive 5.6 miles, then take the right fork onto Pierce Point Road. Drive 3.3 miles on Pierce Point Road to the Abbotts Lagoon Trailhead on the left side of the road.

Information and Contact

There is no fee. Dogs are not allowed. Bikes are allowed. A free park map is available at the Bear Valley Visitor Center on Bear Valley Road. A more detailed Point Reyes map is available from Tom Harrison Maps, 415/456-7940, www.tomharrisonmaps.com. For more information, contact Point Reyes National Seashore, Point Reyes, CA 94956, 415/464-5100, www.nps.gov/pore.

5 MARSHALL BEACH
Point Reyes National Seashore

Level: Easy

Hiking Time: 1.5 hours

Total Distance: 2.4 miles round-trip

Elevation Change: 300 feet

Summary: An easy trail travels to a picturesque beach on the calmer, warmer, Tomales Bay side of the Point Reyes peninsula.

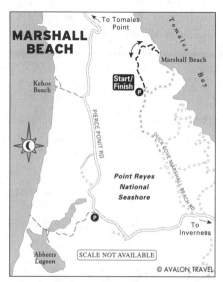

The Marshall Beach Trail is one of the best-kept secrets in Point Reyes. Few visitors know about Marshall Beach because the trailhead is situated on a dirt road to nowhere, at the northeastern tip of the Point Reyes peninsula. Although thousands of visitors pour into neighboring Tomales Bay State Park for its protected bay waters and stunning white beaches, few realize that right next door is Marshall Beach, with all the same advantages but none of the crowds and no entrance fee.

On your first trip to the Marshall Beach trailhead you may question whether you are going the right way. The route leads through dairy cow country with no sign of the coast in sight. Soon the paved road turns to dirt and you continue driving through grassy prairie until you reach a nondescript parking area (really a grassy flat) and a large metal gate. Beyond the gate lies the trail, a dirt road that requires a vigilant lookout for "cow droppings." The unwary will discover that the stuff clings to your boot soles for days.

Have you ever wondered why there are so many cows in this national park? Ranching is considered to be part of the "cultural history" of Point Reyes. Cattle and dairy ranches have operated in the area since the 1850s. The 1962 law that authorized Point Reyes National Seashore made allowances so that the original ranch owners could continue operating within the park's boundaries. Currently, there are six viable dairies in the park, milking about 3,200 cows and producing over five million gallons of milk each year. Just wave and smile at Bessie as you walk to the beach.

The hike to Marshall Beach is a simple out-and-back, with no trail junctions. Just amble down the wide ranch road, which makes a curving descent to the water's edge. There is no shade along the route, except at the edge of Marshall Beach's cove, where a few windswept cypress trees stand guard. Thick lichen hangs from their branches.

Marshall Beach is a nearly perfect beach, with coarse white sand bordering the azure blue water of Tomales Bay. Largely protected from the wind by Inverness Ridge, this small slice of paradise overlooks the hamlet of Marshall on the far side of the bay. The most common visitors to the beach are kayakers who paddle over from Marshall, Inverness, or Tomales Bay State Park to the south. Other hikers are few. On warm days, the calm bay water beckons swimmers.

Essentials for this trip include a picnic, a bathing suit, a good book, and some binoculars for bird-watching. Settle in for a perfect afternoon, then drag yourself away—and back up the hill—when it's time to leave.

Options

If you like the look of Tomales Bay from Marshall Beach, take a drive over to its opposite side and hike on the Tomales Bay Trail. The trailhead is found 1.8 miles north of the town of Point Reyes Station on Highway 1. The mostly level, easy trail passes a couple of freshwater ponds on its way to the southern edge of Tomales Bay, where the bay makes the transition from a large, open water body to narrow creeks, channels, and wetland marshes. At the trail's end, one mile

© ANN MARIE BROWN

The calm waters of Tomales Bay invite swimmers on warm summer days and kayakers year-round.

out, you'll find old railroad trestles and the remains of a lock system on a levee that is no longer used. In the early 1900s, the North Pacific Coast Railroad cut through this marsh.

Directions

From San Francisco, cross the Golden Gate Bridge and drive north on U.S. 101 for 7.5 miles. Take the Sir Francis Drake Boulevard exit west toward San Anselmo, and drive 20 miles to the town of Olema. At Olema, turn right (north) on Highway 1 for about 150 yards, then turn left on Bear Valley Road. Drive 2.2 miles on Bear Valley Road until it joins with Sir Francis Drake Boulevard. Bear left on Sir Francis Drake Boulevard and drive 5.6 miles, then take the right fork onto Pierce Point Road. In 1.2 miles you'll see the entrance road for Tomales Bay State Park. Continue just beyond it to Duck Cove/Marshall Beach Road; turn right and drive 2.6 miles. The road turns to gravel and dirt; stay to the left where it forks. Park in the flat grassy area by the metal trailhead gate.

Information and Contact

There is no fee. Dogs are not allowed. Bikes are allowed. A free park map is available at the Bear Valley Visitor Center on Bear Valley Road. A more detailed Point Reyes map is available from Tom Harrison Maps, 415/456-7940, www.tomharrisonmaps.com. For more information, contact Point Reyes National Seashore, Point Reyes, CA 94956, 415/464-5100, www.nps.gov/pore.

6 JEPSON, JOHNSTONE, AND BEACHES LOOP
Tomales Bay State Park

Level: Easy/Moderate **Total Distance:** 4.2 miles round-trip

Hiking Time: 2.0 hours **Elevation Change:** 500 feet

Summary: Spend a day at three separate beaches along the shores of Tomales Bay and visit a virgin grove of Bishop pines.

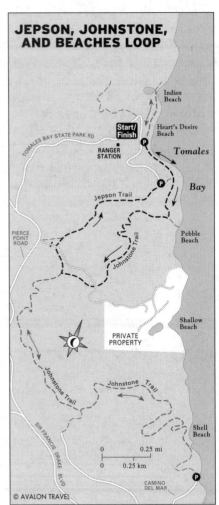

Tomales Bay State Park is 2,200 acres of white sandy beaches, sparkling bay waters, and dense forests filled with botanical marvels. Most visitors come to the park for its easy access to Tomales Bay, a large, sheltered cove that is blessed by unusually balmy weather (unusual for this region of western Marin). Protected by Inverness Ridge, Tomales Bay is often sunny and warm even when the nearby coast is fogged in or windy. The bay waters are usually gentle enough for swimming, an activity that is nearly impossible at the turbulent beaches of neighboring Point Reyes. When the sun shines the water of Tomales Bay turns an exquisite light blue, making the white sand beaches look like a tropical paradise.

Hikers will find still more treasures at the park. A loop route starting from Heart's Desire Beach follows Johnstone Trail to secluded Pebble Beach, then gently climbs to a junction with Jepson Trail and drops back down through a unique forest of Bishop pines. Both legs of the loop are set in a forest so tangled with curving tree branches, huckleberry vines, wax myrtle, toyon,

© ANN MARIE BROWN

Magnificent bay laurel trees form arches over the Jepson Trail.

and ferns that you can often see only a few feet ahead of you. When the loop returns to Heart's Desire Beach, it's possible to add on a short out-and-back walk to Indian Beach.

Start your trip at the south side of Heart's Desire Beach, at the trail sign for Johnstone Trail. Leave the beach-towel and cooler-toting crowds behind as you travel through a forest of oaks, bay, and madrone, gaining frequent views of Tomales Bay through the trees. Pass by Vista Point Group Picnic Area and its stunning view of Heart's Desire Beach and Tomales Bay. At 0.5 mile out, watch for a sign pointing left to the restrooms, where the Johnstone Trail turns right. This spur trail descends to Pebble Beach, a small and secluded curve of beach composed of tiny—guess what?—pebbles. Because it can only be accessed by trail, Pebble Beach usually has much fewer visitors than Heart's Desire Beach. Narrow and only 100 yards long, the scenic cove is backed by a small marsh. Across the bay and to the south, the predominant landform is Black Mountain at 1,280 feet.

After your beach visit, return to the main trail and head uphill on Johnstone Trail. Note the pink lichen growing on the bark of broad oak trees near Pebble Beach. Johnstone Trail winds gradually upward for 1.5 miles, passing through several wet, marshy areas on small wooden bridges. After crossing a private road, it meets up with Jepson Trail, on which you turn right. In a few footsteps you'll cross the private road again. (A small parking area is located near here, at the private road's junction with Pierce Point Road. Hikers who don't want to park in the Heart's Desire area could start their trip from this parking lot and avoid paying the state park entrance fee.)

Jepson Trail makes a more direct descent to Tomales Bay. The trail passes through a virgin grove of Bishop pines, which bear gracefully sculpted limbs and weatherworn trunks. Cousins of the Monterey pine, Bishop pines belong to the family of pines that requires the extreme heat of fire to break open their cones and disperse their seeds. As such, these pines do not reproduce often. Bishop pines are relatively uncommon along the California coast, but Tomales Bay and Point Reyes have healthy stands of them.

Jepson Trail deposits you at the parking lot for the Vista Point Group Picnic Area. Cross it, enter the picnic area, and turn left on Johnstone Trail to head back to Heart's Desire Beach. Then cross to the north side of Heart's Desire and pick up the Indian Nature Trail to Indian Beach (located alongside the restrooms). The path is a 0.5-mile interpretive trail with signs identifying various plants and trees and their uses by the coastal Miwok tribe. You might be surprised to learn that the Miwoks used poison oak to tattoo their skin.

Stay to the right at the fork; you'll climb gently then descend to Indian Beach, an inviting strip of sand that separates an inland marsh from Tomales Bay. Two tall, bark-covered *kotchas* stand guard at the beach; they are replicas of Miwok dwellings.

Birds and wildlife are plentiful both in the marsh and along the shoreline. On one trip, we stood on the footbridge over the marsh and watched a group of bat rays just below our feet in the ocean-bound stream. The rays hovered in the water, moving their fins just enough to hold steady their position in the current while they fed on tiny organisms in the creek.

It's possible to cross the bridge at Indian Beach's north end and loop back to Heart's Desire Beach on a dirt service road, but the more scenic route is to retrace your steps on the Indian Nature Trail.

Options

To lengthen this trip, add on an out-and-back hike to Shell Beach. Follow the first leg of the trip as described, but at the junction of Johnstone and Jepson Trails, turn left to stay on Johnstone Trail for the 2.7-mile distance to Shell Beach. The beach is as lovely as Heart's Desire, Pebble, and Indian, and it's a particular favorite of swimmers. This out-and-back excursion will add 5.4 miles to your day's total. If you want to see Shell Beach without a long walk, you can access it via a 0.25-mile stroll from a parking lot at the end of Camino del Mar (near the junction of Pierce Point Road and Sir Francis Drake Boulevard).

Directions

From San Francisco, cross the Golden Gate Bridge and drive north on U.S. 101 for 7.5 miles. Take the Sir Francis Drake Boulevard exit west toward San Anselmo, and drive 20 miles to the town of Olema. At Olema, turn right (north) on Highway 1 for about 150 yards, then turn left on Bear Valley Road. Drive 2.2 miles on Bear Valley Road until it joins with Sir Francis Drake Boulevard. Bear left on Sir Francis Drake Boulevard and drive 5.6 miles, then take the right fork onto Pierce Point Road. Drive 1.2 miles to the access road for Tomales Bay State Park. Turn right and drive one mile down the park road. Turn left and park at the Heart's Desire Beach parking lot. Johnstone Trail begins at the south end of the beach.

Information and Contact

An $8 day-use fee is charged per vehicle. Dogs and bikes are not allowed. A park map is available at the entrance kiosk or can be downloaded free at www.parks. ca.gov. For more information, contact Tomales Bay State Park, 1208 Pierce Point Road, Inverness, CA 94937, 415/669-1140, www.parks.ca.gov.

☑ ESTERO TRAIL TO SUNSET BEACH   BEST ☾
Point Reyes National Seashore

🦌 🛶 🌼 🏊

ho beach! disappointment

Level: Moderate

Total Distance: 7.8 miles round-trip

Hiking Time: 4 hours   *3h*

Elevation Change: 720 feet

Summary: Water-view hiking alongside Home Bay and Drakes Estero leads to a small, secluded beach.

Hiking the Estero Trail to Sunset Beach is a quintessential Point Reyes experience. It's full of good surprises, including an exemplary display of Douglas iris in spring, a thick forest of Monterey pines, abundant bird sightings, nearly nonstop views of estuary, bay, and ocean, and access to pristine Sunset Beach. Plus, the 7.8-mile round-trip mileage is the perfect length for a not-too-strenuous day hike.

The trail leads from the signboard at the Estero parking lot and crosses a grassy hillside, with little or no indication of what lies ahead. As you hike, look over your left shoulder to observe the regenerated hillsides of Inverness Ridge. After the Point Reyes wildfire of 1995, the ravaged slopes quickly turned from black to green again, and now the trees have gained noticeable height.

© ANN MARIE BROWN

Sandstone boulders come in all shapes and sizes at Sunset Beach.

The trail rounds a corner and descends into a dense stand of Monterey pines, the remainders of an old Christmas tree farm. In another few minutes of walking through the trees, the trail opens out to blue, serene Home Bay, exactly one mile from the trailhead.

Walk across the footbridge on the edge of the bay. You'll be surrounded by bay water if the tide is in, or by mudflats if the tide is out. White egrets that nest in the tall Monterey pines are commonly seen fishing here. On the bridge's far side, the trail rises above Home Bay and crests its first hill. At its peak you'll see where Home Bay opens into much larger Drakes Estero. The view is dependent on the tide, with low tides bringing the most unusual perspective. When the bulk of the seawater recedes, mazelike patterns appear in the mudflats, crisscrossed by thin channels of moving water. Even if the tide is high, wide blue-water views are a pleasure for the eyes.

Shortly you'll drop downhill, then cross another levee in yet another protected cove. The undulating trail continues its up-and-down meander as it parallels the edge of calm Drakes Estero. You'll enjoy nonstop water views as well as nonstop bouquets of Douglas irises in spring. The lavish, sky-blue blooms decorate the grasslands in April and May. If the tide is out, Drakes Estero's mudflats and the oyster beds of nearby Drakes Bay Oyster Farm will be revealed. If the tide is in, you'll see only a wide expanse of azure blue water. You'll climb and descend a total of three hills on this trail; the third is marked by a lone eucalyptus tree on its summit. Near its base, the leafless, colorful lilies known as "pink ladies" bloom in profusion in August.

Chances are good that you will spot some wildlife. Waterfowl and shorebirds can be seen close-up every time the trail dips down to the water's edge.

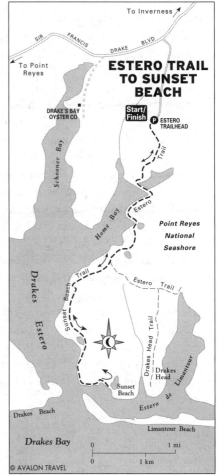

On one trip, I spotted an immense great blue heron, slowly beating his wings and taking off from the ground like a huge, mythical creature. Another time I watched from above as hundreds of bat rays were feeding in the low-tide waters. Occasionally, the tips of their "wings" would poke above the surface as they hovered to stay in position.

Deer also frequent this section of the park, both native black-tailed deer and nonnative fallow (white) and axis (spotted) deer. The nonnatives were purchased from the San Francisco Zoo in the 1940s and brought to Point Reyes by a local rancher. Although many visitors have enjoyed seeing them over the years, they are slowly being eradicated by the National Park Service through a contraceptive program that will eventually render the entire population sterile. The existing fallow and axis deer will live out their lives by about 2020 or 2025 and no future generations will be born. Despite a strong public outcry against this practice, the National Park Service believes eradication is imperative in order to protect the native black-tailed deer from diseases and competition for food.

Unfortunately, a plethora of cows are also found along this trail, and the Park Service supports their presence in Point Reyes. To some, they seem awkward and overbearing in this pastoral setting. In the wet season, their hooves make a rutted, muddy mess out of the ranch road/trail. Wear good boots.

At 2.4 miles out, you'll reach a trail sign for Drakes Head to the left and Sunset Beach straight ahead. Continuing straight on Sunset Beach Trail, the route levels out, passing more patches of springtime Douglas iris. At 1.5 miles from the junction, a large pond separates you from the edge of the bay. Although the freshwater pond in the foreground is calm and still, you can hear the roaring ocean waves ahead. Hike around the pond's left side, following the trail as it becomes narrower and often muddier. (Don't be tempted to head inland into the coastal scrub to bypass the mud. The brushy areas are lined with poison oak.)

In 0.25 mile you reach the place where Drakes Estero empties into the sea. Beautiful Sunset Beach, littered with sculpted sandstone boulders and black crabs scurrying between the rocks, is to your left in about 200 yards. A sandy stretch can be easily accessed when the tide is low. On many days you'll hear the barking of sea lions hauled out on Limantour Spit just across the way. In this special place, it's not unusual for a flotilla of white pelicans to float past like a beautiful mirage.

Options

If you are hiking this trail on a very clear day in Point Reyes, take the left turnoff for Drakes Head at the 2.4-mile mark. You'll head uphill for 0.7 mile, still on Estero Trail, then turn right on Drakes Head Trail at a maze of fences and a large cattle coral. The 1.4-mile trail leads to the edge of the headlands high above the Estero de Limantour. Views from this high perch at land's edge extend out across Limantour Spit and along the length of Drakes Bay. Many hikers consider this to be one of the finest vantage points in all of Point Reyes. It is not uncommon to see sea lions, white pelicans, egrets, and scores of other birds.

Directions

From San Francisco, cross the Golden Gate Bridge and drive north on U.S. 101 for 7.5 miles. Take the Sir Francis Drake Boulevard exit west toward San Anselmo, and drive 20 miles to the town of Olema. At Olema, turn right (north) on Highway 1 for about 150 yards, then turn left on Bear Valley Road. Drive 2.2 miles on Bear Valley Road until it joins with Sir Francis Drake Boulevard. Bear left on Sir Francis Drake Boulevard and drive 7.6 miles to the left turnoff for the Estero Trailhead. Turn left and drive one mile to the trailhead parking area.

Information and Contact

There is no fee. Dogs are not allowed. Bikes are allowed. A free park map is available at the Bear Valley Visitor Center on Bear Valley Road. A more detailed Point Reyes map is available from Tom Harrison Maps, 415/456-7940, www.tomharrisonmaps.com. For more information, contact Point Reyes National Seashore, Point Reyes, CA 94956, 415/464-5100, www.nps.gov/pore.

8 CHIMNEY ROCK   BEST ☾
Point Reyes National Seashore

🏕 🚵 🦌 🌼 👫

Level: Easy   **Total Distance:** 1.4 miles round-trip

Hiking Time: 1 hour   **Elevation Change:** Negligible

Summary: Windswept Chimney Rock is one of Marin County's most celebrated spots for admiring spring wildflowers and waving hello to passing gray whales.

If you like wildflowers, whale-watching, and ocean views, there may be no better springtime hike in Point Reyes than the Chimney Rock Trail. Every year, from late March to early June, colorful wildflowers carpet the rugged coastal bluffs that lead to an overlook of Chimney Rock, an offshore sea stack. This is one of the best flower displays in all of Point Reyes. From December to May you're likely to see elephant seals on the beaches below Chimney Rock and on nearby Drakes Beach, or you may spot the spouts (or fins, or backs, or tails) of gray whales out at sea. Adding to the trail's attractions is a tidepool area at a rocky cove near the parking lot, offering visitors at low tide a chance to inspect the contents of the sea.

The best trip on the Chimney Rock Trail is achieved with some planning. First, know that the wind can blow fiercely here, especially in the afternoons. Although the first half of the trail is on the sheltered side of the headland that faces Drakes Bay, the second half extends onto the thin peninsula of land that separates Drakes Bay from the Pacific Ocean. At the point where the bay and ocean meet, you'll find Chimney Rock—and frequently, a howling wind. Make sure you dress for it. On the positive side, this trail is usually not as windy as nearby Point Reyes Lighthouse, if that's any consolation. Plan a morning trip if possible, and wear a jacket that will deflect the wind.

From the trailhead parking lot, head straight for the Chimney Rock Trail or take a couple of short, worthwhile detours. The detours require a brief descent on the paved road that continues beyond the parking lot. In a few hundred feet you'll come to a dirt trail on the left signed for Elephant Seal Overlook. Follow it, go through a cattle gate, walk about 200 yards, then come out to a fenced overlook with a view of the southern tip of Drakes Beach. This is where elephant seals haul out in the winter and spring months, creating a tremendous cacophony of barking and snorting. Although you are a few hundred feet away from the seals, you can clearly see them brawling with each other and watch their strange, jerking movements as they go from sand to sea and back.

Elephant seals started to colonize the beaches in Point Reyes in 1981 and the

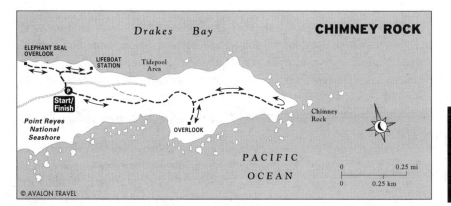

annual seal population has expanded to more than 1,500 individuals. (Elephant seals were nearly extinct from hunting by the year 1900; their comeback in the last century has been remarkable.) The huge male elephant seals arrive in late November to claim the best spots on the beaches; the pregnant females come to shore 2–3 weeks later to give birth and breed. In a few months, the seals disappear back into the ocean and are usually not seen again until the following winter.

After watching the seals' antics, continue down the paved road to see the Point Reyes Lifeboat Station, which was built in 1927 and operated until 1968. Despite the proximity of the Point Reyes Lighthouse, many shipwrecks occurred along the Point Reyes peninsula and the daring crews at the lifeboat station had the job of rescuing survivors. Just beyond the lifeboat station is a rocky beach that is laden with exposed tidepools at low tide. (The daily status of the tides is posted at the Bear Valley, Lighthouse, and Drakes Beach Visitor Centers, and printed in local newspapers.)

With these detours completed, you're ready for the main event: the Chimney Rock Trail. The path is a narrow dirt trail leading from the restrooms at the trailhead parking lot. The route crosses grassy headlands, first along sheltered Drakes Bay, where you can see the tall white cliffs that mark Drakes Beach. Then the trail climbs briefly to the top of the narrow bluffs that divide Drakes Bay from the sea. If it's a windy day, you'll feel it here.

At 0.4 mile, you'll see a faint trail leading off to the right; this path travels 0.1 mile to an overlook of the Point Reyes Headlands Reserve and the Farallon Islands, 20 miles away. The main trail continues another 0.3 mile to a fenced overlook of multiple sea stacks, the largest of which is Chimney Rock. It's impossible to see the rock's "chimney" from here, although you can see it clearly from the south end of Drakes Beach.

On a clear day this overlook is a choice spot to look for passing gray whales. Because the land you're standing on juts out so far from the mainland, whales often pass by quite close to Chimney Rock—sometimes only a few hundred yards offshore. Occasionally they will enter Drakes Bay and hang around for a while. Even if you don't spot one, you'll still be rewarded with stellar ocean views. A small beach just to the left of the trail's end is the temporary winter home of a group of elephant seals. You'll hear them barking and making a ruckus. Do not attempt to descend to any of the beaches near Chimney Rock; the cliffs are steep, rugged, and unstable.

Wildflower lovers, take note. In addition to the more common flowers such as poppies, owl's clover, tidy tips, lupine, checkerbloom, mule's ears, paintbrush, Douglas iris, and footsteps-of-spring that you'll find along the trail, look for the more rare pussy's ears near the end of the Chimney Rock Trail. They're light purple or white and somewhat furry, as you might expect.

Options

If you've driven all the way out to Chimney Rock, you should certainly pay a visit to the nearby Point Reyes Lighthouse. The short walk to reach it (less than 0.5 mile in length) might not be considered a hike except for the fact that you must climb more than 300 steps on your return trip. Plenty of visitors don't make it to the top without resting. The lighthouse is perched on a dramatic coastal promontory that has a reputation for being the windiest and foggiest spot on the entire West Coast. A small museum and visitors center (415/669-1534) presents a fascinating

Hikers taking the windswept walk to Chimney Rock are rewarded with spring wildflowers and gray whale sightings.

glimpse into our coastal history. Make sure you time your trip carefully; the stairs to the lighthouse are open only 10 A.M.–4:30 P.M. Thursday–Monday.

Directions

From San Francisco, cross the Golden Gate Bridge and drive north on U.S. 101 for 7.5 miles. Take the Sir Francis Drake Boulevard exit west toward San Anselmo, and drive 20 miles to the town of Olema. At Olema, turn right (north) on Highway 1 for about 150 yards, then turn left on Bear Valley Road. Drive 2.2 miles on Bear Valley Road until it joins with Sir Francis Drake Boulevard. Bear left on Sir Francis Drake Boulevard and drive 17.6 miles to the left turnoff for Chimney Rock. Turn left and drive 0.9 mile to the trailhead and parking area.

NOTE: During peak whale-watching season (from the last Saturday in December through mid-April), the Park Service usually requires visitors to ride a shuttle bus from Drakes Beach to the Chimney Rock Trailhead on weekends and holidays (on weekdays, you can drive your own car). There is a $5 fee per person. Phone the Bear Valley Visitor Center at 415/464-5100 for current information.

Information and Contact

There is no fee. Dogs are not allowed. Bikes are allowed. A free park map is available at the Bear Valley Visitor Center on Bear Valley Road. A more detailed Point Reyes map is available from Tom Harrison Maps, 415/456-7940, www.tomharrisonmaps.com. For more information, contact Point Reyes National Seashore, Point Reyes, CA 94956, 415/464-5100, www.nps.gov/pore.

beautiful! Make sure to walk through arch along beach.

9 SKY TRAIL AND WOODWARD VALLEY LOOP
Point Reyes National Seashore

took Mt Wittenberg trail back. 5 1/2 h with rest.

BEST ☾

Level: Strenuous

Total Distance: 13.6 miles round-trip

Hiking Time: 7 hours

Elevation Change: 1,600 feet

Summary: This "sampler" loop hike serves up the best of Point Reyes in one long, rewarding day.

There are so many trailheads in Point Reyes National Seashore, and so many trails to choose from, it can be hard to decide how to spend your time in the park. Here's a long day-hike that offers a sampler of the best of Point Reyes, including access to two of the park's most exquisite beaches and some of its loveliest forests and meadows. Start your trip early in the day so you'll have plenty of time to kick back at this trip's main destinations, Kelham and Sculptured Beaches, both superlative stretches of sand and rock.

From the trailhead, follow Sky Trail, a wide dirt road with an initially steep grade, through a forest of Douglas firs. In early spring, the road is lined with dense clusters of light blue forget-me-nots (look for their yellow centers), which thrive in the shade and rich soil here. At a tight curve in the road, where a wooden railing lines the right side, the trees open up sufficiently to allow a

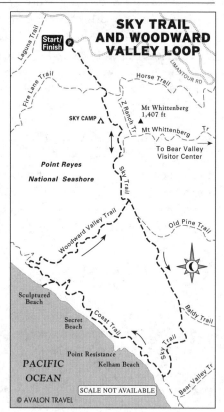

SKY TRAIL AND WOODWARD VALLEY LOOP

clear view to the west of Limantour Beach and Drakes Bay. In less than a half-hour from your car you arrive at Sky Camp, where water and restrooms are available. Overnighters should drop their packs at their chosen site, while day hikers simply continue along Sky Trail for another 4.6 miles all the way to the coast. Much of the route is pleasantly forested, and it's not uncommon to run into a deer or two

© ANN MARIE BROWN

If you time your trip for low tide, you can walk through the tunnel at Sculptured Beach.

along this leg. Also look for four-foot-tall blooming foxgloves in the early spring months. Their showy blossoms are usually white, purple, or pink.

The final stretch of Sky Trail opens out to wide, inspiring views of the coast—you can see all the way to the Farallon Islands on clear days—and after zigzagging downhill for 1.5 miles, you'll find yourself at a junction with Coast Trail. Turn right and walk 0.5 mile to the Kelham Beach turnoff (marked by a giant eucalyptus tree and a horse hitching post, but no trail sign). Follow a narrow, unmaintained spur trail to the beach and enjoy lunch and some playtime on this gorgeous stretch of sand backed by colorful cliffs. Then backtrack to Coast Trail and continue north for 2.5 miles to the Sculptured Beach turnoff. Follow the spur trail down to the water's edge and check out this aptly named beach, which is graced by a series of sandstone boulders, cliffs, arches, and tunnels that have been eroded by the forces of wind and ocean. If you arrive at Sculptured Beach during a very low or minus tide, you can explore the beach to the south, which has some fascinating carved sandstone formations. However, if you arrive during high tide you may wonder what all the fuss is about.

It's usually difficult to say good-bye to Sculptured Beach, but if the afternoon sun is waning, retrace your steps back to Coast Trail and continue north 0.5 mile to the right turnoff for Woodward Valley Trail. A two-mile climb up the coastal bluffs (the ascent is not nearly as difficult as it appears from the bottom) followed by a woodsy walk through beautiful Woodward Valley will bring you back to Sky Trail, where you simply turn left to head back to your car. And so, with a long, deep sigh, here ends another fine day in Point Reyes.

Options

It's possible to convert this day-hike into a backpacking trip with an overnight stay at Sky Camp, one of the four hike-in camps in the park. Because the camp is so close to Sky Trailhead (only 1.3 miles), you can dump off your heavy pack early in the hike and then spend the rest of the day traveling light. Those who want to stay at Sky Camp must obtain a permit from the Bear Valley Visitor Center (phone 415/464-5100 for information),

Directions

From San Francisco, cross the Golden Gate Bridge and drive north on U.S. 101 for 7.5 miles. Take the Sir Francis Drake Boulevard exit west toward San Anselmo, and drive 20 miles to the town of Olema. At Olema, turn right (north) on Highway 1 for about 150 yards, then turn left on Bear Valley Road. Drive 1.7 miles on Bear Valley Road, then turn left on Limantour Road. Drive 3.4 miles on Limantour Road to the Sky Trailhead on the left. Turn left and park in the lot. Begin hiking on the gated dirt road.

Information and Contact

There is no fee. Dogs and bikes are not allowed. A free park map is available at the Bear Valley Visitor Center on Bear Valley Road. A more detailed Point Reyes map is available from Tom Harrison Maps, 415/456-7940, www.tomharrison-maps.com. For more information, contact Point Reyes National Seashore, Point Reyes, CA 94956, 415/464-5100, www.nps.gov/pore.

10 COAST, FIRE LANE, AND LAGUNA LOOP

Point Reyes National Seashore   **BEST** C

Level: Easy/Moderate   **Total Distance:** 5.0 miles round-trip

Hiking Time: 2.5 hours   **Elevation Change:** 450 feet

Summary: A pleasant hike over the coastal hills leads to Santa Maria Beach, where you can choose to spend the night at Coast Camp.

Short of driving your car to Limantour Beach, one of the easiest ways to access a prime stretch of Point Reyes beachfront property is to take a walk on the Coast Trail.

It's also one of the prettiest ways to get there. The Coast Trail departs across the road from the Point Reyes Hostel, skirts the edge of a marshy alder forest, passes a duck-covered pond, then turns south and parallels the ocean for another mile to Coast Camp, a popular backpacking camp. A superlative loop can be made by connecting Coast Trail (2.8 miles to Coast Camp) with Fire Lane and Laguna Trails (1.8 miles back to the trailhead), allowing plenty of time to explore the inviting stretch of sand near Coast Camp known as Santa Maria Beach. Or, if you prefer, do the loop in reverse, saving the easier but longer Coast Trail for last. Both ways are equally pleasant.

The region surrounding Coast Trail was badly burned in the Point Reyes fire

© KEVIN GONG

The scenic Coast Trail is one of the most popular backpacking trails in the Bay Area.

of 1995, but it recovered quickly. Six months after the fire, the trail's surrounding grasslands and hillsides were green with new life as a multitude of ferns, berry bushes, and vines poked up from the ground and grasses blanketed the blackened earth. In only a few years, the coastal scrub regained its rightful place. Today, it's difficult to find any evidence of fire along the trail.

The National Park Service reintroduced tule elk to this region of the park in 1999, and a small herd wanders the hillsides near Limantour Road. You may possibly see elk here, although you have a much greater chance at Pierce Point Ranch and along the Tomales Point Trail in the northern region of the park, where the elk population is much larger (see *Tomales Point Trail* listing in this chapter).

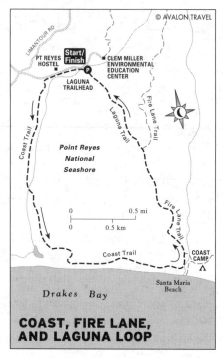

COAST, FIRE LANE, AND LAGUNA LOOP

Starting from the Point Reyes Hostel, the walking is easy on Coast Trail's wide, dirt road, following a slight downhill grade to the coast. When you reach the shoreline, you can head straight for the sand and continue walking southeast, but first-timers beware: It is difficult to spot the trail to Coast Camp from the beach from this direction. The no-fail route is to stay on Coast Trail for another 1.1 miles to Coast Camp. (Backpackers who wish to reserve a spot at the 14-site campground must obtain a permit from Point Reyes headquarters. Advance reservations are necessary, especially in summer.)

At Coast Camp, a narrow foot trail leads from near the restrooms to Santa Maria Beach. Once on the sand, your options are open in either direction—north toward Limantour Beach or south toward Sculptured Beach—with miles of uninterrupted shoreline between. Or, if you're tired of walking, just flop down in the sand.

For your return trip, take Fire Lane Trail north from Coast Camp for one mile to a junction with Laguna Trail. You'll face a substantial climb; keep turning around to check out the ocean views as you gain elevation. At the junction, bear left on Laguna Trail and hike 0.8 mile back to the Laguna Trailhead adjacent to a park ranger's residence, where your car is waiting.

Options

For a completely different hike in the same neighborhood, follow Muddy Hollow Trail to Limantour Beach, then walk along the windswept dunes of Limantour Spit. At the turnoff for the Point Reyes Hostel on Limantour Road, turn right (west) instead of left (east) and drive 0.5 mile to the Muddy Hollow Trailhead. Muddy Hollow Trail leads 1.7 miles to Limantour Beach, passing two bird-filled ponds along the way. At the entrance to the beach, head down to the sand and turn right to hike along Limantour Spit. An out-and-back along this route will make a six- to eight-mile round-trip, depending on how far you follow the narrow spit. Note that this hike is best done in summer or fall; in the rainy months, Muddy Hollow Trail is sometimes closed and often impassable because of wet conditions.

Directions

From San Francisco, cross the Golden Gate Bridge and drive north on U.S. 101 for 7.5 miles. Take the Sir Francis Drake Boulevard exit west toward San Anselmo, and drive 20 miles to the town of Olema. At Olema, turn right (north) on Highway 1 for about 150 yards, then turn left on Bear Valley Road. Drive 1.7 miles on Bear Valley Road, then turn left on Limantour Road. Drive 5.9 miles on Limantour Road to the left turnoff for the Point Reyes Hostel. Turn left, drive 0.5 mile (past the hostel) and park in the lot on the right (Laguna Trailhead). Then walk back up the road 0.3 mile, passing the hostel again. Begin hiking on the dirt road just west of (and across the road from) the hostel. The road is signed as Coast Trail to Coast Camp.

Information and Contact

There is no fee. Dogs are not allowed. Bikes are allowed only on Coast Trail. A free park map is available at the Bear Valley Visitor Center on Bear Valley Road. A more detailed Point Reyes map is available from Tom Harrison Maps, 415/456-7940, www.tomharrisonmaps.com. For more information, contact Point Reyes National Seashore, Point Reyes, CA 94956, 415/464-5100, www.nps.gov/pore.

11 BEAR VALLEY TRAIL TO ARCH ROCK
Point Reyes National Seashore

Level: Easy/Moderate

Hiking Time: 4 hours

Total Distance: 8.2 miles round-trip

Elevation Change: 400 feet

Summary: Point Reyes' most popular trail follows an easy grade from lush Bear Valley to dramatic Arch Rock, a precipitous bluff-top overlook.

The Bear Valley Trail is far and away the most well known and busiest trail in Point Reyes, and for that reason alone many serious hikers avoid it. They fear the crowds at the trailhead, the noise of other chitchatting trail users, and the probable lack of peace in a place as sacred as Point Reyes.

But bypassing the Bear Valley Trail is a big mistake. The trailside scenery is sublime. The easy grade makes it suitable for a family hiking (or biking) trip. And arriving at the trailhead before 9 A.M. assures you of some solitude along the route, even on weekends. Winter is the best season for fewer crowds, and the trail is loveliest then, when the streams are running full and the ferns are in full leafy display.

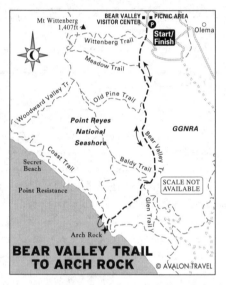

The trail is simple to follow. It begins as a wide dirt road just beyond the Bear Valley Visitor Center and Morgan Horse Ranch. Several trails junction with Bear Valley Trail; stay on the wide, main road and meander your way through a mixed bay and Douglas fir forest, following the path of Bear Valley Creek. Ferns of many kinds adorn the creek's banks, including delicate five-finger ferns. You'll notice a slight uphill grade in the first mile, but the entire route never gains or loses more than 200 feet in elevation.

At 1.5 miles from the trailhead, you reach the edge of large Divide Meadow, a tranquil spot for a rest or a picnic on your return trip. Deer are often sighted here. Divide Meadow marks the divide in this valley: Bear Valley Creek, which flows north, is left behind, but soon the trail parallels Coast Creek, which flows south all the way to the sea. Forest, ferns, and lush streamside foliage keep you in good company as you forge onward. In late spring (typically June), buckeye trees along this stretch bloom with fragrant white flower clusters. In early spring (typically April), the trail is bordered by a profusion of blue forget-me-nots and tasty miner's lettuce, which thrive in these shady growing conditions.

At 3.2 miles, you reach a junction of trails and a bike rack. (Bikes are allowed on Bear Valley Trail only to this point.) Glen Trail leads to the left and Baldy Trail to the right, but you simply continue straight on Bear Valley Trail to Arch Rock. Although at present you are deep in the forest, surrounded by alder, bay laurel, and Douglas fir, you will soon leave the shade. A half-mile farther the trail opens out to coastal marshlands and chaparral, and the ocean appears straight ahead.

Nearing the sea, Bear Valley Trail splits off as it meets up with Coast Trail. Bear left to walk the last stretch of the hike. These final steps are filled with drama as you traverse the top of Arch Rock's precipitous, jade-green bluff jutting out into the sea. Coast Creek, the previously gentle stream you were following, now cuts a deep and eroded gorge on its way to the ocean. An unmaintained spur trail drops along the edge of the gorge to the beach. Some hikers plan their trip so they can descend to the beach, then crawl through Arch Rock's tunnel at the mouth of Coast Creek. But this is possible only when conditions are just right: The tide must be very low, and the water level in Coast Creek must also be low. Most hikers are content to stay on top of Arch Rock and enjoy the view, which takes in numerous rock outcrops, the shoreline below, and the perpetually rolling surf.

I have a long-standing ritual I perform on Arch Rock. I sit on the jagged bluff edge and wait until a sea lion swims by in the surf below. Then I follow its bobbing and rolling progress through the kelp beds and surging waters as far as my eyes will allow. When the sea lion disappears from sight, I wait for another, and then another. It's remarkable how quickly and pleasantly an afternoon can pass this way.

Options

If it's crowded on Arch Rock, you can choose from two more secluded destinations. The easiest option is to backtrack a few hundred feet to Coast Trail, then follow that trail northward for 0.8 mile to Kelham Beach. The spur trail to the beach is marked by a lone eucalyptus tree. (During very low tides, you can simply hike on the sand to Kelham from the tunnel at Arch Rock.) A more challenging trip is to follow Coast Trail southward for 3.6 miles to Wildcat Beach, where Wildcat Camp is located. If you retrace your steps at the end of the day, you will have completed 15.2 miles. But you can cut off one mile on your return by taking

Arch Rock is a high bluff that juts precipitously out to sea.

the Glen Trail Cutoff and bypassing Arch Rock. Or, get a permit from the Bear Valley Visitor Center so you can carry a backpack and spend the night at Wildcat Camp, then hike the return miles the next day.

Directions

From San Francisco, cross the Golden Gate Bridge and drive north on U.S. 101 for 7.5 miles. Take the Sir Francis Drake Boulevard exit west toward San Anselmo, and drive 20 miles to the town of Olema. At Olema, turn right (north) on Highway 1 for about 150 yards, then turn left on Bear Valley Road. Drive 0.5 mile, then turn left at the sign for Seashore Headquarters Information. Drive 0.25 mile and park in the large lot on the left, past the visitors center. Start hiking along the park road, heading for the signed Bear Valley Trail.

Public transportation: The West Marin Stage Bus #68 stops at the Bear Valley Visitors Center daily. For West Marin Stage information, phone 415/226-0855 or visit www.marintransit.org.

Information and Contact

There is no fee. Dogs are not allowed. Bikes are allowed on the first 3.2 miles of Bear Valley Trail. A free park map is available at the Bear Valley Visitor Center on Bear Valley Road. A more detailed Point Reyes map is available from Tom Harrison Maps, 415/456-7940, www.tomharrisonmaps.com. For more information, contact Point Reyes National Seashore, Point Reyes, CA 94956, 415/464-5100, www.nps.gov/pore.

12 BEAR VALLEY, OLD PINE, WOODWARD VALLEY, AND COAST LOOP
Point Reyes National Seashore

🔲 🦌 🌿 🚻 🚌

Level: Strenuous

Total Distance: 13.0 miles round-trip

Hiking Time: 7 hours

Elevation Change: 1,700 feet

Summary: Spend a full day exploring the interior and coast of Point Reyes on this long loop that delivers stellar scenery and a chance at solitude.

If you're looking for an epic day hike in Point Reyes National Seashore, this is it. This scenic loop has plenty of variety; you'll hike past forest, meadows, and ocean beaches over the course of 13 miles. Pack along a hearty lunch and make a day of it.

The trip begins just past the Bear Valley Visitor Center. Follow Bear Valley Trail for 1.5 miles to Divide Meadow (see *Bear Valley Trail to Arch Rock* listing in this chapter for details on this stretch). Leave the crowds behind at the scenic meadow and turn right on Old Pine Trail, which begins next to the restrooms. In contrast to the wide Bear Valley Trail, Old Pine Trail is a narrow footpath closely bordered by dense Douglas firs and an undergrowth of elderberries and huckleberries. It's much less traveled than nearby trails, so you may even have this peaceful forest all to yourself. You'll climb steadily for 1.5 miles through the trees, then descend for just under 0.5 mile. Here, at a trail junction, turn right on Sky Trail. After only 0.3 mile, you'll meet up with Woodward Valley Trail, where you turn left.

Follow Woodward Valley Trail for two lovely miles to the coast, passing through an assortment of shady conifer forests, open hillsides, and grassy meadows. The path is downhill all the way except for occasional short rises. A brief climb brings you to a sweeping overlook point where you can see the Farallon Islands 20 miles out to sea, Double Point and Alamere Falls to the south, Chimney Rock to the north, and a 10-mile-long arc of curving coastline in between. In the last 0.5 mile, you'll switchback quite steeply down the open, chaparral-covered hillside, heading for Drakes Bay and the ocean. The coast views never quit.

At a junction with Coast Trail, turn left and parallel the bluffs along the shoreline. More ocean views are yours for the taking over the next 0.5 mile, until you reach the turnoff for Sculptured Beach (a metal horse-hitching post marks the spot). Turn right here and pay a visit to Sculptured Beach's fascinating eroded sandstone terraces and rocky tidepools. This is a perfect place for lunch and a rest about halfway through the loop. If the tide is low enough, you can head south along the beach and climb around, over, and through a series of arches and tunnels to access smaller, hidden beaches all the way to Point Resistance. Watch your tide table, though; you don't want to attempt this if the tide is coming in instead of going out. If the tide is high, you can always head north toward Santa Maria Beach, a sandy strip of sand that is almost always accessible.

Back on Coast Trail, two miles farther south, is the turnoff for Kelham Beach. Its spur trail is definitely marked by an immense eucalyptus tree—but no trail sign. Kelham Beach, too, is worth a visit, and makes a good alternative lunch spot if Sculptured Beach is crowded. Kelham is a wide, sandy beach with a colorful backdrop of rust-colored, cave-pocketed cliffs.

The final 0.8-mile stretch on Coast Trail is followed by a left turn on Bear Valley Trail just north of Arch Rock. If you've never visited Arch Rock, do so now with a short side trip. A 0.25-mile walk on the spur trail leads to a spectacular ocean overlook on a jagged, grassy bluff.

At Arch Rock you must wave a sorrowful good-bye to the coast. It's time to turn inland and head home on Bear Valley Trail. A 2.6-mile walk along Coast Creek brings you back to Divide Meadow; a final 1.5 miles along Bear Valley Creek returns you to your starting point.

Options

If you want to add a visit to the summit of Mount Wittenberg to this loop, you can start your trip on the Mount Wittenberg Trail from Bear Valley, instead of Old Pine Trail from Divide Meadow. The Mount Wittenberg Trail climbs steeply

A visit to well-named Sculptured Beach is one of the highlights of this long loop hike.

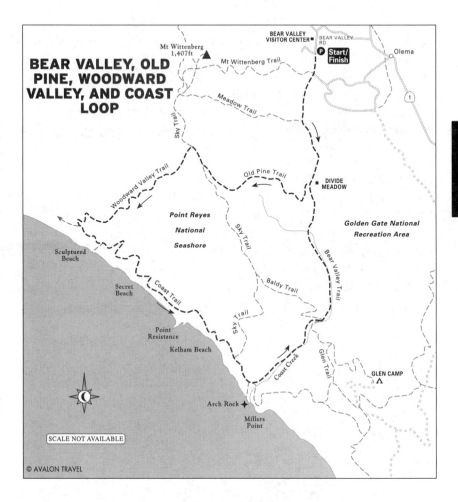

BEAR VALLEY, OLD PINE, WOODWARD VALLEY, AND COAST LOOP

for 1,300 feet to the tallest peak in the national seashore; take the short summit trail on the right to reach the top. Years ago there was a lovely view from this peak; now a tall cluster of conifers crowds the top and obscures the vista. From the base of the summit trail, follow Z Ranch Trail south to Sky Trail, and continue south on Sky Trail to pick up Woodward Valley Trail. The rest of the trail is the same as described previously. This loop is also 12 miles long, but it has a slightly steeper climb.

Directions

From San Francisco, cross the Golden Gate Bridge and drive north on U.S. 101 for 7.5 miles. Take the Sir Francis Drake Boulevard exit west toward San Anselmo, and drive 20 miles to the town of Olema. At Olema, turn right (north) on Highway 1 for about 150 yards, then turn left on Bear Valley Road. Drive 0.5 mile, then turn left at the sign for Seashore Headquarters Information. Drive 0.25 mile and park in the large lot on the left, past the visitors center. Start hiking along the park road, heading for the signed Bear Valley Trail.

Public transportation: The West Marin Stage Bus #68 stops at the Bear Valley Visitors Center daily. For West Marin Stage information, phone 415/226-0855 or visit www.marintransit.org.

Information and Contact

There is no fee. Dogs are not allowed. Bikes are allowed on the first 3.2 miles of Bear Valley Trail. A free park map is available at the Bear Valley Visitor Center on Bear Valley Road. A more detailed Point Reyes map is available from Tom Harrison Maps, 415/456-7940, www.tomharrisonmaps.com. For more information, contact Point Reyes National Seashore, Point Reyes, CA 94956, 415/464-5100, www.nps.gov/pore.

1 3 BARNABE PEAK LOOP BEST ◖
Samuel P. Taylor State Park

Level: Moderate

Hiking Time: 3 hours

Total Distance: 6.0 miles round-trip

Elevation Change: 1,300 feet

Summary: An intimate waterfall, a rainforest-like fern forest, and a summit with a big view in western Marin County.

Although it is a much older public parkland, Samuel P. Taylor State Park is somewhat overshadowed by its large and more famous neighbor, Point Reyes National Seashore. For hikers, that's a bonus: Even when Samuel P. Taylor's campground is filled to the limit on summer weekends, it's rare to find many people on its hiking trails. But that's just fine with those who know and love the park; they can enjoy a little solitude along with the scenery.

The park's best hike is a loop trip to Barnabe Peak, a six-mile trek that leads through a ferny, mossy forest of bay trees, passes by a wet-season waterfall, and

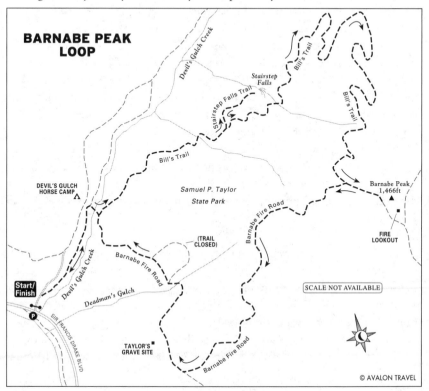

BARNABE PEAK
LOOP

Devil's Gulch Creek

Stairstep Falls Trail

Stairstep
Falls

Bill's Trail

Bill's Trail

Bill's Trail

DEVIL'S GULCH
HORSE CAMP

Samuel P. Taylor
State Park

Barnabe Peak
1,466ft ▲

Barnabe Fire Road

FIRE
LOOKOUT

Devil's Gulch Creek

(TRAIL
CLOSED)

Barnabe Fire Road

Start/
Finish
P

SCALE NOT AVAILABLE

Deadman's Gulch

SIR FRANCIS DRAKE BLVD

TAYLOR'S
GRAVE SITE

Barnabe Fire Road

© AVALON TRAVEL

then bags the summit of Barnabe Peak at 1,466 feet. The trailhead isn't at the main Samuel P. Taylor campground entrance; it's one mile west on Sir Francis Drake Boulevard near Devil's Gulch Horse Camp. Park in the dirt pullout across the road from the camp, then walk up the paved camp road for 100 yards until you reach a trail cutting off to the right along Devil's Gulch Creek, paralleling the road. Follow it and immediately you descend into a stream-fed canyon filled with Douglas firs, tanoaks, bay laurel, and about a million ferns. In April and May, the ground near the stream is covered with forget-me-nots and buttercups.

A few minutes of upstream walking brings you to a footbridge over Devil's Gulch. Just ahead is a huge, hollowed-out redwood tree—the only one of its kind along this stream. Go ahead, climb inside; everybody does it. The tree's charm is irresistible.

Turn right and cross the footbridge, then turn left on its far side, following the sign for Bill's Trail to Barnabe Peak. You'll climb very gently above the creek, marveling at the walls of ferns and the long limbs of mossy oaks and bays, as you gain 350 feet over 0.75 mile. Soon you gain a view of the bald, grassy ridge on the far side of the canyon.

After crossing a bridge over a feeder stream, look for the Stairstep Falls trail junction on your left. Bear left and in 10 minutes of walking, you'll reach the trail's end near the base of Stairstep Falls. True to its name, 40-foot-tall Stairstep Falls drops in three main cascades, with a rocky "staircase" producing dozens of rivulets of water. Trail maintenance crews try to keep the area cleared of fallen trees and branches so you can stand near the base of the falls. It's a charming spot in the wet winter and spring months, perfect for quiet contemplation in the good company of ferns, forest, and water.

When you've seen enough, retrace your steps back to Bill's Trail and continue uphill. This beautifully graded path is popular with local runners, and it's easy to see why: You hardly realize you are climbing as you zigzag your way through dozens of switchbacks. The patient meandering of the path slows you down so you have plenty of time to admire the graceful bay laurels, immense Douglas firs, and prolific ferns.

At 3.7 miles, the trail nears the top of the ridge and opens out to a small meadow. A dip back into the trees is followed by another meadow, and then you are permanently expelled from the shade onto the exposed ridge of Barnabe Peak. Wow! What a view! Tomales Bay and Point Reyes are spread out before you even though you're not yet at the summit. Turn left on the fire road to hike the final 0.25 mile to Barnabe Peak's top, which is easily identified by its fire lookout tower. This lookout, one of only two in Marin County, is fully operational. (The other

© ANN MARIE BROWN

Barnabe Peak's summit vista

tower, on Mount Tamalpais, hasn't been used for decades.) Barnabe Peak's lookout tower is closed to the public, but the view from its base is magnificent.

At the summit, your panorama expands to the south to include Bolinas Ridge and Mount Tamalpais. That sparkling patch of water with the large spillway is Kent Lake in the Marin Municipal Water District. To the east, you can see Mount Diablo. In the foreground lies the town of Lagunitas and the San Geronimo Valley. Are those little tiny boats on Tomales Bay to the west? Yes indeed. The big hill on the southeast side of Tomales Bay is Black Mountain at 1,280 feet.

If you're wondering about this summit's moniker, Barnabe Peak was named for explorer John Fremont's mule. After many great traveling expeditions with Fremont, Barnabe lived out his final days as the pet of the Samuel P. Taylor family. He liked to escape the confines of his corral and go for long walks on these hillsides.

To loop back from the summit, follow the open, exposed fire road back to the point where Bill's Trail joined it, then continue down the fire road from there (this road is sometimes signed as Riding and Hiking Trail). The return leg of the loop is only two miles, compared to the four miles you hiked uphill, so expect a much steeper grade. (Hikers with bad knees might consider going back down the way they came up.) At 1.3 miles from the peak, you'll notice a small white picket fence in a clearing 100 feet off the trail. This is Samuel P. Taylor's grave site; he lived from 1827 to 1896. Taylor was famous for establishing the first paper mill on the West Coast and producing newsprint for the San Francisco dailies. He built the town of Taylorville on the site of the present-day park and opened Camp Taylor, a popular weekend recreational resort.

Options

Another favorite trail at Samuel P. Taylor State Park is the Pioneer Tree Trail, which begins at the Redwood Grove Picnic Area near the park's main campground (one mile east of Devil's Gulch on Sir Francis Drake Boulevard). This 2.7-mile loop curves around one redwood-filled canyon after another, passing by some big trees that are hundreds of years old. The 500-year-old Pioneer Tree has been hollowed out by fire; you can stand inside its massive trunk. To get a good look at how large the Pioneer really is, have a seat on the bench located a few yards uphill, where you gain a wider perspective.

Directions

From San Francisco, cross the Golden Gate Bridge and drive north on U.S. 101 for 7.5 miles. Take the Sir Francis Drake Boulevard exit west toward San Anselmo, then drive about 15 miles (through the towns of Ross, Fairfax, and Lagunitas) to the signed entrance to Samuel P. Taylor State Park's campground. Don't turn here; continue on Sir Francis Drake Boulevard for exactly one more mile. Park in the dirt pullout across the road from Devil's Gulch Horse Camp. Walk across the road and take the paved road toward the campground.

Public transportation: The West Marin Stage Bus #68 stops at the main entrance to Samuel P. Taylor State Park, by the campground (one mile from the Devil's Gulch Trailhead). For West Marin Stage information, phone 415/226-0855 or visit www.marintransit.org.

Information and Contact

There is no fee if you park in the roadside pullout across from Devil's Gulch Horse Camp. An $8 per vehicle day-use fee is charged if you park in the main paved parking areas. Dogs are not allowed. Bikes are allowed on fire roads only. A park map is available at the entrance kiosk at the main campground. Wilderness Press publishes a more detailed map of the park and surrounding areas; order the Point Reyes and West Marin Parklands map online at www.wildernesspress.com. For more information, contact Samuel P. Taylor State Park, P.O. Box 251, Lagunitas, CA 94938, 415/488-9897, www.parks.ca.gov.

14 MOUNT BURDELL
Olompali State Historic Park

Level: Moderate   **Total Distance:** 7.8 miles round-trip

Hiking Time: 4 hours   **Elevation Change:** 1,500 feet

Summary: One of Marin County's least-visited parks is a great place to admire giant oaks and spring wildflowers on the way to the summit of the county's fifth-highest peak.

Olompali is the state park with the funny name that is passed by each day by multiple thousands of commuters on U.S. 101. Located a few miles north of Novato and a few miles south of Petaluma, the park's entrance is right along the freeway corridor. You might expect this would mean that the place is packed with visitors year-round, but in fact, the opposite is true. Olompali is one of the least-visited state parks in the San Francisco Bay Area.

Maybe that's because nobody can pronounce its name. It's oh-LOMP-o-lee, with the accent on the second syllable.

Olompali has a colorful history. This land was a major Miwok trade center for hundreds of years. The Coast Miwoks inhabited at least one site within the present-day park from about 500 A.D. It was perhaps one of the largest Native American sites in what is now Marin County. The name Olompali comes from the Miwok language and means something like "southern village" or "southern people."

In more recent history, the land was owned by the Burdell family, a prominent San Francisco dentist and his wife. In the late 1800s, they built a 26-room

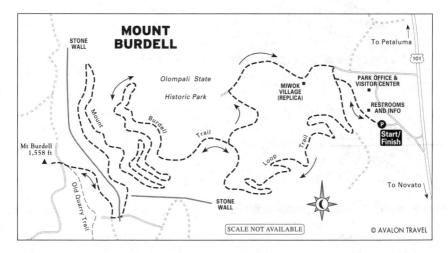

mansion with formal gardens here. In the 20th century, the land was rented to various tenants, including the Grateful Dead in 1966. (One of their album covers shows the rolling hills of Olompali.) In the 1970s, a series of archeological digs in the parkland uncovered an Elizabethan silver sixpence dated 1567, possibly related to Sir Francis Drake's landing in Marin County.

The park's best offering is a gently switchbacked trail that climbs 1,500 feet to the summit of Mount Burdell, a grassy, rounded peak with expansive views of northern Marin County and southern Sonoma and Napa Counties. At 1,558 feet, it's the fifth-highest peak in Marin County.

One caveat: Olompali's inland hills can bake in the summer and early fall. Even though the Mount Burdell Trail is mostly shaded, the hike can be quite hot and unpleasant in the summer months. The best seasons are spring, when the wildflowers bloom, and autumn, when the oaks' leaves turn gold. Clear winter days are also recommended.

Take the trail leading uphill from the parking lot (not the path that heads toward the ranch buildings). Bear left at an obvious fork; a large bridge over Olompali Creek is on the right. You soon leave the sunny grasslands for the wooded eastern slopes of Mount Burdell. Oak savanna gives way to forests of bay laurels, madrones, and deciduous oaks. The only negative is the constant rumble of cars on the highway; at least you can relish the fact that you're not seated in one of them.

At 1.6 miles, the path reaches a major trail junction; turn left on the signed trail for Burdell Mountain Summit. (A closed trail at this junction is the old summit trail; it made a beeline straight uphill and was subject to terrible erosion in winter rains.)

© ANN MARIE BROWN

a hiker takes in the view of the Petaluma River from Mount Burdell's summit

As you continue the ascent, you'll gain peekaboo views of the Petaluma River to the east and its surrounding marshlands. Climb a few more switchbacks and you'll see where the river empties into San Pablo Bay. Small planes take off and land at Gnoss Field airport, just across U.S. 101, and a steady parade of cars streams north and south on the freeway.

Where the switchbacks lead into the mountain's many small canyons, all sights and sounds of civilization disappear. The quiet of the leafy woodland is punctured only by the movements of the black-tailed deer who inhabit it. (On one trip, I counted 37 deer, all in separate groups of twos and threes.)

The trail switchbacks all the way up to a metal gate marking the park's boundary. Here, the parkland adjoins Burdell Mountain Open Space Preserve. Pass through the gate, then follow the trail to the paved Burdell Mountain Ridge Fire Road. Views open up to the southwest of the tree-lined streets of Novato and the shimmering blue water of Stafford Lake. Far off to the south, you can see the tips of the tallest buildings in downtown San Francisco. If you follow the paved road all the way to the mountain's AT&T transmitter towers, you can walk around them and look westward to Nicasio and Point Reyes. But the best view comes from the north side of the summit ridge. At a low stone wall along the 1,500-foot ridgeline, you can see east toward the Petaluma River and San Pablo Bay and north toward Napa and Sonoma. This wall was built by Chinese laborers in the 1870s to mark the border between two large ranchos.

On your return trip, retrace your steps back down to the main junction and then follow the opposite side of the park's short loop. You'll descend through a canopy of oaks and bays, pass a meandering creek, then reach a replica of a Miwok village that was built by park volunteers and local Native Americans. Finally the trail curves down through the Burdell ranch buildings and finishes out at the parking lot. A visit to the historic ranch buildings is a worthwhile side trip; there are two 19th-century barns, a blacksmith shop, and a saltbox house. Look for Kitchen Rock southeast of the older barn; it contains Native American grinding holes of varying sizes, in which the Miwok would grind acorn meat into flour.

Options

If you'd like to visit the summit of Mount Burdell but want to avoid paying the park entrance fee, or if you are hiking with your dog, start your trip from the Mount Burdell Open Space Preserve trailhead at the end of San Andreas Drive in Novato (off San Marin Drive). Here, dogs are permitted and access is free. A series of wide fire roads (San Andreas, Middle Burdell, and Cobblestone) will escort you to the top in 2.8 miles. After late winter and early spring rains, don't miss a visit to Hidden Lake, a seasonal pond at the junction of Middle Burdell and Cobblestone fire roads. The resident tree frogs sing a deafening chorus. The lake is also home to an assortment of rare plants.

Directions

From San Francisco, cross the Golden Gate Bridge and drive north on U.S. 101 for 28 miles to Novato. Continue another 2.5 miles north of Novato on U.S. 101;

the park entrance is on the west side of the highway. Note: The park is accessible only to southbound traffic from U.S. 101. Driving north, you must continue past the park entrance, take the Redwood Landfill overpass, then head back south on U.S. 101 to the entrance.

Information and Contact

An $8 day-use fee is charged per vehicle. Dogs and bikes are not allowed. Park maps are sometimes available at the trailhead. A detailed map of the area is available from Pease Press, 415/387-1437, www.peasepress.com (ask for the *Trails of Northeast Marin County* map). For more information, contact Olompali State Historic Park, P.O. Box 1016, Novato, CA 94948, 415/892-3383, www.parks.ca.gov.

15 BASS LAKE, DOUBLE POINT, AND ALAMERE FALLS

BEST **(**

Point Reyes National Seashore

🚶 🦌 🌷 🏊 🌊

Level: Moderate	**Total Distance:** 8.4 miles round-trip
Hiking Time: 4 hours	**Elevation Change:** 550 feet

Summary: One of California's most spectacular waterfalls and an inviting swimming lake are found along this trail on the southern tip of Point Reyes.

Quick—which California waterfall leaps off high coastal bluffs and cascades gracefully down to the sand and surf below? Most people think of famous McWay Falls in Big Sur, one of the most frequently visited and photographed waterfalls in the state. But don't forget the other coastal cataract that makes the same dramatic plunge from earth to sea, 150 miles up the coast in western Marin County. That's Alamere Falls in Point Reyes National Seashore.

There may be no finer way to spend a spring day than to hike to Alamere Falls with stops along the way at Bass Lake and Double Point. If you time your trip for a clear, sunny day, when the bush lupine and Douglas iris are in full bloom and the waterfall is flowing enthusiastically, this trail's scenery will knock your socks off.

Start hiking on Coast Trail from the Palomarin Trailhead in Point Reyes, the southernmost trailhead in the national seashore. Despite its off-the-beaten-track location near the town of Bolinas, the trailhead parking lot is often full of cars. Some of these visitors are here to backpack the 15-mile Coast Trail, a highly recommended two-day trip. You'll follow a portion of that route on this hike.

Coast Trail is a wide dirt road that begins in stands of eucalyptus. The first mile is nearly level and serves up frequent ocean views, putting you in good spirits for the rest of the trip. Then Coast Trail turns inland, climbing slightly to a

Alamere Falls makes a graceful cascading drop to the Pacific Ocean.

© ANN MARIE BROWN

junction with Lake Ranch Trail at 2.1 miles. Stay on Coast Trail as it veers left and passes a couple of seasonal ponds, which are often covered with paddling waterbirds. At 2.6 miles, you'll skirt the north edge of Bass Lake. Swimming and picnicking opportunities are plentiful at the large blue lake; just follow the unsigned spur trail on the left amid the Douglas firs. (The trail is located about 100 yards past the point where you first glimpse the lake.) On warm spring and summer weekends, you'll leave much of the traffic on this busy trail at Bass Lake.

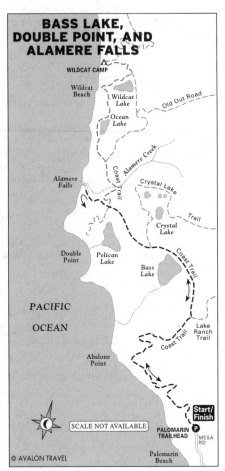

A short distance farther is another trail junction where the unmaintained Crystal Lake Trail heads to tiny Crystal and Mud Lakes. Continue straight on Coast Trail, now heading toward the ocean. Three-quarters of a mile beyond Bass Lake, prepare yourself for a stunning view of Pelican Lake, perched on a coastal bluff to your left. The Pacific Ocean forms its backdrop. After curving past the lake, an unmarked and usually overgrown left spur trail leads to the northern edge of Double Point. If you take the spur, you'll come to a rocky overlook with views of the ocean and Stormy Stack, a big offshore rock outcrop. This is a splendid spot for whale-watching.

Just beyond this spur, a trail sign points straight ahead for Wildcat Camp and a second overgrown spur leads left, heading for the coastal bluffs and Alamere Falls. (So many hikers have missed this turnoff over the years that the Park Service finally put a sign at the junction.) Follow the 0.4-mile spur trail, which is quite narrow and usually encroached by poison oak and coastal scrub, until it meets up with Alamere Creek and continues to the cliff edge. Although you are now practically on top of the waterfall, you can see little of its watery theatrics.

To see more, many hikers cross the creek and scramble down the bluffs to the beach, but park rangers try to discourage this because of the potential dangers of the constantly crumbing cliffs. Instead, they suggest that if you want to see Alamere Falls from the bottom, backtrack to Coast Trail and continue hiking 1.9 miles north to Wildcat Camp, then follow the trail to its neighboring beach. A one-mile stroll southward along brayed tan sand brings you safely to the base of Alamere Falls, where its full drama unfolds. During and just after the rainy season, the waterfall cascades 50 feet in a wide, effusive block over its cliff, then streams across the sand to the sea.

Options
Ambitious hikers should continue another 1.9 miles beyond Alamere Falls on Coast Trail to Wildcat Beach and Wildcat Camp. Along the way, you'll pass two more lakes, Ocean and Wildcat, although neither is as large as Pelican or Bass Lake. If you get a permit, you can spend the night at Wildcat Camp. If you hike this as a day trip, you'll have a 12.4-mile day.

Directions
From San Francisco, cross the Golden Gate Bridge and drive north on U.S. 101 for four miles. Take the Mill Valley/Stinson Beach/Highway 1 exit and continue straight for one mile to a stoplight at Shoreline Highway (Highway 1). Turn left on Shoreline Highway and drive 12 miles to Stinson Beach, then continue north on Highway 1 for another 5.5 miles to the left turnoff for Bolinas Road, which is often not signed (it's across from a big white farmhouse). Turn left and drive 2.1 miles to Mesa Road. Turn right and drive 5.8 miles to the Palomarin Trailhead.

Information and Contact
There is no fee. Dogs and bikes are not allowed. A free park map is available at the Bear Valley Visitor Center on Bear Valley Road. A more detailed Point Reyes map is available from Tom Harrison Maps, 415/456-7940, www.tomharrison-maps.com. For more information, contact Point Reyes National Seashore, Point Reyes, CA 94956, 415/464-5100, www.nps.gov/pore.

16 KENT, GRIFFIN, AND ZUMIE LOOP TRAILS

Audubon Canyon Ranch/Martin Griffin Preserve   **BEST** C

Level: Easy/Moderate

Total Distance: 3.0 miles round-trip

Hiking Time: 1.5 hours

Elevation Change: 800 feet

Summary: A bird-watching experience that is guaranteed to thrill birders and nonbirders alike, combined with a peaceful hike away from the crowds.

When I pulled into the parking lot at Audubon Canyon Ranch, I thought I was in the middle of a major event. A row of cars lined the driveway, more cars kept pulling in, and somebody was trying to direct all the traffic. Was it John Muir's birthday or something?

No, just a busy birding day at the ranch. One of three preserves in Marin and Sonoma Counties run by Audubon Canyon Ranch, the Martin Griffin Preserve is an amazing spot to see wildlife—great egrets and herons, especially—up close and very personal. The preserve is one of the most significant and most studied nesting sites on the West Coast. From Henderson Overlook, a hike-in bird-watching platform, visitors can witness the miracle of more than 100 pairs of these large shorebirds—with wingspans up to six feet long—nesting in the tops of redwood trees.

The preserve is open on weekends and holidays only from mid-March to mid-July. With visitation periods so limited, there's no way to avoid the crowds at the parking lot, except perhaps to show up on a rainy day. Fortunately, most visitors make only very short trips to and from the egret overlook. If you're willing to

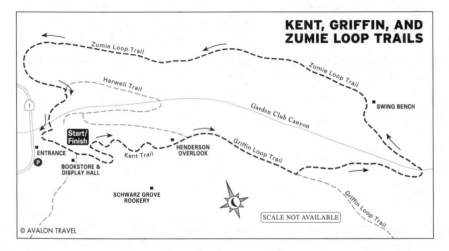

KENT, GRIFFIN, AND
ZUMIE LOOP TRAILS

Zumie Loop Trail

Zumie Loop Trail

Harwell Trail

SWING BENCH

Garden Club Canyon

Start/
Finish

ENTRANCE

Kent Trail

HENDERSON
OVERLOOK

Griffin Loop Trail

BOOKSTORE &
DISPLAY HALL

SCHWARZ GROVE
ROOKERY

Griffin Loop Trail

SCALE NOT AVAILABLE

© AVALON TRAVEL

hike a little farther, you can explore a beautiful protected wildlife preserve and find some solitude as well.

Start your trip by visiting the must-see Henderson Overlook. Take the Alice Kent Trail, which begins behind the preserve's buildings. It climbs moderately and pleasantly for 0.5 mile, and about halfway up you'll get your first glimpse of snow-white great egrets, nesting in their treetop colony on the neighboring hillside. At the overlook platform is a set of viewing benches, stacked like bleacher seats at a football game. Audubon volunteers set up sighting scopes; visitors take turns looking at the birds.

What you see through the scopes depends on what month it is. By May, the egret eggs have usually hatched. Looking through the scopes you can see the baby egrets in their nests. Typically you'll see two or three baby birds per nest, all clamoring for food. If you show up in late March or April, you'll see the adult birds (both male and female) incubating the eggs. In late June or July, you may see young egrets learning to fly. In any month, the sighting scopes allow a beautiful magnified view of the adult egrets in their white, feathered finery. So large that they appear almost clumsy, the adult birds make the redwood branches sway and droop dramatically when they take off and land.

The egrets' delicate feathers are the reason for their near extinction. The birds were massively hunted in the early 1900s to provide plumage for ladies' hats. Efforts of the Audubon Society eventually resulted in legislation that protected the birds.

This wooded nesting site received a similar rescue from annihilation. In 1961, the redwood grove where the herons and egrets nest was scheduled to be logged. Adjacent Bolinas Lagoon was to be dredged and developed as a marina, and a four-lane freeway was to be built between the nesting site and lagoon feeding grounds. Fortunately, the president of the Marin Audubon Society negotiated a deal with the landowner to purchase the property and save it from development.

Lucky visitors will get to see great blue herons nesting, in addition to the great egrets. Typically there are less than a dozen pairs of herons in the preserve, compared to more than 100 egret pairs. The herons begin nesting a month earlier than the egrets.

After you've marveled at the birds, continue beyond the overlook on Griffin Loop Trail, which leads uphill through an oak and bay forest. The path heads straight up with no switchbacks for 0.5 mile. When you reach the marked intersection of Griffin Loop Trail and Zumie Loop Trail, go left and follow Zumie Loop Trail downhill into a fern-filled redwood forest along Garden Club Canyon's small stream. After 0.25 mile, you'll swing away from the creek and follow the ridge on a narrow path. Climbing ever so slightly, the trail tops out at a high, open bluff. Have a seat on the strategically placed wooden swing, which is wide enough for two or more, and enjoy the expansive view of Bolinas Lagoon. Sway back and forth to your heart's content as you review the day's wonders.

Finally, follow the trail downhill along the sloping hillside. The path curves gently all the way back to Audubon Ranch headquarters, providing sweeping coastal views all the way. Just before returning to the ranch you'll have the chance to stop at one more great birding observation point, the Clem Miller Lookout. From here you have a wide view across Bolinas Lagoon, where the usual cabal of shorebirds—from sandpipers to osprey to pelicans—go about their business.

© ANN MARIE BROWN

The great egret is a graceful flyer.

Options

Another recommended hike is to remain on Griffin Loop Trail beyond the Henderson Overlook and traverse a 2.7-mile loop around Picher Canyon. Similar to the loop already described, the Griffin Loop leads through a mix of dense forests and open ridge tops with views of Stinson Beach, Bolinas Lagoon, and the coast.

Directions

From San Francisco, cross the Golden Gate Bridge and drive north on U.S. 101 for four miles. Take the Mill Valley/Stinson Beach/Highway 1 exit and continue straight for one mile to a stoplight at Shoreline Highway (Highway 1). Turn left on Shoreline Highway and drive 12 miles to Stinson Beach, then continue north on Highway 1 for another 3.7 miles. Look for the entrance to Audubon Canyon Ranch on the right. (It's 0.5 mile beyond the entrance signed Volunteer Canyon.)

Information and Contact

Martin Griffin Preserve is open 10 A.M.–4 P.M. on weekends and holidays only, mid-March–mid-July. There is no fee, although a $15 donation is appreciated. Dogs and bikes are not allowed. A free trail map is available at the trailhead. A detailed map of the area is available from Tom Harrison Maps, 415/456-7940, www.tomharrisonmaps.com (ask for the *Pine Mountain* map). For more information, contact Audubon Canyon Ranch, 4900 Highway 1, Stinson Beach, CA 94970, 415/868-9244, www.egret.org.

17 CASCADE CANYON

BEST €

Marin County Open Space District

Level: Easy

Total Distance: 1.5 miles round-trip

Hiking Time: 1 hour

Elevation Change: 100 feet

Summary: A family-friendly hike to a scenic waterfall, with an option for a more strenuous walk to a second cataract and deep pools upstream.

Here's proof that the true measure of a waterfall is not how big it is or how much water flows over it, but the overall impression it creates. Little Cascade Falls in Fairfax is no Niagara, but it is perfectly situated in a rocky grotto nestled in a deep, forested canyon. Once you arrive, you may be so charmed that you never want to leave.

At its start, the path through Cascade Canyon doesn't seem like it could possibly lead to a waterfall. To reach the trailhead, you drive along a narrow road through a suburban neighborhood. Parking is limited and difficult; take care to obey all signs and don't block anyone's driveway. At the hike's start, you follow an often dry and dusty fire road (except, of course, in the peak of the rainy season). The water in this stretch of San Anselmo Creek is rarely more than a few inches deep. Things may not look promising.

But they get better. Keep San Anselmo Creek on your left as you hike, avoiding the wide fire road wherever possible and following the single-track hiking paths that roughly parallel it. Cross a wooden footbridge at 0.5 mile and veer right into an oak and bay forest, still walking alongside Cascade Creek. The stream has many quiet pools and charming rock cascades.

In 0.25 mile, you'll round a bend and hear the sound of falling water, then get your first glimpse of the waterfall. Cascade Falls tumbles 18 feet over a rough rock face into a small pool below. The pool is surrounded by many large and small mossy rocks, perfectly placed for waterfall-watching.

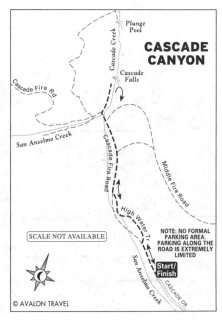

CASCADE CANYON

Plunge Pool

Cascade Creek

Cascade Falls

Cascade Fire Rd

San Anselmo Creek

Cascade Fire Road

Middle Fire Road

High Water Tr

San Anselmo Creek

SCALE NOT AVAILABLE

Start/ Finish

CASCADE DR

NOTE: NO FORMAL PARKING AREA. PARKING ALONG THE ROAD IS EXTREMELY LIMITED

© AVALON TRAVEL

Options

If you'd like to see more of Cascade Canyon, you could follow the informal trail up and over Cascade Falls. But the path quickly becomes rough, steep, and lined with poison oak. A better option is to backtrack 0.25 mile to the footbridge you crossed on the way in, then turn right (west) on Cascade Fire Road. In only 100 yards, you'll see a single-track trail on the right signed as No Bikes. (It's shortly beyond another single-track trail on the left). Built by local Fairfax trail rebels, this 1.7-mile trail was initially labeled illegal by Marin Municipal Water District officials and was scheduled for closure in early 1996. But public support for the trail was so strong that the Water District eventually decided to leave it alone, and now it's a favorite of local hikers, bikers, and dog walkers.

Follow this narrow path up a wooded ridge on a steady but moderate grade. The climb relents at spots where the trail opens out to grassy, open slopes with views of the opposing ridge. Finally the trail heads downhill to rejoin Cascade Creek. Where it forks, turn right and walk about 100 feet, then cross the creek. You'll come out at the brink of a beautiful two-tiered waterfall and swimming hole sometimes referred to as the Plunge, the Ink Well, or just plain Upper Falls. Your round-trip distance will be about five miles.

Directions

From San Francisco, cross the Golden Gate Bridge and drive north on U.S. 101 for 7.5 miles. Take the Sir Francis Drake Boulevard exit west toward San Anselmo,

A footbridge takes hikers right to the lip of Cascade Falls.

© ANN MARIE BROWN

then drive six miles to the town of Fairfax. Turn left by the Fairfax sign (on Pacheco Avenue), then turn right immediately on Broadway. In one block, turn left on Bolinas Road (on some signs it is labeled Bolinas-Fairfax Road). Follow Bolinas Road for 0.3 mile to a three-road intersection. Bear right on Cascade Drive (the middle road) and continue for 1.5 miles. The road becomes very narrow and ends at Elliott Nature Preserve. Parking is extremely limited. Park alongside the road (be careful to avoid blocking driveways and obey the No Parking signs in the last 100 feet before the trailhead). Begin hiking at the gate.

Information and Contact

There is no fee. Leashed dogs are allowed. Bikes are allowed only on fire roads. Detailed maps of the area are available for free by download at www.marinopen-space.org, or can be purchased from Tom Harrison Maps, 415/456-7940, www.tomharrisonmaps.com (ask for the *Pine Mountain* map). For more information, contact the Marin County Open Space District, 3501 Civic Center Drive, Room 415, San Rafael, CA 94903, 415/499-6387, www.marinopenspace.org.

18 BON TEMPE AND LAGUNITAS LAKE LOOP
Marin Municipal Water District

🦌 🛩 🌿 🐴 🚻

Level: Easy   **Total Distance:** 5.0 miles round-trip

Hiking Time: 2.5 hours   **Elevation Change:** 200 feet

Summary: A mellow walk around two of Marin County's loveliest lakes, with an option for a little shoreline fishing.

When most people think of public parkland around Mount Tamalpais, they think of the towering redwoods of Muir Woods National Monument, or the grasslands, forests, and stunning coastal views of Mount Tamalpais State Park. But fewer people know that five sparkling lakes are also part of the Mount Tam landscape. Located in the Mount Tamalpais watershed on the northwest side of the mountain, the five lakes are Alpine, Bon Tempe, Phoenix, Kent, and Lagunitas. Together they present five more reasons why the Mount Tamalpais area is so ideal for outdoor recreation.

The best lakes for a hiking excursion are Bon Tempe and Lagunitas. By linking together a couple of trails, you can walk all the way around both lakes' perimeters in a couple of hours. The best seasons are winter, spring, and early summer, when the reservoirs are filled to the brim (and sometimes overflowing down their spillways).

Start your trip by walking uphill to Bon Tempe Dam. From the top, you'll gain views of bright blue Bon Tempe Lake on your left and the marshes and lowlands of Alpine Lake on your right. The unmistakable profile of Mount Tamalpais looms to the southeast. The long, wide dam is a worthy bird-watching site. In addition to the more common cormorants, egrets, ducks, and coots, osprey are often spotted at Bon Tempe Lake. The large raptors are amazing fishers, with razor-sharp eyes that can spot a fish in the lake from high up in the air. They plunge feet first into the water for their prey. Black-tailed deer are also commonly seen around the lake's edges.

Bon Tempe Lake is stocked with trout by the Department of Fish and Game November–April. However, because the lake is a reservoir, no boating, swimming, or wading is allowed. Fishing is permitted from the shoreline only, and yes, plenty of trout are caught here. Although your dog is allowed to accompany you at the lake, he or she must be kept leashed and out of the water.

Walk across the dam, then pick up the single-track trail that leads left along the lakeshore. It climbs imperceptibly as it travels into a dense mixed forest of oaks, madrones, firs, and redwoods. This peaceful, shady stretch of trail is punctuated

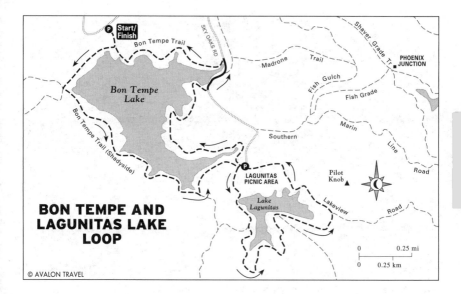

BON TEMPE AND LAGUNITAS LAKE LOOP

© AVALON TRAVEL

by the sound of water lapping against the shore. In about a mile, the trail leaves the forest and enters a grassy marsh area where you can look westward over the entire lake—all the way back to your starting point at the dam. This vista is particularly lovely if the sun is sinking low in the sky.

The trail heads back into the redwoods for a short distance, then emerges near the parking lot for neighboring Lake Lagunitas. Shortly before the pavement, turn right on a wide fire road. After 0.25 mile, the road climbs above Lake Lagunitas' earthen dam. Built in 1873, this dam makes Lagunitas the oldest of the Marin lakes. Follow the wide road as it circles the edge of the 22-acre lake; at all junctions, just follow the path that stays near the water. The shallower edges of the lake are crowded with reeds, tules, and cattails. Families of ducks are often seen paddling along the surface in spring.

Pass a couple of rangers' residences along the north edge of Lake Lagunitas, then take the fire road downhill past the picnic area to the parking lot. Here you must locate the final leg of the loop along Bon Tempe Lake; head west across the parking lot to access the trail. Where the fire road splits off with a single-track trail leading left along the lake, follow the single-track. (Once again, just ignore all trails that don't stay close to the water.) There's only one short section on Bon Tempe Lake's north side where a feeder stream and marsh force your path to move away from the water; you'll have to walk along the edge of paved Sky Oaks Road for 200 yards. Where you see a gravel pullout for cars on the right side of the road, look to your left to find the single-track trail again, which returns to the water's edge.

© ANN MARIE BROWN

Bon Tempe Lake is a tranquil place for hikers and anglers.

The final mile along the north shore of Bon Tempe Lake is the best stretch of the trip in springtime. The sunny, grassland slopes are covered with wildflowers, particularly patches of blue and white Douglas irises.

Options
When the lakes are full in winter and spring, a noteworthy option is to hike across Bon Tempe Dam and then turn right on the wide dirt road. Stay right on this road and it leads you to the edge of long and narrow Alpine Lake and the start of Kent Trail, which curves along the lake's shore. Two miles from the dam, turn left to stay on Kent Trail and hike steeply uphill for a mile. Turn left on Stocking Trail and follow it 0.6 mile to Rocky Ridge Fire Road, where you turn left and drop back down to Bon Tempe Dam. The total loop distance is 5.7 miles.

Directions
From San Francisco, cross the Golden Gate Bridge and drive north on U.S. 101 for 7.5 miles. Take the Sir Francis Drake Boulevard exit west toward San Anselmo, then drive six miles to the town of Fairfax. Turn left by the Fairfax sign (on Pacheco Avenue), then turn right immediately on Broadway. In one block, turn left on Bolinas Road (on some signs it is labeled Bolinas-Fairfax Road). Drive 1.5 miles on Bolinas Road to Sky Oaks Road, where you bear left. Drive straight for 0.4 mile to the ranger station and entrance kiosk, then continue 0.3 mile to a

fork in the road. Bear right on the gravel road. (The left fork takes you to Lake Lagunitas.) Drive 0.6 mile until you reach another fork, then bear left and park in the gravel parking area next to a gated fire road. Start hiking at the gate, heading uphill to Bon Tempe Dam.

Information and Contact

An $8 day-use fee is charged per vehicle. Leashed dogs are allowed. Bikes are allowed only on fire roads. Maps are available from Tom Harrison Maps, at 415/456-7940, www.tomharrisonmaps.com (ask for the *Pine Mountain* map). For more information, contact Sky Oaks Ranger Station at 415/945-1181 or Marin Municipal Water District, 220 Nellen Avenue, Corte Madera, CA 94925, 415/945-1438, www.marinwater.org.

19 CARSON FALLS   BEST ◖
Marin Municipal Water District

Level: Easy/Moderate   **Total Distance:** 3.4 miles round-trip

Hiking Time: 1.5 hours   **Elevation Change:** 800 feet

Summary: A four-tiered waterfall drops over greenstone basalt and provides habitat for the threatened foothill yellow-legged frog.

Quiz question: Name three waterfalls located on or nearby Mount Tamalpais, all within six miles of each other, that begin with the letter C.

Answer: Cascade Falls in the Marin County Open Space lands off Bolinas-Fairfax Road (see *Cascade Canyon* listing in this chapter), Cataract Falls near Laurel Dell, just over the border from Mount Tamalpais State Park (see *Cataract Trail to Cataract Falls* listing in this chapter), and Carson Falls in Marin Municipal Water District.

It's a good idea to learn them all and know which is which, because it saves a lot of confusion when you tell your coworkers at the water cooler about the great waterfall you hiked to over the weekend. Carson Falls? Isn't that the one with the trail that starts at Alpine Dam and climbs the whole way? No, that's Cataract. Cataract Falls? Isn't that the one that falls in a long, stair-stepped plunge through a steep, rocky canyon? Sorry, that's Carson. Cascade Falls? Isn't that the one that's just outside the Fairfax suburbs? Well, you got one right.

To set the record straight, Carson Falls is an unusual waterfall found in the middle of a dry grassland canyon in Marin Municipal Water District lands, high above Alpine and Kent Lakes on the northwest slope of Mount Tamalpais. It's a long chain of four pool-and-drop cataracts that pour into rock-lined pools. Located a few miles outside the town of Fairfax, it's just far enough off the beaten path that it gets somewhat less traffic than other waterfalls in Marin County. However, since brand-new trail signs and

Carson Falls cascades in several tiers over greenstone basalt.

© ANN MARIE BROWN

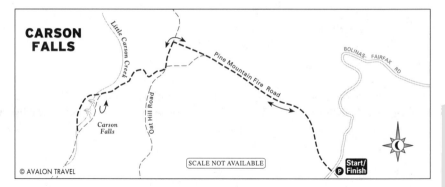

a reconstructed section of trail were put in to place in 2009, the waterfall is seeing a lot more visitors than it used to (and now it's easier to find, too).

The trailhead is located along the north side of Bolinas-Fairfax Road at 1,078 feet in elevation. From the gravel parking area, cross Bolinas-Fairfax Road and pick up Pine Mountain Fire Road at the large Marin Municipal Water District signboard. Climb uphill for one mile, gaining slightly more than 300 feet in elevation. Be sure to pause and look over your right shoulder as you ascend to take in the sweeping view of Mount Diablo, San Pablo Bay, Marin County, the East Bay, and even the Richmond Bridge. The climb will get your heart pumping, but the views are more than fair compensation for your efforts.

Keep your eyes and ears attuned for mountain bicyclists on this fire road. They sometimes come flying downhill at breakneck speed, most often after experiencing the agony and ecstasy of climbing nearby Pine Mountain.

After a mile of climbing, you reach a high point on the ridge and a junction. Look due north for a surprising view of Mount St. Helena in Napa, 45 miles distant, then turn left on Oat Hill Road, also a fire road. In only 0.25 mile, you'll see a sign for the Carson Falls turnoff on your right. Here you'll leave the fire roads behind and walk on the gorgeous new stretch of single-track that was built in 2007 and 2008, replacing the badly eroded path that once existed. The trail switchbacks gently downhill into the Carson Creek watershed through a forest of oaks and madrones. A bevy of sword ferns grace the understory.

This pleasant, shady stretch deposits you on a narrow, artfully constructed footbridge above Carson Falls. Don't expect that usual thunderous moment of "Wow! A waterfall!" Carson Falls is more subtle and mysterious than that—especially since you arrive at its crest, not at its base. This waterfall reveals its pleasures slowly, one pool at a time. To see it in its entirety, cross the footbridge, then follow the rocky path downhill, dropping in elevation along with the stream. Use caution heading down the steep footpath, especially when the rocks are wet in the rainy season. Carson Falls' green-grey rock looks like serpentine, but it's actually a type of greenstone basalt.

The pools of Carson Falls are home to threatened amphibians, including the foothill yellow-legged frog, which has been listed as a federal and state species of special concern. The frogs have disappeared from nearly 50 percent of their historic range in California and Oregon. Here in the Mount Tam watershed, only two populations exist, including this one at Carson Falls. To help protect these creatures, keep yourself and any canine companions out of the water, especially March–June when the frog eggs and tadpoles are most vulnerable.

Instead, pick any rock near one of the waterfall pools, have a seat, and listen to the water music for a while. Even in summer, when Carson Falls is reduced to a mere trickle, a visit here feels restorative, like resting in a Zen garden with the sound of the wind and the tinkling of water as your only companions.

Options

Another unusual sight in the region of Carson Falls is a stand of dwarf Sargent cypress trees off San Geronimo Ridge Road. The Sargent cypress is a rare evergreen that grows in scattered groves around Mount Tamalpais. It is usually stunted in size when rooted in serpentine soil, which is the case here. Cypress trees that are more than 100 years old may be only a few feet tall. To see them, continue straight on Pine Mountain Road at its junction with Oat Hill Road (the route is mostly level from here). In just under 0.5 mile, you'll come to a junction of roads; the 1,762-foot summit of Pine Mountain is off to the left. Go straight on San Geronimo Ridge Road and reach the miniature Sargent cypress forest in 0.6 mile.

Directions

From San Francisco, cross the Golden Gate Bridge and drive north on U.S. 101 for 7.5 miles. Take the Sir Francis Drake Boulevard exit west toward San Anselmo, then drive six miles to the town of Fairfax. Turn left by the Fairfax sign (on Pacheco Avenue), then turn right immediately on Broadway. In one block, turn left on Bolinas Road (on some signs it is labeled Bolinas-Fairfax Road). Drive 3.8 miles on Bolinas Road, past the golf course, to the trailhead parking on the left side of the road. Park and walk across the road to the trailhead.

Information and Contact

There is no fee. Leashed dogs are allowed. Bikes are allowed only on fire roads. Maps are available from Tom Harrison Maps at 415/456-7940, www.tomharrisonmaps.com (ask for the *Pine Mountain* map). For more information, contact Sky Oaks Ranger Station at 415/945-1181 or Marin Municipal Water District, 220 Nellen Avenue, Corte Madera, CA 94925, 415/945-1438, www.marinwater.org.

20 CATARACT TRAIL TO CATARACT FALLS

Marin Municipal Water District   **BEST**

Level: Easy/Moderate   **Total Distance:** 3.2 miles round-trip

Hiking Time: 1.5 hours   **Elevation Change:** 800 feet

Summary: A series of magical waterfalls, cascades, and pools are revealed on this ever-popular trail on the "back side" of Mount Tamalpais.

From the first rains in November until the final runoff in April or May, the multiple cascades of Cataract Falls plunge down the fern-covered hillsides of western Mount Tamalpais. Cataract Trail, which traces a path alongside Cataract Creek, offers hikers easy access to the handsome series of falls.

Reaching the trailhead at Alpine Lake requires a long and winding drive on narrow Bolinas-Fairfax Road, but it's a scenic cruise through the countryside. You're more likely to stop for deer crossing the road than traffic. After parking at the hairpin turn just beyond Alpine Dam, begin hiking at the sign for Cataract Trail. You're treated to lake views for the first 0.25 mile before the trail enters a dense forest of redwoods, ferns, maples, and tanoaks. Soon the path heads steeply uphill through the woodland, at times ascending on rock stairsteps.

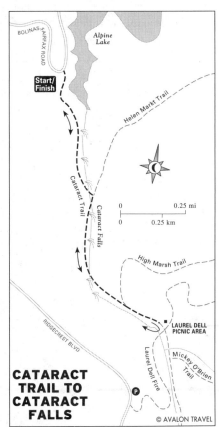

Cataract Falls is not one waterfall, but several. The series of cascades is spread out over 1.6 miles of Cataract Trail, so hike as much of it as you like. Soon after the trail leaves the lake and begins to climb, you will start seeing waterfalls. Half a dozen cascades are found in the first 0.75 mile between the lake's edge and a narrow footbridge crossing Cataract Creek. After a good rain, the canyon comes to life with the continual sound and sight of waterfalls.

Every curve and turn of the trail presents a new watery surprise. The unveiling of each cascade is so exciting that it's easy to ignore the steepness of the climb.

Most of the cascades are only 20–30 feet high, but each is completely different in shape and appearance. Their common denominator, besides the life-giving flow of Cataract Creek, is that each one is completely surrounded by ferns. The last waterfall appears just before a junction with High Marsh Trail; this is the most impressive of the group and the one most people consider to be the "true" Cataract Falls. Here, Cataract Creek makes a dramatic tumble over car-sized boulders as it rushes downhill. From the big fall, it's less than 0.25 mile uphill on Cataract Trail to Laurel Dell, a picnic area near a large, grassy clearing. Have lunch or a snack at Laurel Dell, then turn around and hike back down Cataract Trail, witnessing the waterfall show all over again.

During the rainy season, the multiple cascades of Cataract Falls are a sight to behold.

Options

You can extend this hike into a 7.5-mile loop by continuing on Cataract Trail to High Marsh Trail. Follow High Marsh Trail gently uphill for 2.2 miles, gaining surprising views of San Pablo Bay. At a confusing series of trail junctions near High Marsh and Willow Meadow, turn left (north) on Kent Trail and head downhill for 1.4 miles, nearly to the edge of Alpine Lake. Turn left on Helen Markt Trail and hike two miles through redwoods to the lower stretch of Cataract Trail. Turn right and walk 0.5 mile back to your car. If you choose to make this loop, be sure to bring a good map with you. Numerous unsigned junctions along the route can lead you off in the wrong direction.

Directions

From San Francisco, cross the Golden Gate Bridge and drive north on U.S. 101 for 7.5 miles. Take the Sir Francis Drake Boulevard exit west toward San Anselmo, then drive six miles to the town of Fairfax. Turn left by the Fairfax sign (on

Pacheco Avenue), then turn right immediately on Broadway. Drive one block and turn left on Bolinas Road (on some signs it is labeled Bolinas-Fairfax Road). Drive 7.8 miles on Bolinas Road to the dam at Alpine Lake. Cross the dam and continue 0.1 mile farther to the hairpin turn in the road. Park in the pullouts along the turn; the trailhead is on the left.

Information and Contact

There is no fee. Leashed dogs are allowed. Bikes are not allowed. Maps are available from Tom Harrison Maps at 415/456-7940, www.tomharrisonmaps.com (ask for the *Pine Mountain* map). For more information, contact Sky Oaks Ranger Station at 415/945-1181 or Marin Municipal Water District, 220 Nellen Avenue, Corte Madera, CA 94925, 415/945-1438, www.marinwater.org.

21 SHORELINE TRAIL
China Camp State Park

🛫 🚣 ⊛

Level: Easy/Moderate

Total Distance: 7.0 miles round-trip

Hiking Time: 3 hours

Elevation Change: 100 feet

Summary: This nearly level trail along the edge of San Pablo Bay is the perfect outing for birders, bay-watchers, and history enthusiasts.

Most people know China Camp State Park as a historic park that showcases the remains of a Chinese shrimp fishing village from the 19th century—a place that's popular for school field trips. But China Camp also boasts a scenic location on San Pablo Bay, which allows blue-water vistas at every turn of the park's Shoreline Trail. With more than 1,500 shoreline acres, plus a dense forest of oaks, bays, and madrones, the park is an island of natural beauty just outside the busy city of San Rafael.

China Camp is also a rare animal in the California State Park system. It's one of the few state parks that allows mountain bike riders on its single-track trails. Most bikers and hikers mind their manners and get along fine, but be forewarned that if you don't like sharing the trail with bikes, avoid visiting on weekends when the park sees its heaviest use.

An out-and-back trip on the park's Shoreline Trail entails walking seven scenic and nearly level miles. Bird-watchers won't want to be caught without binoculars; the variety of species you'll see is impressive.

Begin on Shoreline Trail from the Back Ranch Meadows Campground parking lot. You'll walk past a cattail-filled marsh and have immediate views of the tranquil blue waters of San Pablo Bay. Wide-open grasslands are punctuated by a few spreading valley oaks.

In only 0.25 mile, cross San Pedro Road and take Turtle Back Nature Trail. When bay waters were higher, Turtle Back was an island, but now it's a shoreline hill surrounded by saltwater marsh. In late autumn, the marsh's pickleweed turns a brilliant red color, highlighting wide views of San Pablo Bay. Ancient duck blinds dot the water's edge. From Turtle Back, you can see Jake's Island to the north, another shoreline hill that was once an island. Two other such hills exist to the east, Bullet Hill and Chicken Coop Hill.

Return to the main Shoreline Trail and continue hiking east. You'll parallel North San Pedro Road until the path heads inland, then curve around to an open meadow and the park's group picnic area, Miwok Meadows. Follow its wide dirt road back toward the bay. Pick up single-track Shoreline Trail again, continuing eastward. More open bay views are followed by a stint in a leafy oak and bay forest. North San Pedro Road drops out of sight and earshot as the trail leads through the woodland canopy.

Three miles out, you'll switchback downhill to China Camp State Park's ranger station (a mobile home), then cross the service road to pick up the trail on the opposite side. In slightly more than 0.5 mile, cross North San Pedro Road carefully, then head down to China Camp Historic Area, the site of a 19th-century Chinese fishing village. China Camp was one of more than 30 such villages that sprung up on the shores of San Francisco and San Pablo Bays in the 1870s. The Chinese villagers fished for plentiful grass shrimp in spring, summer, and fall. In winter, they mended their nets and worked on their boats. Some of the shrimp were sold at local markets, but most were exported to China. Eventually laws were passed that forbid the Chinese method of shrimp fishing with bag nets. In 1905, the export of dried shrimp was also banned, and this village, along with others like it, was soon abandoned.

A pier and four buildings, filled with furniture and tools from the day-to-day life of the shrimp camp, are all that remains of the village. They are fascinating to explore. A sandy beach to the west of China Camp is a first-rate bird-watching

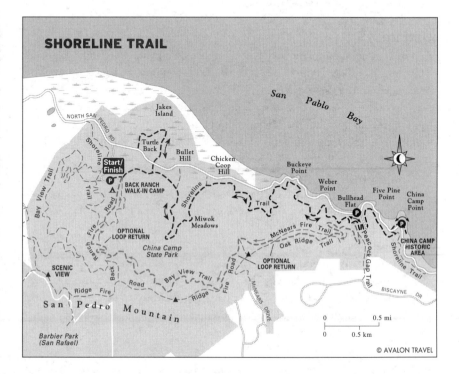

© ANN MARIE BROWN

Rat Rock stands guard along the shoreline of China Camp.

spot. Great egrets and snowy egrets fish in the marsh areas and offshore of Rat Rock Island. The beach is also popular with waders and swimmers in summer; the bay water is calm and relatively warm.

Options

A more strenuous tour of the park is an 11-mile loop on Shoreline Trail, Oak Ridge Trail, and Bay View Trail. This longer hike leads you into the backcountry of the park, far from the cars traveling North San Pedro Road. Follow the first half of the trip outlined earlier to China Camp Historic Area. Then retrace your steps to the junction uphill of the ranger station and bear left on Peacock Gap Trail. Climb uphill, then turn right on Oak Ridge Trail. Connect to Ridge Fire Trail, then Bay View Trail. From these trails' higher elevations, your bay views are far more expansive. Deciduous oaks and even some redwoods offer shade at points along the route. A right turn on Back Ranch Fire Road and a steep descent will return you to within a few yards of your car.

Directions

From San Francisco, cross the Golden Gate Bridge and drive north on U.S. 101 for 11 miles to San Rafael. Take the North San Pedro Road exit and drive east for 3.5 miles. Turn right at the sign for Back Ranch Meadows Campground and park in the campground parking lot. Shoreline Trail is located on the bay side of the lot, signed as No Dogs.

Information and Contact

A $5 day-use fee is charged per vehicle. Dogs are not allowed. Bikes are allowed. A trail map is available for $1 at the ranger station, or free by download at www. parks.ca.gov. A detailed map of the area is also available from Pease Press at 415/387-1437, www.peasepress.com (ask for the *Trails of Northeast Marin County* map). For more information, contact China Camp State Park, 101 Peacock Gap Trail, San Rafael, CA 94901, 415/456-0766, www.parks.ca.gov.

22 VERNA DUNSHEE TRAIL AND GARDNER LOOKOUT

Mount Tamalpais State Park

BEST ◖

Level: Easy

Total Distance: 1.4 miles round-trip

Hiking Time: 1 hour

Elevation Change: 170 feet

Summary: One of the Bay Area's most famous peaks is circled by an easy loop trail that offers 360-degree views.

If it's a clear day and you're in the mood to feel on top of the world, head for the summit of Mount Tamalpais and the Verna Dunshee Trail. The trail is short, accessible to wheelchairs and strollers, and features absolutely top-notch views of Marin County, San Francisco, and points far beyond as it loops around the mountain's summit. To add a little challenge to the trip, you can also hike the short but steep path to the tip-top of Mount Tamalpais East Peak, where a closed fire lookout tower allows for an all-in-one-glance panoramic view.

The drive up Mount Tamalpais is part of the adventure. From Pantoll Road upward, the mountainside views are compelling enough that you have to remind yourself to keep your eyes on the pavement. Close attention is essential, because the summit road is narrow, winding, and leaves little room for error.

When at last you reach Mount Tamalpais' high ridgeline, you pass the mountain's West Peak first. That's the one with the "huge white golf balls," or radar dishes, at 2,560 feet in elevation. Next you pass the lower Middle Peak, and finally you wind up at the road's end at the parking lot for Mount Tam's East Peak. The East Peak is the highest summit of the three at an elevation of 2,571 feet. (This

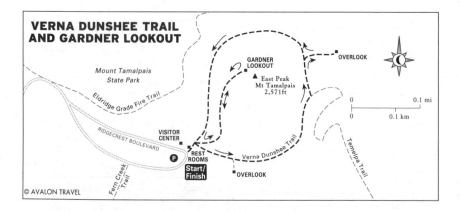

may not sound especially high, but when you consider that the peak is surrounded primarily by ocean, bay, and sea-level land, it's a considerable vertical rise.)

Leave your car and walk past the visitors center. If you show up on a weekend day, the center will be open and you can obtain an interpretive brochure keyed to numbers painted on the asphalt on the Verna Dunshee Trail. Locate the trail just to the right of the restrooms; you'll walk counterclockwise on the paved loop.

In the first few yards of trail, the manzanita grows so high and dense that the views are obscured. But not for long. Soon you emerge from the chaparral and your views extend all the way south to San Francisco and southwest to the Pacific Ocean. On the best days, the Farallon Islands are visible some 25 miles out to sea.

As you head eastward, views of southern Marin County expand to include Richardson Bay, Angel Island, and Tiburon. Before you know it, you're looking at the San Rafael-Richmond Bridge and across to the East Bay. Mount Diablo looms in the background. Far beyond it and rarely seen is the snowy Sierra crest.

About halfway through the loop, Temelpa Trail cuts off to the right; stay on the paved path and in a few more yards take the unsigned dirt path that leads along a northeast ridge of the summit. This puts you on a promontory directly overlooking southern and eastern Marin County. The tall buildings of downtown San Francisco glitter in the distance like the Emerald City.

Back on the main trail, you begin to circle around to the north, now looking toward San Rafael, Sonoma, and Napa. Yes, that's Mount St. Helena near Calistoga far to the northwest. The lake shimmering in the foreground is Bon Tempe Lake near Fairfax. Mount Tam's West Peak obscures the western view, so finish out your loop by heading south to the visitors center, then make a sharp left turn on the Gardner Lookout Trail.

The first leg of Gardner Lookout's ascending path is lined with old railroad ties. These serve as reminders of the days when the "Crookedest Railroad in the World" operated on Mount Tamalpais. In the early 1900s, no visit to San Francisco was complete without a ride on this train, which traveled up the mountain through a thrilling 281 curves. Alas, the railroad's reign sadly ended with the advent of the automobile and the first road built to the mountain's summit.

The Gardner Lookout Trail makes a few steep switchbacks up to East Peak's summit and its closed fire lookout tower, which was built in 1937. Although you can't walk up to the tower's deck (it's lined with barbed wire), the view from its base is superb. Wander around on the East Peak's summit boulders until you find the best spot to soak in the scenery. Be sure to bring a jacket with you; the wind often blows up here on even the balmiest days of summer. And you might want to time your trip for late in the day: The East Peak of Mount Tamalpais is one of the finest places in the Bay Area to watch the sun set.

Options

If the short Verna Dunshee Trail is too tame for your hiking sensibilities, you can turn it into a longer and much more strenuous loop. Follow Verna Dunshee Trail as detailed, but turn off after 0.25 mile at the signpost for Temelpa Trail. Hope you brought your hiking poles; this recklessly steep descent drops 700 feet in just under a mile. When you meet up with Vic Haun Trail (also called Old Plane Trail), turn right and hike downhill for another 0.5 mile to a junction with Hoo-Koo-E-Koo Fire Road. Turn westward (right), climb gently, and in 0.7 mile bear right to follow a stretch of Old Railroad Grade. Watch for the Fern Creek Trail turnoff 0.3 mile farther, then turn right and head back uphill, gaining another 700 feet over 0.7 mile on the way back to the East Peak

Gardner Lookout on Mount Tam's East Peak

© ANN MARIE BROWN

parking area. If this grade is too steep for you, join the club. You can always exit Fern Creek Trail 0.3 mile uphill, turn left on Tavern Pump Trail for 0.3 mile, then turn right on Old Railroad Grade for the last 0.5 mile to the parking lot. This will add 0.5 mile to your trip but smooth out the grade to a somewhat more manageable level. The Temelpa–Fern Creek loop is 3.4 miles or 3.9 miles, depending on how you do it.

Directions

From San Francisco, cross the Golden Gate Bridge and drive north on U.S. 101 for four miles. Take the Mill Valley/Stinson Beach/Highway 1 exit and continue straight for one mile to a stoplight at Shoreline Highway (Highway 1). Turn left on Shoreline Highway and drive 2.5 miles, then turn right on Panoramic Highway. Drive 0.9 mile to a four-way intersection. Take the middle road (straight), continuing on Panoramic Highway for 4.3 more miles to Pantoll Road. Turn right on Pantoll Road and drive 1.4 miles to its intersection with Ridgecrest Boulevard. Turn right on Ridgecrest Boulevard and drive 2.9 miles to the East Peak parking area.

Information and Contact

An $8 day-use fee is charged per vehicle. Dogs and bikes are not allowed. A trail map is available at the summit visitors center or Pantoll Ranger Station for $1, or free by download at www.parks.ca.gov. Maps of the area are also available from Tom Harrison Maps, 415/456-7940, www.tomharrisonmaps.com (ask for the *Mount Tam* map). For more information, contact Mount Tamalpais State Park, 801 Panoramic Highway, Mill Valley, CA 94941, 415/388-2070, www.mttam.net.

23 MATT DAVIS AND STEEP RAVINE LOOP

Mount Tamalpais State Park   **BEST** [

🏕️ 🌸 ⛵ 🚌

Level: Moderate   **Total Distance:** 7.8 miles round-trip

Hiking Time: 4 hours   **Elevation Change:** 1,500 feet

Summary: This moderate loop delivers the best of Mount Tamalpais' world-famous scenery, with flower-covered grasslands, coastal views, a dense redwood forest, and a cascading stream.

Matt Davis Trail curves a long, graceful arc from Mount Tam's Pantoll Ranger Station to the sea at Stinson Beach. Steep Ravine Trail makes a dramatic ascent alongside a boisterous stream in a steep-sided redwood canyon. Combine these two trails with a brief stretch on the Dipsea Trail and you have one of the best loop hikes in the San Francisco Bay Area.

It's a classic Mount Tamalpais day hike, showing off the best of the state park's attributes. On weekends, the route can be quite busy, particularly the scenic but narrow stretch of Steep Ravine Trail. (Many visitors hike this trail out-and-back, especially in the rainy season when Webb Creek is running hard.) On weekdays, you're likely to have much less company, except for a few Marin locals who walk or run the loop on a regular basis. Here's one of their secrets: If you start your hike around 10 A.M., you can reach the bottom of Matt Davis Trail at Stinson Beach right around noon. Don't bother packing a picnic lunch, because you can buy a hamburger (or most anything else) at Stinson and have a leisurely lunch on the beach. After refueling, you spend the afternoon hiking back uphill on Dipsea and Steep Ravine Trails. Now how's that for a fine day?

The loop begins near Pantoll Ranger Station on Mount Tamalpais. Exit the Pantoll parking lot, cross Panoramic Highway to the start of Pantoll Road, and pick up Matt Davis Trail on the southwest side of Pantoll Road. A bench in the first 50 feet of trail invites you to sit and enjoy a partial view of the coast. This is the last open viewing spot you'll have for a while; the trail quickly leads into the trees.

Matt Davis Trail laterals along the slope of Mount Tamalpais some 1,500 feet above the ocean, maintaining an even, easy grade. After a long stretch in a mossy oak and bay woodland, the trail breaks out into grasslands, introducing panoramic views of San Francisco to the south and Point Reyes to the north. In some areas it's hard to move onward; it's tempting to stay put and relish the vistas. At 1.6 miles, the trail splits: Coastal Trail to the right and Matt Davis Trail to the left. Head left and begin your descent to Stinson Beach.

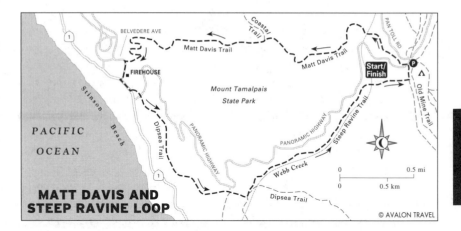

Hike downhill 0.7 mile through an enchanting forest of Douglas firs, oaks, and the graceful branches of bay laurel. Look for tall stalks of colorful red and yellow columbine along this shaded stretch in spring. At a signed turnoff for Table Rock, follow a spur trail a few feet to a large, flat boulder that overlooks the town of Stinson Beach and its long strip of sand and surf. Listen to the sound of the waves and enjoy a snack or stretching break before the final mile downhill to Stinson.

Back on the main trail, begin a series of short switchbacks accented with wooden stairs to soften the steep drop. Redwood railings edge the trail. Just below Table Rock, hike down Bischopf's Steps (named for the trail builder who carefully constructed this stretch) and pass a delightful small cataract along Table Rock Creek. The cascading stream serenades you as you descend; you'll cross it repeatedly on wooden footbridges. Its noise competes with the roar of nearby ocean breakers.

A sign states "Caution: Rattlesnake Area" just before the trail reaches the park boundary. Turn left at the signed boundary and junction, cross a footbridge, and reach an unsigned fork in 100 yards. Bear right and walk down to Belvedere Avenue in Stinson Beach, now four miles from your start at Pantoll. It's decision time: Do you want to forge ahead on the loop or make a stop at Stinson Beach for a hamburger and a suntan?

For the latter, follow Belvedere Avenue downhill about 200 feet, past the community center and firehouse, to Highway 1. Turn right and head for the shops, restaurants, and beach access in Stinson. To continue on the loop, turn left on Highway 1 instead. Walk 200 feet along the left side of the highway to an obvious trail that begins with a set of wooden stairs. Follow this path, which crosses Panoramic Highway as it stretches downhill from Mount Tamalpais, and you are now on the Dipsea Trail for the return leg of your loop.

In contrast to the Matt Davis Trail's steep forested canyon, Dipsea Trail traverses sunny, exposed slopes. The trail makes a gradual climb through coastal scrub and grasslands, affording nonstop ocean views over your right shoulder, then heads into a dense bay laurel forest. In 1.3 miles, Dipsea Trail joins with Steep Ravine Trail. Turn left on Steep Ravine and begin a more serious climb along Webb Creek, rising 1,000 feet in two miles. Redwoods and Douglas firs tower over the cascading stream. In spring, colorful Chinese houses, calypso orchids, and trillium bloom in the shady understory. Wooden footbridges cross the creek a half-dozen times. You'll need to duck and scramble under fallen redwood trunks, then climb a 10-foot ladder over a tricky trail stretch where Webb Creek is constricted by large boulders. All the while, you'll pause repeatedly to admire the myriad crystal pools and small waterfalls on Webb Creek and the multitude of ferns at streamside. Look for sword ferns, huge woodwardia ferns, and delicate five-finger ferns.

Too soon, the trail ends at the parking lot at Pantoll Ranger Station. But the entire loop is so good, you may be tempted to turn around and hike it all over again.

Options

An unusual feature of this loop is that it works well heading in either direction, and starting at either end. If you prefer your uphill at the start, not the finish,

begin this loop in Stinson Beach (leave your car at the Stinson Beach parking lot, or in a legal space downtown). You can refill your water bottles at Pantoll Ranger Station, almost halfway through the loop. Make your lunch stop at one of the coastal viewpoints just off the Matt Davis Trail. The grade on Matt Davis Trail is somewhat easier than on Steep Ravine, so for the easiest loop, head uphill on Matt Davis and return downhill on Steep Ravine.

Directions

From San Francisco, cross the Golden Gate Bridge and drive north on U.S. 101 for four miles. Take the Mill Valley/Stinson Beach/Highway 1 exit and continue straight for one mile to a stoplight at Shoreline Highway (Highway 1).

© ANN MARIE BROWN

Steep Ravine's lush canyon

Turn left on Shoreline Highway and drive 2.5 miles, then turn right on Panoramic Highway. Drive 0.9 mile to a four-way intersection. Take the middle road (straight), continuing on Panoramic Highway for 4.3 more miles to the Pantoll Ranger Station and parking lot. Turn left to park in the lot, then take the steps on the northwest side of the lot, cross Panoramic Highway, and access Matt Davis/Coastal Trail near the start of Pantoll Road, on its southwest side. Limited parking is also available in the small dirt parking lot at the start of Pantoll Road. The trail begins across the road from this parking lot.

Public transportation: The West Marin Stage Bus #61 stops at Pantoll Ranger Station at Mount Tamalpais State Park. For West Marin Stage information, phone 415/226-0855 or visit www.marintransit.org.

Information and Contact

An $8 day-use fee is charged per vehicle if you park at the paved parking lot at Pantoll Ranger Station. If you park legally in any pullout along the road, there is no fee. Dogs and bikes are not allowed. A trail map is available at Pantoll Ranger Station for $1, or free by download at www.parks.ca.gov. Maps of the area are also available from Tom Harrison Maps, 415/456-7940, www.tomharrisonmaps. com (ask for the *Mount Tam* map). For more information, contact Mount Tamalpais State Park, 801 Panoramic Highway, Mill Valley, CA 94941, 415/388-2070, www.mttam.net.

24 MOUNTAIN THEATER AND WEST POINT INN LOOP

Mount Tamalpais State Park and Marin Municipal Water District

🏞 🌐 🚌

Level: Easy/Moderate | **Total Distance:** 5.0 miles round-trip

Hiking Time: 2.5 hours | **Elevation Change:** 500 feet or 1,300 feet

Summary: Travel back in time and explore some of Mount Tam's history on this gentle loop hike.

This Mount Tamalpais trail is for history lovers. Marin's beloved mountain was once the home of the "Crookedest Railroad in the World," which weaved its way from Mill Valley to Mount Tam's summit through eight miles and 281 curves. The gravity car railroad, a popular tourist attraction, put Mount Tamalpais on the map in the late 1800s. This five-mile loop hike visits historic mountain sites and supplies first-rate views and scenery along the way.

Start your trip at Pantoll Ranger Station. Cross Panoramic Highway and pick up paved Old Stage Road to the right of Pantoll Road. A 0.25-mile walk brings you to a series of junctions; take the path signed as Easy Grade Trail to Mountain Theater. You'll climb steadily for 0.8 mile, soon losing the noise of the nearby road as you head deeper into oak woodland. A surprise awaits when you come out of the trees and onto the stage of Mountain Theater—you'll find yourself staring up at rows of stone bench seats in a tree-shaded amphitheater.

Formally named the Sidney Cushing Memorial Theater after the builder of the Mount Tamalpais Scenic Railway, Mountain Theater is an open-air, natural stone amphitheater that seats up to 3,500 people. Reconstructed in the 1930s by the Civilian Conservation Corps, the theater has hosted the annual *Mountain Play* every summer since 1913. A Marin County tradition, the *Mountain Play* brings playgoers up the slopes of Mount Tam carrying blankets and picnic baskets for an afternoon of theater.

Walk to the far side of the stage, then up along the right (east) side of the rock bench seats. Near the top of the theater, on your right, is Rock Spring Trail. Follow it and enjoy a level stroll with frequent views toward the coast and San Francisco. In 1.5 miles, the trail makes an easy descent to West Point Inn. The inn was built by the railroad in 1914 as a restaurant and stopover for passengers who were getting off the train and picking up the stagecoach to ride down to Stinson Beach or Bolinas.

After the rail days ended, the building came under the jurisdiction of the Marin Water District, and it is now operated by a nonprofit group. You can purchase drinks and snacks at West Point Inn (415/388-9955, www.westpointinn.com, 11 A.M.–6 P.M. Tues.–Sun. in summer; until 5 P.M. in winter). Restrooms and picnic areas are available all the time. The inn holds Sunday pancake breakfasts once a month from April to October (check the website for a schedule) and has five cabins and seven rooms for rent. Although there is no electricity, propane is used for light, heat, and refrigeration. A small sign on West Point Inn's front door conveys its simple philosophy: "You may use the parlor if you keep it tidy."

The inn's real draw is not the parlor but the view from its deck, which takes in a wide expanse of San Francisco Bay, the Bay Bridge and Richmond Bridge, Larkspur Landing, and San Francisco. On a clear day, the view is hard to forget.

To complete a five-mile loop, you have two options: You can follow Nora Trail from the front of the inn steeply downhill for 0.5 mile to Matt Davis Trail. Turn right on Matt Davis and hike back to the base of Old Stage Road near Pantoll Ranger Station. Although this is a scenic trail with coastal views and a nice stand of redwoods, it suffers from too much road noise from Panoramic Highway, especially on weekend afternoons. A quieter alternative that affords equally fine

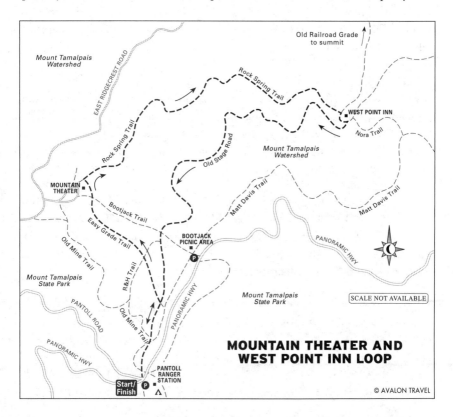

MOUNTAIN THEATER AND WEST POINT INN LOOP

© AVALON TRAVEL

Hikers, bikers, and history lovers will enjoy a stop at West Point Inn.

views is to follow Old Stage Road downhill from the inn for two miles back to Pantoll. This trail is not for hikers only, however; you'll share it with mountain bikers, so be on alert.

Options

If you seek a more strenuous hike, you can add on a trek to the summit of Mount Tamalpais for an 8.5-mile semi-loop trip. At West Point Inn, continue uphill on Old Railroad Grade for 1.5 steep, rocky miles to the East Peak parking lot. The wide trail is exposed and brushy, with occasional Douglas firs and Bishop pines mixed in with the chaparral. Views of the summit above and the forested slopes below provide continual inspiration.

Once at the 2,571-foot summit, you can hike the short, view-filled Verna Dunshee Trail or walk up to the closed Gardner Fire Lookout (see *Verna Dunshee Trail and Gardner Lookout* listing in this chapter). Both paths will reward you with some of the Bay Area's best views. Then retrace your steps to West Point Inn, and finish out the trip as described earlier.

Directions

From San Francisco, cross the Golden Gate Bridge and drive north on U.S. 101 for four miles. Take the Mill Valley/Stinson Beach/Highway 1 exit and continue straight for one mile to a stoplight at Shoreline Highway (Highway 1). Turn left on Shoreline Highway and drive 2.5 miles, then turn right on Panoramic Highway. Drive 0.9 mile to a four-way intersection. Take the middle road (straight), continuing on Panoramic Highway for 4.3 more miles to the Pantoll Ranger Station and parking lot. Turn left to park in the lot, then walk across Panoramic Highway to the start of Pantoll Road. Take the paved road on the right, signed Authorized Vehicles Only; this is the start of Old Stage Road.

Public transportation: The West Marin Stage Bus #61 stops at Pantoll Ranger Station at Mount Tamalpais State Park. For West Marin Stage information, phone 415/226-0855 or visit www.marintransit.org.

Information and Contact

A $8 day-use fee is charged per vehicle if you park at the paved parking lot at Pantoll Ranger Station. If you park legally in any pullout along the road, there is no fee. Leashed dogs are allowed on parts of the loop that are located in Marin Water District lands, but in Mount Tamalpais State Park they are permitted only on Old Stage Road. Bikes are allowed only on Old Stage Road and Old Railroad Grade. A trail map is available at Pantoll Ranger Station for $1, or free by download at www.parks.ca.gov. Maps of the area are also available from Tom Harrison Maps at 415/456-7940, www.tomharrisonmaps.com (ask for the *Mount Tam* map). For more information, contact Mount Tamalpais State Park, 801 Panoramic Highway, Mill Valley, CA 94941, 415/388-2070, www.mttam.net.

25 COASTAL, CATARACT, AND OLD MINE LOOP

Mount Tamalpais State Park

BEST [

Level: Moderate

Total Distance: 6.8 miles round-trip

Hiking Time: 3 hours

Elevation Change: 700 feet

Summary: It's all about the vistas and the wildflowers on this guaranteed-to-please day hike on Mount Tamalpais.

Is it a clear day in the San Francisco Bay Area? If so, then your mission is obvious: Lace up your hiking boots and head for this loop trail in Mount Tamalpais State Park. The Coastal, Cataract, and Old Mine Loop offers the best of all worlds—secluded forest groves laced with small, coursing streams, wide grasslands covered with lupine and poppies in the spring, and grand vistas of city and sea. And don't forget to pack your lunch. Tempting picnic spots are as abundant as black-tailed deer on Mount Tamalpais.

© ANN MARIE BROWN

Coastal Trail crosses the rolling slopes of Mount Tamalpais, which are carpeted with wildflowers in spring.

Start your trip on the Matt Davis/Coastal Trail near Pantoll Ranger Station. After an initial glimpse at the ocean near the trail's start, you'll head into a dense mixed hardwood forest and remain there for just shy of a mile. The beauty is close at hand—thick moss growing like fur on the bay laurel trees, dense ferns clustered on the banks of seasonal streams, and dappled sunlight filtering through the canopy of leaves.

Just as your eyes grow accustomed to the low light of the forest, the trail suddenly opens out to wide, sloping grasslands and bright sunshine. In spring, the mountain's wildflowers burst into colorful display, spurred on by cooling fog and plentiful sunlight. The blue and gold of poppies and lupine will make you feel a rush of patriotism for California's state colors. Because you can see so far and wide down the grassy slopes of Mount Tamalpais, views are extraordinary. The Pacific Ocean glitters in the distance. From this perspective, you may spot deer on a hillside a mile away, or a couple of miniature hikers having lunch on a rock, looking like pieces out of a model train set.

From your vantage point on the Coastal Trail, the mountain slopes drop 1,500 feet to the ocean. The farther you walk, the wider your view becomes until it finally stretches from the San Francisco skyline in the south to Stinson Beach and Bolinas in the north, then still farther north to the Point Reyes peninsula. If you ever wanted to explain to someone how immense the ocean is relative to the size of the land, this would be the place to do it.

Don't miss following an unmarked spur trail on the left at 1.6 miles in, just before the Coastal Trail/Matt Davis Trail fork. A short climb to a grassy knoll brings you to Coastal Trail's best view of the day, encompassing the entire Marin County coast. Soak in the scenery for as long as you please, then return to the main trail. At the nearby fork, Matt Davis Trail heads downhill to Stinson Beach (see *Matt Davis and Steep Ravine Loop* listing in this chapter). Take the right fork on Coastal Trail, continuing gently uphill.

Where Coastal Trail meets a wide fire road at 3.3 miles out, turn right and climb steeply uphill for a brief stretch. Look for a side trail cutting off the fire road to the left; this will deliver you to paved Ridgecrest Boulevard at its junction with Laurel Dell Fire Road. Cross the paved road (watch for cars), then take Laurel Dell Fire Road. The dirt and gravel road makes a gentle descent through a mossy, shady bay forest to the edge of Cataract Creek. Watch for a right turnoff on Cataract Trail; a footbridge will carry you across the creek. If you miss it, you can stay on the fire road until it crosses the creek near Laurel Dell, then pick up Cataract Trail on its far side.

Cataract Trail parallels its namesake stream, passing within arm's length of the mossy trunks of bays and tan oaks in a dense forest canopy. The trail opens out to a meadow near Rock Spring, then deposits you at the Rock Spring parking lot. Cross Ridgecrest Boulevard again and pick up Mountain Theater Fire Road on its far side, a few yards to the left. A brief, steep climb and a right turn on Old Mine Trail takes you to high views of San Pablo Bay, the Richmond Bridge, and San Francisco. Perhaps this vista is so striking because the glittering, urban cityscape contrasts sharply with Cataract and Coastal Trails' all-natural beauty. A few large boulders on a grassy knoll make an ideal viewing platform.

Follow Old Mine Trail back downhill for one mile to paved Old Stage Road. The path drops 500 feet through a series of steep switchbacks. Finally, turn right on Old Stage Road and walk back to your car at Pantoll Ranger Station.

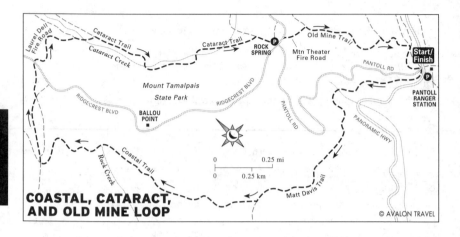

COASTAL, CATARACT, AND OLD MINE LOOP

© AVALON TRAVEL

Options

Another great trail loop that starts at Pantoll Ranger Station is the 3.6-mile Dipsea and Steep Ravine Loop. This loop starts from the Pantoll parking lot (you don't need to cross Panoramic Highway). Follow the paved trail from the far end of the parking lot a few hundred feet to Old Mine Trail. In 0.5 mile, go left on a fire road, then almost immediately right on Dipsea Trail. This trail is the part of the famous seven-mile Dipsea Race that is run from Mill Valley to Stinson Beach every spring. At two miles from the start, you'll cross a bridge and go right on Steep Ravine Trail for the climb back uphill. For more details on redwood-lined Steep Ravine Trail, see *Matt Davis and Steep Ravine Loop* listing in this chapter.

Directions

From San Francisco, cross the Golden Gate Bridge and drive north on U.S. 101 for four miles. Take the Mill Valley/Stinson Beach/Highway 1 exit and continue straight for one mile to a stoplight at Shoreline Highway (Highway 1). Turn left on Shoreline Highway and drive 2.5 miles, then turn right on Panoramic Highway. Drive 0.9 mile to a four-way intersection. Take the middle road (straight), continuing on Panoramic Highway for 4.3 more miles to the Pantoll Ranger Station and parking lot. Turn left to park in the lot, then take the steps on the northwest side of the lot, cross Panoramic Highway, and access Matt Davis/Coastal Trail near the start of Pantoll Road, on its southwest side. Limited parking is also available in the small dirt parking lot at the start of Pantoll Road. The trail begins across the road from this parking lot.

Public transportation: The West Marin Stage Bus #61 stops at Pantoll Ranger Station at Mount Tamalpais State Park. For West Marin Stage information, phone 415/226-0855 or visit www.marintransit.org.

Information and Contact

An $8 day-use fee is charged per vehicle if you park at the paved parking lot at Pantoll Ranger Station. If you park legally in any pullout along the road, there is no fee. Leashed dogs are allowed on Cataract Trail and Laurel Dell Fire Road only (Marin Municipal Water District land). Bikes are not allowed. A trail map is available at Pantoll Ranger Station for $1, or free by download at www.parks. ca.gov. Maps of the area are also available from Tom Harrison Maps at 415/456-7940, www.tomharrisonmaps.com (ask for the *Mount Tam* map). For more information, contact Mount Tamalpais State Park, 801 Panoramic Highway, Mill Valley, CA 94941, 415/388-2070, www.mttam.net.

26 BENSTEIN, MICKEY O'BRIEN, AND CATARACT LOOP
Marin Municipal Water District

Level: Easy/Moderate **Total Distance:** 4.0 miles round-trip

Hiking Time: 2 hours **Elevation Change:** 500 feet

Summary: Get away from the weekend crowds on this woodsy loop hike from Mount Tam's Rock Springs Trailhead.

If you are longing for a quiet walk in the woods, maybe with a little picnicking or a nature lesson along the way, this trail loop is just right. Lots of people come to Mount Tamalpais to see the tall coastal redwoods or take in the sweeping coastal views, but there's much to be said for a simple woodland hike offering a little exercise, some solitude, and the comforting sounds of the birds and your own breathing.

The plethora of cars parked at Rock Spring parking area on the weekends might concern you, but fear not. Rock Spring is a major hub of trails; most hikers have set out on other paths to the scenic lookout at O'Rourke's Bench or the historic Mountain Theater. On one weekend trip, the only people I saw on this trail were a group of hikers who looked to be in their 70s. They were speeding up Benstein Trail as if they were going to a fire, arguing all the way about what species of oriole they had just seen. They passed me near Potrero Meadow and I never caught up with them.

Start by walking north from the parking area, traveling on Cataract Trail until it splits—Cataract to the left and Benstein to the right. Take Benstein Trail northeast, heading immediately into a tan oak and Douglas fir forest where you'll likely be greeted by the drumming of woodpeckers.

Trail markers point you toward Potrero Meadow. Benstein Trail ascends steadily until it reaches a junction with Rock Spring and Lagunitas Fire Road. Take the fire road left for only a few dozen yards. Join Benstein Trail again where it veers off to the left, back on single-track.

Prepare for a sudden scenery change as you come out of the hardwoods and onto the rocky back side of this ridge. You'll enter a contrasting world of manzanita, chemise, small Sargent cypress trees, and serpentine rock. Serpentine, California's state rock, is formed when water mixes with peridotite. It's a pretty grayish green on Mount Tamalpais, although in other areas it's mostly gray. Spend some time examining the foliage growing here; it consists of plants that require few nutrients and are often dwarfed in size, which is typical of a serpentine environment.

The most fascinating flora are the miniature cypress trees, which mature when they are only a few feet tall. Ironically, two of the world's largest Sargent cypress trees—over 80 feet tall—grow near here on the Mickey O'Brien Trail.

Descending from this gravelly, exposed ridge, follow Benstein Trail north for 0.25 mile until you reach Laurel Dell Fire Road. (A picnic area can be found across the road at Potrero Meadow if anyone in your party is getting hungry.) Turn left on the fire road and hike about 50 yards. You'll gain a brief view of Bon Tempe Lake and the Marin watershed to the north.

Turn left on another fire road at a trail sign for Barth's Retreat. Barth's Retreat is an old camp that was built by poet, musician, and hiker Emil Barth in the 1920s. He was an avid Mount Tamalpais trail builder. Turn right and cross a bridge, pass by yet another picnic area, then continue straight. You are now on Mickey O'Brien Trail heading west along Barth's Creek in a thick forest of oak, bay, and Douglas fir. This is one of the best sections of the loop, especially when the stream is running strong, creating an enchanting melody of water sounds. Mickey O'Brien Trail, named for the 1920s president of the Tamalpais Conservation Corps, leads you gently downhill toward Laurel Dell, a grassy meadow.

Just before the dell, Mickey O'Brien Trail ends at an intersection with Cataract

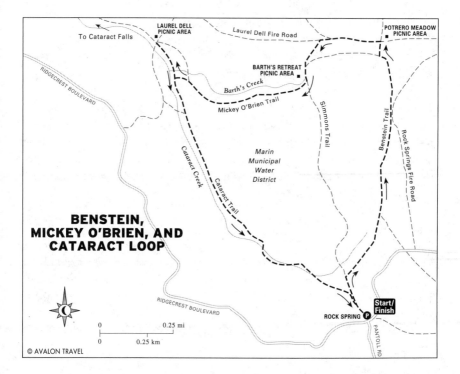

© ANN MARIE BROWN

Benstein Trail is just right for a peaceful walk in the woods.

Trail. The latter is your ticket back to Rock Spring. Turn left on Cataract; it's just over a mile to the parking lot. If you want to make a side trip to picnic at Laurel Dell, go right for 150 yards, have your lunch, then follow Cataract home.

In winter and spring, you can add on a visit to Cataract Falls from Laurel Dell. Just follow Cataract Trail northwest from the far end of the dell, then begin a steep descent through redwoods and Douglas firs. Watch for an intersection with High Marsh Trail on the right; continue straight and shortly you'll reach the uppermost cascade of Cataract Falls. Cataract Trail curves in tightly, bringing you right alongside the stream. Water tumbles over huge boulders as it rushes downhill. Pick a rock and watch the show. If you like, you can continue downhill along Cataract Trail, visiting as many of the trail's cascades as you wish. Remember that the return trip to Laurel Dell is all uphill. (See *Cataract Trail to Cataract Falls* listing in this chapter for more details.)

Options
An easy way to extend this trip into a six-mile loop is to continue straight across Laurel Dell Fire Road toward Potrero Camp and Potrero Meadow. Pick up Kent Trail and follow it north one mile to High Marsh Trail, where you turn left. High Marsh Trail travels 2.1 miles and intersects with Cataract Trail just above the largest cascade of Cataract Falls and shortly below Laurel Dell. Turn left and follow Cataract Trail all the way back to Rock Spring.

Directions

From San Francisco, cross the Golden Gate Bridge and drive north on U.S. 101 for four miles. Take the Mill Valley/Stinson Beach/Highway 1 exit and continue straight for one mile to a stoplight at Shoreline Highway (Highway 1). Turn left on Shoreline Highway and drive 2.5 miles, then turn right on Panoramic Highway. Drive 0.9 mile to a four-way intersection. Take the middle road (straight), continuing on Panoramic Highway for 4.3 more miles to Pantoll Road. Turn right on Pantoll Road and drive 1.4 miles to its intersection with Ridgecrest Boulevard, where there is a large parking area called Rock Spring. Park there and take the signed Cataract Trail from the north side of the lot.

Public transportation: The West Marin Stage Bus #61 stops at Pantoll Ranger Station at Mount Tamalpais State Park. From there, you'll need to walk up Pantoll Road for 1.4 miles to the Rock Spring parking lot. For West Marin Stage information, phone 415/226-0855 or visit www.marintransit.org.

Information and Contact

There is no fee to park at Rock Spring. Leashed dogs are allowed. Bikes are not allowed. Maps are available from Tom Harrison Maps at 415/456-7940, www.tomharrisonmaps.com (ask for the *Mount Tam* map). For more information, contact Sky Oaks Ranger Station at 415/945-1181 or Marin Municipal Water District, 220 Nellen Avenue, Corte Madera, CA 94925, 415/945-1438, www.marinwater.org. Information is also available from Mount Tamalpais State Park, 801 Panoramic Highway, Mill Valley, CA 94941, 415/388-2070, www.mttam.net.

27 OCEAN VIEW, LOST TRAIL, AND FERN CREEK LOOP

Muir Woods National Monument

Level: Easy/Moderate

Total Distance: 3.4 miles round-trip

Hiking Time: 1.5 hours

Elevation Change: 800 feet

Summary: A short but steep hike in Muir Woods shows off its famous coastal redwoods and coursing stream.

The redwoods at Muir Woods National Monument are true beauties. The foliage growing in the big trees' understory—bays, tan oak, thimbleberry, sword ferns, and sorrel—is lush and green year-round. Redwood Creek, which cuts through the center of the park, is a pristine, coursing stream.

No doubt about it, Muir Woods is a winner. Its only drawback is its popularity. This tiny national monument, not much larger than a few city blocks, is visited by more than one million people each year.

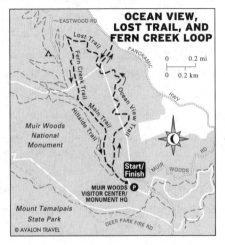

OCEAN VIEW, LOST TRAIL, AND FERN CREEK LOOP

© AVALON TRAVEL

How do you hike in the park and see its magnificent trees without getting run over by the crowds? Summer is the busiest time, of course, so it's best to avoid May–September altogether. Weekends tend to be more crowded than weekdays, but weekdays bring school groups. (Thirty sixth-graders on a field trip can be rather boisterous.) The best choice? Try to show up early in the morning, as in 8 A.M., when the park gates open. During the week, the school buses and tour buses don't usually arrive until 9 or 10 A.M. On weekends, most visitors don't show up until midmorning. An 8 A.M. start any day of the week should give you at least a two-hour window of peace among the redwoods. Winter and early spring are the least crowded and also the loveliest seasons, when Redwood Creek runs full and high.

And don't worry about visiting on a rainy day; just pack along your rain gear. A redwood forest is the best place to hike in the rain. You'll be partially protected by the big trees, and the drops of water on every fern, branch, and leaf only accentuate their beauty.

Start your trip from the entrance gate to Muir Woods near the small visitors center. The park's main trail is a wide, boardwalk-lined trail that is mostly flat and runs along the bottom of the canyon, passing the most impressive redwoods. You'll walk the entire length of this trail on your return. For now, bear right and in about 100 yards you'll reach a fork with Ocean View Trail. Follow this trail up the hillside to the right.

The path is completely forested, but the redwood trees are younger and smaller than in the canyon below and interspersed with many Douglas firs. Ocean View Trail climbs moderately, curving around the canyon until it reaches an unsigned junction with Lost Trail on the left at 1.5 miles. Note this junction, then continue straight for 200 yards until Ocean View Trail emerges from the forest just below Panoramic Highway, a busy road. A large boulder rests on the hillside between the trail and the road; this is the best spot to obtain a long-distance vista. On a sunny day, it's a nice viewpoint, looking out over the forests of Muir Woods below.

When you've had your fill of sunshine, return to the shade of the woods and the Lost Trail junction. Bear right on Lost Trail, now heading downhill. Similar to Ocean View Trail, Lost Trail weaves through a young redwood, Douglas fir, and bay forest. Soon it descends more steeply on railroad-tie stairsteps, and in 0.7 mile it connects with Fern Creek Trail. Fern Creek is a seasonal tributary to Redwood Creek, the main stream that flows through Muir Woods' canyon. Fern Creek Trail follows Fern Creek's delightful course for 0.5 mile, crossing it on two footbridges.

Near the end of Fern Creek Trail you pass a sign marking the border of Muir Woods National Monument. In a few more steps you're at the base of the Kent Memorial, a very large Douglas fir tree dedicated to the man who was responsible for the creation of this park.

There's a wonderful story about Congressman William Kent. He and his wife purchased this land and granted it to the federal government in 1905 under the condition that it be named for the naturalist John Muir. When President Theodore Roosevelt suggested the forest be named "Kent Woods" instead, Kent refused, saying he believed that naming the forest after himself was an implication that immortality could be bought, not earned.

"So many millions of better people have died forgotten," Kent wrote. "I have five good, husky boys that I am trying to bring up to a knowledge of democracy. If these boys cannot keep the name of Kent alive, I am willing it should be forgotten."

Roosevelt wrote back: "By George, you are right. Good for you, and for the five boys who are to keep the name of Kent alive. I have four boys who I hope will do the same thing by the name of Roosevelt."

Roosevelt officially created Muir Woods National Monument in 1908. The loop trail ends with a 0.75-mile walk from the Kent Memorial back down the park's wide main trail to your starting point. For more information on Muir Woods' main trail, see *Bootjack, Ben Johnson, and Hillside Trail Loop* listing in this chapter.

Options

A slightly longer hike from Muir Woods is a 4.2-mile loop that combines Ocean View, Redwood, Sun, and Dipsea Trails. Follow Ocean View Trail uphill almost to Panoramic Highway as described earlier in this listing, then turn right on Redwood Trail. Shortly you'll gain the ocean views you didn't get on Ocean View Trail. In one mile you reach an unusual-looking building called the Tourist Club (415/388-9987, www.touristclubsf.org), a branch of the Nature Friends organization. The club was founded in the early 1900s by German immigrants; the private hiking group offers refreshments most weekends 1–5 P.M. Near the club, Redwood Trail connects to Sun Trail, which runs 0.7 mile to a junction with Dipsea Trail. Turn right on Dipsea, which crosses Muir Woods Road and drops back down to Muir Woods parking lot in one mile.

Directions

From San Francisco, cross the Golden Gate Bridge and drive north on U.S. 101 for four miles. Take the Mill Valley/Stinson Beach/Highway 1 exit and continue straight for one mile to a stoplight at Shoreline Highway (Highway 1). Turn left

A gentle climb up Ocean View Trail leads hikers away from the Muir Woods crowds.

© ANN MARIE BROWN

on Shoreline Highway and drive 2.5 miles, then turn right on Panoramic Highway. Drive 0.9 mile and turn left on Muir Woods Road. Drive 1.5 miles to the Muir Woods parking area.

Public transportation: On summer weekends and holidays only, the West Marin Stage Bus #66 stops at Muir Woods National Monument. Direct connections are available to and from the Golden Gate Sausalito Ferry. For West Marin Stage information, phone 415/226-0855 or visit www.marintransit.org. Also on summer weekends and holidays May–Sept. Golden Gate Transit operates the Route 66 shuttle service between Marin City and Manzanita Park and Ride to Muir Woods. Round-trip fares (westbound) are $3 for adults and $1 for youth (ages 6–18), seniors, and disabled; exact cash only accepted. For information, phone 415/451-4650 or visit www.goldengate.org.

Information and Contact

There is a $5 entrance fee per adult. Children ages 15 and under enter free. Dogs and bikes are not allowed. A trail map ($1) is available at the entrance station or by free download at www.nps.gov/muwo. Detailed maps of the area are available from Tom Harrison Maps, 415/456-7940, www.tomharrisonmaps.com (ask for the *Mount Tam* map). For more information, contact Muir Woods National Monument, Mill Valley, CA 94941, 415/388-2595, www.nps.gov/muwo.

28 BOOTJACK, BEN JOHNSON, AND HILLSIDE TRAIL LOOP BEST 【

Muir Woods National Monument and Mount Tamalpais State Park

🦌 🚌

Level: Moderate   **Total Distance:** 6.4 miles round-trip

Hiking Time: 3 hours   **Elevation Change:** 1,100 feet

Summary: Tour the main thoroughfare at Muir Woods National Monument to see the famous trees, then leave the crowds behind as you explore quieter woods and meadows.

Muir Woods National Monument is filled with gems, like its virgin grove of coast redwoods and pristine Redwood Creek, which flows through the monument. But Muir Woods is small. If you want to hike any distance, you must leave the monument's borders and explore the adjoining lands of Mount Tamalpais State Park. This loop trail starts and ends in the monument and explores the best of it, then makes a brief tour of the equally dense redwood forest beyond its boundary.

The loop begins on the main thoroughfare in Muir Woods, a wide, boardwalk-lined path through the big trees that is usually packed with people. (For tips on how to avoid the Muir Woods crowds, see *Ocean View, Lost Trail, and Fern Creek Loop* listing in this chapter.) Follow the main trail as it parallels Redwood Creek and relax in the knowledge that you will soon leave most visitors behind. (You know you're in a heavily visited urban park when signs proclaim: "Help keep the creek clean. Do not throw coins in the water.")

If you've visited the coast redwood forests in Redwood National Park and its neighboring state parks, you may be surprised to find that the redwoods in Muir Woods are not as big. Whereas the trees around Redwood National Park grow to 20 feet in diameter, the broadest tree in Muir Woods is only 13.5 feet in diameter. What the Muir Woods redwoods lack in girth, however, they make up for in setting: They thrive in a steep, lush, stream-filled canyon that appears almost mystical on a foggy or rainy day. The monument's highlights include the dense stands of ancient redwoods in the Cathedral Grove and Bohemian Grove. The latter has some of the tallest trees in the park at 250 feet.

If you haven't visited Muir Woods in a long time, you'll notice that the main trail has been substantially modified. Bridges are in place and the Park Service removed a substantial length of pavement, installing a boardwalk made of recycled redwood to help protect the big trees' fragile roots. The boardwalk was moved a few yards away from Redwood Creek to help the fish that return to it each year to spawn. If you visit the park in winter, you may be lucky enough to

© ANN MARIE BROWN

The main trail at Muir Woods leads along the valley floor past the largest redwoods.

spot some of the native wild population of steelhead trout or coho salmon. The fish are born in Redwood Creek, live out their adult lives in the Pacific Ocean, then return here to breed and die.

Continue down the main trail, passing the Fern Creek Trail and Camp Alice Eastwood Trail turnoffs. In a few more yards you reach the pavement's end at a junction with Bootjack Trail, which continues on a smooth dirt path along the stream to the right. You are now one mile from Muir Woods' entrance, and you've likely left the crowds far behind.

Bootjack Trail makes an easy to moderate ascent along Redwood Creek, passing a cornucopia of splashing cascades in winter. The trail stays close to the water's edge, making this a perfect rainy season hike for white-water lovers. The forest is a dense mix of big-leaf maples, bays, and redwoods. Bootjack Trail steepens a bit, then travels up wooden stairs fashioned from old park signs, until it tops out at Van Wyck Meadow, 1.3 miles from Muir Woods. The postage stamp–sized meadow has a big boulder to sunbathe on and a brown sign stating "Van Wyck Meadow, population 3 steller jays."

Enjoy this peaceful spot and its sunshine, then turn left on TCC Trail to head back into the woods. (The path is signed as TCC Trail to Stapelveldt Trail.) TCC Trail meanders on a nearly level course through young, slender Douglas firs for 1.4 miles. Most noticeable is the silence—for the first time on this loop hike, you're nowhere near a boisterous creek. Cross a bridge and where you reach two junctions immediately following one another (both for Dipsea Trail), bear left at both. You'll wind up on Stapelveldt Trail heading for Ben Johnson Trail in 0.5 mile.

Now you're back in a wetter forest again, featuring many graceful, mossy bay trees. At the junction with Ben Johnson Trail turn left to find yourself back in the redwoods. Many of these trees rival the size and beauty of those on the monument's main trail.

In the last mile of the trip, you have a choice: Turn left to walk the main canyon trail back to the park entrance, or turn right to walk Hillside Trail above the canyon. Hillside Trail deposits you at Bridge 2 on the main trail, where you turn right and walk the last few yards back to your car.

Options

On busy weekend days at Muir Woods, hikers who want to see the big redwoods might do well to walk into the national monument instead of driving. To do so, park at the trailhead across from Mountain Home Inn on Panoramic Highway. (Continue past the Muir Woods Road turnoff for about 1.5 miles to the parking lot on the left.) Take Alice Eastwood Road downhill to Alice Eastwood Group Camp, then follow Plevin Cut and Camp Eastwood Trails into Muir Woods. Wander among the big trees as you please, then head back uphill on Fern Creek Trail and Lost Trail. This is a three-mile round-trip (plus you can add on more miles while you are in the monument).

Directions

From San Francisco, cross the Golden Gate Bridge and drive north on U.S. 101 for four miles. Take the Mill Valley/Stinson Beach/Highway 1 exit and continue straight for one mile to a stoplight at Shoreline Highway (Highway 1). Turn left on Shoreline Highway and drive 2.5 miles, then turn right on Panoramic Highway.

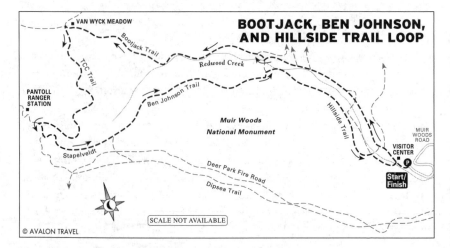

Drive 0.9 mile and turn left on Muir Woods Road. Drive 1.5 miles to the Muir Woods parking area.

Public transportation: On summer weekends and holidays only, the West Marin Stage Bus #66 stops at Muir Woods National Monument. Direct connections are available to and from the Golden Gate Sausalito Ferry. For West Marin Stage information, phone 415/226-0855 or visit www.marintransit.org. Also on weekends and holidays May–Sept. Golden Gate Transit operates the Route 66 shuttle service between Marin City and Manzanita Park and Ride to Muir Woods. Round-trip fares (westbound) are $3 for adults and $1 for youth (ages 6–18), seniors, and disabled; exact cash only accepted. For information, phone 415/451-4650 or visit www.goldengate.org.

Information and Contact

There is a $5 entrance fee per adult. Children ages 15 and under enter free. Dogs and bikes are not allowed. A trail map ($1) is available at the entrance station or by free download at www.nps.gov/muwo. Detailed maps of the area are available from Tom Harrison Maps, 415/456-7940, www.tomharrisonmaps.com (ask for the *Mount Tam* map). For more information, contact Muir Woods National Monument, Mill Valley, CA 94941, 415/388-2595, www.nps.gov/muwo.

29 MUIR BEACH/COASTAL TRAIL
Golden Gate National Recreation Area

🏠 🌸 🏊 🐕

Level: Strenuous   **Total Distance:** 7.0 miles round-trip

Hiking Time: 4 hours   **Elevation Change:** 1,800 feet

Summary: Nonstop coastal views are yours for the taking on this spectacular bluff trail that skirts the edge of the Marin Headlands.

The Coastal Trail in the Marin Headlands runs along the bluffs from Muir Beach to Rodeo Beach, then heads inland around Point Bonita and meanders a bit until it winds up at the Golden Gate Bridge. It's 11 miles one-way to hike the whole thing, but there's a better, shorter option for beach lovers. The stretch that stays closest to the ocean for the longest distance runs between Muir Beach and Tennessee Beach in southern Marin County. An out-and-back hike from the trailhead at Muir Beach provides a seven-mile round-trip with three beaches to visit and nonstop coastal views.

Know before you go: This is not a level, easy walk. Coastal Trail climbs, then descends, then climbs again, at times with a vengeance. An advantage to starting your trip at Muir Beach is that if you tire of the trail's continual ups and downs, you can always skip the final descent to Tennessee Beach and the ensuing return climb. An abbreviated walk on the Coastal Trail is almost as good as the whole thing.

Start by locating the trail, which is on the southwest side of the Muir Beach parking lot, near the restrooms. Walk across a footbridge over a marsh to reach the signed Coastal Trail. Take the wide fire road to the right and immediately make a steep, quick climb up a ridge. Follow the single-track spur to the right to reach the trail's first overlook point, where you can catch your breath and enjoy a view to the north of Muir Beach's picturesque, semicircular cove and small community of homes. In spring, poppies, lupine, and tidy tips bloom in abundance along the coastal bluffs.

Then regain the main path at a major junction of trails; you'll stay to the right along the coast. (For the next two miles, Coastal Trail is a single-track trail for hikers only. Mountain bikers aren't permitted; they must keep to the fire roads.)

Coastal Trail descends, bestowing wide views of the crashing surf below. Straight ahead to the south you can observe the line of ridges and valleys and pick out your final destination at Tennessee Cove. An intermediate destination is reached at two miles from the trailhead; watch for a spur trail leading to tiny, rocky Pirate's Cove. (Just before the spur, the main trail heads inland to curve around the cove's inlet stream.) Follow the short but steep spur path to what must be Marin County's smallest and most secluded beach. Rest up while you're there; the next 0.5 mile is a steep ascent that gains 550 feet.

March your way uphill through the sweaty climb. A series of wooden stairs make the work a little easier. At the end of the ascent, you'll reach a junction of trails and a rewarding overlook point. Here, on a flat, high bluff, you're provided with a 360-degree panorama of the Pacific Ocean to the west, Tennessee Valley and its blue lagoon to the south, Bolinas and Point Reyes to the north, and the San Francisco skyline to the southwest. To the east are the pastoral rolling hills of the Golden Gate National Recreation Area.

Consider your position carefully before continuing onward to Tennessee Valley. If you're tiring out, this high point makes an excellent turnaround, and most of your return trip will be downhill. But if you have energy to burn, head steeply downhill on the wide dirt road to Tennessee Valley, then turn right on Tennessee

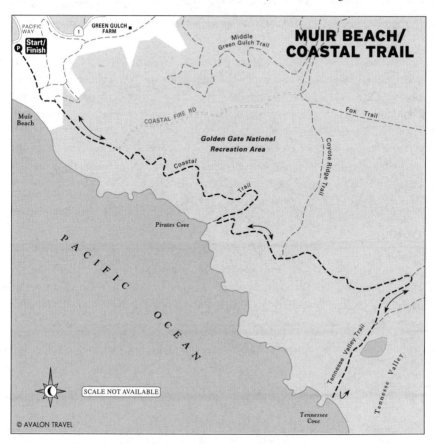

Hiking the Coastal Trail from Muir Beach ensures nonstop ocean views all the way.

Valley Trail and take a level stroll to the beach. You'll pass by a bird-covered lagoon and an abundance of coastal chaparral along the way. (For more information on Tennessee Beach, see *Tennessee Valley Trail* listing in this chapter.) Enjoy your stay at this postcard-perfect, black-sand beach, then shore up your energy for the hilly return trip.

Note that your dog may accompany you on this hike right up to the point where Coastal Trail joins Tennessee Valley Trail, but canines must do an about-face where the trails junction. Although dogs are allowed at Muir Beach, they are not permitted at Tennessee Beach, nor on its trail.

Options

There are more beaches to explore just north of Muir Beach. To access them, drive north on Highway 1 for 1.2 miles to the Muir Beach Overlook. Park in the lot, then follow Owl Trail as it heads north and downhill to Slide Ranch, one mile away. The ranch, a popular destination for school field trips, is an educational center with farm animals and vegetable gardens. Continue past the ranch to two beach spur trails; one leads 0.25 mile to North Beach and the other travels the same distance to South Beach. Take your pick. Both "beaches" are rocky coves with crashing waves and much coastal drama, although neither has much to offer in the way of sand.

Directions

From San Francisco, cross the Golden Gate Bridge and drive north on U.S. 101 for four miles. Take the Mill Valley/Stinson Beach/Highway 1 exit and continue straight for one mile to a stoplight at Shoreline Highway (Highway 1). Turn left on Shoreline Highway and drive 5.2 miles, then turn left on Pacific Way (by the Pelican Inn). Drive 0.5 mile on Pacific Way to the Muir Beach parking lot. The trail begins on the southwest side of the lot near the restrooms.

Information and Contact

There is no fee. Dogs are allowed on Coastal Trail up to its junction with Tennessee Valley Trail. Bikes are allowed only on fire roads. A detailed map of the area is available from Tom Harrison Maps, 415/456-7940, www.tomharrisonmaps.com (ask for the *Mount Tam* or *Southern Marin* map). A free map is also available at the Marin Headlands Visitor Center, Fort Barry, Building 948, Sausalito, CA 94965, 415/331-1540, or by download at www.nps.gov/goga. The Marin Headlands Visitor Center is open 9:30 a.m.–4:30 p.m. daily.

30 TENNESSEE VALLEY TRAIL
Golden Gate National Recreation Area

🦌 ✈️ 🏵️ 🏊 👪

Level: Easy

Hiking Time: 2 hours

Total Distance: 4.0 miles round-trip

Elevation Change: 150 feet

Summary: A family-friendly walk to a dramatic black-sand beach in the Marin Headlands.

The Tennessee Valley Trail is one of the most popular trails in the Golden Gate National Recreation Area and probably the most heavily used trail in all of Marin County. But don't let the crowds scare you away. Time your trip for an early morning or a weekday and you'll enjoy a peaceful, easy walk to a postcard-quality beach.

Aside from the first-class scenery, the main reason for the crowds at Tennessee Valley is its proximity to the homes of thousands of San Francisco and Marin residents. Mount Tamalpais is only a few miles up the road from Tennessee Valley, but it's a steep, winding drive to get there. Tennessee Valley is in the flats, close to town and U.S. 101. Plus, Tennessee Valley Trail is open to bikers as well as hikers, and it's a popular route for runners and parents pushing baby strollers.

© ANN MARIE BROWN

the black-sand beach at Tennessee Cove

Fortunately the route is wide enough so there's plenty of room for everybody. Trail conflicts are rare to nonexistent.

The trail begins as a paved route by Miwok Stables, where horses can be rented and riding lessons are held. Shortly the pavement forks left and the main trail continues straight as a wide dirt road. The mostly level path follows a creek bed between tall grassy ridges lined with coastal chaparral. Rabbits, deer, and bobcats are often seen in the early morning. In spring, poppies, lupine, and tidy tips pepper the grasslands. Your destination is two miles away at Tennessee Cove, where a small, black-sand beach is bracketed by high cliffs. This picturesque pocket beach is where the steamship *Tennessee* wrecked in dense fog on its way to San Francisco in 1853. The ship was carrying cargo, mail, and 600 passengers. Miraculously

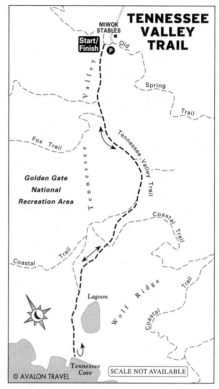

all lives were saved, although the rough surf soon tore the ship to pieces.

While the beach is the trail's prime attraction, a bird-filled, blue lagoon along the way is a close runner-up. The trail forks before the lagoon; bikers must stay on the wide road to the right but hikers take the single-track to the left, which leads along the water's edge. Bird-watching is usually productive. The trails rejoin 0.5 mile later as they near Tennessee Beach.

At the beach, rolling waves crash on dark sands, pelicans soar overhead, and an offshore rock is battered by continual breakers. Although Tennessee Beach is a great spot for surf-watching, don't think about swimming here, even on the rare days when the air and sun are warm enough to tempt you. The surf is extremely treacherous. If you tire of reposing on the beach and wish to see the world from a pelican's perspective, a short trail leads up the northwestern bluff nearly 200 feet to an overlook at an old military bunker.

Options

Both hikers and mountain bikers favor a 5.3-mile loop that starts at Tennessee Valley Trailhead. Follow the Tennessee Valley Trail to 0.5 mile before the beach (or go check out the surf while you're here), then make a short but strenuous climb up Coastal Trail. At the summit, catch your breath and enjoy the views, then turn right and climb more gently, eventually joining Coyote Ridge Road. A final right turn and downhill stint on Miwok Trail will bring you back to Tennessee Valley Trailhead. A lot of cross-country runners power out this hilly loop on Saturday mornings.

If you'd rather stay close to the coast, you can combine this stroll with a more strenuous up-and-down hike on Coastal Trail, either heading south to Rodeo Beach or north to Muir Beach (see *Muir Beach/Coastal Trail* listing in this chapter).

Directions

From San Francisco, cross the Golden Gate Bridge and drive north on U.S. 101 for four miles. Take the Mill Valley/Stinson Beach/Highway 1 exit and continue straight for 0.6 mile to Tennessee Valley Road on the left. Turn left and drive two miles to the trailhead.

Information and Contact

There is no fee. Dogs are not allowed. Bikes are allowed. A detailed map of the area is available from Tom Harrison Maps, 415/456-7940, www.tomharrison-maps.com (ask for the *Southern Marin* map). A free map is also available at the Marin Headlands Visitor Center, Fort Barry, Building 948, Sausalito, CA 94965, 415/331-1540, or by download at www.nps.gov/goga. The Marin Headlands Visitor Center is open 9:30 A.M.–4:30 P.M. daily.

31 LAGOON TRAIL   BEST 🄲
Golden Gate National Recreation Area

Level: Easy   **Total Distance:** 1.75 miles round-trip

Hiking Time: 1 hour   **Elevation Change:** Negligible

Summary: Pack the bird-watching binoculars for this walk alongside Rodeo Lagoon from the Marin Headlands Visitor Center to the beach.

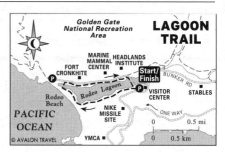

You have to look long and hard to find a hiking trail in the Marin Headlands that is nearly level. Or you can head directly for the Lagoon Trail at Rodeo Lagoon and spare yourself a lot of searching. The trail begins conveniently at the Marin Headlands Visitor Center, where you can get a few natural and cultural history lessons before heading out on the scenic, easy path.

From the northwestern edge of the parking lot, start walking directly toward the ocean and Rodeo Beach. A trail veers off to the right, but continue straight ahead, marching toward the sea. Hiking on a wide gravel path, you can hear the rhythm of the ocean waves and watch the birds in Rodeo Lagoon. This natural lagoon is separated from the ocean by a narrow strip of beach. Winter storm waves occasionally wash over the beach, resulting in a mixed freshwater and saltwater environment that makes Rodeo Lagoon a happy home for brown pelicans, snowy egrets, diving wood ducks, and other waterbirds. Red-winged blackbirds and other songbirds like it, too.

For a brief stretch, the foliage alongside the trail is very dense and high, and you can't see far in any direction. Walk past a feeder stream where horsetail ferns grow in thick clusters. The trail begins to climb, rising 100 feet above the lagoon and opening up your views. Across the water, you can see the buildings of the Headlands Institute and the Marine Mammal Center. The latter is a nonprofit organization that rescues and rehabilitates injured marine animals.

Where the trail drops back down again, nearly at the edge of Rodeo Beach, you are greeted by springtime poppies and deep blue lupine. The National Park Service is working diligently to remove invasive mats of nonnative ice plant from this area and give the native flowers a chance to flourish.

Follow the sandy trail straight out to the beach, or climb up on the bluffs on your left for a broad view of rocky sea stacks and the coast to the south. Most prominent is Bird Island, a giant sea stack that is only barely disconnected from the coast. Because of its separation, Bird Island is inaccessible to ground predators such as foxes, bobcats, raccoons, and people. It serves as a major rest stop for seabirds—as many as 1,200 brown pelicans have been counted on the island at one time. Bird Island is a small paradise for serious bird-watchers.

If you head straight for Rodeo Beach, you'll find it peopled by a collection of anglers, dog walkers, bird-watchers, and beach lovers. When it's sunny on Rodeo Beach, it's often windy. When it's foggy, it's generally still and peaceful. Look closely at the tiny, colorful pebbles on the beach. Some are semiprecious stones such as carnelians, jasper, and agates, but because this beach is in a national park, collecting them is prohibited. Swimming at the beach is not recommended because of riptides, although you will see hardy surfers riding the waves. The lagoon, also, is off-limits for swimming.

To finish out your trip, you can loop back by exiting the beach on a long footbridge, then walking along the north side of the lagoon, paralleling the road. I'd recommend a turnaround instead; just reverse your steps and enjoy this path all over again.

Options

If you'd like to see more of the beaches of the Marin Headlands, several short trails will take you there. The trail to Kirby Cove and Kirby Campground begins near Battery Spencer, 0.3 mile from the start of Conzelman Road. The one-mile trail (a wide road) leads downhill to a beach with a spectacular view of the Golden Gate Bridge. Two more beach trails are found at parking lots on the one-way section of Conzelman Road. Each trail is about 0.5 mile in length.

Directions

From San Francisco, cross the Golden Gate Bridge on U.S. 101 and take the first exit north of the bridge, Alexander Avenue. Turn left and loop back under the freeway, then turn right on Conzelman Road. (Coming southbound on U.S. 101, take the last Sausalito exit just before the Golden Gate Bridge.) Drive one mile on Conzelman Road, then turn right on McCullough Road and drive 0.9 mile. Turn left on Bunker Road and drive two miles. (Follow the signs for the Marin Headlands Visitor Center.) Park at the visitors center and locate the Lagoon Trail marker near the restrooms on the west side of the parking lot.

Public transportation: MUNI Bus #76 stops at the Marin Headlands Visitor Center on Sundays and holidays only. For MUNI information, phone 415/701-2311 (or just 311 in San Francisco) or visit www.sfmta.com.

© ANN MARIE BROWN

Lagoon Trail carves an easy, level path to scenic Rodeo Beach.

Information and Contact

There is no fee. Leashed dogs are allowed. Bikes are not allowed. A detailed map of the area is available from Tom Harrison Maps, 415/456-7940, www.tomharrisonmaps.com (ask for the *Southern Marin* map). A free map is also available at the Marin Headlands Visitor Center, Fort Barry, Building 948, Sausalito, CA 94965, 415/331-1540, or by download at www.nps.gov/goga. The Marin Headlands Visitor Center is open 9:30 A.M.–4:30 P.M. daily.

32 COASTAL TRAIL AND HILL 88 LOOP

BEST ◖

Golden Gate National Recreation Area

Level: Moderate

Total Distance: 5.5 miles round-trip

Hiking Time: 3 hours

Elevation Change: 1,000 feet

Summary: A hike high above the Marin Headland's busiest beach to an overlook with an unbeatable coastal view.

At one time, the Coastal Trail at Rodeo Beach was a paved road, but over the years, weather and erosion have taken their toll. The trail has been rebuilt, rerouted, and reworked so many times that today the path is a patchwork: part paved road, part dirt road, part single-track, and part wooden stairs. But its destination remains the same. The Coastal Trail leads from Rodeo Beach to the top of mighty Hill 88 in the Marin Headlands, providing what many consider to be the finest views in the Golden Gate National Recreation Area—a park rife with memorable views.

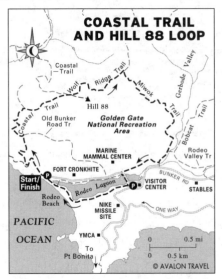

Even better, once you reach the top you don't have to turn around and retrace your steps. A convenient 5.5-mile loop can be made by descending via Wolf Ridge Trail and Miwok Trail, then cruising alongside Rodeo Lagoon back to your car. On a clear day when the fog has vanished from the Golden Gate, this loop trip may be the best possible way to spend an afternoon.

One more incentive, if it's needed: Spring wildflowers along Wolf Ridge are exemplary. The April–June show features grasslands peppered with colorful shooting stars, California poppies, and fringe cups.

The trip begins at the big parking lot by Rodeo Beach in the Marin Headlands. Start hiking on the gated, paved road that leads uphill along the coastal bluffs. A bonus is that you can bring your dog along on this trail; just be sure to keep him or her leashed. Bikes share sections of the route as well, but there's plenty of room for everybody.

Take the first left cutoff signed as Coastal Trail, only 100 yards up the road. This spur leads up a few easy switchbacks to an overlook perched a few hundred feet above the sea. Spectacular? Yes, indeed. Consider it a preview of the vistas to come. A maze of paths lead along the ocean bluffs, but none of them are through-trails. Return to the pavement again and continue uphill, soon approaching Battery Townsley. One of several dismantled military installations in the Marin Headlands, Battery Townsley was built during World War II to protect the coast against a possible aerial attack. Townsley was the first battery on the Pacific Coast to fire a 16-inch projectile.

Explore the battery's old concrete structures, then climb some more. The clanging bell of an offshore fog signal provides background music for your walk. You'll leave the pavement near an obvious landslide (the paved road was washed out) then continue uphill on single-track trail and wooden stairs. Up, up, and up. Is this starting to feel like a workout? Yes, but the views inspire you all the way. It's a total of 2.3 miles and a 1,000-foot elevation gain from Rodeo Beach to the summit.

Finally you top out at the paved road again. A wide dirt road continues uphill to the west past more abandoned military buildings. It's tempting to follow it to the high hill right above you, but hold off: Hill 88 is even higher, and not far off. Stay to the right on the pavement, heading east. The grade mellows as you follow the backbone of narrow Wolf Ridge. Note the junction with Wolf Ridge Trail and Coastal Trail to Tennessee Valley on your left; you'll take Wolf Ridge Trail for the return leg of your loop.

For now, continue straight on the pavement for the final third of a mile to the summit of Hill 88. The junky, rusting bunkers and square, cinder-block structures won't hold your attention. Instead it's the view. An enormous expanse of ocean and bay is visible, plus Mount Diablo to the east, Montara Mountain to the south, Mount Tamalpais to the northwest, Tennessee Valley to the west, and a multitude of landmarks in the city of San Francisco—Twin Peaks, Ocean Beach, the tall buildings of downtown, and so on. Hill 88's best viewpoint is an old cement gun placement facing south, which makes a perfect overlook platform.

After you've seen enough, retrace your steps down the pavement to the junction with Wolf Ridge Trail. Turn right and head steeply downhill for 0.75 mile. You'll gain views of Mount Tamalpais, Tennessee Valley, and pristine Gerbode Valley. As you admire the green valley floor, consider the fact that in the 1960s, developers planned a community of several thousand homes to be built in Gerbode Valley. Although the gateposts had already been set, dedicated conservationists fought the development plan and won. Chalk up a victory for the hawks, bobcats, and butterflies.

At the next junction, turn right on Miwok Trail. Wolf Ridge Trail is open to

A hike to the top of Hill 88 gives a wide perspective on Rodeo Beach and the mouth of the Golden Gate.

hikers only, but you'll probably share wide, smooth Miwok Trail with mountain bikers. After 1.5 miles of downhill walking (with a near guarantee of spotting deer, hawks, and other creatures), you'll reach the base of Hill 88 and a junction of trails. Follow Miwok Trail for another 0.4 mile to its end at a large building across from Rodeo Lagoon. Cross Bunker Road to the lagoon's edge, then take the trail alongside it for a little more than 0.5 mile back to Rodeo Beach.

Options

The 6.8-mile Miwok and Bobcat Loop is well loved by a nearly equal mix of hikers and mountain bikers, especially in the springtime when the Marin Headlands put on their annual wildflower show. (Bikes are not allowed on the entire loop; for part of it they follow a different route.) Start on Miwok Trail from the northeast edge of Rodeo Lagoon (the trail begins on the right side of a cluster of buildings). Follow it steeply uphill for 3.3 miles to a junction with Bobcat Trail, where you turn right. Bobcat Trail loops 2.7 miles back downhill to Miwok Trail; follow Miwok Trail for the last 0.4 mile to your car. You'll pass the turnoff for Hawk Camp along the way; backpackers with a permit can spend the night here.

Directions

From San Francisco, cross the Golden Gate Bridge on U.S. 101 and take the first exit north of the bridge, Alexander Avenue. Turn left and loop back under the freeway, then turn right on Conzelman Road. (Coming southbound on U.S. 101, take the last Sausalito exit just before the Golden Gate Bridge.) Drive one mile on Conzelman Road, then turn right on McCullough Road and drive 0.9 mile. Turn left on Bunker Road and drive 2.4 miles to the end of the road at Rodeo Beach.

Public transportation: MUNI Bus #76 stops at Fort Cronkhite/Rodeo Beach on Sundays and holidays only. For MUNI information, phone 415/701-2311 (or just 311 in San Francisco) or visit www.sfmta.com.

Information and Contact

There is no fee. Leashed dogs are allowed. Bikes are allowed on Coastal Trail and Miwok Trail, but not on Wolf Ridge Trail. A detailed map of the area is available from Tom Harrison Maps, 415/456-7940, www.tomharrisonmaps.com (ask for the *Southern Marin* map). A free map is also available at the Marin Headlands Visitor Center, Fort Barry, Building 948, Sausalito, CA 94965, 415/331-1540 or by download at www.nps.gov/goga. The Marin Headlands Visitor Center is open 9:30 A.M.–4:30 P.M. daily.

33 POINT BONITA LIGHTHOUSE
Golden Gate National Recreation Area

Level: Easy

Hiking Time: 1 hour

Total Distance: 1.0 mile round-trip

Elevation Change: 100 feet

Summary: An unforgettable walk across a mini-suspension bridge to a historic lighthouse perched atop a rock outcrop.

Okay, this isn't the Bay Area's longest hike. It's so short and easy, let's just call it a walk. But the trail to Point Bonita Lighthouse must be considered one of the Bay Area's most unforgettable paths, if not for its unique destination and historical interest, then for its heart-stopping scenery.

A 0.5-mile walk takes you from the Point Bonita trailhead along a thin backbone of land to the Marin Headlands' southern tip, where the Point Bonita Lighthouse shines its mighty beacon. As you walk this knife-thin ridge, the realization hits you that Point Bonita is really out there, as in just barely attached to the rest of the continent. It's a place unlike any other in the Bay Area.

Constructed in 1855, Point Bonita was the third lighthouse built on the West Coast, after the Alcatraz and Fort Point Lighthouses. (Marin County's other famous lighthouse at Point Reyes was built in 1870.) Point Bonita's original glass lens has been in continuous use for nearly 150 years, shining a light that can be seen for 18 miles out to sea. Prior to the lighthouse's construction, mariners frequently sailed right by San Francisco Bay without even noticing it, particularly in heavy fog. As settlers and gold seekers poured into the Golden Gate with the Gold Rush in 1848, a lighthouse was needed to make the port's entrance more visible.

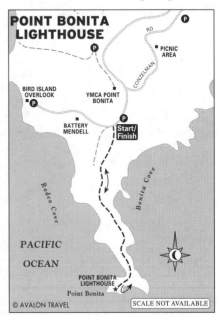

Your trip begins with a glance at your calendar. Is it Saturday, Sunday, or Monday? Can you get there between 12:30 and 3:30 P.M.? The Point Bonita Lighthouse and the trail that accesses it are open only during these hours, so you can't just show up whenever you

© KEVIN GONG

Point Bonita's lighthouse and suspension footbridge are precariously perched.

feel like it. Next, glance at the skies. Although the lighthouse is open to visitors in any weather except extreme high winds, it's best to save your trip for a clear day when the coast and bay vistas will be optimal.

Finally, you ought to borrow your great aunt's convertible, because the drive to the lighthouse along Conzelman Road is one of the most breathtaking in all of California. If you've never driven this remarkable road on the edge of the Marin Headlands, you're in for a treat. (You can also drive to the lighthouse via Bunker Road in the Marin Headlands, but it's nowhere near as thrilling.)

Once you're at the trailhead, the trip is self-explanatory. The trail is wide, paved, and easy, with a slight downhill grade to the lighthouse. Views of the Golden Gate Bridge, San Francisco, and the immense blue bay are exceptional to begin with, but just wait until you proceed along Point Bonita's curving tip of land that juts precipitously into the bay. The panorama just keeps expanding.

In your first few steps, you'll pass the worn metal rails of an abandoned life-saving station. The station was established in 1899 to aid shipwrecked boats. Despite the warning beacon of the lighthouse, hundreds of vessels have been lost near the entrance to the Golden Gate. Long before the U.S. Coast Guard came into existence, the daring crews at this lifesaving station had the hazardous job of rescuing lives and property in treacherous seas. The "surfmen" (as they were called) would row out to sea in rowboats to search for shipwreck survivors. Their foreboding motto was "You have to go out, but you don't have to come in." Too often they didn't.

After walking less than 0.25 mile, you reach the trail's famous hand-dug tunnel, a six-foot-high, 50-foot-long hole bored through a pillow basalt formation. (The tunnel is the point where the Park Service closes off the trail when the lighthouse is closed.) Tall people have to duck when passing through; kids usually run back and forth a few times.

On the tunnel's far side, the trail continues along a thin backbone of volcanic rock, then reaches a series of boardwalks and a mini–suspension bridge. Yes, it's just like the Golden Gate Bridge, but a lot smaller and white, not orange. The piece of land connecting Point Bonita to the coast is so minimal, and has been so badly worn by the ravages of waves and weather, that it's just shy of being disconnected. Point Bonita will eventually become an island, a rocky sea stack just off the coast.

Only two people at a time are permitted on the 40-yard-long suspension bridge; otherwise it gets a little tippy. If you have to wait a minute to get on, you're lucky. From the bridge's entrance the views of the Golden Gate and the lighthouse are perfectly framed. A lot of photo snapping happens here.

Finally you arrive at Point Bonita's lighthouse. You can explore its lower floor, talk to the volunteers who staff it, and learn all kinds of facts about the hard life of a lighthouse keeper. Then again, you might just stand around on its deck and gaze in wonder at the crashing waves, black-sand coves, and the magnificent Golden Gate.

Options

For more easy walking, combine this hike with a saunter on the loop trail around Rodeo Lagoon (see *Lagoon Trail* listing in this chapter).

Directions

From San Francisco, cross the Golden Gate Bridge on U.S. 101 and take the first exit north of the bridge, Alexander Avenue. Turn left and loop back under the freeway, then turn right on Conzelman Road. (Coming southbound on U.S. 101, take the last Sausalito exit just before the Golden Gate Bridge.) Follow Conzelman Road all the way to its end (the road becomes one-way) at the Point Bonita Lighthouse parking area. (You can also reach the lighthouse from the Marin Headlands Visitor Center on Bunker Road; follow the brown signs for one mile.)

Information and Contact

The Point Bonita Lighthouse and trail are open only 12:30–3:30 P.M. on Saturday, Sunday, and Monday. There is no fee. Dogs and bikes are not allowed. A free map is available at the Marin Headlands Visitor Center, which is open 9:30 A.M.–4:30 P.M. daily. For more information, contact the Marin Headlands Visitor Center, Fort Barry, Building 948, Sausalito, CA 94965, 415/331-1540, www.nps.gov/goga.

34 PHYLLIS ELLMAN TRAIL BEST ◖

Ring Mountain Open Space Preserve

🔭 🦌 ✈ 🌸 🎴 🐕

Level: Easy/Moderate **Total Distance:** 3.0 miles round-trip

Hiking Time: 1.5 hours **Elevation Change:** 600 feet

Summary: A special preserve tucked amid burgeoning development offers surprising tranquility, big bay views, and a chance to see rare species of wildflowers.

The Nature Conservancy's Ring Mountain Preserve is located smack in the middle of the Corte Madera suburbs, not far from Paradise Drive's paradise of shopping malls. But while the surrounding development may seem discouraging, Ring Mountain Preserve is a heavenly slice of open space. It features a wealth of grassland wildflowers, fascinating rock outcrops, and outstanding views.

The Nature Conservancy acquired this hillside land tucked between neighborhood developments in order to protect the Tiburon mariposa lily, which grows nowhere else in the world.

PHYLLIS ELLMAN TRAIL

Ring Mountain Open Space Preserve

PARADISE DRIVE

Start/Finish

Phyllis Ellman Trail

TAYLOR DRIVE

Taylor Ridge Fire Road

PETROGLYPH ROCK

TURTLE ROCK

Ring Mountain 602ft ▲

WATER TANK

REED RANCH RD

SCALE NOT AVAILABLE

© AVALON TRAVEL

Six other species of Ring Mountain wildflowers grow in few other areas, landing them spots on the rare plant list. These special flora share Ring Mountain with many more common wildflowers and grasses, as well as bay trees, live oaks, deer, grey fox, rabbits, quail, and songbirds. To see the preserve at its best, you must visit in spring when the grasslands are in bloom, and preferably on a clear day.

Phyllis Ellman Trail, combined with a path named simply Loop Trail, circles the preserve. You'll see a sufficient amount of signposts in this preserve, but very few that bear trail names. (Just remember to head uphill for the outbound leg and downhill on the way back.) The trail forks within a few yards of the trailhead; take the left side of the loop first, saving the right side for your return. Things may not look all that promising at first, but just be patient. Ignore the neighboring houses and the busy road behind you, start climbing, and take your time—there's nowhere to go but up.

As you ascend, be sure to turn around every few minutes to check out the view at your back. You gain elevation quickly, and with every few footsteps your vista will expand to include more of the North and East Bays. Ring Mountain is situated directly across the bay from two easy-to-identify landmarks: the Larkspur Ferry Terminal and San Quentin Prison. As you scan the horizon, you'll see the East and West Brother Islands near Richmond, the East and West Marin Islands near San Rafael, Point San Pedro, the Richmond Bridge, and parts of the East Bay. The islands are perhaps the most intriguing sight. This is the only park in Marin where you can simultaneously see the Marin Islands, which are state owned and unoccupied, and the East and West Brother Islands (the former features a lighthouse and tiny inn).

There's also plenty to see right by your feet. Large and small rock outcrops jut out from the hillside, adding contrast to the grasslands. Flower lovers should watch for sky lupine with clusters of dark blue flowers, blue-eyed grass, western larkspur, Douglas iris, light blue flax, pink onions, tarweed, yarrow, owl's clover, and the yellow spikes of false lupine. California poppies are the most prevalent bloomers. If you want to see the rare Tiburon mariposa lily, you must show up in late May, after many of the other wildflowers have finished their bloom. Even then, you must look carefully for this precious plant. Its mottled flowers are camouflaged against the surrounding grasses.

You'll be in open sunshine for most of this walk, but as you gain the ridge the trail passes by small, inviting groves of live oaks. As the climb tops out, the trail meets up with a wide fire road on Taylor Ridge. You'll see a large water tank and a handful of immense houses to your left, and a prominent serpentine outcrop

A hiker and his dog examine the Native American rock carvings.

straight ahead. This is known as Turtle Rock, although from here it's difficult to see why—the top of the rock resembles a turtle, but only when seen from one angle. Climb on top of Turtle Rock for a fabulous view to the south of San Francisco, Angel Island, Alcatraz, Tiburon, and Sausalito. The whole of the East and North Bays remains visible in the opposite direction. You can see both San Francisco Bay and San Pablo Bay at the same time.

After enjoying the view from the big rock overlook, head west (right) on the fire road for a short distance to a four-way junction of trails. From the junction, leave the fire road and walk west downhill for about 40 yards to examine Petroglyph Rock (there's a post-and-rail fence and interpretive signboard on the rock's west side). This large outcrop was carved with inch-deep, horseshoe-shaped markings by Native Americans approximately 3,000 years ago. (Sadly, the rock has also been carved by vandals in more recent years.) Additional carvings are found on at least 30 other outcrops in the preserve. A midden on the lower part of the mountain suggests that Miwok Indians were living on Ring Mountain as early as 370 B.C.

From Petroglyph Rock, follow Phyllis Ellman Trail back downhill for the return leg of your loop. The bay vistas will continue to inspire you all the way downhill.

Options
For a view-filled trip without a lot of effort, continue past the Phyllis Ellman trailhead for just under a mile, then turn right on Taylor Road and drive to its end. This is the trailhead for Taylor Ridge Fire Road, which connects to Phyllis Ellman Trail along the ridge top. Start your hike here and follow the ridgeline out as far as you please before turning back.

Directions
From San Francisco, cross the Golden Gate Bridge and drive north on U.S. 101 for seven miles to Corte Madera. Take the Paradise Drive exit and head east for 1.6 miles (through a residential neighborhood). The preserve trailhead is on the right. Park in the gravel pullouts on the side of the road.

Information and Contact
There is no fee. Leashed dogs are allowed. Bikes are not allowed. Detailed maps of the area are available for free by download at www.marinopenspace.org, or can be purchased from Tom Harrison Maps, 415/456-7940, www.tomharrisonmaps.com (ask for the *Southern Marin* map). For more information, contact Marin County Open Space District, 3501 Civic Center Drive, Room 415, San Rafael, CA 94903, 415/499-6387, www.marinopenspace.org.

35 PERIMETER TRAIL
Angel Island State Park

🚶 🚵 🌊 🍽 🚻 🚌

Level: Easy

Hiking Time: 2.5 hours

Total Distance: 5.5 miles round-trip

Elevation Change: 200 feet

Summary: The most desirable real estate in the Bay Area is yours for the day on this easy trail that circles Angel Island and passes numerous historic sites.

The Perimeter Trail at Angel Island State Park may be the most spectacular easy hike in the entire San Francisco Bay Area. How easy? It's mostly paved and nearly level, so you can push a baby stroller around the whole thing. How spectacular? The Bay Area has plenty of first-rate trails, but what sets this one apart is that it's on an island in the middle of the bay. The 360-degree views alone are reason enough to make the journey.

What comes as a surprise to first-time visitors is how fun it is just getting to Angel Island—walking up the ferry boat gangway, finding a spot on the open-air top deck or inside the cozy lower deck, and watching the mainland diminish as the boat pulls away from the harbor. Even the most jaded can hardly keep from smiling as they smell the salt air and feel the cool bay breeze.

In about 20 minutes from Tiburon and 40 minutes from San Francisco or the East Bay, your ferry docks at Ayala Cove. Walk to your right, past the island's café and bike rental kiosk. (Commercial services vary seasonally; to find out what is currently open for business on the island, visit www.angelisland.com or phone 415/897-0715.) The picnic area at Ayala Cove is usually packed with people, but you'll quickly leave them behind. Take the well-signed trail to the left of the picnic tables, which switchbacks gently uphill to join the main Perimeter Trail.

Perimeter Trail is a wide, paved road, although the pavement deteriorates to gravel and dirt in some places. Because the road loops around the island, you can head either right or left. If you go left, heading clockwise around the island, you will face most of the oncoming bicyclists, who usually ride in the opposite direction. (The trail is wide enough to easily handle all its users, but it helps when hikers see bikers coming.)

You'll have only one major hill to face on the southeast side of the island. The views will more than compensate for the energy expenditure. Heading clockwise, you begin with a panorama of Tiburon and its Mediterranean-looking waters, then the Richmond Bridge and the northern tip of San Pablo Bay. Far beyond are the hills of Napa and Sonoma Counties. The panorama changes with every

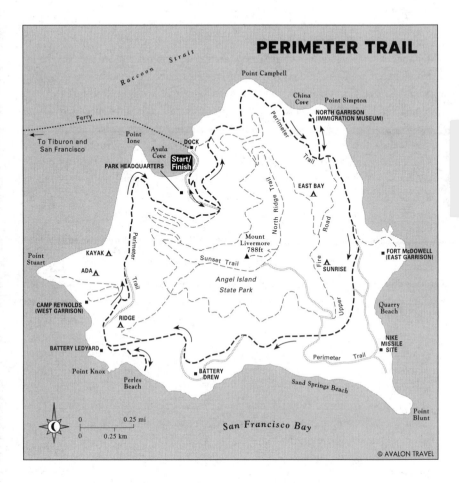

PERIMETER TRAIL

Raccoon Strait

Point Campbell

China Cove

Point Simpton

NORTH GARRISON
(IMMIGRATION MUSEUM)

Ferry

To Tiburon and
San Francisco

Point Ione

DOCK

Ayala Cove

Start/Finish

PARK HEADQUARTERS

Perimeter Trail

EAST BAY ▲

North Ridge Trail

Fire Road

Mount Livermore 788ft ▲

Point Stuart

KAYAK ▲

ADA ▲

Perimeter Trail

Sunset Trail

Angel Island State Park

Fire

SUNRISE ▲

FORT McDOWELL
(EAST GARRISON) ■

CAMP REYNOLDS
(WEST GARRISON) ■

RIDGE ▲

Upper

Quarry Beach

NIKE MISSILE SITE ■

BATTERY LEDYARD ■

Point Knox

Perles Beach

BATTERY DREW ▲

Perimeter Trail

Sand Springs Beach

Point Blunt

0   0.25 mi

0   0.25 km

San Francisco Bay

© AVALON TRAVEL

few steps. You have to keep analyzing and reanalyzing what you're seeing, because your perspective is so different from the center of San Francisco Bay than it is from its edges.

One of the best viewpoints is on the southeast side of the loop, at an open stretch where you glimpse the Bay Bridge and Golden Gate Bridge simultaneously, plus everything in between and on either side, including Alcatraz, which lies directly ahead. You're viewing the whole line of cities from Berkeley to San Francisco to Sausalito, a 180-degree scene.

Numerous historical side trips are possible on Perimeter Trail. Angel Island has a long and varied history as a military outpost, a Russian sea otter hunters' site, and an immigrant detention center. The visitors center near the picnic area at Ayala Cove has brochures and exhibits on the island's history. One recommended side trip is a visit to Camp Reynolds (also called West Garrison) on the island's southwest side. Established in 1863, Camp Reynolds was built to protect the Bay Area from Confederate sympathizers during the American Civil War. A dozen years later, it was used as a staging area for troops fighting various "wars" against Native Americans in the West. The camp remained in use by the military through World War II. You can walk its parade grounds and visit some of its remaining buildings, including a chapel, mule barn, hospital, and barracks.

Another important site is the old immigration station at China Cove, where Asian immigrants were detained for long, arduous periods in the years following World War I. This so-called "Ellis Island of the West" qualifies as the saddest chapter in Angel Island's history. During World War II, German, Italian, and Japanese prisoners of war were confined here.

My favorite side trip on Angel Island is the 0.5-mile walk to Perles Beach, a windy strip of sand with an amazing vista facing south toward Alcatraz and San Francisco. You'll find the turnoff for its dirt road at an overlook point above Battery Ledyard, where everyone stops on the roadside benches to admire the Golden Gate Bridge view. Another popular beach is Quarry Beach on the island's east side, which is larger, more protected from the wind, and better for sunbathing than Perles Beach.

Keep in mind that the weather can be fickle at Angel Island and the fog can come in on a moment's notice. Come prepared with an extra jacket, even on sunny days. A pleasant bonus for day hikers is that if you didn't bother to pack a lunch, you can buy one at the café near the boat dock (closed in winter). The outside deck is inviting, but most likely you'll want to choose your own private picnic spot somewhere on the island.

Options

If you'd like to see more of Angel Island's panoramic views, you can hike an inner loop trail high above the Perimeter Trail. A dirt fire road circles the island's interior; connect to it via a trail by the fire station on the north side of the island, or by the single-track North Ridge Trail. Because the Upper Fire Road is situated higher in elevation, it doles out even more expansive views than Perimeter Trail. Upper Fire Road is a four-mile loop.

Directions

Ferry service to Angel Island is available from Tiburon, San Francisco, and Oakland/Alameda. For Tiburon departures, contact Tiburon Ferry, 415/435-2131, www.angelislandferry.com. For Oakland or Alameda departures, contact East Bay Ferry, 510/522-3300, www.eastbayferry.com. For San Francisco departures, contact Blue and Gold Fleet, 415/705-8200, www.blueandgoldfleet.com.

© KEVIN GONG

Views of passing freighters, Alcatraz, and downtown San Francisco can be seen from Angel Island's Perimeter Trail.

Information and Contact

Ferry fees and schedules vary according to your city of departure ($13.50–$18 per person, round-trip). All ferry fees include entrance to Angel Island State Park. Dogs are not allowed. Bikes are allowed on Perimeter Trail. A park map is available for $2 at the ferry landing on the island, or by free download at www.angelisland.org. A detailed map is available from Tom Harrison Maps, 415/456-7940, www.tomharrisonmaps.com (ask for the *Angel Island* map). For more information, contact Angel Island State Park, P.O. Box 318, Tiburon, CA 94920, 415/435-1915 or 415/435-5390, www.angelisland.org.

36 NORTH RIDGE AND SUNSET TRAIL LOOP
Angel Island State Park   BEST ☾

🏛 🌲 🚌

Level: Easy/Moderate   **Total Distance:** 4.5 miles round-trip

Hiking Time: 2 hours   **Elevation Change:** 780 feet

Summary: Visit the summit of Mount Livermore, the highest point on Angel Island, on this view-filled half-day hike.

You want to visit Angel Island, but you can't bear to hike on pavement? You don't like sharing the trail with bikers and you want a hikers-only path? No problem. There are two completely different ways to hike Angel Island: One path is on the wide, paved Perimeter Trail, which circumnavigates the island. The other path is the dirt and mostly single-track North Ridge and Sunset Trail Loop, which travels to the island's highest point, the summit of Mount Livermore. For the former, see *Perimeter Trail* listing in this chapter. For the North Ridge and Sunset Trail Loop, read on.

The hardest part of this trip is in the first 10 minutes after you get off the boat. While everyone else disembarks and heads to the right toward Ayala Cove and the island's concession stands (there's a café, bike and Segway rentals, tram tours, and more), you'll head the other way. North Ridge Trail starts on the north side of the ferry dock, just to the left of the restrooms. It begins with a quick, steep climb of more than 100 steps, leading past a couple of well-placed picnic tables (with a great view) and then up to the paved Perimeter Road.

Cross the road, pant a few times, then pick up North Ridge Trail on its far side. Now the path is more like a trail and less like a staircase. The single-track is well graded and alternates through sunny chaparral-covered slopes and a shady, fern-filled canopy of live oaks. At just over one mile up the trail, the path traverses the northern flank of Mount Livermore, passing a surprising grove of nonnative Monterey pines. Views widen as you climb, and Tiburon and Belvedere begin to fade into the distance.

Where North Ridge Trail junctions with Sunset Trail and the trail to the summit, bear right and follow the summit trail uphill. Climbing a 0.25-mile brings you to the hill's previously flat, but now pointed, 788-foot summit. How did Mount Livermore get its pointed peak? In 2002, California State Parks went to great effort and expense to replace the top 16 feet of the mountain, which had been shaved off to make room for a Nike missile base in the 1950s. They also got rid of the old, ugly road that led to the summit and put in this hiking trail with its much kinder grade. A few picnic tables are found at and just below the summit, as well as interpretive signs that point out the landmarks of the bay. What landmarks? These and more: Berkeley, Mount Diablo, San Leandro, Alameda, Mission Peak

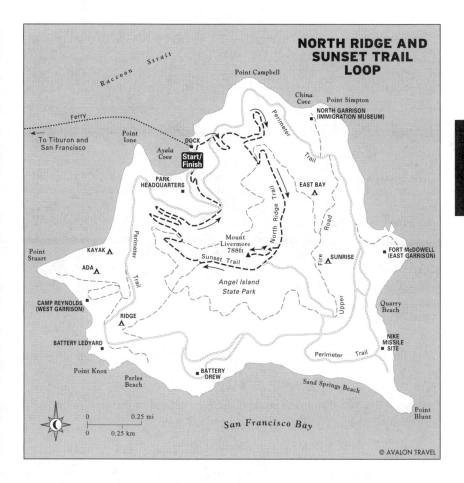

NORTH RIDGE AND
SUNSET TRAIL
LOOP

(38 miles away), Mount Hamilton (56 miles away), Santa Clara, Mountain View, San Francisco's Telegraph Hill, Alcatraz Island, Montara Mountain, Twin Peaks, the Golden Gate Bridge, Mount Tamalpais, Tiburon, Belvedere, San Quentin Prison, and Mount St. Helena in Napa (57 miles away).

With a view like that, it's not surprising that Mount Livermore's few picnic tables are in high demand on sunny weekend days. After you've lunched or just enjoyed the view, head back down the summit trail. Pick up Sunset Trail at the junction with North Ridge Trail, and enjoy another 0.5 mile of open views as you descend through the grasslands. The trail heads into a forest of oaks and bays, switchbacking gently downhill to another wide viewpoint and a crossing of Perimeter Road. You can follow the paved road back downhill to Ayala Cove, or take the forested single-track just to the right of it.

Highly observant hikers may notice evidence of a wildfire that burned more

© ANN MARIE BROWN

The summit of Mount Livermore rewards hikers with views of Tiburon, Belvedere, and San Pablo Bay.

than 400 acres here—more than half the island—in October 2008. But the vegetation has largely recovered, and now it takes a careful eye to discern the fire's path. Many oaks and pines were lost, but a fresh crop of chapparal and grasslands covered the earth in a vibrant green cloak. As is typical in the years following a wildfire, the spring wildflowers now bloom in full glory.

Options

One of the best ways to explore Angel Island is by spending the night at one of its backpacking camps. Advance reservations are required; phone 800/444-7275 or visit www.reserveamerica.com. Three popular sites are located at the Ridge camps on the west side of the island, where the views of San Francisco and the Golden Gate Bridge are divine, but the wind can howl. If you just want to make sure you sleep in a wind-protected spot, the East Bay campsites on the island's east side are the best choice. Other good options are the three east-side Sunrise camps, which offer great views of Treasure Island and the East Bay. However, because these sites are very close together, they are best suited for groups. All three camping areas require a hike of only 1–2 miles each way. Tables, food lockers, running water, pit toilets, and a barbecue are located at each site. No wood fires are allowed; you must bring charcoal or a backpacking stove.

Directions

Ferry service to Angel Island is available from Tiburon, San Francisco, and Oakland/Alameda. For Tiburon departures, contact Tiburon Ferry, 415/435-2131, www.angelislandferry.com. For Oakland or Alameda departures, contact East Bay Ferry, 510/522-3300, www.eastbayferry.com. For San Francisco departures, contact Blue and Gold Fleet, 415/705-8200, www.blueandgoldfleet.com.

Information and Contact

Ferry fees and schedules vary according to your city of departure ($13.50–$18 per person, round-trip). All ferry fees include entrance to Angel Island State Park. Dogs are not allowed. Bikes are allowed on the island, but not on this loop. A park map is available for $2 at the ferry landing on the island, or by free download at www.angelisland.org. A detailed map is available from Tom Harrison Maps, 415/456-7940, www.tomharrisonmaps.com (ask for the *Angel Island* map). For more information, contact Angel Island State Park, P.O. Box 318, Tiburon, CA 94920, 415/435-1915, www.angelisland.org.

EAST BAY

© ANN MARIE BROWN

BEST HIKES

If it's sun-filled days of hiking you seek, your best prospects in the San Francisco Bay Area are in the East Bay. Here, a bit farther from the ocean's influence, is the Bay Area's driest microclimate, where even the infamous summer fog rarely penetrates. The East Bay landscape is comprised of a mix of oak-dotted hills, grassy ridgelines, forested valleys, and rock-studded peaks. Each year, shortly after the winter rains, the grass-covered hills and ridges turn a brilliant green, then play host to myriad wildflowers for a too-brief blaze of color before the dry heat of summer turns the landscape gold, then brown.

Two major East Bay counties — Alameda and Contra Costa — are home to 2.5 million people, many of whom find escape from the region's ubiquitous freeways and office complexes in the lands managed by the East Bay Regional Park District (EBRPD). With more than 100,000 acres of land under its jurisdiction, the District's 65 separate parks and preserves contain a whopping 1,150 miles of trails. The EBRPD system comprises nearly a dozen freshwater lakes, 40 miles of Bay shoreline, two islands, and hundreds of acres of undeveloped inland hills and valleys. Running across the length of it is the East Bay Skyline National Trail, a 31-mile scenic route that was the first of its designation located outside of federal lands.

Each of the District's parklands is notable in its own right and boasts its own unique features. If you're a history buff, the ghost town sites and abandoned shafts at Black Diamond Mines Regional Preserve will tunnel your curiosity. Bird-watchers flock to the shores of San Francisco Bay at Coyote Hills Regional Park, while would-be sailors prefer the water views from the high grassland hills above Carquinez Strait. Geology fans won't want to miss a trip to Sibley Volcanic Regional Preserve, where they can explore an extinct volcano, or Las Trampas Regional Wilderness, where they can search for ancient clamshells embedded in the park's high rocky ridges. And for tree lovers, the dense groves of coastal redwoods at Redwood Regional Park are the East Bay's answer to more famous redwood parks around the Bay, like Muir Woods and Big Basin.

The state of California also has a hand in managing the East Bay's bountiful natural resources. Anchoring the northeast corner of the East Bay is mighty 3,849-foot Mount Diablo, the centerpiece of Mount Diablo State Park. While the mountain's amazing summit view is the park's claim to fame, Mount Diablo offers plenty more to enjoy, including the sedimentary rock formations of Rock City and the wintertime waterfalls of Donner Canyon. And due to some strategic land acquisitions in the 1980s and '90s, the state park is now part of a contiguous corridor of East Bay open space that includes Round Valley Regional Preserve, Morgan Territory Regional Preserve, Brushy Peaks Regional Preserve, and the Los Vaqueros Watershed – all of which are laced with myriad trails for our hiking pleasure.

Those unfamiliar with the East Bay's parklands might think of this region only as home to a spider's web of freeways with numbers that end in 80 and traffic-clogged cities like Oakland, Alameda, Concord, and Walnut Creek. But for those willing to lace up their boots and start walking, there is a surprising abundance of wild country to be found in the East Bay.

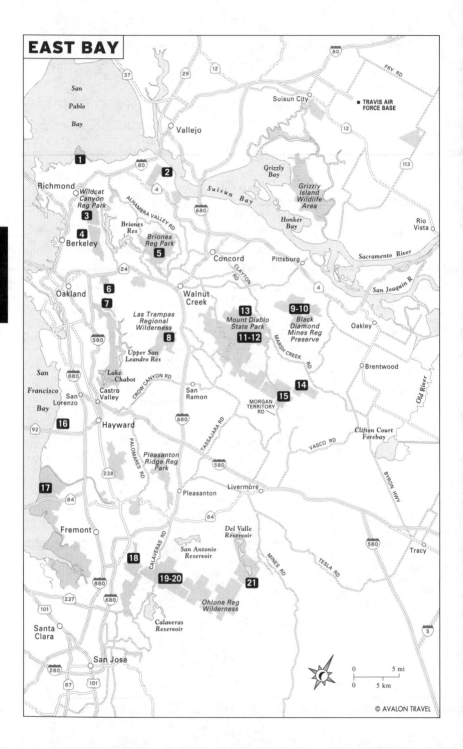

EAST BAY

TRAIL NAME	LEVEL	DISTANCE	TIME	ELEVATION	FEATURES	PAGE
1 Bay View Loop	Easy	5.0 mi rt	2.5 hr	Negligible	🖼️🥾🏊	214
2 Two Trails at Carquinez Strait	Easy	1.0–3.0 mi rt	1.0–2 hr	150 ft	🖼️🥾	217
3 San Pablo Ridge and Wildcat Creek Loop	Moderate	6.8 mi rt	3 hr	1,200 ft	🖼️🥾	221
4 Wildcat Peak and Laurel Canyon Loop	Easy	3.5 mi rt	1.5 hr	500 ft	🖼️🥾	224
5 Briones Loop Tour	Moderate	7.0 mi rt	4 hr	1,400 ft	🖼️🥾	227
6 Huckleberry Path	Easy	1.7 mi rt	1 hr	400 ft	🥾	231
7 Stream, Fern, and West Ridge Trail Loop	Easy/Moderate	4.8 mi rt	2.5 hr	700 ft	🖼️🥾	234
8 Rocky Ridge and Devil's Hole Loop	Moderate	6.8 mi rt	3.5 hr	1,200 ft	🖼️🥾	237
9 Rose Hill Cemetery Loop	Easy	2.5 mi rt	1 hr	400 ft	🥾	240
10 Stewartville and Ridge Trail Loop	Moderate	7.0 mi rt	3.5 hr	1,500 ft	🖼️🥾	243
11 Mount Diablo Grand Loop	Butt-Kicker	10.0 mi rt	5 hr	2,900 ft	🖼️🥾	247
12 Rock City and Wall Point Summit	Easy	3.5 mi rt	1.5 hr	500 ft	🖼️🥾	251
13 Back and Donner Canyon Loop	Moderate	7.0 mi rt	3.5 hr	1,100 ft	🖼️🥾	254
14 Round Valley Loop	Easy	6.0 mi rt	3 hr	200 ft	🥾	257
15 Morgan Territory Loop	Moderate	7.0 mi rt	3.5 hr	1,200 ft	🥾	260
16 Cogswell Marsh Trail	Easy	3.6 mi rt	1.5 hr	Negligible	🥾	263
17 Bayview and Red Hill Loop	Easy	4.8 mi rt	2.5 hr	200 ft	🥾	266
18 Mission Peak	Strenuous	6.6 mi rt	3.5 hr	2,000 ft	🖼️🥾	269
19 Sunol Loop Tour	Strenuous	7.5 mi rt	3.5 hr	1,800 ft	🥾	273
20 Maguire Peaks Loop	Moderate	5.5 mi rt	3 hr	800 ft	🥾	277
21 Murietta Falls	Butt-Kicker	12.0 mi rt	7 hr	3,500 ft	🥾	280

1 BAY VIEW LOOP
Point Pinole Regional Shoreline

Level: Easy

Total Distance: 5.0 miles round-trip

Hiking Time: 2.5 hours

Elevation Change: Negligible

Summary: Easy walking not far from East Bay cities leads to close-up bay views and a glimpse at Point Pinole's varied history.

Point Pinole Regional Shoreline is a little park with a big heart, a place of tranquility not far from the urban bustle of the East Bay. Few visitors other than avid anglers and dog walkers make the trip to the tip of Point Pinole, but those who do are surprised at this small park's varied offerings. In addition to inspiring bay views, a fascinating history, and good pier fishing, the park has volleyball courts, picnic areas, and more than 12 miles of winding dirt trails suitable for hiking or mountain biking.

Don't be put off by the drive into the park. Point Pinole Regional Shoreline has some odd neighbors, including Chevron's oil refineries and a juvenile detention center. The Southern Pacific Railroad runs right alongside the park. But once you're inside the gates of Point Pinole, all is peaceful. On two weekend visits here, we found the place largely deserted except for a few hikers, dog walkers, and bike riders.

Start your hike on the main paved trail by the entrance kiosk. You'll notice a small mound planted with flowers and a plaque denoting the site of the Giant Powder Company from 1892 to 1960. When terrible explosions ruined its Berkeley and San Francisco factories, Giant Powder moved to remote Point Pinole to manufacture dynamite. Here they built a thriving company town and local railway. More than two billion pounds of dynamite were produced here before the Regional Parks acquired the property in 1973.

Follow the paved road for 200 yards to

Point Pinole entices hikers with grass-lined trails that lead to blue bay waters.

© JOHN KLEINFELTER

a railroad bridge. Cross the bridge and take the signed trail on the left, Bay View Trail. The wide dirt trail skirts the edge of Point Pinole's peninsula and supplies continuous views of San Pablo Bay. To the southwest, plumes of gas and steam rise from Chevron's oil refineries. To the west, Mount Tamalpais looms over Marin County. In the foreground are miles of open bay water, interrupted only by the San Rafael–Richmond Bridge and East and West Brother Islands. A few duck blinds dot the shoreline. Seabirds gather on the mudflats during low tide.

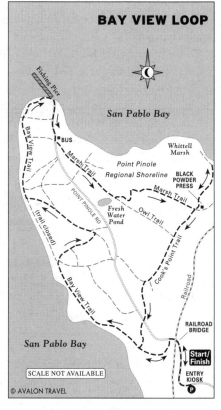

The path moves away from the bay and into a eucalyptus grove for a brief stretch, then returns to the meeting of land and sea. Just under two miles from the trailhead, the path curves around the tip of Point Pinole's peninsula to reach its 0.25-mile-long fishing pier. Walk out to the pier's end, then sit and sniff the salty air while you admire the views of Mount Diablo on your far right and Mount Tamalpais on your left. Look back toward shore and note the rugged coastal bluffs rising 100 feet above the bay. Point Pinole is the only place on this side of San Pablo Bay with shoreline cliffs; elsewhere the water is surrounded by flatlands.

The pier's Plexiglas shelters provide protection for anglers and hikers when the wind howls. If you're interested in fishing, note that you don't need a license to pier fish here. For those with luck, the catch may include sturgeon, striped bass, and kingfish.

From the pier, follow the paved road 100 yards south to a wooden bus shelter. (Shuttle buses ride this paved route from the parking lot to the pier every hour 7:30 A.M.–2:30 P.M. For $1, anglers who don't want to walk to the pier can catch a ride.) Beyond the bus shelter, take the signed Marsh Trail on the left. In just under 0.5 mile, a small pond appears on your right; turn left by the pond to stay on Marsh Trail.

Now facing eastward, your perspective on the bay is totally different. The Carquinez Bridge appears, as well as Vallejo and Napa. A large salt marsh lined with pickleweed borders the trail. The wide, gentle waters of San Pablo Bay remain constant.

At the junction of Marsh Trail and Cook's Point Trail is an odd structure sheltering a large hunk of metal. It's a black powder press remaining from the days of Giant Powder Company. Head past it on Marsh Trail to the edge of the bay, or make a short loop to the right along the shoreline if you wish. Bird-watching is usually rewarding near the salt marsh.

The return leg of the loop is Cook's Point Trail. This path will lead you all the way back to the park's picnic areas. From there it's a short stroll over the railroad bridge and back to your car.

Options

If you enjoy the bay shoreline at Point Pinole, check out the trails at Miller-Knox Regional Shoreline at Point Richmond, near the foot of the Richmond–San Rafael Bridge. (Access is off I-580 and Dornan Drive/Garrard Boulevard.) The park is well known for kite flying because of its consistent winds, and two loop trails provide hiking choices. On the bay side of the park, a one-mile loop circles a lagoon. On the inland side (across Dornan Drive), an access trail leads uphill to a two-mile loop on Old Country Road, West Ridge Trail, Crest Trail, and Marine View Trail. Don't miss a visit to False Gun Vista Point and East Vista Point—high knolls that offer views of the San Francisco skyline and Mount Tamalpais.

Directions

From I-80 in Richmond, exit at Richmond Parkway. Follow Richmond Parkway to the Giant Highway exit. Turn right and drive 0.75 mile to the park entrance on the left. Or, from U.S. 101 in Marin, take the Richmond–San Rafael Bridge east (I-580), then take the first exit east of the bridge, signed for Castro Street and Richmond Parkway. Drive 4.3 miles on Richmond Parkway to the Giant Highway exit. Take the exit and drive 0.5 mile, then turn right on Giant Highway. Drive 0.75 mile to the park entrance on the left.

Public transportation: AC Transit Bus #71 stops at the park entrance. For AC Transit information, phone 510/891-4700 or visit www.actransit.org.

Information and Contact

A $3 day-use fee is charged per vehicle on weekends and holidays. Leashed dogs are allowed ($2 dog fee) except on the pier. Bikes are allowed. A free map is available at the entrance kiosk or by download at www.ebparks.org. For more information, contact East Bay Regional Park District, 2950 Peralta Oaks Court, P.O. Box 5381, Oakland, CA 94605, 888/327-2757, www.ebparks.org.

2 TWO TRAILS AT CARQUINEZ STRAIT

Carquinez Strait Regional Shoreline

🏕 🌸 🐕 🚻 🚌

Level: Easy

Total Distance: 1.0–3.0 miles round-trip

Hiking Time: 1–2 hours

Elevation Change: 150 feet

Summary: Two appealing trail segments explore the grassland bluffs bordering the narrow waterway between San Pablo and Suisun Bays.

Although San Francisco Bay and San Pablo Bay are as familiar as the local freeways to most Bay Area residents, the waterway at Carquinez Strait is far less known. Even the name "Carquinez Strait" sounds foreign and exotic. The northeastern arm of the conglomeration of waterways that constitute the bay and river delta, Carquinez Strait forms the narrow passageway between San Pablo and Suisun Bays. It's the meeting place of the Sacramento and San Joaquin Rivers, where they join together to flow to the Pacific Ocean through the Golden Gate.

The bluffs above Carquinez Strait are a wonderful place for an easy hike. Carquinez Strait Regional Shoreline encompasses 1,415 acres of land on the strait's south side. The park's main two parcels are located along Carquinez Scenic Drive near the cities of Crockett and Martinez. Both areas have pleasant trails to explore and plentiful scenery along the waterway. Unfortunately, they aren't contiguous, because the middle section of Carquinez Scenic Drive washed out in a landslide in

Benches found along the Carquinez Strait bluffs make view-filled resting spots.

1982. So the people of Martinez have one slice of the bluffs above Carquinez Strait and the people of Crockett have a separate slice. Both are worth a visit.

To see the western area of the park, drive to the Bull Valley Staging Area near Crockett, just a few miles from the Carquinez Bridge. From the parking lot, take the trail at the cattle gate by the portable toilet. Head east along the grassy bluffs, which are littered with owl's clover every spring. The green hills lie in sharp contrast to the bright blue of the strait. You may hear the sound of a commuter train roaring past on the tracks that hug the shoreline, or the horn of a tugboat working the waterway. Part of the joy of this walk is watching the ships, large and small, journey in and out of the strait. You might see anything from a windsurfer to a freighter.

Where the wide double-track trail forks, bear left and walk through a planted eucalyptus grove until your view of the strait is unobstructed again. At a second junction, bear left again; the right fork is the return of a short loop through a eucalyptus grove. You might skip the loop and walk back the way you came; the views of the strait are well worth a second look. At points, you'll find a few well-positioned benches and picnic tables with wide views to the north, east, and south. Benicia State Recreation Area is visible across the strait, as well as the houses and businesses of the town of Benicia, but what captures your attention is the wide expanse of blue waterway.

Consider the story of Carquinez Strait. Hundreds of thousands of king salmon once passed through here on their way to the Sacramento and San Joaquin Rivers to spawn. Native Americans lived off their abundance for centuries. In the 1800s, white settlers set up commercial fishing operations and canneries along the strait. Salmon ran the economy of this area until the mid-20th century, when laws were passed that banned all commercial fishing east of the Carquinez Bridge. Although this was a great victory for the conservation movement and the future of fish populations, it made ghost towns of the once bustling communities along Carquinez Strait.

To see the eastern area of the park, drive to the Carquinez Strait East Staging Area in Martinez. Follow the Hulet Hornbeck Trail from the far end of the equestrian parking lot (don't take the Rankin Park Trail from the left side of the lot). You'll head uphill through a shady ravine filled with oaks, bays, and eucalyptus. In 0.3 mile, turn left and walk the two-mile Franklin Ridge Loop. You'll leave the

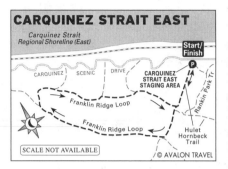

CARQUINEZ STRAIT EAST

trees in the canyon below; up on the ridge, native grasslands sway and dance in the breeze and raptors soar overhead. Lucky hikers may spot a bobcat or fox as it darts across the trail. From atop Franklin Ridge, you can see Mount Tamalpais to the west and Mount Diablo to the east, plus the grassy ridges of Briones and Las Trampas Regional Parks to the south. Combined with the long blue stretch of Carquinez Strait to the north, the overall effect is stunning.

Options

Another trail to hike in the Martinez area is the Mount Wanda Trail near the John Muir National Historic Site. The trail leads from an entrance gate near the Park and Ride lot on Franklin Canyon Road and Alhambra Avenue. It is a one-mile uphill trek to the two highest points in the park, Mount Wanda at 660 feet and Mount Helen at 640 feet, named for Muir's two daughters. Muir often took the girls on outings in this part of his ranch to teach them about the natural world. Pick a cool day to visit (temperatures frequently rise above 100°F here in the summer). Or sign up for one of the ranger-led full moon hikes, which are held June–September (see www.nps.gov/jomu for details).

Directions

For the Crockett trailhead: From Highway 4 west of Martinez, exit at Cummings Skyway. Turn right on Crockett Boulevard, then right again on Pomona Street. As you head east, Pomona Street becomes Carquinez Scenic Drive. Continue two miles to the Bull Valley Staging Area on the left. (If you are coming from I-80, exit on San Pablo Avenue or Pomona Street in Crockett and follow Pomona Street east as described.)

For the Martinez trailhead: From Highway 4 in Martinez, take the Alhambra Avenue exit and drive north through Martinez for two miles. Turn left on Escobar Street, drive three blocks, then turn right on Talbart Street, which becomes Carquinez Scenic Drive. Drive 0.4 mile to the Nejedly Staging Area on the right. Begin hiking on the Hulet Hornbeck Trail from the far end of the horse trailer parking lot.

Public transportation to the Martinez trailhead (Nejedly Staging Area): County Connection Bus #116 runs from Pleasant Hill BART. County Connection Buses

#108 and #118 run from Concord BART. All buses stop at the Park and Ride lot on Alhambra Avenue in Martinez. Walk the final 0.5 mile to the trailhead by following the driving directions described earlier. For more information, phone 925/676-7500 or visit www.cccta.org.

Information and Contact

There is no fee. Leashed dogs and bikes are allowed. Free trail maps are available at the entrance kiosk or by download at www.ebparks.org. For more information, contact East Bay Regional Park District, 2950 Peralta Oaks Court, P.O. Box 5381, Oakland, CA 94605, 925/228-0112 or 888/327-2757, www.ebparks.org.

3 SAN PABLO RIDGE AND WILDCAT CREEK LOOP

Wildcat Canyon Regional Park

🏕 🛶 🌿 🐴 🚌

Level: Moderate

Hiking Time: 3 hours

Total Distance: 6.8 miles round-trip

Elevation Change: 1,200 feet

Summary: Enjoy rolling hills, waving grasslands, and wide-angle views of the bay.

Never judge a trail by its trailhead, sage hikers say. When you park your car at Wildcat Canyon Regional Park's Alvarado staging area, you'll think, "Aha, a forested hike through eucalyptus and oaks." But looks are deceiving at Wildcat Canyon. What begins as a tree-shaded paved trail quickly becomes a dirt path through the grasslands that takes you up 1,000 feet for wide views of the San Francisco Bay Area.

Begin your hike by walking 0.5 mile on Wildcat Creek Trail, an old paved road that begins on the east side of the parking lot. At the trail sign for Belgum Trail, turn left and begin climbing up the grassy hillside. The wide dirt path makes a moderate ascent, passing two stately palm trees that mark an old homestead. The surrounding hills are dotted with nonnative purple thistles, which in autumn and winter bear dried, puffy pom-poms. They grow as tall as four feet high. Several slopes at Wildcat Canyon are covered with entire armies of them; their spine-

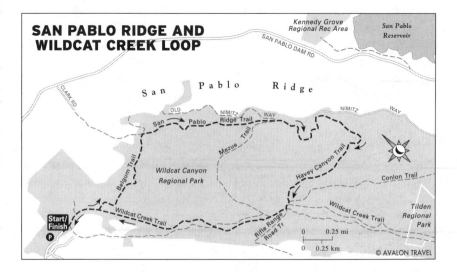

SAN PABLO RIDGE AND WILDCAT CREEK LOOP

© AVALON TRAVEL

San Pablo Ridge offers views of the East Bay, San Francisco, and beyond.

tipped leaves provide thorough protection against grazing cattle. In spring, you'll find big yellow mule's ears and plenty of blue-eyed grass.

Keep looking over your right shoulder as you hike. In short order you'll gain enough elevation to be rewarded with wide-angle views of the San Francisco Bay Area, from Vallejo to San Francisco and the southern East Bay. On a clear day, it's fun to pick out all the famous landmarks: Bay Bridge, Transamerica Pyramid, Twin Peaks, Golden Gate Bridge, Angel Island, and so on. (When it comes to views, I've always preferred a sea of conifers to a sea of civilization. Still, this vista—truly an urban view—makes a lasting and memorable impression.)

In less than a mile, Belgum Trail meets up with a junction of several trails, both formal and informal. Bear left to stay on Belgum Trail (don't take the hard left on Clark-Boas Trail). After curving around the north side of a grassy hill, turn right on San Pablo Ridge Trail. The short climb that follows is memorably steep. But once you complete it, you've gained San Pablo Ridge and the rest of the walk is an easy cruise.

No matter how calm and warm it was when you started your hike, it's likely to be windy on top of the ridge. Numerous raptors and songbirds, including red-winged blackbirds, take advantage of the lofty breezes up here.

You just cruise along, stopping when you feel like it to enjoy the sights from your top-of-the-ridge perch. At a cattle gate, the trail turns from dirt to pavement. You're leaving San Pablo Ridge Trail and following Nimitz Way Trail, a paved path that is popular with bicyclists and hikers. (Most of them access the trail from Inspiration Point in Tilden Regional Park.) The trail hugs the ridge top, and the vistas keep changing with every footstep. There's San Pablo Reservoir and Briones Reservoir behind it, plus looming Mount Diablo, all on your left. Then there's San

Francisco Bay, the Golden Gate Bridge, and Angel Island on your right. At every turn in the trail, over every hill, you get a slightly different twist on the view. The Richmond Bridge drops into sight, the Gold Coast comes into frame up ahead, then San Francisco disappears and the Brother Islands come into view. Suddenly Napa and Carquinez show up to the north. And so it goes.

After 0.75 mile on paved Nimitz Way, turn right on Havey Canyon Trail. The path narrows as it descends, closely following a spring-fed stream. You'll leave the sunshine and wide open grasslands for a forest of willows, oaks, bay laurel, and a plethora of vines. The trail drops gently over 1.5 miles, never leaving the canopy of shade until it bottoms out at Wildcat Creek Trail. Turn right to finish out your loop, walking a level 1.5 miles back to your car.

Options
Northeast of Wildcat Canyon Regional Park lies Sobrante Ridge Regional Preserve (access is off Castro Ranch Road in El Sobrante). From the trailhead staging area, follow Sobrante Ridge Trail as it curves around the ridge, then heads due south. In addition to enjoying the expansive ridge-top views, you should take two short side trips: one on the tiny Broken Oak Trail Loop, and the other on Manzanita Trail to access the short Manzanita Loop. Sobrante Ridge is home to one of the last stands of the rare and endangered Alameda manzanita, a chaparral-type shrub, and this loop leads through a large grove of it. The out-and-back trip, including the Manzanita Loop, is 2.4 miles.

Directions
From I-80 heading north in Richmond, take the Amador/Solano exit and drive three blocks east on Amador. Turn right on McBryde Avenue and drive 0.5 mile to the entrance to Wildcat Canyon Regional Park. (Bear left where the road forks.) The trail begins on the far side of the parking lot and is paved at the start. (Heading south on I-80, take the McBryde Avenue exit and go east.)

Public transportation: AC Transit Bus #68 stops at McBryde Avenue and Arlington Boulevard. Walk uphill on McBryde Avenue a short distance to the park entrance. For AC Transit information, phone 510/891-4700 or visit www.ac-transit.org.

Information and Contact
There is no fee. Leashed dogs and bikes are allowed. Free trail maps are available at the parking area or by download at www.ebparks.org. For more information, contact East Bay Regional Park District, 2950 Peralta Oaks Court, P.O. Box 5381, Oakland, CA 94605, 510/236-1262 or 888/327-2757, www.ebparks.org.

4 WILDCAT PEAK AND LAUREL CANYON LOOP

BEST [C]

Tilden Regional Park

Level: Easy

Total Distance: 3.5 miles round-trip

Hiking Time: 1.5 hours

Elevation Change: 500 feet

Summary: This easy trail to the summit of Wildcat Peak makes a perfect leg-stretching hike for a Sunday afternoon.

Most people think of Tilden Park as a place to take the kids. The park has pony rides, a carousel, a miniature train, a swimming beach at Lake Anza, and lots of other diversions that keep children occupied and happy. But over on the northwest edge of the park lies the Tilden Nature Area, a very different part of Tilden Park. Here the only amenities are trail signs and the only diversions are the natural beauty and the views.

Start your trip at the Tilden Environmental Education Center at the northwest end of Central Park Drive. Take a look around this marvelous visitors center, then walk out its back door to access Laurel Canyon Trail. Its trailhead is located to the left of Little Farm and to the right of Jewel Lake Nature Trail. Oddly, Laurel Canyon Trail isn't signed with its name, but with a symbol: a narrow bay laurel leaf and a berry. You'll follow these iconographic trail markers through several junctions.

Start hiking gently uphill through a eucalyptus grove. The narrow, well-built trail dips and rolls, gaining elevation very slowly. In the rainy season, Laurel Creek runs nearby, making delightful water music. You'll reach several junctions in the first 0.5 mile, but just keep following the laurel leaf symbols. The path departs the eucalyptus and enters a dense grove of canyon oaks and bay laurels. Leaves crunch underfoot as you tunnel your way through the forest. Where the trees open up, look up to your left and you'll spot your destination: Wildcat Peak.

A mile up the trail, take the trail fork signed to Nimitz Way. Where Laurel Canyon Trail tops out at a wide dirt road (Laurel Canyon Road), turn right and continue uphill for a short distance to Nimitz Way. This paved multiuse trail runs along the ridge top from Inspiration Point in Tilden Regional Park to Wildcat Canyon Regional Park. It's one of the East Bay's greatest bicycle trails. Turn left and follow Nimitz Way for just under 0.5 mile, then turn left on Wildcat Peak Trail. The dirt trail makes a 0.5-mile climb to the summit of Wildcat Peak, elevation 1,250 feet. (This is the steepest section of the loop, but even so, it's quite easy.)

Wildcat Peak's summit vista is surprising. From the stone overlook platform on top, you can see all of San Pablo Reservoir, the edge of Briones Reservoir, and mighty Mount Diablo to the east. San Pablo Bay appears to the north. To the west, you gain a wide view of famous landmarks. San Francisco Bay sparkles in the sunlight. Mount Tamalpais, Angel Island, the Golden Gate Bridge, the Richmond Bridge, the Bay Bridge, and downtown San Francisco are easily recognizable. You're directly across from Brooks Island, a large, flat island south of Richmond that was once owned by a private hunting club and is now managed by the East Bay Regional Park District.

Wildcat Peak's stone overlook is marked with a sign denoting the Rotary Peace Grove below, a living memorial of giant sequoia trees dedicated to people who have worked for world peace. The grove was a joint project between the Rotary Club of Berkeley and the East Bay Regional Park District.

From Wildcat Peak, head back downhill on Wildcat Peak Trail (its trail signs are marked with a rounded peak). The path descends open, grassy slopes. When

© ANN MARIE BROWN

San Pablo Reservoir as seen from Wildcat Peak

you reach Sylvan Trail (marked with three trees), turn left. Follow Sylvan Trail through a eucalyptus grove back to the visitors center.

Options
The best spring wildflower trail in Tilden Regional Park is Sea View Trail. Even if you miss the flower show, the wide and easy trail is pleasant in any season because it travels along a high ridgeline, affording marvelous views. Most of the flowers are easily identified, common varieties: mule's ears, California poppies, silver bush lupine, California buttercups, and checkerbloom. Hike out as far as you like and back; a suggested destination is a picnic table on a high knoll with a sweeping, 360-degree view, about two miles from the start. The trailhead for Sea View Trail is on Lomas Cantadas, just off Grizzly Peak Boulevard, by Tilden Park's steam trains.

Directions
From I-580 in Berkeley, take the University Avenue exit and go east. Drive two miles to Oxford Street and turn left. Drive 0.5 mile to Rose Street and turn right. Drive one block and turn left on Spruce Street. Drive 1.7 miles on Spruce Street. Immediately after crossing Grizzly Peak Boulevard, turn left on Canon Drive. Drive 0.5 mile and turn left on Central Park Drive. Follow Central Park Drive for 0.25 mile to its end by the Tilden Nature Area and Environmental Education Center. The trail begins behind the education center.

Public transportation: On weekends and holidays, AC Transit Bus #67 stops at the Environmental Education Center. On weekdays, you must disembark at Spruce Street and Grizzly Peak Boulevard, then walk northeast on Canon Drive 0.25 mile to enter the park. For AC Transit information, phone 510/891-4700 or visit www.actransit.org.

Information and Contact
There is no fee. Dogs and bikes are not allowed. A free map is available at the visitors center or by download at www.ebparks.org. For more information, contact Tilden Regional Park at 510/544-2233. Or contact East Bay Regional Park District, 2950 Peralta Oaks Court, P.O. Box 5381, Oakland, CA 94605, 888/327-2757, www.ebparks.org.

5 BRIONES LOOP TOUR
Briones Regional Park

🏕️ 🌸 🥾 🐕

Level: Moderate

Hiking Time: 4 hours

Total Distance: 7.0 miles round-trip

Elevation Change: 1,400 feet

Summary: This pastoral loop hike in Briones' less-visited northern section leads past a miniature waterfall, two duck ponds, and miles of cow-populated grasslands.

Briones Regional Park is more than 6,000 acres of grasslands and oaks that were once part of Rancho San Felipe, a Spanish land grant. In the mid-1800s, this was an important fruit-growing region. Today it's the grassy home of grazing cows and frequently visited by hikers, mountain bikers, dog walkers, and horseback riders.

I wouldn't want to be accused of overselling Briones. Its sunny exposure, wide dirt roads, and large expanse of open grasslands are perhaps better suited to bikers and equestrians than to hikers. But on a breezy spring day when the wildflowers are blooming and the grasslands are glowing green, well, it wouldn't be hard to wax poetic about the place. And considering the fact that Briones is bordered on three sides by freeways—Highway 4, I-680, and Highway 24—it's a miracle that this giant open space even exists. For residents of Martinez, Concord, Pleasant

© KEVIN GONG

From the top of Briones Peak, you can enjoy the view of Mount Diablo or just take a nap.

Hill, Walnut Creek, and Lafayette, Briones is only a stone's throw away and a welcome vacation from urban life.

Briones has three main staging areas—Bear Creek, Alhambra Creek, and Lafayette Ridge—but this loop hike starts at a less developed trailhead at the end of Briones Road. As the crow flies, it's only about a mile from the Alhambra Creek Staging Area, but it's much higher in elevation. Your car does some of the climbing for you. Also, no fee is charged at the Briones Road trailhead.

Start your hike on Old Briones Road, a gated dirt road that leads from the parking area. The initial stretch heads through a dense grove of canyon oaks. In autumn, their leaves turn bright gold and capture the low afternoon sun. In just over 0.5 mile of gentle climbing, you'll reach a hiker's gate and leave the trees behind.

It's a different world on the other side of the gate—wide open expanses of grasslands with an occasional cluster of cows adding variety to the scene. At a junction with Spengler Trail, bear right to stay on Old Briones Road. You'll pass two small ponds, whimsically named Maricich Lagoons. They are naturally occurring vernal pools. One-third of a mile farther brings you to another junction; bear right on Briones Crest Trail. (You might consider going straight uphill for 100 yards to a gate with a lovely view of the valley below.)

Briones Crest Trail leads you past Sindicich Lagoons—two more vernal pools, one on either side of the trail. As the dirt road begins to climb, you gain views to the north of Carquinez Strait, Suisun Bay, San Pablo Bay, and the Benicia–Martinez Bridge. The industrial waterfront of Martinez lies in the foreground. Hey, what are all those ships lined up down there? That's the "Mothball Fleet"—old military ships that have been put out to pasture. Also in sight are the oil refineries along Contra Costa County's shoreline, often referred to as the Oil Coast.

At 1.5 miles, Briones Crest Trail joins with Mott Peak Trail. Bear left, descend a bit, then leave the trail and hike uphill to the summit of Mott Peak, elevation 1,424 feet. (It's not the high hill lined with a fence; it's the one beside it to the west.) A climb to Mott Peak's grassy summit produces a 360-degree vista. In addition to views of Suisun Bay, Carquinez Strait, and smaller waterways to the north, the panorama includes miles of open parkland to the south and west, framed by the distant outline of Mount Tamalpais. Ever-present Mount Diablo towers over the eastern scenery, which includes the suburbs of Concord and Walnut Creek.

Mott Peak isn't the highest point in the park; Briones Peak is 60 feet higher. But Mott Peak is a balder summit and offers a better view. It was named for William Penn Mott, champion of parks. During Mott's long career, he worked as the general manager of the East Bay Regional Park District, then as director of California State Parks, and finally as director of the National Park Service.

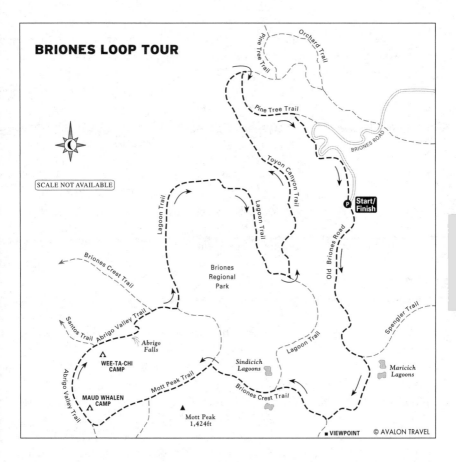

When you've seen enough, return to Mott Peak Trail and head west, meeting up with Abrigo Valley Trail in 0.5 mile. In winter, the cheerful presence of Abrigo Creek is a welcome sight. Turn right and pass two campgrounds, Maud Whalen and Wee-Ta-Chi. Pay close attention to the creek just beyond Wee-Ta-Chi Camp. Look and listen carefully and you may spot Abrigo Falls dropping 15 feet over a rock face into a narrow, cave-like canyon. The waterfall is nearly hidden, and if the stream isn't flowing strong, it can be difficult to spot. It's located at the point where the trail makes a short, steep climb. (Where the trail makes a hairpin turn to the left and moves away from the creek, you've passed it.)

Continue another 0.25 mile to Abrigo Valley Trail's junction with Briones Crest Trail; bear right and then left shortly thereafter on Lagoon Trail. Follow Lagoon Trail for 1.2 miles, looping around to Toyon Canyon Trail. You'll enter a live oak forest, a nice change of pace from the sunshine and grasslands. Turn left on Toyon Canyon Trail and continue gently downhill for one mile, then turn right on Pine Tree Trail. You'll have to climb a bit to finish out the loop. When you see the paved road you drove in on, follow the single-track trail that parallels it back to the parking area and your car.

Options

To see Abrigo Falls via a shortcut, or to start your Briones trip from a different trailhead, head for the Bear Creek Staging Area off Happy Valley Road and Bear Creek Road. When the kiosk is staffed, there's a $3 fee per vehicle. Walk an easy 1.3 miles up the dirt road that is Abrigo Valley Trail to find Abrigo Falls. A half-mile farther, Abrigo Valley Trail meets up with the Briones Crest Trail. Turn right and hike for 0.5 mile along Briones Crest for stellar views of Mount Diablo, Suisun Bay, San Pablo Bay, and Point Pinole. Then retrace your steps or loop back on Mott Peak Trail for a four-mile round-trip.

Directions

From Highway 4 in Martinez, take the Alhambra Avenue exit. Turn south on Alhambra Avenue, drive 0.5 mile and bear right on Alhambra Valley Road. Drive 1.2 miles, then turn right to stay on Alhambra Valley Road. In about 75 yards, turn left on Briones Road and continue 1.5 miles to the trailhead.

Information and Contact

There is no fee at the Briones Road trailhead. Leashed dogs and bikes are allowed. Free trail maps are available at the entrance kiosk or by download at www.ebparks.org. For more information, contact East Bay Regional Park District, 2950 Peralta Oaks Court, P.O. Box 5381, Oakland, CA 94605, 888/327-2757, www.ebparks.org.

6 HUCKLEBERRY PATH

Huckleberry Botanic Regional Preserve

Level: Easy

Hiking Time: 1 hour

Total Distance: 1.7 miles round-trip

Elevation Change: 400 feet

Summary: A peaceful trail in the Berkeley hills shaded by a dense tree canopy and filled with plants of ecological interest.

Trailheads along Skyline Boulevard in the Berkeley hills are about as common as the million-dollar houses clinging to steep hillsides. Home to several regional parks and a large section of the 31-mile East Bay Skyline National Trail, Skyline Boulevard is a weekend recreationist's paradise. Mountain bikers, dog walkers, runners, hikers—everybody finds a trail to suit their desires.

This being the case, your chance of finding solitude anywhere in these parks on a Saturday or Sunday is next to nil. Parking lots usually fill up before noon at Sibley Volcanic Regional Preserve and Skyline Gate at Redwood Regional Park. Late arrivals must squeeze into pullouts along the road.

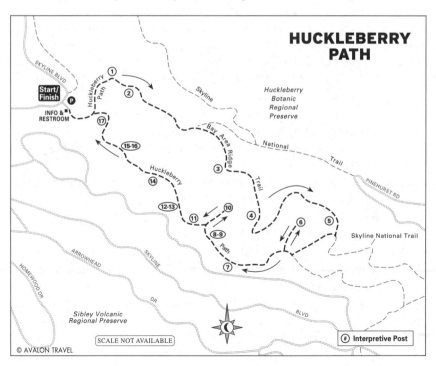

But one park on Skyline Boulevard presents a greater chance for peace and quiet (plus a parking space): Huckleberry Botanic Regional Preserve. Unlike its neighboring parks, Huckleberry is designated for hikers only. No bikes, horses, or dogs are allowed; this reduces the number of visitors dramatically. Even joggers are discouraged. People come here because they are serious about one thing: nature.

The park is home to a large number of native plants that are extremely rare in the East Bay, plus some that are extremely rare, period. Even hikers who know nothing about botany will appreciate one obvious fact: Unlike most of the East Bay Regional Parks, there aren't any eucalyptus trees here.

The main trail is called simply Huckleberry Path, and it's a well-built, narrow, meandering footpath that weaves its way through dense foliage. A self-guided trail brochure is available for free at the trailhead; it corresponds to numbered posts along the path. Unless you're a botanist by trade, carrying a brochure will greatly enhance your experience at the preserve.

Huckleberry Path is a loop with a total distance of only 1.7 miles. (To hike the loop in the proper direction, bear left at the first junction.) At 0.5 mile, stay right to continue on the Huckleberry Path as it merges with the Bay Area Ridge Trail. After interpretive post 5, bear right to continue on the Huckleberry Path back to the trailhead. You can easily tack on another 0.75 mile to the loop, where the trail connects with a trailhead at Pinehurst Road. Or, since part of the Huckleberry Path is the East Bay Skyline National Recreation Trail, you can take the Skyline National Trail northward to Sibley Preserve (about two miles) or southward to Redwood Regional Park (one mile).

Take your pick of the add-on trails or simply choose to linger within the boundaries of Huckleberry. Stay for a while at the sunny, manzanita-lined overlook by interpretive post 6, where the view of Mount Diablo is inspiring. Or take time to study or photograph the preserve's rare plants, such as western leatherwood (look for leathery branches and bright yellow flowers December–March), and tall pallid manzanita with its delicate, pink, bell-like blossoms. Or perhaps best of all, time your trip so you can sample the preserve's namesake huckleberries, which fruit in late summer and early fall.

Any season is a good time to visit this preserve. The trail is completely shaded by long-limbed bay laurels plus some madrones and oaks, so it remains cool even in the heat of summer. Plentiful sword and wood ferns "green up" and come to life after winter rains. Spring wildflowers are always worth a special visit; look for purple Douglas iris in the early months and orange bush monkeyflower as summer approaches.

Many types of ferns can be found in the shady regions of Huckleberry Regional Preserve.

© ANN MARIE BROWN

Options

Only a short drive north from Huckleberry Preserve is Sibley Volcanic Regional Preserve, off Skyline Boulevard. This park is the home of Mount Round Top, an ancient volcano that was the source of most of the lava rock found in the ridges of the East Bay hills. The two-mile Round Top Loop Trail and Volcanic Trail are keyed to an interpretive brochure that explains the various geological features to be seen.

Directions

From Highway 24 near Orinda, take the Fish Ranch Road exit immediately east of the Caldecott Tunnel. (You must be in the right lane as you exit the tunnel.) Drive one mile northwest on Fish Ranch Road to Grizzly Peak Boulevard. Turn left and drive 2.4 miles to Skyline Boulevard. Turn left and drive 0.5 mile to the park entrance on the left (past Sibley Volcanic Regional Preserve).

Alternatively, from I-580 in Oakland, take the Park Blvd. exit; turn north and drive for about 2 miles to the intersection with Mountain Blvd. Turn left on Mountain Blvd., then right on Snake Rd. Follow Snake Rd. for 2 miles to Skyline Blvd. Turn left on Skyline and drive 0.25 mile to the park entrance and lot on the right.

Public transportation: AC Transit Bus #59A runs from 19th Street BART and Lake Merritt BART to the Montclair Transit Center. From there, AC Transit Bus #5 runs to Colton Boulevard and Ridgewood Drive. Walk from Colton Boulevard north to Skyline Boulevard, then turn left and head to the park (total 0.5-mile walk). For AC Transit information, phone 510/891-4700 or visit www.actransit.org.

Information and Contact

There is no fee. Dogs and bikes are not allowed. Free trail maps are available at the entrance kiosk or by download at www.ebparks.org. For more information, contact East Bay Regional Park District, 2950 Peralta Oaks Court, P.O. Box 5381, Oakland, CA 94605, 888/327-2757, www.ebparks.org.

7 STREAM, FERN, AND WEST RIDGE TRAIL LOOP

BEST ℂ

Redwood Regional Park

🏃 🐕 🚌

Level: Easy/Moderate

Total Distance: 4.8 miles round-trip

Hiking Time: 2.5 hours

Elevation Change: 700 feet

Summary: The East Bay's answer to Muir Woods and Big Basin are the prized redwoods of Redwood Regional Park.

Cathedral redwoods, also known as fairy rings, are found at Redwood Regional Preserve.

© ANN MARIE BROWN

They don't call this place Redwood Regional Park for nothing. The dark, shaggy-barked trees grow more than 100 feet tall and their shady canopy covers a vast expanse of the park. A walk among these lofty trees is the perfect antidote to too much time spent in Emeryville office buildings or on East Bay freeways.

The redwoods here aren't first growth. Rather, they are the second-generation offspring of the original trees that once towered over this canyon. Between 1840 and 1860, logging companies constructed lumber mills and mill workers built shantytowns in what is now Redwood Regional Park. They logged the virgin redwoods to provide lumber for the growing cities of San Francisco and San Jose. In 20 years, all the giant trees in a five-square-mile area were felled.

Some botanists believe this grove's original redwoods may have been the largest the world has ever known. The massive trees were used as navigational guides by ships sailing into San Francisco Bay before the construction of lighthouses. Located high on a ridge 16 miles from the Golden Gate, the redwoods were prominent enough to steer sailors away from Blossom Rock, submerged in the bay between Alcatraz and San Francisco. (The actual "landmark trees" were located in what is now Roberts Regional Recreation Area, next door to Redwood Park. The site is denoted by a state historic plaque.)

The redwoods aren't the only prizes of Redwood Regional Park. Redwood Creek,

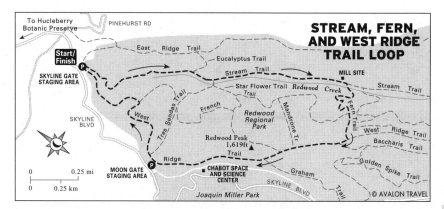

which bisects the park, is home to rainbow trout that are descendants of the original, pure strain of rainbows—the ones the species is named after. In addition, the park is bordered by two high ridges to the east and west. Both afford expansive views.

Start your trip at the Skyline Gate Staging Area on Skyline Boulevard. Three trails lead from the parking lot—East Ridge, Stream, and West Ridge. You'll start on Stream Trail and return on West Ridge Trail.

Stream Trail, a wide fire road that is closed to bikes, makes a quick drop from the trailhead. The first 0.75 mile is a mellow, shaded descent through a mixed forest of oaks, madrones, ferns, and huckleberries, punctuated by occasional tall eucalyptus. Farther downhill you enter a redwood grove and remain under the spell of the big trees for a long, dreamy stretch. In the rainy season, the sight and sound of splashing Redwood Creek enlivens the dark canyon. A split-rail fence lines the stream's bank; it's an attempt to keep people, dogs, and horses away from the fragile riparian habitat.

At 1.5 miles, you'll pass two camping and picnicking areas in a row—Mill Site on the left and Fern Hut on the right. (The camps' stone buildings were built by the Works Progress Administration in the 1930s.) A few feet past Fern Hut is the right turnoff for Fern Trail. Follow it steeply uphill. A half-mile of heavy breathing will bring you to West Ridge Trail; turn right again.

What's this, sunshine? Yes indeed. After a long stretch of shaded greenery, the trail opens out on sunny West Ridge. Hike northwest, climbing a bit more. An interesting side trip is possible 0.5 mile out on the ridge. Take the right fork, then the left fork immediately following, to hike up to the top of Redwood Peak, elevation 1,619 feet. As you might guess from its name, you won't get much of a summit view. The redwoods hide most everything except for a glimpse northeast toward Moraga and San Leandro Reservoir. But the peak is littered with interesting sandstone boulders. Under the canopy of redwoods, the rocks make fine seats for lunch or quiet contemplation.

Backtrack to West Ridge Trail. Heading northwest, you'll pass the edge of the archery range in Roberts Recreation Area. The path climbs a bit farther to a eucalyptus grove, then suddenly a surprising vista of Oakland, San Francisco, and the bay appears. Depending on the day's visibility, this can be a breathtaking sight. The tall buildings of Oakland and San Francisco appear amazingly close. The bay's bridges look like delightful miniatures in a train set.

West Ridge Trail's final stretch passes by the observatory at the worthwhile Chabot Space & Science Center (10000 Skyline Blvd., 510/336-7300, www.chabotspace.org, Wed.–Thurs. 10 A.M.–5 P.M., Fri.–Sat. 10 A.M.–10 P.M., Sun. 11 A.M.–5 P.M., $14.95 admission). The last mile is a delightfully easy cruise back to Skyline Gate through a shady forest of bay laurel, madrone, and Monterey pine. Watch for peekaboo views of monolithic Mount Diablo through the trees.

Options

A very pleasant section of the East Bay Skyline National Recreation Trail runs from the Skyline Staging Area at Redwood Regional Park to Bort Meadow in Anthony Chabot Regional Park. With a car shuttle, you can hike this 7.8-mile one-way distance. Most hikers follow the route by starting out on West Ridge Trail, then cutting off on French Trail and following it through the redwoods until it rejoins West Ridge Trail. At the MacDonald Gate Staging Area, you follow MacDonald Trail up to a high ridge above Grass Valley and then down to Bort Meadow.

Directions

From I-580 in Oakland, take the 35th Avenue exit and turn north. Drive 2.4 miles (35th Avenue will become Redwood Road). Turn left on Skyline Boulevard and drive 3.7 miles to the Skyline Gate Staging Area. (Skyline Boulevard makes a sharp right turn after the first 0.5 mile.) The staging area is located at the intersection of Skyline and Pine Hills Drive.

Public transportation: AC Transit Bus #60 stops at Moon Gate at Redwood Regional Park. The final mile of this loop, West Ridge Trail, runs right past Moon Gate. For AC Transit information, phone 510/891-4700 or visit www.actransit.org.

Information and Contact

A $5 day-use fee is charged per vehicle. Leashed dogs are allowed ($2 dog fee). Bikes are allowed on West Ridge Trail. A free park map is available at the Skyline Gate Staging Area or by download at www.ebparks.org. For more information, contact East Bay Regional Park District, 2950 Peralta Oaks Court, P.O. Box 5381, Oakland, CA 94605, 888/327-2757, www.ebparks.org.

8 ROCKY RIDGE AND DEVIL'S HOLE LOOP
Las Trampas Regional Wilderness

Level: Moderate   **Total Distance:** 6.8 miles round-trip

Hiking Time: 3.5 hours   **Elevation Change:** 1,200 feet

Summary: A hidden canyon tucked amid burgeoning development offers surprising tranquility and a healthy hill climb.

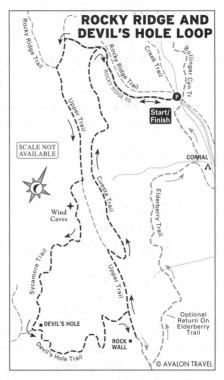

ROCKY RIDGE AND DEVIL'S HOLE LOOP

SCALE NOT AVAILABLE

Start/Finish

CORRAL

Wind Caves

DEVIL'S HOLE

ROCK WALL

Optional Return On Elderberry Trail

© AVALON TRAVEL

If you have some energy to burn, Las Trampas is a great place to tromp around. Quite simply, all trails at Las Trampas go up. The park is composed of two parallel ridges—Rocky Ridge and Las Trampas Ridge—bisected by Bollinger Creek. The park road and its many trailheads lie along the creek canyon, which means that no matter where you start hiking, sooner or later you'll have to climb one of the ridges.

But no matter; the rewards for doing so are great. An interesting 6.8-mile loop hike can be taken on the park's western ridge, Rocky Ridge. Starting from the end of Bollinger Canyon Road at the main staging area, you hike uphill on paved Rocky Ridge Road. Don't let the pavement discourage you; you'll leave it shortly. The ascent is a bit steep, but if you turn around to catch your breath about 0.25 mile up the trail, you'll see the summit of Mount Diablo poking up over the park's eastern ridge, Las Trampas.

At 0.5 mile up the trail, two single-track trails meet up with the paved trail, one shortly after the other. Take the upper trail, signed as Rocky Ridge Trail. You've climbed to nearly 2,000 feet in elevation. From this high ridge top, the interstate sounds like a distant rumble, but mostly your ears are filled with the whistling of wind in the rye grass. Bald Rocky Ridge is covered with grasslands, while parallel Las Trampas Ridge is lined with chaparral and bay laurel. In spring,

Rocky Ridge's grasslands are littered with ubiquitous poppies, blue-eyed grass, and brodiaea. The ridge-top winds are fierce, but the grassland flowers are tenacious. Like the willow tree, they have learned to bend in the breeze. Bright yellow mule's ears and purple nonnative thistles add to the show.

At the next junction, take Upper Trail. (A gate on your right leads through East Bay Municipal Utility District lands; the area can be hiked only with a permit.) Follow Upper Trail south along the ridge. On your left, you look down at the park's stables, buildings, and road. To your right is a barbed wire fence. But have patience; in a few minutes the fence disappears and you gain far-reaching views to the west and south. The large water body in the foreground is Upper San Leandro Reservoir. Your vista takes in the East Bay and extends down the Peninsula. To the west, views expand across San Francisco Bay to Mount Tamalpais in Marin.

A few scattered bay laurel trees grow along the top of the ridge, their lower limbs wrapped tightly around sandstone rocks. The closer you look at them, the more impossible it becomes to tell if the trees grew over the rocks or if the rocks grew out of the trees.

Take the right turnoff for Sycamore Trail downhill and then up again toward the huge rock outcrop 0.25 mile away. As you approach it, leave the trail and scramble up the formation to explore its wind-sculpted caves. Exercise caution; the outcrop is jealously guarded by clumps of poison oak and bay laurel. Note the rock's many varieties of colorful lichen in bright shades of orange, green, and gray. With some careful maneuvering, climb all the way to its summit, where you are presented with far-reaching views, a headstrong wind, and a great place for lunch. All you can see from here is wild land—no buildings, roads, or anything "civilized."

Continue on Sycamore Trail (it is often quite narrow and overgrown with grasses) for another mile to Devil's Hole on Cull Creek. Set in a box canyon, Devil's Hole's rock-lined cascades are a delightful sight after a period of rain. Sycamore, bay laurel, and live oaks shade the stream. Then take signed Devil's Hole Trail steeply back uphill to Upper Trail. Hike southward on Upper Trail for another third of a mile; views range to the south toward Livermore. Keep watching on your right for what appears to be a low rock wall. Examine its rocks closely for embedded clamshells, proof positive that this area was once undersea. (This also explains the sandstone on top of the ridge.)

The most direct route back to the parking area is to loop back on Elderberry Trail. But cows often graze along this trail, and if that insults your wilderness sensibilities, backtrack on Upper Trail for 0.5 mile to single-track Cuesta Trail. Then take Cuesta Trail back downhill to paved Rocky Ridge Road. Spring wildflowers are abundant in the grasslands surrounding Cuesta Trail.

Well-named Rocky Ridge provides big views of East Bay wildlands.

Options

From the same staging area, head straight on Bollinger Canyon Trail and climb steeply up to Las Trampas Peak, elevation 1,827 feet (bear left on Las Trampas Trail at 1.2 miles, then continue another 0.5 mile to the summit). The highest point on Las Trampas Ridge, Las Trampas Peak provides first-rate views of Mount Diablo, Carquinez Strait, and Ygnacio and San Ramon Valleys. Make your return a semi-loop by following Las Trampas Trail past 1,787-foot Vail Peak (more views) to Chamise Trail.

Directions

From I-680 in San Ramon, take the Crow Canyon Road exit west. Drive 1.3 miles to Bollinger Canyon Road, then turn right (north). Drive 4.5 miles on Bollinger Canyon Road to its end at the main parking area at Las Trampas Regional Wilderness. (Go past the stables and the Little Hills Picnic Ranch.)

From I-580 in Castro Valley, take Crow Canyon Road north to Bollinger Canyon Road. Turn left (north) on Bollinger Canyon Road and proceed as described earlier.

Information and Contact

There is no fee. Leashed dogs are allowed. Bikes are allowed on fire roads only. A free map is available at the visitors center or by download at www.ebparks.org. For more information, contact East Bay Regional Park District, 2950 Peralta Oaks Court, P.O. Box 5381, Oakland, CA 94605, 510/544-3276 or 888/327-2757, www.ebparks.org.

9 ROSE HILL CEMETERY LOOP
Black Diamond Mines Regional Preserve

Level: Easy

Hiking Time: 1 hour

Total Distance: 2.5 miles round-trip

Elevation Change: 400 feet

Summary: Wander through a little-known slice of East Bay history on this fascinating walk through Black Diamond's cemetery.

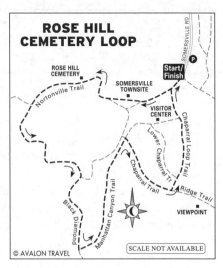

From 1860 to 1906, the Mount Diablo Coal Field was the largest coal-mining district in California. Located near present-day Antioch in what is now Black Diamond Mines Regional Preserve, this productive coalfield on the northern side of Mount Diablo prompted the digging of 12 major mines and the growth of five townships. Nearly four million tons of coal was extracted from the earth in less than 50 years. Much of this mining history, and a large acreage of rolling grassland hills and chaparral-clad slopes, is preserved at Black Diamond Mines.

A good introduction to the park can be gained by hiking the Nortonville Trail to a preserved pioneer cemetery, then looping back on Black Diamond Trail, Manhattan Canyon Trail, and Chaparral Trail for a sampling of the region's native flora.

From the parking lot at the end of Somersville Road, begin hiking on Nortonville Trail, a wide paved road that's an extension of the road you drive in on. Head toward the picnic area, then bear right at the fork just before it. The trail is a wide dirt road leading uphill to Rose Hill Cemetery. You are in the townsite of Somersville, which extended throughout this basin from the area of the present-day parking lot to Rose Hill. What was once a thriving mining town is now just a large open area.

Leave the trail to explore inside the cemetery's fence. You'll note that most of the graves are from the late 1800s, and most of the dead are Welsh. Although the Mount Diablo miners and their families came from all over the world, Rose Hill Cemetery was a Protestant graveyard. Some of the epitaphs are still visible, like this one: "'Tis God lifts our comforts high or sinks them in the grave. He gives and when he takes away, he takes but what he gave."

When you've explored enough, exit the cemetery on its far side and rejoin the dirt road, continuing your uphill climb through wide open grasslands. The native grasses bloom in spring with annual wildflowers such as owl's clover and brodiaea. Turn left on Black Diamond Trail and note the views you're gaining to the north of Suisun Bay. Piles of mine tailings are visible along the hillsides. Where the trail starts to descend, watch for a single-track path on the left signed "to Manhattan Canyon Trail." (Take the second cutoff, not the first.) This narrow trail makes several tight, steep switchbacks downhill until it junctions with Chaparral Loop Trail. Turn right on Chaparral Loop, a steep roller-coaster trail with a few uphill stretches that will raise your heart rate. You stroll among the good company of manzanita and monkeyflower. A few coulter pines make an appearance here; they are at the northernmost edge of their range.

At a junction with Ridge Trail, consider a short out-and-back (and uphill) jaunt to gain some impressive views of Mount Diablo. Take any of the short spurs off the Ridge Trail to reach the best viewpoints. To the north, you have more wide views of Carquinez Strait and Suisun Bay, and you can look back west to the graveyard on the hill. With a stiff breeze blowing through the ridge's pines, this could be an excellent place for a picnic. Return to Chaparral Loop Trail and turn right to return to the parking lot.

Options

On weekends only April–November each year, two portals to the past are open at Black Diamond Mines. One is the Greathouse Visitor Center, located in an underground chamber excavated in the 1920s, which contains old photographs, displays, and artifacts from this region's coal-mining era. (The visitors center is undergoing reconstruction and will reopen in 2011.) The other is the Hazel-Atlas Mine, which mined silica sand to make jars, bottles, and glasses. Visitors can take a guided tour (noon and 3 P.M. weekends Mar.–Nov., first-come first-served, $3 per person) with a

headstone at Rose Hill Cemetery

ranger or docent, heading 800 feet into the mine to see ore chutes, the mine boss's office, and other mine workings. Advance reservations (call 510/544-2750) are accepted weekends Apr.–Nov. (11 A.M., 1 and 2 P.M.), although some spots are available on a first-come, first-served basis.

Directions
From Highway 4 in Antioch, take the Somersville Road exit south. Drive 3.8 miles on Somersville Road to the end of the road and the trailhead. (You'll pass the park entrance kiosk at three miles, then continue another 0.75 mile to the trailhead.)

Information and Contact
A $5 day-use fee is charged per vehicle on weekends and holidays. Leashed dogs are allowed ($2 dog fee). Bikes are allowed on fire roads only. A free map is available at the entrance kiosk or by download at www.ebparks.org. For more information, contact East Bay Regional Park District, 2950 Peralta Oaks Court, P.O. Box 5381, Oakland, CA 94605, 510/544-2750 or 888/327-2757, www.ebparks.org.

10 STEWARTVILLE AND RIDGE TRAIL LOOP

BEST 🄲

Black Diamond Mines Regional Preserve

🚻 🌸 📷 🐕

Level: Moderate

Total Distance: 7.0 miles round-trip

Hiking Time: 3.5 hours

Elevation Change: 1,500 feet

Summary: Some steep ups and downs lead to an 1860s mining tunnel and big views of Carquinez Strait.

Black Diamond Mines Regional Preserve is a strange mix of elements—human history combined with natural history, wild green hills juxtaposed with industrial complexes north of the park, rare species of plants commingled with nonnative flora planted by settlers in the late 1800s. The 3,700-acre park has many moods and puts on different faces in changing seasons and weather conditions. This seven-mile loop reveals some of its highlights and adds some good exercise to the bargain.

Begin your trip at the trailhead at the end of Somersville Road. Take the paved road from the gate at the parking lot, walk about 50 yards, then turn left on signed Stewartville Trail. Named for one of the coal-mining towns that thrived in this area in the late 1800s, Stewartville Trail is a wide dirt road that climbs moderately and steadily uphill. As you hike through open grasslands, you'll pass some

The open, exposed hills of Black Diamond Mines Preserve make it easy to see where you're heading.

nonnative trees that the miners planted—pepper, eucalyptus, almond, and locust. The almond trees produce fragrant flowers in the spring.

A 0.5-mile climb brings you to a cattle gate at a high point on Stewartville Trail. Go through the gate and admire the deep, green, grassy valley below you. The good news is that you're going to hike into that bucolic valley; the bad news is that you'll have to climb back out of it. On the far side of the gate, turn right to stay on Stewartville Trail. (The return of your loop is Ridge Trail, on your left.) Mount Diablo looms large to the south.

As you start to descend, watch for the single-track cutoff for Miners Trail; bear left on this trail and leave the wide roads behind. Miners Trail is a narrow, well-built footpath that descends along the shoulder of the canyon wall, cutting across its steep slope. It leads through a surprising grove of gnarled foothill pines and coulter pines. Black Diamond Mines Preserve is noted as the northernmost location of coulter pines, black sage, desert olive, and dudleya.

Where Miners Trail touches down to the valley floor, continue straight ahead to rejoin Stewartville Trail. Down in this valley, you'll hear nothing but wind and the sound of your own breathing. It's hard to imagine that this wide-open space was once the site of a bustling community.

Bear left on wide Stewartville Trail. In 0.5 mile you'll pass Stewartville Trail Camp, a hike-in camp that can be reserved by individuals or groups who are willing to hike, bike, or ride horses into the camp. At a junction with single-track Star Mine Trail, consider adding on a 1.5-mile loop trip to see the closed-off tunnel of Star Mine, one of the last active coal mines in the area. (The loop will bring you back to Stewartville Trail.) Or continue straight ahead for 0.25 mile, passing an outcropping of colorful boulders that is lined with swallow's nests, to the left turnoff for Prospect Tunnel.

The tunnel's spur trail leads a few hundred yards to an obvious opening in the hillside. You can explore about 150 feet into the mine shaft before you reach a steel gate. The air inside its sandstone walls is a little musty, but always cool. Tall hikers will have to duck their heads. Daylight penetrates the entrance, but a flashlight is necessary if you want to travel more than a few feet. The tunnel was driven in the 1860s by miners in search of coal ("black diamonds").

Back on the main path, follow Stewartville Trail for nearly a mile farther, climbing gently, then make a sharp left turn on Ridge Trail. You're leaving the valley now and beginning the steep ascent back to the trailhead. The roller-coaster Ridge Trail dips down occasionally but more often rises steeply. The climb is eased by the sudden appearance of views to the north of Carquinez Strait, Suisun Bay, Pittsburg, and Antioch.

When at last Ridge Trail returns you to the gate at Stewartville Trail, consider a rest on the bench by the gate. Once again, pause to admire the green valley below. Then it's an easy 0.5-mile stroll back down Stewartville Trail to the trailhead.

Options

Sometimes you just don't want to see another soul, and that's not always easy to do in the San Francisco Bay Area. But there's a hiking trail in Black Diamond Mines that is rarely visited because it's not in the main trail region of the park. The loop is a figure eight around Lougher Ridge, and it begins behind a park residence across the road from the main park office. If you hike just the outside of the figure eight, it's a three-mile loop, but one of the best areas is the cross-section, which provides high views from a 1,100-foot ridge. What's so great about Lougher Ridge Loop? Grasslands, spring wildflowers, views to Carquinez Strait, and most importantly, solitude.

Directions

From Highway 4 in Antioch, take the Somersville Road exit south. Drive 3.8 miles south on Somersville Road to the end of the road and the trailhead. (You'll

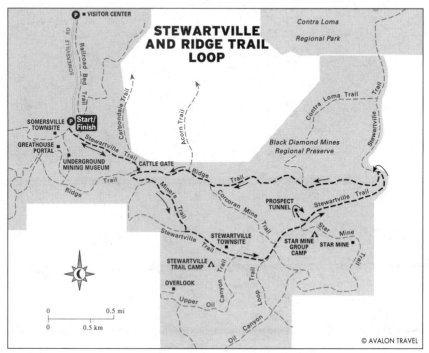

pass the park entrance kiosk at three miles, then continue another 0.75 mile to the trailhead.)

Information and Contact

A $5 day-use fee is charged per vehicle on weekends and holidays. Leashed dogs are allowed ($2 dog fee). Bikes are allowed on fire roads only. A free map is available at the entrance kiosk or by download at www.ebparks.org. For more information, contact East Bay Regional Park District, 2950 Peralta Oaks Court, P.O. Box 5381, Oakland, CA 94605, 510/544-2750 or 888/327-2757, www.ebparks.org.

11 MOUNT DIABLO GRAND LOOP   BEST €

Mount Diablo State Park

Level: Butt-Kicker

Total Distance: 10.0 miles round-trip

Hiking Time: 5 hours

Elevation Change: 2,900 feet

Summary: For an unforgettable day, circumnavigate the tallest peak in the East Bay and visit its two neighboring summits, Eagle Peak and North Peak.

Most everybody thinks about making a trip to 3,849-foot Mount Diablo from time to time. After all, you see it from just about everywhere in the Bay Area. It's not the tallest mountain around San Francisco Bay (Mount Hamilton near San Jose is 360 feet taller), it just has a way of making its presence known, looming in the background of the lives of millions of East Bay residents.

When your time to visit Mount Diablo arrives, make your first stop at the top. Drive to the summit and see what it's like to look at the greater Bay Area from Mount Diablo, rather than vice versa. Park as close to the top as possible, then walk up to the observation deck above the Summit Museum for a 360-degree vista. On the clearest days, you can see all the way to the Sierra Nevada and Mount Lassen. If the museum is open (hours are 10 A.M.–4 P.M. daily), stop in for an education on the mountain's flora and fauna.

© KEVIN GONG

A hiker conquers the Mount Diablo Grand Loop.

After being thoroughly wowed by the summit view, you'll be inspired to hike this 10-mile loop around the peak, which adds in two side trips to equally inspiring Eagle Peak and North Peak. The route includes substantial ups and downs, but you'll be rewarded with sweeping views and a variety of mountain flora.

Drive back downhill to Juniper Campground, park outside the camp, and walk through it to access Deer Flat Road. Head out on the wide fire road and enjoy immediate vistas to the west. On good days, San Francisco is clearly visible. With luck, you're hiking in spring, when the grassland wildflowers explode in color. Poppies and lupine headline the show. As you circumnavigate the mountain through a variety of terrain, different flowers will show themselves. Lucky hikers will spot Mount Diablo fairy lanterns, which grow nowhere else in the world. They have yellow, waxy-looking, nodding heads on stalks about five inches high. More prevalent are bright yellow narrowleaf goldenbush, purple hooker's onions (brodiaea), purple fields of clarkia, red larkspur, and delicate mariposa lilies. If you visit after the March–May flower season has passed, you'll still have California laurel, magnificent oaks, and foothill pines to keep you company along the trail.

Bear right at the road's first junction, onto Meridian Ridge Trail at 0.75 mile out. The descent steepens and in another 0.75 mile, you reach oak-shaded Deer Flat. (It's marked by the junction where Mitchell Canyon Road heads off to the

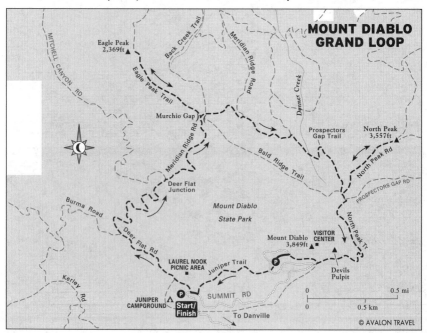

left.) In springtime, look for patches of light blue bird's eye gilia. In any season, watch and listen for the wealth of birdlife at Deer Flat.

Keep heading downhill on Meridian Ridge Trail, entering a canyon filled with ceanothus and bay trees. Cross tiny Deer Flat Creek and your downhill stint has ended; you'll be climbing for the next few miles.

At Murchio Gap, take the Eagle Peak Trail left for an out-and-back 0.8 mile to 2,369-foot Eagle Peak. The trail leads along the narrow backbone of Bald Ridge with steep drop-offs on both sides and wide views all the way. Many hikers consider this stretch to be the best part of the entire loop. From Eagle Peak's rocky summit, most impressive are the vistas of the Sacramento and San Joaquin Delta, Honker Bay, and Suisun Bay. Mount Diablo's North Peak, which you will soon visit, appears as an imposing pinnacle. Leave a note in the summit register, then retrace your steps to Murchio Gap.

At the gap, take your pick between following both Meridian Ridge Road and Prospectors Gap Trail or single-track Bald Ridge Trail (on the far side of the road). Both routes make their way to Prospectors Gap near North Peak. Bald Ridge Trail has many steep up and down sections with loose, rocky soil, so if you aren't wearing your best hiking boots, stay on the fire road. But the narrow trail does pass some fascinating serpentine outcrops and dense groves of manzanita. Just above the distinct saddle at Prospectors Gap, you gain an interesting view of the rock quarries north of the park, the bays and delta, and the towns of Antioch and Pittsburg. At the gap, you have open views to the east and west.

If you have the energy, take North Peak Road from Prospectors Gap out and back 0.8 mile to North Peak. Mount Diablo has two summits: the main one with the paved road to the top and North Peak, which is 292 feet shorter at 3,557 feet. If it's a clear day, North Peak is your best bet for catching a glimpse of the Sierra.

Then follow single-track North Peak Trail to the right (south), along the rocky eastern slope of Mount Diablo. This is a particularly good area for spring wildflowers. The trail weaves in and out of chaparral and grasslands, interspersed with scraggly-looking foothill pines. Views extend southwest to the windmills in Livermore and east to the Central Valley. You pass directly below the large rock outcrop called Devil's Pulpit on Mount Diablo's summit.

Where North Peak Trail ends at the paved park road, take Summit Trail uphill to the Lower Summit parking lot, then follow Juniper Trail downhill for one mile back to your car. Or, if you're tired of climbing by the time you reach the park road, just follow the road downhill for a mile.

There are two important elements to keep in mind when hiking at Mount Diablo: First, carry plenty of water with you. Second, never hike in the blazing afternoon heat of summer. The best seasons to visit are winter, when you may be surprised to find snow on the summit, and spring, when the grasses are green and the wildflowers put on their show. Mount Diablo's sunsets, sunrises, and moonrises are spectacular in any season.

Options

This trail can be made shorter and easier by skipping the two side trips to Eagle Peak and North Peak. This will shave 3.2 miles and 1,200 feet of elevation gain off your round-trip. However, if you don't want to miss the exciting hogback trail to Eagle Peak, you can hike there and back following the trail notes described earlier in this listing. A turnaround at its scenic summit (instead of continuing on the loop) makes a 6.3-mile round-trip.

Directions

From I-680 at Danville, take the Diablo Road exit and head east. Follow Diablo Road for 2.9 miles (you must turn right at 0.7 mile to stay on Diablo Road). At a stop sign at Mount Diablo Scenic Boulevard, turn left. Drive 3.7 miles on Mount Diablo Scenic Boulevard (it becomes South Gate Road) to the park's southern entrance station. Continue to the junction with Summit Road, then turn right and drive to the summit (a total of 7.3 miles). After visiting the summit, drive back down Summit Road for 2.5 miles to Juniper Campground and Laurel Nook Picnic Area. Park outside the campground in the wide turnout along the road, then walk through the camp to pick up Mitchell Canyon/Deer Flat Road at its far end, near site 23.

Alternatively, from I-680 in Walnut Creek, take the Treat Boulevard exit and go east for 1.2 miles. Turn right on Bancroft Road, which crosses Ygnacio Valley Road and becomes Walnut Avenue. Drive 1.6 miles on Walnut Avenue, then turn right on Oak Grove Road. Turn left immediately on North Gate Road and continue to the junction with Summit Road. Turn left and drive to the summit (a total of 12 miles).

Information and Contact

A $6 day-use fee is charged per vehicle. Dogs are not allowed. Bikes are allowed on fire roads. A park map is available at the entrance station and summit visitors center, or by free download at www.parks.ca.gov. A more detailed map is available for $7.50 at www.mdia.org. For more information, contact Mount Diablo State Park, 96 Mitchell Canyon Road, Clayton, CA 94517, 925/837-2525 or 925/837-0904, www.mdia.org or www.parks.ca.gov.

12 ROCK CITY AND WALL POINT SUMMIT

Mount Diablo State Park   **BEST** 🄲

Level: Easy   **Total Distance:** 3.5 miles round-trip

Hiking Time: 1.5 hours   **Elevation Change:** 500 feet

Summary: A playground of sandstone rock formations awaits exploration on the slopes of Mount Diablo.

If you're a kid or a kid at heart, you'll love Rock City in Mount Diablo State Park. Set among clusters of tall manzanita, foothill pines, madrones, and live oaks, Rock City is a jumble of eroded sandstone outcroppings that form a playground for hikers and rock climbers.

Rock City was formed 40–50 million years ago during the Eocene period, when Mount Diablo was buried under a great sea. Eventually the waters receded and the sand that was left behind hardened into a ridge of rocks that was exposed during the more recent growth of Mount Diablo. This rocky ridge has been weathered and eroded by centuries of wind and rain, creating odd-shaped boulders with small caves and Swiss cheese–style holes. They're fun to look at and easy to photograph.

Rock City's boulders ignite the imagination. It isn't long before you notice that one rock resembles a barking sea lion, another looks like an elephant, and still another imitates a hippopotamus. Many paths wind over and around the sculpted rock formations, so you can just explore without having to follow a set trail.

Most visitors find their way to Sentinel Rock, a tall pinnacle of sandstone with

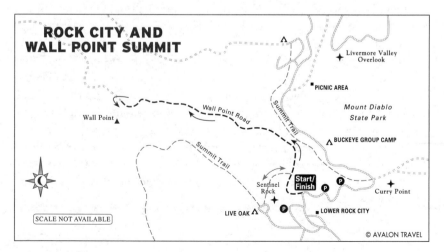

on top of Sentinel Rock at Rock City

stairsteps leading to its summit. Because the rock's drop-offs are quite steep, the park has installed steel cables along the stairsteps and at the summit. No, it's not Half Dome, but it's a fun climb to the top, from which you will tower over the live oaks and foothill pines in the valley below. Sentinel Rock is located about 0.25 mile from the main Rock City parking lot, heading in a northwest direction through numerous other wind-sculpted boulders. Another 0.25 mile beyond Sentinel Rock are the Wind Caves, a ridge of tan-colored rocks riddled with holes and caverns.

If you find yourself feeling annoyed at the hundreds of names and initials carved into the soft sandstone, take heart. This sandstone is so soft, the graffiti is worn off in a few decades.

Hikers who yearn to walk farther than the short paths in Rock City can set out on Wall Point Road for a three-mile round-trip to the summit of Wall Point. Wall Point Road is visible from various points in Rock City; it's the wide fire road leading northwest (on your right as you head to Sentinel Rock). If you follow the spiderweb of paths heading west from Sentinel Rock, you'll eventually end up on one that connects to the fire road. If you don't find your way, just head back to the Rock City parking lot, then walk 100 yards north on the main park road. Across from the ranger's residence, on the west side of the road, is the start of Wall Point Road.

The trail starts out mostly level and offers views of Sentinel Rock, Rock City, and "real" cities far to the west. In just under a mile you reach a saddle with a view over Dan Cook Canyon to the south. A half-mile of climbing leads to the road's high point near the peak of bald Wall Point. Masses of poison oak guard a narrow use trail that leads to its summit; take it if you dare.

Birders, bring your binoculars for this walk. Wall Point is considered to be one of the best birding spots on the mountain.

Options

Anyone looking for a short and easy trail on Mount Diablo shouldn't miss the Fire Interpretive Trail at the mountain's summit. From Rock City, continue uphill to park headquarters, then turn right on Summit Road and head for the trailhead on the north side of the road above the lower summit parking lot. This 0.7-mile loop circles the summit with only the slightest of climbs. As you might expect, the trail serves up nonstop views of miles of Northern California terrain far, far below. Rock outcrops and wildflowers along the trail will also hold your interest.

Directions

From I-680 at Danville, take the Diablo Road exit and head east. Follow Diablo Road for 2.9 miles (you must turn right at 0.7 mile to stay on Diablo Road). At a stop sign at Mount Diablo Scenic Boulevard, turn left. Drive 3.7 miles on Mount Diablo Scenic Boulevard (it becomes South Gate Road) to the park's southern entrance station. Continue 0.8 mile farther to the Rock City parking area on the left, signed as Rock City/Live Oak. Park in any of the main picnic area parking lots, and begin hiking at the sign for Big Rock, Sentinel Rock, and Wind Caves. Or, walk up the paved loop road to campsite 20; a trail begins just behind it.

Information and Contact

A $6 day-use fee is charged per vehicle. Dogs are allowed only in the Rock City picnic area. Bikes are allowed on fire roads. A park map is available at the entrance station and summit visitors center, or by free download at www.parks.ca.gov. A more detailed map is available for $7.50 at www.mdia.org. For more information, contact Mount Diablo State Park, 96 Mitchell Canyon Road, Clayton, CA 94517, 925/837-2525 or 925/837-0904, www.mdia.org or www.parks.ca.gov.

13 BACK AND DONNER CANYON LOOP

Mount Diablo State Park   **BEST** ☾

Level: Moderate   **Total Distance:** 7.0 miles round-trip

Hiking Time: 3.5 hours   **Elevation Change:** 1,100 feet

Summary: A moderate hike leads to a series of surprising waterfalls on the brush-covered slopes of Mount Diablo's less-visited side.

Waterfalls on Mount Diablo? It may be hard to believe, but a trip to Clayton in the rainy season and a hike along the back side of this rugged, arid mountain reveals half a dozen gushing cascades. Scattered along the hillsides on two forks of Donner Creek, the falls drop in a canyon that is notoriously dry, steep, and hot as Hades most of the year. Pick the right day, though, soon after a good rain, and it's water, water everywhere.

Luckily, even if the falls aren't flowing, a hike through Mount Diablo's Back and Donner Canyons is a pleasure. A visit on any day except for the hottest days of summer allows you to get to know the mountain more intimately. Unlike many of Mount Diablo's trails, this seven-mile loop follows single-track paths most of the way, weaving in and out of the mountain's deep northern canyons. Diablo's fascinating geology and vegetation are close at hand.

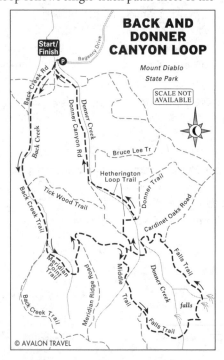

BACK AND DONNER CANYON LOOP

Mount Diablo State Park

SCALE NOT AVAILABLE

© AVALON TRAVEL

The trailhead is located at the end of Regency Drive, a suburban neighborhood in Clayton. (You don't have to pay the state park day-use fee here.) Walk down to Donner Creek beyond the street barrier and through the gated park boundary. Take the fire road on the right signed as Back Creek Road. (Or follow its neighboring single-track trail, which soon rejoins Back Creek Road.)

Although the hike begins in grasslands and oaks, it won't stay that way for long. In 0.5 mile, Back Creek Road meets up with its namesake stream, and shortly thereafter the road narrows to

The foothill pine with its heavy cones reigns supreme in Donner Canyon.

single-track. As soon as the trail drops down to proper hiking width, the vegetation closes in. Back Creek Trail climbs gently but steadily amid eroded rock formations and dense stands of sage, toyon, yerba santa, and monkeyflower, heading due south toward the mountain's summit. Watch for an abandoned mine tunnel, only a few feet deep, on the left side of the trail.

At the point where the canyon divides, turn left on Meridian Point Trail and climb more steeply through chaparral until the path tops out at Meridian Point. From the high overlook at this junction with Meridian Ridge Road, you gain a wide view of the town of Clayton and a glimpse of Suisun Bay to the northwest.

Follow Meridian Ridge Road downhill for 0.25 mile to single-track Middle Trail. Turn right on Middle Trail; you've left Back Canyon and are now entering Donner Canyon. The steep buttress of Mount Diablo's North Peak towers above at 3,557 feet.

Watch for the left turnoff for Falls Trail, then follow this rough, narrower trail for 1.25 miles as it winds along the steep slopes of Donner Creek. Whereas Back Creek is only a small stream, Donner Creek can become a wide torrent during the rainy season. Where the loop trail reaches its southernmost point and starts to curve to the northeast, you'll cross a fork of Donner Creek and start seeing waterfalls. Most are about 20 feet high, although one impressive 30-foot free fall drops over jagged, red-brown rock. The trail stays about 100 feet distant from the cascades, so you won't get to admire them up close. You do get the extraordinary experience of seeing as many as five waterfalls at once in a very small area.

Note the occasional foothill pines along Falls Trail; their cones are extremely dense and can weigh up to four pounds. Among the eroding rock formations, you'll find scattered juniper trees bearing bright blue winterberries.

Where Falls Trail crosses the eastern fork of Donner Creek, the cascades are left behind. Watch out for steep drop-offs as you hike downhill out of Donner Canyon, enjoying more northward views of Clayton and Suisun Bay.

At Falls Trail's end, turn left on Cardinet Oaks Road. You'll make five knee-jarring, steep switchbacks downhill, cross Donner Creek again, then turn right on Donner Canyon Road at Cardinet Junction. To finish out your hike, simply follow Donner Canyon Road all the way back to the trailhead, or a better option is to turn right on single-track Hetherington Loop Trail. This narrow path tunnels through bay laurel trees and skirts Donner Creek, eventually returning you to Donner Canyon Road. Then it's a level stroll through pastoral oaks, buckeyes, and grasslands back to the Regency Drive trailhead.

Options

Another first-rate destination that is accessible from the Regency Drive Trailhead is Mount Olympia, a rugged rock outcrop with captivating views. Follow Donner Canyon Road to Middle Trail, then take Middle Trail to Prospectors Gap Road. Turn left and climb steeply until you reach Prospectors Gap. There, turn left and follow North Peak Road and then North Peak Trail to 2,946-foot Mount Olympia. Loop back on zigzagging Mount Olympia Road to Cardinet Oaks Road, which will bring you back to Donner Canyon Road. This trip isn't for the faint of heart, however: It's a challenging 9.9-mile hike with approximately 3,000 feet of elevation gain.

Directions

From I-680 heading north in Walnut Creek, take the Ygnacio Valley Road exit. Drive east on Ygnacio Valley Road for 7.5 miles to Clayton Road. Turn right on Clayton Road and drive 2.9 miles (it becomes Marsh Creek Road, but don't turn right at the sign for Marsh Creek Road) to Regency Drive. Turn right and drive 0.5 mile to the end of the road and the trailhead.

Or, from I-680 heading south in Walnut Creek, take the Treat Boulevard exit and go east. In one mile, turn right on Bancroft Road. In another mile, turn left on Ygnacio Valley Road and drive five miles to Clayton Road. Continue as described.

Information and Contact

There is no fee at the Regency Drive trailhead. Dogs are not allowed. Bikes are allowed on fire roads. A park map is available by free download at www.parks.ca.gov. A more detailed map is available for $7.50 at www.mdia.org. For more information, contact Mount Diablo State Park, 96 Mitchell Canyon Road, Clayton, CA 94517, 925/837-2525 or 925/837-0904, www.mdia.org or www.parks.ca.gov.

14 ROUND VALLEY LOOP   BEST 【

Round Valley Regional Preserve

Level: Easy   **Total Distance:** 6.0 miles round-trip

Hiking Time: 3 hours   **Elevation Change:** 200 feet

Summary: A pleasant cool-weather trek through a pastoral park that serves as an important habitat for wildlife.

If you ever start to feel like the East Bay is too crowded, too congested, or has too much concrete, take a trip a little farther east to the back side of Mount Diablo. Here, on the far eastern edge of the Bay Area, just before the bay's geography converges with that of the San Joaquin Valley, are wide-open spaces, spring wildflowers, and stately valley oaks.

Round Valley is a pastoral landscape of oaks and grasslands.

Welcome to Round Valley Regional Preserve, one of the newest additions to the East Bay Regional Park system. It's the 2,000-acre home of nesting golden eagles, burrowing owls, chubby ground squirrels, and the endangered San Joaquin kit fox. In spring, the grassy hills of Round Valley turn a brilliant green and are sprinkled with grassland wildflowers. The small miracle of Round Valley Creek flows with unmodulated passion until late spring or early summer, when it drops to meager pools along the streambed. In midsummer, temperatures at Round Valley can soar to more than 100°F, so be sure to plan your visit for the cooler months.

From the preserve's staging area, the trail starts out with a long bridge over Marsh Creek. At the far side of the bridge, turn right on Miwok Trail. Immediately you face the only two sizable hills of the day. Hike up and over them, then relax—the remaining miles in the preserve are almost completely level.

In its first 0.5 mile, wide Miwok Trail meets up with Round Valley Creek. If you've timed your trip for winter or spring, the stream will be running cool and clear alongside you for much of your hike.

You'll notice the remains of old ranching equipment along the dirt trail. This land was farmed by the Murphy family from 1873 until 1988, when it was sold to the East Bay Regional Parks. Prior to the Murphy's ownership, the Round Valley area was home to Native Americans, who probably used the land as a meeting and trading place between San Joaquin Valley tribes and East Bay hill tribes.

You're bound to see dozens of chubby ground squirrels scurrying around the grasses and popping in and out of their burrows. These plentiful squirrels are a chief reason that golden eagles nest in Round Valley. They're a critical part of the food chain. The squirrels' burrow holes double as homes for other animals, such as burrowing owls.

Lucky hikers may spot an endangered San Joaquin kit fox. The tiny foxes are at the northern edge of their range in Round Valley. For the few remaining foxes, this land is rare and valuable habitat that could aid in the survival of their species.

Stay on Miwok Trail throughout the length of the preserve—almost three miles—then turn right on Murphys Meadow Trail. In one mile, turn right again, remaining on Murphys Meadow Trail and looping back on the far side of Round Valley Creek. When you reach a junction with Fox Tail Trail in just under a mile, look for a good place to cross the creek (there is no formal trail). Miwok Trail is just on the other side, about 100 feet away. Cross the stream carefully, then rejoin Miwok Trail and turn left to head back to the trailhead.

Options
Round Valley Regional Preserve is also the staging area for one of the most exciting tours in the East Bay Regional Parks: a guided tour to Vasco Caves Regional Preserve, home to wind- and water-carved sandstone formations marked with Native American rock art, endangered plants and animals, vernal pools, and a landscape that has been visited by relatively few Bay Area hikers. A shuttle bus leaves from the Round Valley parking lot for the drive to Vasco Caves, where a naturalist guide leads tours through the caves. Advance reservations (call 888/327-2757) are required; tours are scheduled a few days each month.

Directions
From I-580 in Livermore, take the Vasco Road exit and drive north for 14 miles. Turn left (west) on Camino Diablo Road and drive 3.6 miles. Camino Diablo Road merges with Marsh Creek Road; continue 1.6 miles to the Round Valley parking area on the left.

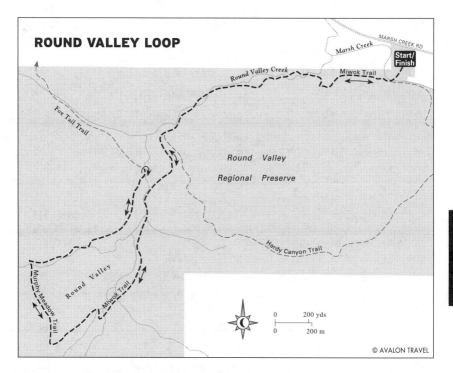

Alternatively, from I-680 heading north in Walnut Creek, exit at Ygnacio Valley Road and drive east for 7.5 miles to Clayton Road. Turn right on Clayton Road. In the town of Clayton, Clayton Road becomes Marsh Creek Road; continue east past Morgan Territory Road and Deer Valley Road to the Round Valley parking area on the right. (It's about 12 miles from Clayton.)

Information and Contact

There is no fee. Dogs are not allowed. Bikes are allowed. Free maps are available at the trailhead parking area or by download at www.ebparks.org. For more information, contact East Bay Regional Park District, 2950 Peralta Oaks Court, P.O. Box 5381, Oakland, CA 94605, 888/327-2757, www.ebparks.org.

15 MORGAN TERRITORY LOOP BEST

Morgan Territory Regional Preserve

Level: Moderate

Hiking Time: 3.5 hours

Total Distance: 7.0 miles round-trip

Elevation Change: 1,200 feet

Summary: A varied loop in the green hills of Morgan Territory offers expansive views, a walk through oak woodland, and myriad spring wildflowers.

Morgan Territory—even the name sounds wild, like a holdover from the Old West. If you're wondering if anything wild could still exist in Contra Costa County, wonder no more. Come to Morgan Territory and rediscover the wild East Bay.

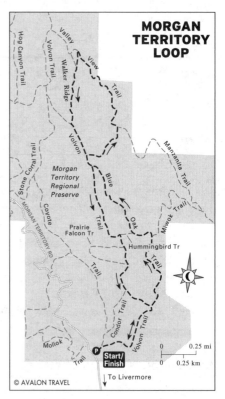

The drive to the trailhead is a trip in itself. First make sure you are traveling in the cooler months of the year, because the open hills around Livermore bake in the summer. (If you're visiting in the warm season, make sure you arrive *very* early in the morning.) Follow narrow, winding Morgan Territory Road north of Livermore to the preserve's main trailhead. Try not to get so wowed by the views that you drive right off the curvy road. Watch for cars coming the opposite way; the road is so narrow that usually somebody has to pull over to let the other car pass.

At the trailhead parking lot, you've climbed to 1,900 feet in elevation. (Okay, so your car has done the work.) You're greeted by grassy hillsides and usually a fair breeze. Pick up a free trail map and follow Volvon Trail uphill and through a cattle gate. This first climb allows for no warm-up, but fear not, the trail mellows at the top.

After 0.5 mile on Volvon Trail, bear right on Blue Oak Trail and prepare yourself for a few glimpses of the San Joaquin Valley far to the east. When you aren't facing east, you have great views of Mount Diablo to the west. (Now that's a change for Bay Area residents—seeing Mount Diablo in the *west*.) The dirt road rolls gently up and down small hills. The ruts and holes underfoot are caused by the trampling feet of cattle. You'll probably see a few bovines somewhere along the path. If you're lucky, you'll see a few deer as well, or maybe a coyote.

True to its name, Blue Oak Trail features some magnificent oak trees, interspersed with rocks coated with colorful lichens. Dozens of spots invite you to throw down your day pack, wander among the trees, and spread out a picnic. This is especially true if you're visiting during the wildflower bloom. More than 90 flower species blossom along Morgan Territory's grassy hillsides, creating an unforgettable sight in good wildflower years. The most common flowers are California poppies, brodiaea, blue-eyed grass, mariposa lilies, elegant clarkia, and larkspur. This is oak woodlands, so there are lots of woodpeckers and songbirds, but this is also prime raptor country.

Stay on Blue Oak Trail for 1.3 miles until you reach a cattle gate at a portable toilet. Go through the cattle gate and turn right on Valley View Trail. (The path straight ahead will be the return of your loop.) A rather quick and steep descent on Valley View Trail leads you to remarkable views to the east of the San Joaquin Valley. On the clearest days, the snowcapped Sierra Nevada Mountains can be seen far beyond, more than 100 miles away. Mount Diablo shows its face to the west, and Mount St. Helena in Napa appears to the north. After relishing the vista, turn right on Volvon Loop Trail to start your return, climbing back uphill

© ANN MARIE BROWN

An ancient oak harbors clumps of mistletoe at Morgan Territory Regional Preserve.

to the cattle gate. From there you have an easy hike on Volvon Trail all the way back to the trailhead and parking lot.

A couple of tips to make your hike at Morgan Territory ideal: One, pick a cool day. Two, make sure you take one of the park's free trail maps (or download one before you set out from home) to help negotiate your way through numerous junctions. This park is huge—more than 4,000 acres. And three, carry plenty of water and a suitable picnic to spread out under the shade of the biggest oak you can find.

Options

This East Bay is also one of the best parks for bird-watching year-round and wildflower-viewing in the spring. Los Vaqueros Reservoir is located southeast of Morgan Territory Regional Preserve. You can hike from one park to the other, or you can drive to Los Vaqueros' two main trailheads and staging areas. One is at the north end of Los Vaqueros Road, off Vasco Road in Livermore; the other is at the south end of Walnut Boulevard near Brentwood. First-timers should stop in at the interpretive center off Walnut Boulevard. The huge reservoir's western and northern shores are laced with 55 miles of hiking trails. Fishing is also popular.

Directions

From I-580 in Livermore, take the North Livermore Avenue exit and turn left (north). Drive north for 4.3 miles, then turn right on Morgan Territory Road. Drive 5.7 miles to the entrance to Morgan Territory Preserve on the right. (The road is narrow and steep.)

Or, from I-680 heading north in Walnut Creek, take the Ygnacio Valley Road exit and drive east for 7.5 miles to Clayton Road. Turn right on Clayton Road. In the town of Clayton, Clayton Road becomes Marsh Creek Road; continue east for about five miles and turn right (south) on Morgan Territory Road. Drive 9.5 miles to the entrance to Morgan Territory Preserve on the left.

Information and Contact

There is no fee. Leashed dogs and bikes are allowed. Free trail maps are available at the trailhead or by download at www.ebparks.org. For more information, contact East Bay Regional Park District, 2950 Peralta Oaks Court, P.O. Box 5381, Oakland, CA 94605, 925/757-2620, 510/544-2750 or 888/327-2757, www.ebparks.org.

16 COGSWELL MARSH TRAIL
Hayward Regional Shoreline

Level: Easy

Hiking Time: 1.5 hours

Total Distance: 3.6 miles round-trip

Elevation Change: Negligible

Summary: Ponder the importance of San Francisco Bay to human beings and wildlife on this bird-rich stroll along the wetlands.

COGSWELL MARSH TRAIL

To Park Office

San Francisco Bay

Cogswell Marsh

JOHNSON'S LANDING

(RESTRICTED ROADS)

Start/ Finish

BREAKWATER AVE

To San Mateo

0   0.25 mi
0   0.25 km

© AVALON TRAVEL

Hayward Regional Shoreline is a place to consider two things: wetlands and birds. A full appreciation of either requires more than a casual glance, and as you hike around the bay shore's 3.6 miles of perfectly level, gravel trails, you'll have ample opportunity for slow, careful study.

Start your trip with a visit to the interpretive center at the trailhead, then take the wide dirt trail from the building's back side. The path skirts along a freshwater marsh until it reaches the shoreline of San Francisco Bay. Although Highway 92 and the San Mateo Bridge are close by at the trail's start, they are quickly left behind as the path heads northward. The San Francisco skyline can be seen across the water to the northwest.

As you walk, consider the wetlands around San Francisco Bay. We've built houses, factories, and roads around most of the bay's perimeter; concrete rip-rap lines much of the rest. Thousands of acres of bay marshes have been diked, drained, filled, dredged, and destroyed to build salt mines, carve out space for airports and highways, or create huge ports.

But despite the damage they have suffered, the bay's wetlands are still the best friend the Bay Area could have. The many streams and waterways at the bay's edge hold millions of gallons of water, protecting us from flood damage during harsh winter storms. Much of the fish and shellfish we eat spend part of their lives in the bay's wetland areas. In addition, at least one-third of the nation's rare and endangered species are dependent on wetland areas such as those around the bay for nesting, feeding, or growing habitat. Without these wetlands, some endangered species would face extinction.

© ANN MARIE BROWN

This long footbridge at the edge of the bay attracts anglers and bird-watchers.

The coastal mudflats around San Francisco Bay have been reduced to 10 percent of their original size. The bay's salt marshes have been reduced to 15 percent of their original size. Although many people think these flat, mucky areas are suitable only for landfill, mudflats and salt marshes are among the most nutrient-rich and productive habitats on earth.

That's why some forward-thinking people got together in the 1970s to rebuild Hayward Shoreline. The area was dramatically altered in the 1850s when dikes and levees were built to increase salt production. In the process, a huge expanse of wetlands became dry land. Only a generation ago, environmental engineers redesigned and reclaimed 400 acres of freshwater, brackish water, and saltwater marshes in one of the largest marsh restoration projects on the West Coast. Through careful science, humans tried to reconstruct what Mother Nature had originally made.

The effort is paying off. For starters, Hayward Regional Shoreline is now crawling with birds. Even the most novice bird-watcher strolling along the levees will soon notice many distinct and varied species on the waterways. Tall, elegant great egrets share the mudflats with their smaller cousins, the snowy egret. Black-necked stilts race around on their remarkably long, thin, pink-red legs. Avocets use their distinctive curved bills to scoop through the nutrient-rich waters. Migrating ducks line the freshwater ponds and waterways. Other commonly seen species are terns, willets, cormorants, sandpipers, and pelicans. A perennial crowd-pleaser are the flocks of magnificent white pelicans, which are much larger than the more common brown pelicans.

After 1.2 miles of easy walking, with no trail junctions to distract you from your bird and wetland studies, you reach a fork in the trail. Bear left and cross the long footbridge. A short distance farther is a bench with a view of the water. Loop back on the trail to the right, which travels through restored Cogswell Marsh.

Options

Hayward Shoreline puts you in intimate contact with the bay, but to the southeast lies a park that can take you almost 1,000 feet above it. At Garin Regional Park, off Highway 238 at Garin Avenue south of Hayward, the Vista Peak Loop curves past Vista Peak at 934 feet and Garin Peak at 948 feet. Both summits offer wide views of the East Bay and South Bay, where few other nearby landmarks attain this height. The Vista Peak Loop is a 1.6-mile loop that begins 0.5 mile from the parking lot, making a 2.6-mile round-trip.

Directions

From I-880 in Hayward, take the Highway 92 exit west. Drive 1.7 miles and take the Clawiter Road exit. Cross Clawiter Road and turn left immediately on Breakwater Road. Drive one mile on Breakwater Road to the Hayward Regional Shoreline interpretive center.

Information and Contact

There is no fee. Dogs are not allowed. Bikes are allowed. A free map is available at the trailhead or by download at www.ebparks.org. For more information, contact East Bay Regional Park District, 2950 Peralta Oaks Court, P.O. Box 5381, Oakland, CA 94605, 510/783-1066 or 888/327-2757, www.ebparks.org.

17 BAYVIEW AND RED HILL LOOP   BEST ◖

Coyote Hills Regional Park

Level: Easy   **Total Distance:** 4.8 miles round-trip

Hiking Time: 2.5 hours   **Elevation Change:** 200 feet

Summary: The home of the Ohlone people for more than 2,000 years, Coyote Hills is now a place to enjoy bay and marsh views and abundant bird sightings.

If you ever have occasion to drive across the Dumbarton Bridge from the South Bay to the East Bay, a few things will catch your attention—like the huge electrical towers that straddle the water and the dismantled, decaying railroad bridge that parallels Dumbarton. The bay itself seems impossibly huge and blue in contrast to the density of the cities and freeways that surround it. But urban-weary eyes come to rest on the soft green knolls of Coyote Hills Regional Park. Situated on your left as you head east across the bay, the park's tule marshes, creeks, and acres of grassland hills beckon you to pull off the freeway and explore.

A 1,000-acre patch of open space along the edge of San Francisco Bay, Coyote Hills was the homeland of the Ohlone tribe for more than 2,000 years. The Ohlone fished bay waters for food and cut willow branches along the creeks to build their homes. Today the park is a wildlife sanctuary, both a permanent home

Boardwalks lead across the marsh at Coyote Hills.

© ANN MARIE BROWN

and a temporary rest stop for thousands of resident and migratory birds.

Binoculars are a worthwhile accessory for this trail, but many of the birds are so close that you don't even need them. On one short walk at Coyote Hills, we watched a great egret stalk and catch a field mouse 20 yards from us, then fly off with it in his beak. Moments later, a peregrine falcon soared overhead, shortly followed by a red-tailed hawk swooping and floating over the grasslands. In winter, great egrets and snowy egrets displaying exquisite white plumage are as common as human visitors to the park.

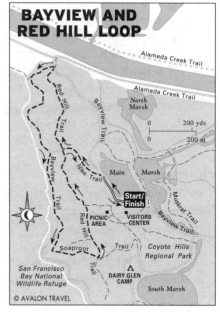

The park has a paved multiuse trail along its hillsides, allowing hikers, baby stroller–pushers, wheelchair users, and bikers access to breathtaking bay and marsh views. But hikers who prefer earthen paths to pavement won't be disappointed. Red Hill Trail climbs to the top of the park's grassy hills for panoramic views and a close-up look at some odd rock formations—outcrops of reddish gold chert once part of the ocean floor.

It's a park for wandering, with or without a formal plan. Start your trip at the Coyote Hills Visitor Center, which is open Wednesday through Sunday and has some interesting displays on the natural and cultural history of the area. Then follow the gated, paved road—Bayview Trail—heading north from the visitors center parking lot.

Leave the pavement in 100 yards as you turn left on wide Nike Trail, heading toward the bay. In 0.25 mile, turn right on Red Hill Trail to begin a 2.3-mile loop on Red Hill and Bayview Trails. Hike up and over a grassy hill, then drop back down to the water's edge. Rejoin paved Bayview Trail and stroll southward along the bay, only 50 feet above the water's edge. After a full mile of nonstop views, you'll round Glider Hill and see the turnoff for Soaproot Trail. Turn left on Soaproot, then left again on Red Hill Trail to finish out your loop. As you hike to the top of Red Hill, consider the fact that when San Francisco Bay's waters were higher (before dikes were built in the late 1800s), Red Hill and its neighboring hills were islands.

After exploring Red Hill and its red-colored rock formations, return to the junction with Nike Trail and retrace your steps to the visitors center parking lot. Then head off in the opposite direction, walking 50 yards south on the road you drove in on. Watch for a wooden boardwalk crossing the tule-lined marsh on your left. Follow the boardwalk through a labyrinth of tules, cattails, and sedges. (Children love this maze-like walk.) Where the marsh opens up, ducks and other waterfowl are easily spotted. The path leads to an Ohlone shell mound. The largest of four shell mounds in the park, this debris pile supplies archaeological proof that the Ohlone inhabited this area for at least 2,200 years.

Options

If you enjoyed the bird-watching opportunities at Coyote Hills, head to neighboring Don Edwards San Francisco Bay National Wildlife Refuge (510/792-0222, www.fws.gov/desfbay), on the south side of Highway 84 off Thornton Avenue. Two of the largest egret nesting colonies in Northern California are located at the refuge. Start your trip at the visitors center (10 A.M.–5 P.M. Tues.–Sun.), then set out on the signed trails that follow boardwalks above the bay's tidal flats.

Directions

From I-880 in Newark, take Highway 84 west for two miles. Take the Paseo Padre Parkway exit, turn right (north) and drive one mile to Patterson Ranch Road. Turn left and drive 1.5 miles to the visitors center parking lot at Coyote Hills.

Information and Contact

A $5 day-use fee is charged per vehicle. Leashed dogs are allowed ($2 dog fee) except in the marsh area. Bikes are allowed. A free map is available at the entrance kiosk and visitors center, or by download at www.ebparks.org. For more information, contact East Bay Regional Park District, 2950 Peralta Oaks Court, Oakland, CA 94605, 510/795-9385 or 888/327-2757, www.ebparks.org.

18 MISSION PEAK   BEST ◖
Mission Peak Regional Preserve

🏠 🐴 🚌

Level: Strenuous   **Total Distance:** 6.6 miles round-trip

Hiking Time: 3.5 hours   **Elevation Change:** 2,000 feet

Summary: A challenging hike to a popular summit near Fremont, where hang gliders soar past at eye level.

The grassy slopes of 2,517-foot Mission Peak are a requisite hike for outdoor lovers in Alameda County. On any sunny weekend day with good visibility, hundreds of East and South Bay residents make the pilgrimage to Mission Peak's summit. At the top, they enjoy first-rate views of the South Bay, the northern Santa Cruz Mountains, the Peninsula, San Francisco, and even the summits of the Sierra Nevada. Along the way, they are entertained by colorful hang gliders and paragliders taking off from Mission Peak's slopes, then soaring with the thermals high overhead.

The trail to Mission Peak is a wide, exposed fire road, so be sure to wear your sunscreen. Also, forget hiking on hot days. Some of the grades are quite steep, and with its shadeless slopes, the peak can bake in summer. Although the trail has a reputation for being a butt-kicker, it's only 3.3 miles to the summit from the main Fremont trailhead, and even children can make the trip in cool weather. Just remember to bring along plenty of water and snacks, and take your time.

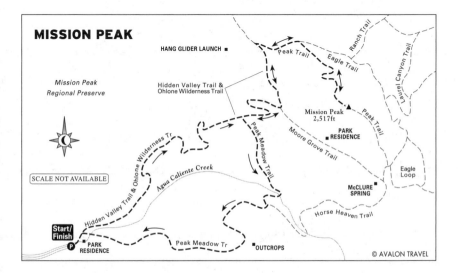

MISSION PEAK

Mission Peak Regional Preserve

SCALE NOT AVAILABLE

HANG GLIDER LAUNCH ■

Hidden Valley Trail & Ohlone Wilderness Trail

Peak Trail

Ranch Trail

Eagle Trail

Laurel Canyon Trail

Mission Peak 2,517ft

Peak Trail

PARK ■ RESIDENCE

Moore Grove Trail

Hidden Valley Trail & Ohlone Wilderness Tr

Agua Caliente Creek

Peak Meadow Trail

Eagle Loop

McCLURE ■ SPRING

Horse Heaven Trail

Start/ Finish
P PARK RESIDENCE

Peak Meadow Tr

■ OUTCROPS

© AVALON TRAVEL

One way to make the trip easier is to stay on the trail. Mission Peak Regional Preserve is lined with well-marked fire roads, including a section of the 31-mile Ohlone Wilderness Trail. But these roads diverge into a spiderweb of use trails, most of which cut the switchbacks and head straight up the mountain. If you ignore the use trails and stay on the wide, signed, multiuse path, you'll enjoy a much more pleasant grade up the mountain.

From the trailhead, start by taking the left fork, which is signed as Hidden Valley Trail and Ohlone Wilderness Trail. Almost immediately you'll spot a parallel use trail on your left; it will meet up with the main trail in less than a mile at a rocky outcrop with a wide view of the South Bay. Many people just walk up to this viewpoint and then turn around. You'll stay on the wide fire road, sweating through a few steep stretches for the first 1.5 miles. The view gets wider and more impressive with every twist and turn. The Coyote Hills are a standout; they are the only landmarks in the foreground with any elevation. The rest of the South Bay is remarkably flat.

At a junction with Ohlone Wilderness Trail marker 2, note the right fork for Peak Meadow Trail. You'll follow this on your return. For now, bear left to stay on Hidden Valley Trail/Ohlone Wilderness Trail and enjoy an easier grade. The road enters into a grassy meadow directly below Mission Peak's fractured and rocky summit. Scattered rocks are evidence of ancient landslides.

The road winds around the northwest side of the mountain. At a cattle gate, turn right and follow Peak Trail, another wide fire road. Views are of Mount Diablo and the wildlands of Sunol and Pleasanton Ridge. The launch site for hang gliders is just downhill to your left; you'll see it as you rise up the summit flank.

In 0.25 mile, reach a second junction where Peak Trail bears right and makes the final steep summit climb. The last 0.25 mile is a rocky single-track path; it leads to a metal post lined with pipes that serve as sight scopes. Look through them and note all the landmarks. To the north are Mount Diablo, Pleasanton Ridge, Livermore, San Antonio Reservoir, and Sunol Regional Wilderness. To the west are Mount Tamalpais, San Francisco, Redwood City, the Dumbarton Bridge, and Coyote Hills. To the south are Mount Loma Prieta and the Santa Cruz Mountains. To the east are Santa Clara County, Mount Hamilton, Lick Observatory, and Rose Peak in the Ohlone Wilderness. On the clearest days, it's possible to make out the snowy peaks of the Sierra Nevada, far to the east. While you are admiring all this majesty, it's not uncommon to see a hang glider or paraglider fly by at eye level.

For your return trip, head back downhill the way you came. Before turning left at the cattle gate for Hidden Valley/Ohlone Wilderness Trail, continue straight ahead for a few hundred feet to the hang glider launch site. It's fascinating to

On a windswept winter day, hikers take in the view using the sighting scope on top of Mission Peak.

watch these colorful, delicate human birds take off and soar overhead. Then take Hidden Valley/Ohlone Wilderness Trail back downhill to marker 2. Turn left on Peak Meadow Trail, a less-traveled fire road. This path almost guarantees solitude for the rest of your trip, plus it offers a pleasant stint through the oak-forested canyon of Agua Caliente Creek. Don't miss a side trip to the rock outcrops one mile down Peak Meadow Trail (on your left). The view to the south from these rocks is almost as good as Mission Peak's summit view.

Options

For a somewhat mellower hike to Mission Peak, begin at the trailhead at Ohlone College in Fremont. The grade is less steep from this direction, although the trailhead isn't easy to locate behind the campus buildings. (Park in lot D or H; make sure you pay the parking fee.) The route follows Peak Trail (part of the Bay Area Ridge Trail) for 2.4 miles as it contours along the mountain's lower slopes, then ascends to the summit. The final 0.75 mile to the top is the same as the route described earlier. The distance of the two trails to Mission Peak are about the same, but the trailhead elevation at Ohlone College is higher, shaving off some of the climb.

Directions

From I-880 in Fremont, take the Warren Avenue/Mission Boulevard exit and drive east 1.5 miles. Turn right on Stanford Avenue and drive 0.5 mile to the trailhead parking area.

Alternatively, from I-680 in Fremont, take the Durham Road exit and drive east for one mile. Turn right on Mission Boulevard, drive 0.75 mile, then turn left on Stanford Avenue. Drive 0.5 mile to the trailhead parking area.

Public transportation: AC Transit Bus #217 stops at the corner of Stanford Avenue and Mission Boulevard. Walk 0.5 mile up Stanford Avenue to the trailhead. AC Transit Buses #210, #217, and #218 also stop at Ohlone College, the optional trailhead for this hike to Mission Peak. For AC Transit information, phone 510/891-4700 or visit www.actransit.org.

Information and Contact

A $3 day-use fee is charged per vehicle. Leashed dogs and bikes are allowed. A free map is available at the trailhead or by download at www.ebparks.org. For more information, contact East Bay Regional Park District, 2950 Peralta Oaks Court, P.O. Box 5381, Oakland, CA 94605, 510/544-3246 or 888/327-2757, www.ebparks.org.

19 SUNOL LOOP TOUR

BEST (

Sunol Regional Wilderness

🏕 ✈ 🌲 🐾

Level: Strenuous

Total Distance: 7.5 miles round-trip

Hiking Time: 3.5 hours

Elevation Change: 1,800 feet

Summary: Wildflowers abound in the spring and Alameda Creek flows year-round on this scenic loop in the Sunol countryside.

A trip to Sunol is a trip to the country. Unlike many other East Bay parks, Sunol Regional Wilderness isn't bordered by neighborhoods or major thoroughfares. You can't reach it any other way than by driving slowly on a narrow, country road. When you hike the grassy, oak-studded hills of Sunol, all you see are more grassy, oak-studded hills, and an occasional glimpse at shimmering Calaveras Reservoir. Sunol is bordered by San Francisco Water District lands to the north and south and the Ohlone Regional Wilderness to the east. It is protected land surrounded by protected land. And that's what makes it good.

This hike follows a 7.5-mile loop tour of Sunol that reveals many of the park's best features. It is steep in spots, so come prepared for a hike that has a few challenging moments. (Plenty of water and a few snacks will get you through it easily.) You should also check the temperature: Sunol is lovely in fall, winter, and spring, but it's often too hot on summer days.

From the parking lot just east of the ranger station and visitors center, begin your hike by crossing the long footbridge over Alameda Creek. This is Alameda County's largest stream, and it can swell to 30 feet wide after winter rains. On the far side of the footbridge, turn right for Canyon View Trail and pass two trail junctions in the next few hundred yards. You're following one leg of Indian Joe Nature Trail, but don't turn left where the nature trail leads uphill. Instead, keep

The grassy hills of Sunol are most inviting in the springtime.

hiking eastward with Alameda Creek on your right. At a third junction (signed with a post in the middle of the path marked Ohlone Wilderness Regional Trail), bear left and head uphill and away from the creek. Shortly you reach a clearly marked fork and the start of your loop, where Indian Joe Creek Trail veers left and Canyon View Trail continues straight ahead. This mess of junctions in the first 0.25 mile is annoying, but it's over with now.

Follow narrow Canyon View Trail as it roller-coasters up and down through grassy hillsides and oak woodland. Springtime brings a remarkable display of flowers along the path. Most impressive are the huge, yellow blooms of mule's ears, but you'll also find plentiful California poppies, elegant clarkia, mariposa lilies, owl's clover, brodiaea, and gilia. Birding, too, is excellent throughout Sunol. The park is renowned for its yellow-billed magpies and acorn woodpeckers.

As you progress, you'll gain views to your right of Alameda Creek's steep, miniature canyon. One pleasant mile of strolling through the grasslands will bring you to Canyon View Trail's junction with Cerro Este Road and wide Camp Ohlone Road. Cross the latter to pay a visit to Little Yosemite, a narrow gorge on Alameda Creek that is choked with car-sized boulders. Little Yosemite would be best explored by taking off your shoes, but sadly, no swimming or water contact is allowed. The creek is on San Francisco Water District land. However, you may scramble down to the water's edge, sit on a rock, and admire Alameda Creek's clear green pools. Watch for the small trout that dart through the stream and listen to the music of tumbling waterfalls.

From Little Yosemite, prepare for a serious climb over the next mile on Cerro Este Road. Sticky monkeyflower and purple nightshade line the road's steep banks. The shadeless ascent on the fire road may seem uninspiring, but turn around occasionally as you climb and you'll glimpse long-distance views of Calaveras Reservoir to the south. The only downer in the vista is Camp Ohlone Road, which looks too much like a paved street, even though it's a gravel road.

Your ascent ends at Cerro Este Overlook, a grassy knoll at 1,720 feet in elevation, signed by a large stone marker. Catch your breath and enjoy the wide views of the park and Calaveras Reservoir, then bear left on Cave Rocks Road. You have an easy 0.5-mile walk before turning right on single-track Eagle View Trail, which winds along the slope of Sunol's high ridge. A gentle ascent through chaparral and sage over the course of a mile will bring you to Vista Grande Overlook at a junction with Vista Grande Road. This high point (1,680 feet) is actually 40 feet lower than Cerro Este, but the view is even more impressive because of the ridge's steep drop-offs. A gnarled oak tree and another stone marker denote the spot. This might be your best bet for a lunch break.

Turn west on Vista Grande Road and descend rather steeply along the ridgeline. A few curves and twists bring you down to High Valley Road; turn left and walk toward the huge barn you've been looking at from above. The barn is the site of High Valley Camp, a hike-in campground for groups. Bear left to stay on the road north of the barn and walk 0.5 mile to the right turnoff for Indian Joe Creek Trail. (This single-track trail was not signed on our visit; watch for it immediately after crossing a stream canyon.)

Follow Indian Joe Creek Trail all the way downhill and back to the start of your loop. Be sure to go slow and enjoy this last leg, which may be this loop's prettiest stretch. A highlight is Cave Rocks, 0.25 mile down the path, where huge fractured basalt boulders create a playground for rock climbers and ambitious hikers. Other highlights are the crunching noise of autumn leaves underfoot, the springtime sounds of birdsongs, and the gurgling of Indian Joe Creek. In any season, this narrow footpath is the perfect finish to a fine day at Sunol.

Options

If you'd like to enjoy more time on the trail than just a day-hike in Sunol will allow, there are two options. Large groups backpack to High Valley Camp, which can be seen in the hike described. Individual backpackers head for the Sunol Backpack Camping Area, near the junction of Backpack Road and McCorkle Trail. The best way to get there is to hike 3.5 miles from park headquarters on the single-track McCorkle Trail, enjoying fine views of Calaveras Reservoir along the way. Reservations are required for the backpack camp (phone 888/327-3257, $5 fee per person). Many hikers use this camp as a first-night stopover before continuing on longer trips into the Ohlone Regional Wilderness.

Since you're not allowed to play in the water at Sunol's Little Yosemite, here's an East Bay adventure that's all about playing in the water: a guided kayak trip to Brooks Island and a two-mile hike around its shoreline. Tours to the 373-acre island, located 45 miles away just off Richmond Harbor, are held a couple of times each month; public access is limited to these trips. Make reservations with the East Bay Regional Park District (call 888/327-2757) and sign up for an outfitter-led trip (fee includes kayak rental). The all-day adventure includes an easy, short paddle to the island in stable single or double kayaks, followed by a guided hike. There are also trips available for experienced paddlers who own their own boats.

Directions
From I-680 south of Pleasanton, take the Highway 84/Calaveras Road exit. Turn left on Calaveras Road and drive south 4.2 miles. Turn left on Geary Road and drive 1.7 miles to the park entrance. Continue another 0.25 mile to the entrance kiosk, then drive 100 yards past the visitors center to the parking lot across from the horse rental area. The trail begins on the left side of the restrooms at the footbridge.

Information and Contact
A $5 day-use fee is charged per vehicle on weekends and holidays. The visitors center is open 7 A.M.–sunset daily (closed Thanksgiving and Christmas). Leashed dogs are allowed ($2 dog fee). Bikes are allowed only on fire roads. A free map is available at the entrance kiosk or by download at www.ebparks.org. For more information, contact East Bay Regional Park District, 2950 Peralta Oaks Court, P.O. Box 5381, Oakland, CA 94605, 510/544-3249 or 888/327-2757, www.ebparks.org.

20 MAGUIRE PEAKS LOOP
Sunol Regional Wilderness

Level: Moderate

Total Distance: 5.5 miles round-trip

Hiking Time: 3 hours

Elevation Change: 800 feet

Summary: Explore the wilder side of Sunol Regional Wilderness on this moderate loop off Welch Creek Road.

As you drive south on I-680 near Pleasanton, you can't help notice the odd-shaped Maguire Peaks slanting outward from the round, grassy hills. The two side-by-side peaks aren't conical, like most peaks, or even rounded. Instead they're fin-shaped, like two obtuse triangles. Their summits point sideways, then upward. After a little while staring at these odd little mountains, you may find yourself longing to explore them.

You can hike to the peaks from the main Sunol Regional Wilderness entrance on Geary Road, but a shorter option is to start from the trailhead in the Sunol "backcountry" along Welch Creek Road. If the main part of Sunol is too developed for your tastes, you'll love the Welch Creek area. You won't find picnic areas, horse rentals, or a visitors center there; in fact, you won't even find a parking lot. Welch Creek Road is an incredibly narrow, single-lane road with only a few tiny pullouts for cars (you must obtain a parking permit for these pullouts from the

A hiker pauses to enjoy the view from the top of Maguire Peaks.

main park entrance). Leave your car by the 0.72 mile marker and take the single-track Lower Maguire Peaks Trail from the cattle gate.

The first stretch of trail travels up a creek canyon that is so lush and shady that it harbors huge yellow banana slugs. Ferns and wildflowers line the forest floor; the branches of bay laurels and oaks form a dense canopy overhead. The Lower Maguire Peaks Trail is well built and quaintly signed with rusted arrow markers.

Soon you climb out of this delightful canyon into a more open area of oaks and grasslands. At a trail junction, two paths lead uphill to meet up with an old ranch road. Take either one and join wide Maguire Peaks Road, which circumnavigates the two peaks. Go left on the road to make a clockwise circle.

Those who don't like hiking on dirt roads will find this one to be an exception. It's pleasantly overgrown by low grasses and it hasn't been rutted, eroded, or overrun by cows. It makes easy and pleasant walking. Heading west through open grasslands, you'll climb a bit to gain the Maguire Peaks' ridgeline. The sloping hills are peppered with occasional oaks and bay laurels, but for the most part, you're out in the sunshine. If you're fortunate enough to visit on a day when the wind blows, you'll be convinced that the grasses are alive. They tumble, roll, and travel with the wind like migrating creatures. In spring, be on the lookout for wildflowers. I've seen orange monkeyflower, paintbrush, larkspur, blue-eyed grass, mariposa lilies, and blue dicks, as well as huge yellow mule's ears.

When you crest the western ridge of Maguire Peaks, you're rewarded with views of huge San Antonio Reservoir to the north and the city of Pleasanton beyond, framed by Mount Diablo. After all the solitude you've had and the wild land you've been traversing, the sight of civilization is surprising. Head for a rocky outcrop on the ridge's high point where you'll find the widest views and the best picnic spot. Keep your eyes on the skies. Hawk sightings and even eagle sightings are fairly common around Maguire Peaks.

When you've seen enough, continue on your stroll around the perimeter of Maguire Peaks. It's tempting to make an ascent to the top, but you'll have to blaze your own trail to do so. (Beware of rattlesnakes, especially in springtime.) The summits of the peaks are lined with wind-sculpted basalt rock.

The eastern sides of the peaks are more vegetated than the western sides, particularly with large oaks and bay laurel. Poison hemlock grows 12 feet high in places. Too many nonnative thistles are evidence of the ranching that has taken place here. As in many East Bay parks, cows graze on Maguire Peaks. Fortunately, the area isn't overrun with them.

A long downhill returns you to the start of your loop. Turn left to regain the single-track trail back to your car.

An insider's tip: Maguire Peaks Loop is one of the nicest trails in the East Bay for a sunset hike. Just remember to bring a flashlight in case it gets dark before you get back to your car.

Options

If you'd like to see the Maguire Peaks from a different perspective, head over to the town of Sunol and Pleasanton Ridge Regional Park, a strip of land on a high ridge. Trailhead access is off Foothill Road in Sunol. From the staging area, head gently uphill on Oak Tree Trail, then cut off on the hikers-only Woodland Trail. A one-mile stint brings you to the ridgeline and appropriately named Ridgeline Trail. Follow it northwest (right) for as far as you please, enjoying wide views of Sunol Valley, the twin Maguire Peaks, and Mission Peak in Fremont.

Directions

From I-680 south of Pleasanton, take the Highway 84/Calaveras Road exit. Turn left on Calaveras Road and drive south 4.2 miles. Turn left on Geary Road and drive 1.7 miles to the park entrance. Pay your entrance fee at the kiosk and obtain a parking permit for Welch Creek Road, then turn around and drive out Geary Road for 1.7 miles back to Calaveras Road. Bear right on Calaveras Road and drive 0.25 mile to Welch Creek Road. (Welch Creek Road is narrow and easy to miss; look for it on your right as you drive north on Calaveras Road.) Drive 0.7 mile on Welch Creek Road to the trailhead on the left, at the cattle gate. Park in the pullout along the road.

Information and Contact

A $5 day-use fee is charged per vehicle on weekends and holidays. Leashed dogs are allowed ($2 dog fee). Bikes are not allowed on this loop. A free map is available at the park entrance kiosk or by download at www.ebparks.org. For more information, contact East Bay Regional Park District, 2950 Peralta Oaks Court, P.O. Box 5381, Oakland, CA 94605, 510/544-3249 or 888/327-2757, www.ebparks.org.

21 MURIETTA FALLS   BEST ◖
Ohlone Regional Wilderness

🪂 🎒 🏞️ 🐕

Level: Butt-Kicker   **Total Distance:** 12.0 miles round-trip

Hiking Time: 7 hours   **Elevation Change:** 3,500 feet

Summary: Hoping to spot a 100-foot-tall ephemeral waterfall, hikers endure a supremely challenging climb and descent in Ohlone Regional Wilderness.

Everybody loves a waterfall, but do you love waterfalls enough to be willing to grunt out a 3,500-foot elevation change? Think it over. If your answer is yes, you're heading for a fine adventure in Ohlone Regional Wilderness, culminating in a visit to 100-foot Murietta Falls.

If your answer is "not sure," the first half-hour on this trail will be challenging enough to make up your mind, one way or the other.

Ohlone Regional Wilderness is one of the Bay Area's special places. No public roads lead through its nearly 10,000 acres. You have to hike just to reach its boundary, starting either from Sunol Regional Wilderness to the west or Del Valle Regional Park to the north. To be more specific, you have to hike uphill.

In the same vein, Murietta Falls is one of the Bay Area's most special waterfalls. That's partly because it's much taller than other local falls and partly because it's hard enough to reach that most people never make the trip. The difficulty doesn't lie just in the trail's many steep ups and downs, its sunny exposure, and its 12-mile-long round-trip distance. The real difficulty is that the waterfall has an extremely short season and must be seen immediately following a period of rain. More than a few hikers have made the long trip to Murietta and then been disappointed to find only a trickle of water. March is often the best month to see the fall flowing, but it depends on the current year's rain pattern. Depending on when the rains come, Murietta's top flow could happen anywhere from January to April. Keep your eyes on the skies.

One thing to remember: This trail is absolutely not suitable for a warm or hot day. It offers very little shade coupled with a ton of climbing.

The only easy thing about this trail is that it's remarkably well signed. Just pay attention at all junctions and keep following the red markers for Ohlone Wilderness Trail in the first five miles. Also, you must purchase a wilderness permit in order to hike on the Ohlone Wilderness Trail. With your permit you get a free map, which comes in quite handy.

The trail starts by climbing and stays that way for 2.4 miles. (Don't forget to stop and sign in at the wilderness register one mile in.) There are only a very few spots where the wide dirt road levels off. Otherwise, it's up, up, up all the way to the top of Rocky Ridge, a 1,670-foot gain from the trailhead. Then all of a sudden you start an incredibly steep descent—steep enough so that you'll wish you'd brought your trekking poles. You drop 530 feet in about 0.5 mile. The good news is that you're heading for water; listen for its welcoming sound. The wide fire road narrows to single-track for the first time all day as you descend into the beautiful stream canyon of Williams Gulch. The sound of the cascading creek is so refreshing and inviting that you may suddenly remember why you are doing this hike after all. The 0.5-mile stretch of path that cuts through the stream canyon is pure, refreshing pleasure.

You might as well enjoy it, because next you're going to climb out of the canyon in a 1,200-foot ascent. The single-track trail is surprisingly well graded with some good switchbacks, however, so this climb isn't nearly as bad as some of the dirt road stretches. The path is fairly well shaded. Prolific miner's lettuce and pink shooting stars grow alongside it.

You'll get a hint that you're nearing the falls when you start to notice rock outcrops along the trail. For the first four miles the landscape is mostly grasslands and massive oak trees, some with diameters that rival the size of giant redwoods. (The only exception

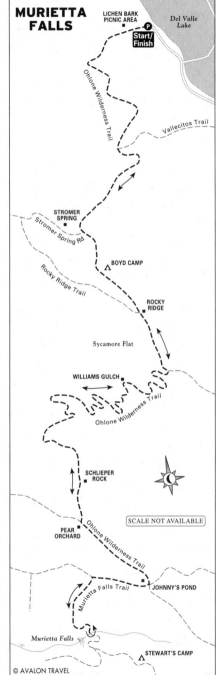

to the oak savannah terrain is in riparian Williams Gulch.) But suddenly large rock outcrops start to pop up out of nowhere. One of these, on the left side of the trail, is signed as Schlieper Rock. It is named for Fred Schlieper, a silversmith from the 1940s. His ashes are scattered at the rock.

The trail also levels out substantially as you near the falls. At this 3,000-foot elevation, you'll gain some wonderful views to the north and west. (On our trip, we were amazed to see snow on the high ridges around us, and even a few lingering white patches right along the trail.)

At 0.7 mile beyond Schlieper Rock you'll reach Johnny's Pond. Just beyond the small pond, turn right at the sign for Murietta Falls (signpost 35). Hike 0.25

A long, hard hike leads to Murietta Falls.

mile farther, then turn left and start paying close attention to your surroundings. In just under 0.5 mile, you'll reach a hairpin turn in the road. If you've timed your trip well, you'll note a few streams of water crossing the road. Leave the trail and follow the main stream downhill to your right; it will deliver you to the brink of the falls in a few hundred feet.

A good use trail makes a steep descent to the base of the falls. Follow it carefully—you've come this far, you might as well get the full effect. The waterfall's cliff, an incredible rocky precipice with a 100-foot drop, is composed of greenstone basalt. At its base is a wide, round, shallow pool. Many good picnicking spots are found nearby. If you made it this far, you deserve to eat well. Pull out that turkey and avocado sandwich.

Bird-watchers, take note: The trailside oak savannah is home to many resident and migratory birds. I counted more western bluebirds on this walk than I had seen in my entire life previously. Not uncommonly, bald eagles are seen commanding the skies above this trail.

Options

Four miles beyond Murietta Falls is 3,817-foot Rose Peak, a towering summit that is only 32 feet lower than Mount Diablo, but much less known. Its summit view takes in the ridges and valleys of the Ohlone Wilderness, plus San Francisco Bay, the Santa Clara Valley, the Santa Cruz Mountains, and several of the Bay Area's major peaks. Accessing Rose Peak from the Murietta Falls Trailhead would be an epic 20-mile day hike, so the obvious choice is to get a permit to camp along the Ohlone Wilderness Trail. Campsites are found at Stewart's Camp, just beyond Murietta Falls on Greenside Trail, and at Maggie's Half Acre, a short distance north of Rose Peak.

Directions

From I-580 in Livermore, take the North Livermore Avenue exit and turn right (south). Drive south through the town of Livermore for 3.5 miles (North Livermore Avenue becomes Tesla Road) and turn right on Mines Road. Drive 3.5 miles on Mines Road to its junction with Del Valle Road. Continue straight at the fork, now on Del Valle Road. Drive 3.2 miles to the entrance kiosk at Del Valle Regional Park. Purchase a wilderness permit at the entrance kiosk, then continue 0.75 mile to the dam and cross it. Turn right and drive 0.5 mile to the Lichen Bark Picnic Area. Take the trail signed as Ohlone Trail.

Information and Contact

A $6 day-use fee is charged per vehicle. Hikers on the Ohlone Wilderness Trail must purchase a $2 wilderness permit, which includes a detailed trail map. (You may purchase a permit in advance by mail at the address that follows, or on the day of your hike at the park entrance station.) Maps are also available by download at www.ebparks.org. Leashed dogs are allowed ($2 dog fee). Bikes are not allowed. For more information, contact East Bay Regional Park District, 2950 Peralta Oaks Court, P.O. Box 5381, Oakland, CA 94605, 510/544-3246 or 888/327-2757, www.ebparks.org.

PENINSULA AND SOUTH BAY

© ANN MARIE BROWN

BEST HIKES

The Peninsula and South Bay may be recorded

in the history books as the focal point of the dot-com boom and bust, but those who live here know it better for its rolling inland hills, rugged coastline, towering redwood forests, miles of ranch and farming country, and soothing wealth of open spaces. Spanning a stretch of land that runs north to south from San Francisco to Santa Cruz, and east to west from San Francisco Bay to the Pacific coast, it's an urban wilderness like no other.

At the northern tip of this region is the city of San Francisco, a seven-mile-square metropolis that is one of the world's most popular tourist destinations. A surprise to many is that San Francisco also offers a few "wilder" attractions for those who want to experience the city with a day pack on their backs, such as the spectacular 11-mile Coastal Trail, with its postcard views of the Golden Gate Bridge, and the Agave Trail on Alcatraz Island, a paradise for bird-watchers.

The San Mateo and Santa Cruz shoreline boasts some of California's most scenic stretches of sand. Sure, this coast is wind-whipped and often foggy, but it's also remarkably dramatic, with rocky sea stacks protruding from the waves and eroded marine terraces dropping off sharply to the sea. The coast's massive reefs are pocketed with tidepools teeming with life, but they only reveal their treasures during the lowest tides of the year. Long stretches of brayed tan sand invite a walk at sunset, sunrise, or any time. Highway 1 runs along the coastline, providing easy access to beaches and parks, but once you travel south of Half Moon Bay, the towns are few and far between. Here, the coast belongs mostly to the gray whales and the elephant seals. Visitors who want to see these amazing sea creatures don't have to look very far at two of the coast's loveliest parks, Año Nuevo State Reserve and Wilder Ranch State Park.

The Santa Cruz Mountains run almost the entire length of the Peninsula and South Bay. Much of these hills are undeveloped, although a handful of highways crisscross their forested slopes. In between the roads are miles of parklands, including four of California's state parks that were so designated to protect the coastal redwoods: Big Basin, Henry Cowell, the Forest of Nisene Marks, and Portola Redwoods. More redwood groves can be visited in several San Mateo County parks, including Sam McDonald, Memorial, and Pescadero Creek.

Perhaps the Peninsula and South Bay's biggest bonanza for nature lovers is the wealth of preserves managed by the Midpeninsula Regional Open Space District, which borders Skyline Boulevard (Highway 35), running across the spine of the northern Santa Cruz Mountains. Here, nearly 40 trailheads are found within a 50-mile stretch of road, providing access to more than 300 miles of trails. On the ocean side of Skyline Ridge, dense groves of redwoods and Douglas firs soak up the coastal fog. The bay side is a mosaic of grasslands interspersed by oak and bay woodlands. Deer, coyotes, and bobcats are commonly seen. Some of the best wildflower viewing in the entire Bay Area is possible here, most notably at Russian Ridge and Long Ridge.

Heading inland and farther south along the Peninsula, the landscape changes noticeably. The weather in and around San Jose is much warmer and drier than it is to the north and west, and the character of its parks reflects that. Two huge inland parks – Henry W. Coe State Park and Joseph D. Grant County Park – protect a large portion of the sun-baked inland hills. Their combined acreages create an important wilderness oasis in a region that has been rapidly consumed by development.

With its wide range of ecosystems and microclimates, the Peninsula and South Bay provides everything that the rest of the Bay Area has to offer, but in a smaller, more accessible package. Any trail a hiker might desire, from redwoods to coast to sunny inland hills, is available here and waiting to be explored.

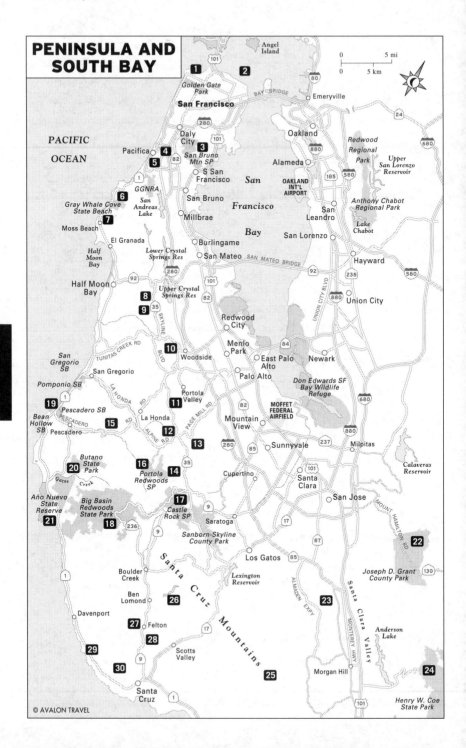

PENINSULA AND SOUTH BAY

PACIFIC OCEAN

0   5 mi
0   5 km

San Francisco

Golden Gate Park

Angel Island

BAY BRIDGE

Emeryville

Daly City

Oakland

Redwood Regional Park

Upper San Lorenzo Reservoir

Pacifica

S San Francisco

San Bruno Mtn SP

Alameda

OAKLAND INT'L AIRPORT

San Andreas Lake

San Bruno

Millbrae

GGNRA

Gray Whale Cove State Beach

Moss Beach

El Granada

Half Moon Bay

San
Francisco
Bay

San Leandro

San Lorenzo

Anthony Chabot Regional Park

Lake Chabot

Burlingame

Lower Crystal Springs Res

San Mateo

SAN MATEO BRIDGE

Hayward

Half Moon Bay

Upper Crystal Springs Res

Redwood City

Menlo Park

Union City

San Gregorio SB

San Gregorio

Woodside

East Palo Alto

Palo Alto

Newark

Don Edwards SF Bay Wildlife Refuge

Pomponio SB

Bean Hollow SB

Pescadero SB

Pescadero

La Honda

Portola Valley

MOFFET FEDERAL AIRFIELD

Mountain View

Butano State Park

Portola Redwoods SP

Cupertino

Sunnyvale

Milpitas

Calaveras Reservoir

Santa Clara

Año Nuevo State Reserve

Big Basin Redwoods State Park

Castle Rock SP

Saratoga

Sanborn-Skyline County Park

San Jose

Joseph D. Grant County Park

Boulder Creek

Los Gatos

Lexington Reservoir

Ben Lomond

Santa
Cruz
Mountains

Davenport

Felton

Scotts Valley

Santa Clara Valley

Anderson Lake

Morgan Hill

Santa Cruz

Henry W. Coe State Park

© AVALON TRAVEL

TRAIL NAME	LEVEL	DISTANCE	TIME	ELEVATION	FEATURES	PAGE
1 Land's End Coastal Trail	Easy	3.5 mi rt	2 hr	250 ft		291
2 Alcatraz Island's Agave Trail	Easy	1.0 mile rt	1 hr	100 ft		294
3 Summit Loop Trail	Easy/Moderate	3.1 mi rt	1.5 hr	725 ft		298
4 Three Trails to Sweeney Ridge	Moderate	4.0 or 5.0 mi rt	2–3 hr	750 ft or 1,000 ft		302
5 Brooks Falls Loop	Easy	2.6 mi rt	1.5 hr	500 ft		306
6 Montara Mountain Summit	Strenuous	7.4 mi rt	4 hr	2,200 ft		309
7 Tidepool Walk	Easy	Up to 5.0 mi rt	1–2 hr	Negligible		313
8 Purisima Grand Loop	Strenuous	10.0 mi rt	5.5 hr	1,600 ft		316
9 Tafoni and Fir Trail Loop	Easy/Moderate	6.0 mi rt	3 hr	600 ft		320
10 Bear Gulch and Alambique Loop	Easy/Moderate	5.4 mi rt	2.5 hr	600 ft		323
11 Windy Hill Loop	Moderate	8.0 mi rt	4 hr	1,100 ft		327
12 Russian Ridge Loop	Easy/Moderate	4.4 mi rt	2 hr	550 ft		330
13 Black Mountain and Stevens Creek Loop	Moderate	6.0 mi rt	3 hr	1,300 ft		333
14 Peters Creek and Long Ridge Loop	Easy/Moderate	4.6 mi rt	2 hr	400 ft		336
15 Heritage Grove and Hiker's Hut Loop	Easy/Moderate	5.0 mi rt	2.5 hr	600 ft		339
16 Peters Creek Grove	Strenuous	13.0 mi rt	7 hr	1,400 ft		342
17 Saratoga Gap and Ridge Trail Loop	Easy/Moderate	5.2 mi rt	2.5 hr	600 ft		345
18 Berry Creek, Silver, and Golden Falls	Strenuous	10.4–12.0 mi rt	5–6 hr	1,900 ft		349
19 Sequoia Audubon Trail	Easy	2.4 mi rt	1 hr	Negligible		353
20 Butano Grand Loop	Strenuous	11.0 mi rt	6 hr	1,300 ft		356
21 Año Nuevo Point Trail	Easy	3.0 mi rt	2 hr	Negligible		359
22 Antler Point Loop	Strenuous	8.8 mi rt	5 hr	1,800 ft		363

TRAIL NAME	LEVEL	DISTANCE	TIME	ELEVATION	FEATURES	PAGE
23 Coyote Peak Loop	Easy	4.0 mi rt	2 hr	500 ft		367
24 Flat Frog, Middle Ridge, and Fish Trail Loop	Moderate	7.8 mi rt	4 hr	1,000 ft		370
25 Waterfall Loop Trail	Easy/Moderate	3.5 mi rt	2 hr	700 ft		374
26 Loch Trail and Highlands Loop	Easy/Moderate	5.2 mi rt	3 hr	700 ft		377
27 Fall Creek Loop	Moderate	8.0 mi rt	4 hr	1,500 ft		380
28 Observation Deck and Big Rock Hole Loop	Moderate	6.4 mi rt	3.5 hr	1,000 ft		384
29 Old Landing Cove Trail	Easy	2.5 mi rt	1.5 hr	Negligible		388
30 Loma Prieta Grade and Bridge Creek Loop	Moderate	7.0 or 9.0 mi rt	4-5 hr	600 ft		391

1 LAND'S END COASTAL TRAIL
Golden Gate National Recreation Area

Level: Easy

Hiking Time: 2 hours

Total Distance: 3.5 miles round-trip

Elevation Change: 250 feet

Summary: A hike along the edge of one of San Francisco's wealthiest neighborhoods delivers an unbeatable Golden Gate view.

What is the wildest place in San Francisco? While some might argue for the South of Market nightclubs, I vote for the Land's End Coastal Trail. It's hard to believe you can find a city trail that feels so natural and remote, but here it is. The path delivers million-dollar views of crashing surf, offshore outcrops, the Golden Gate Bridge, and the Marin Headlands. Wildlife and wildflowers abound.

Coastal Trail begins near Ocean Beach and winds its way north and east along the ocean bluffs to China and Baker Beaches. (It also runs south along Ocean Beach to Sloat Boulevard, but this section is paved and heavily used by tourists, in-line skaters, cyclists, and beach bums of all kinds. Although it's an enjoyable stroll, it's not a nature experience.) In its entirety, Coastal Trail is 11 miles long, although not all of it is contiguous and some of it follows city streets. This 3.5-mile round-trip follows its "wildest" section from the Merrie Way parking lot above the Cliff House to 32nd Avenue and El Camino del Mar. Take a hike here and for a brief while you may forget you're in a major metropolitan area.

The ocean views from the parking lot make a satisfying first impression. As you lace up your hiking boots, watch for a Golden Gate–bound freighter or the

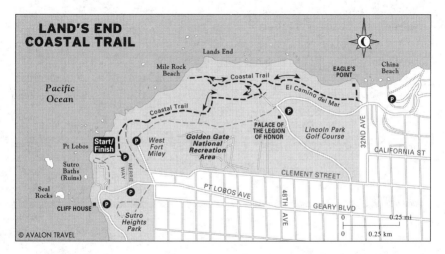

spout of a gray whale, and lend an ear to the chorus of barking sea lions. Then take the trail from the north end of the lot that dips into a canopy of cypress trees. Immediately you'll spot a couple of spur paths on the left; these lead a few hundred feet to ocean overlooks—perfect spots for sunset-watching. Take the right fork to connect to the wide main trail, which is the remains of the roadbed for Adolph Sutro's 1888 steam train.

Sutro was a San Francisco entrepreneur who wanted to make his Cliff House Restaurant and adjoining bathhouse more accessible to working-class folks. He built the railroad and charged people only a nickel to ride. Unfortunately, numerous landslides made maintaining the railway too expensive, and in 1925 he shut it down.

Today the former rail trail supplies postcard views of the Golden Gate Bridge, Marin Headlands, Pacific Ocean, and San Francisco Bay. The path is lined with windswept cypress trees that have taken on strange, stiff forms, as if they've been hair-sprayed into shape. If you look closely at the ocean waters below the trail, you might spot the remains of several Golden Gate shipwrecks. Point Lobos and Mile Rock, two submerged rocks, have taken many casualties off Land's End. Today both rocks are marked with buoy signals.

In 0.5 mile you'll see a right fork, where a gated road heads uphill to the Palace of the Legion of Honor art museum. Continue straight on the main path. In another 50 yards is a narrow trail on the left marked with a leashed dog symbol. Follow this stair-stepped path steeply downhill for 0.25 mile to Mile Rock Beach, named for the red-and-white fog signal in the middle of the bay. The small beach, strewn with driftwood and rounded rocks, is popular with sunbathers. On summer weekends, be prepared for an anatomy lesson: Not everyone wears clothes here. From Mile Rock Beach you can take side trails east and west along the bluffs, but use caution. The soil is continually eroding and the paths are not maintained.

Back on the main trail, you'll reach a fence at Painted Rock Cliff and a section of trail leading uphill, designated for hikers only. Ascend the stairsteps into a grove of eucalyptus, then continue on a narrower trail as it curves along the edge of ocean bluffs, affording more Golden Gate views. Trailside anise grows 10 feet tall and the coastal scrub is aromatic after winter rains.

The trail winds up at Eagle's Point, a dramatic ocean overlook near 32nd Avenue and across from Lincoln Park Golf Course. Follow its winding staircase down the bluffs for the best views of the day, then retrace your steps back to your car.

Options

When you return to the Merrie Way parking lot, consider a walk on the abandoned rail trail into Sutro Heights Park. A short path loops around the remains of

© ANN MARIE BROWN

view of Golden Gate Bridge from the Land's End Coastal Trail

Sutro's estate. To access it, walk through the Merrie Way lot and cross Point Lobos Avenue. (It's about 100 yards uphill.) Be sure to stop at the loop's far end, just below a rock parapet that was built in 1880 as a viewing platform. From here, you are directly above the Cliff House, looking out toward the Farallon Islands.

Another worthy side trip leads from the west side of the Merrie Way parking lot, down a set of stairs to the concrete ruins of the Sutro Baths. The saltwater bathhouse was a popular San Francisco attraction until 1966, when it burned to the ground. The neighboring Cliff House underwent a major renovation in 2004, returning it to its original neoclassical design and adding a new wing with more space for visitors to enjoy the site's spectacular ocean views. If you haven't visited, it's worth a special trip.

Directions

In San Francisco, head west on Geary Boulevard to 48th Avenue, where Geary becomes Point Lobos Avenue. Continue on Point Lobos Avenue for half a block to the Merrie Way parking lot on the right, just above Louis' Restaurant. The trail leads from the north side of the parking lot.

Public transportation: MUNI Buses #38 and #38L stop at Point Lobos and 48th Avenue. Walk west on Point Lobos for a short distance to the Merrie Way parking lot. For MUNI information, phone 415/701-2311 (or just 311 in San Francisco) or visit www.sfmta.com.

Information and Contact

There is no fee. Leashed dogs are allowed. Bikes are allowed on part of the Coastal Trail. A free map is available by contacting Golden Gate National Recreation Area, Fort Mason, Building 201, San Francisco, CA 94123, 415/561-4700, or by free download at www.nps.gov/goga. For more information, phone the GGNRA Presidio Visitor Center at 415/561-4323.

2 ALCATRAZ ISLAND'S AGAVE TRAIL BEST ◖

Golden Gate National Recreation Area

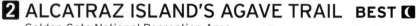

Level: Easy

Hiking Time: 1 hour

Total Distance: 1.0 mile round-trip

Elevation Change: 100 feet

Summary: Stow away to an island in San Francisco Bay and see a part of "The Rock" that most tourists never see.

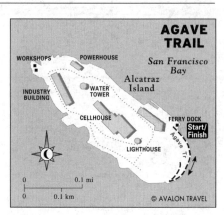

Everyone who has ever been to San Francisco knows about Alcatraz Island, but very few people know about Alcatraz Island's Agave Trail.

Agave? Isn't that the tall, funny-looking plant that's the key ingredient in tequila? Yes, the very same.

The agaves were planted on Alcatraz Island by prison guards and their families in the 1930s and 1940s. Although Alcatraz was little more than a big, barren rock in the middle of the bay, the people who called it home were determined to grow gardens and make the place hospitable. So while the prisoners paced in their jail cells, the guards and their families formed a gardening association, imported topsoil from Angel Island and exotic plants from around the world, and set out to make the island grow. Their work paid off: The agaves and other ornamental flora flourished. Today they frame the island's incomparable views of San Francisco and the Golden Gate.

You can visit Alcatraz and its famous prison almost any day of the year, but if you want to walk the short Agave Trail, you must show up between late September and early February. The rest of the year the trail is closed to protect nesting birds. Colonies of black-crowned night herons and snowy egrets build their nests in trees and bushes around the island each spring. In summer, the prison's concrete parade ground is filled with the nests and chicks of western gulls, making this one of the largest western gull nesting sites on the West Coast. The birds build more than 450 nests on Alcatraz each year.

The timing of the trail's open season works out beautifully, because autumn and winter usually produce the clearest, fog-free days on the bay. Also, the summer tourist crowds are nonexistent, so it's relatively easy to get a seat on an Alcatraz ferry (except in the weeks around Thanksgiving and Christmas). On late fall and winter weekdays, you can often just show up at Pier 33 and get on the next boat. Not so the rest of the year.

Keep in mind that this trip is more like a walk than a hike. You won't need your $200 hiking boots, but you will need your camera. The scenery is incredible.

After an easy and scenic boat ride across San Francisco Bay, you disembark at the landing on the east side of the island. Most everybody heads to the right and up the hill to tour the prison, using audio headsets to listen to a 45-minute self-guided tour of Alcatraz cellhouse. The tour features the voices of actual prisoners and prison guards, and makes the old walls of the prison come to life. However, if your plan for today is simply to walk the Agave Trail and not tour the cellhouse, you can ask a ranger on the dock for a partial refund on your ferry fee, then head left instead of right, passing some picnic tables and a gated chain-link fence. On the fence's far side is a sign marking the Agave Trail.

The path's first stretch is level, concrete, and wheelchair accessible. You saunter only a few feet from the water's edge, watching as boats sail by and seagulls fly overhead. Gentle lapping waves spill onto the walkway. Unforgettable views of downtown San Francisco and the Bay Bridge unfold. As you curve around to the south side of the island, you'll pass the large sign seen on your ferry ride, warning that "persons procuring or concealing escape of prisoners are subject to prosecution and imprisonment."

Agave Trail leads along the base of a steep hillside covered with agave plants. Their strange shapes make marvelous outlines against the bright blue sky. At

Agaves line this trail of the same name on historic Alcatraz.

the end of the trail's level stretch, you can see some of Alcatraz's rocky tidepools during low tides. A rare occurrence in San Francisco Bay, these tidepools were formed from artificial rubble created by years of blasting and building on the island. Although you can't access the tidepools, at low tide you can lean over the railing and glimpse anemones shimmering in the sun.

Artful flagstone stairsteps lead uphill to the prison's parade grounds, which were once ringed by the houses of guards and their families. Those homes were demolished in 1971, and the building remains were scattered across the open concrete yard in huge rubble piles. Very soon these piles became homes for burrowing owls, night herons, deer mice, and salamanders.

From the parade grounds, your view expands to take in all of the Golden Gate Bridge and parts of the Marin Headlands. San Francisco shines to the south. If you can pull yourself away from the scenery, walk across the parade grounds and along the north side of the barracks to join the main paved trail leading to the cellhouse. There are several buildings to explore and many more views of the bay and mainland to see.

Options

If you think you've "been there, done that" at Alcatraz, sign up for an evening tour of the island. These visits include a narrated boat tour around the island, the same self-guided audio tour that is available on day tours, special programs on a variety of Alcatraz topics, and dramatic sunset and nighttime views of the San Francisco skyline. The price is slightly higher than what it costs to visit during the day, but it's worth it. Evening tours are held Thursday–Monday only and last about 2.5 hours. Make reservations with Alcatraz Cruises (415/981-7625, www.alcatrazcruises.com).

Directions

Alcatraz Island can be accessed via Alcatraz Cruises ferry from Pier 33 in San Francisco, which is located on The Embarcadero near Bay Street. Parking is available at more than a dozen fee lots nearby.

Public transportation: The MUNI "F" line runs along the Embarcadero and stops at the ferry terminal. For MUNI information, phone 415/701-2311 (or just 311 in San Francisco) or visit www.sfmta.com.

Information and Contact

The Agave Trail is open only late September–early February, when bird nesting season begins. The rest of Alcatraz Island is open year-round except for Thanksgiving, Christmas, and New Year's Day. The ferry fee is $26 per adult (ages 12–61), which includes the 45-minute audio tour of Alcatraz cellhouse. Tickets for children and seniors are discounted. Purchase Alcatraz tickets in advance through Alcatraz Cruises (415/981-7625, www.alcatrazcruises.com). Advance tickets are strongly recommended in the summer months and during holiday periods. Dogs and bikes are not allowed. For more information, contact Golden Gate National Recreation Area, Fort Mason, Building 201, San Francisco, CA 94123, 415/561-4700, www.nps.gov/alcatraz.

3 SUMMIT LOOP TRAIL BEST C
San Bruno Mountain State and County Park

Level: Easy/Moderate

Total Distance: 3.1 miles round-trip

Hiking Time: 1.5 hours

Elevation Change: 725 feet

Summary: Get some perspective on San Francisco while exploring San Bruno Mountain's rugged natural beauty just minutes from the city.

San Bruno Mountain is located a few miles off U.S. 101, adjacent to South San Francisco and I-280 in Daly City. More specifically, it's situated about 1,200 feet above the Cow Palace, that huge entertainment arena that houses everything from monster truck shows to well-bred cat competitions. The bald, grassy mountain overlooks Candlestick Park and the business complexes on U.S. 101. Does this seem like an unlikely place for a nature preserve? You bet. But San Bruno Mountain is full of surprises.

The Summit Loop Trail takes you on a tour of the mountain, providing a mix of city and bay views. Hikers who show up in spring will find the hillsides brimming with wildflowers. Some of them serve a dire role: San Bruno Mountain is prime habitat for the endangered mission blue butterfly. Three kinds of native lupine grow here that are crucial to the development of the butterfly's larva. The mission blue butterfly exists only on San Bruno Mountain, in the Marin Headlands, and around San Francisco's Twin Peaks.

San Bruno Mountain is also home to two more endangered butterflies, the San Bruno elfin and the San Francisco silverspot, as well as rare and endangered plants including Pacific manzanita, San Bruno Mountain manzanita, Diablo rock rose, San Francisco owl's clover, and dune tansy. The 2,700-acre park is carefully managed with a habitat conservation plan to protect the precious species. A legal agreement between the public and local developers, the plan limits the amount and type of building that can be done on San Bruno Mountain's slopes. Although developers have contested the conservation plan in court, it has always been upheld. Meanwhile, hikers are welcome to share the hillsides with the rare and precious plants and butterflies.

After turning into the park, pass through the entrance kiosk, then turn right to follow the park road under Guadalupe Canyon Parkway for the trailhead on the south side. Check out the San Bruno Mountain Botanical Garden, a native plant garden maintained by park volunteers, then begin hiking at the signboard. Bear right for Summit Loop Trail. In 100 yards, you'll reach a second junction; this is where you choose which leg of the loop to follow uphill. A right turn will lead you across the paved summit road and counterclockwise for the easiest grade. A left turn will take you on the shortest route to the summit, still with a very mild grade.

The shorter left route will earn you dramatic views almost immediately. In just a few minutes of climbing, San Francisco and its bay appear. Mount Diablo looms large in the background. The panorama keeps changing with every switchback up the slope. Vistas are unobstructed because San Bruno Mountain is almost entirely grasslands, with just a few stands of eucalyptus and some low-growing chaparral. Although native grasslands have become increasingly rare in the Bay Area due to grazing and the introduction of nonnative species, San Bruno Mountain is home to more than 20 species.

Just beyond a junction with Dairy Ravine Trail, a left spur leads to a strategically positioned bench on a knoll with a wide-angle view. North to south you can see Twin Peaks, San Francisco's downtown, the Cow Palace, Monster Park, the Bay Bridge, the East Bay hills, and Oyster and Sierra Points. You can hear the rushing sound of the freeway, but perched high on this oasis you feel oddly insulated from it.

Keep climbing and you'll soon approach the antenna-covered summit. Where

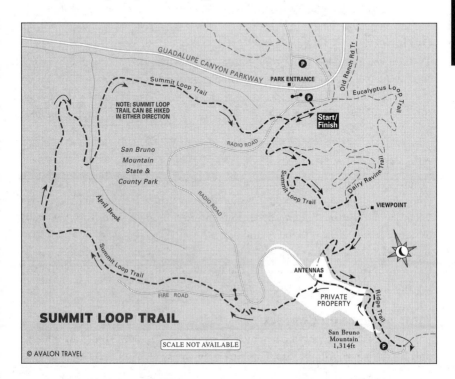

SUMMIT LOOP TRAIL

Ridge Trail heads left, follow it for more outstanding bay views and a scenic final stretch. At a junction with a fire road, turn right and walk the last few steps uphill. Ridge Trail continues for 2.5 miles to San Bruno Mountain's East Peak. This makes a terrific out-and-back hike, if you want to add on a few miles. In addition to providing more incomparable views of the bay, Ridge Trail is bordered by two unusual manzanita species: the endemic coastal manzanita and kinnikinnick, which is near the southern edge of its range.

At the summit, the radio towers barely diminish the drama of the view. From the summit parking lot you can wander around and admire a 360-degree panorama. This will be your first look at the coast; you'll enjoy more western views on the return leg of the loop.

When you've seen enough, head downhill on the paved road for 0.25 mile to where Summit Loop Trail crosses the pavement. Bear left, taking the signed trail on the right side of a gated road. Enjoy more ocean vistas, plus glimpses of Mount Tamalpais and the Marin Headlands to the north. If you're hiking in spring, the park's best displays of wildflowers are found on this western slope. Look for lupine, poppies, Douglas iris, goldfields, pennyroyal, and owl's clover, among many others. More unusual species include broadleaf stonecrop and wild pansy. You'll be accompanied by wildflowers and ocean views all the way back downhill.

Options

The best way to explore San Bruno Mountain is on a guided hike with San Bruno Mountain Watch, a nonprofit stewardship group. Free guided walks are held on occasional Saturdays throughout the year, and almost every Saturday during the spring wildflower bloom. Phone 415/467-6631 or visit www.mountainwatch.org for a current schedule.

Directions

From U.S. 101 south of San Francisco, take the Brisbane/Cow Palace exit (or if you are traveling north, take the Bayshore Boulevard/Cow Palace exit) and drive 1.8 miles on Bayshore Boulevard, heading toward the Cow Palace. Turn left (west) on Guadalupe Canyon Parkway and drive 2.3 miles to the park entrance. Turn right and drive past the entrance kiosk, then loop back underneath the road to the parking area and trailhead on the south side of Guadalupe Canyon Parkway; the trailhead is next to the native plant garden.

Information and Contact

A $5 day-use fee is charged per vehicle. Dogs are not allowed. Bikes are allowed only on the paved summit road. Free park maps are available at the entrance kiosk,

Hikers get a new perspective on San Francisco from San Bruno Mountain.

or by free download at www.eparks.net. A detailed map of the area is available from Pease Press, 415/387-1437, www.peasepress.com (ask for the *Trails of the Coastside and Central Peninsula* map). For more information, contact San Bruno Mountain State and County Park, 555 Guadalupe Canyon Parkway, Brisbane, CA 94005, 650/992-6770, www.eparks.net.

4 THREE TRAILS TO SWEENEY RIDGE
Golden Gate National Recreation Area

Level: Moderate

Total Distance: 4.0 or 5.0 miles round-trip

Hiking Time: 2-3 hours

Elevation Change: 750 feet or 1,000 feet

Summary: Visit one of the Bay Area's most important historical sites and enjoy a stunning 360-degree panorama from the top of Sweeney Ridge.

Has the fog vanished from San Francisco? Good. Is it morning? Good. These are the two crucial elements for a trip to Sweeney Ridge and the San Francisco Bay Discovery Site. Why? Zero fog is imperative in order to fully appreciate the stupendous views from the top of the ridge. Morning is the critical time to hike because if the weather is clear, by midday the wind is probably going to howl.

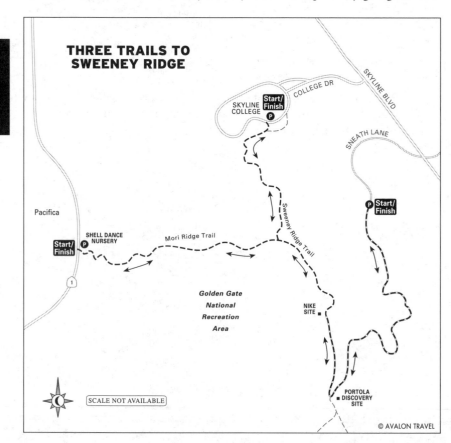

THREE TRAILS TO
SWEENEY RIDGE

SKYLINE BLVD

COLLEGE DR

SKYLINE
COLLEGE

Start/
Finish

SNEATH LANE

Start/
Finish

Pacifica

SHELL DANCE
NURSERY

Mori Ridge Trail

Sweeney Ridge Trail

Start/
Finish

1

Golden Gate
National
Recreation
Area

NIKE
SITE

PORTOLA
DISCOVERY
SITE

SCALE NOT AVAILABLE

© AVALON TRAVEL

Pick a still, sunny morning (most likely to occur in spring or fall) and you're in line for a great hiking trip.

You have three good trail choices. The paved route from Sneath Lane in San Bruno is open to hikers, bikers, and dogs, and has a very easy grade. It features views of San Andreas Lake and the prominent landmarks of South San Francisco and the northern peninsula. The path from Skyline College is a dirt trail, closed to bikes but open to dogs and hikers, which supplies views of the ocean and Pacifica's coastline (parking can be difficult at the college on weekdays). The trail from Shell Dance Nursery in Pacifica is a bit longer and steeper than the others—five miles round-trip instead of four, and a 1,000-foot elevation gain instead of 750 feet. It's open to hikers, bikers, and dogs, and it also offers grand coastal views.

All three trails lead to the same result: an incredible 360-degree panorama from the top of Sweeney Ridge. This vista takes in the Pacific coastline and San Francisco Bay, as well as the landmass to the east, north, and south. It was here, at the 1,200-foot summit on top of Sweeney Ridge, that Gaspar de Portolà and the Portola Expedition arrived at San Francisco Bay on November 4, 1769. A stone monument commemorates the event. Alongside it is a second monument in memory of Carl Patrick McCarthy, who, as the sign states, "personally brought 11,863 visitors to this discovery site" and was instrumental in obtaining protective status for Sweeney Ridge. Carved on the granite marker are the outlines of all the major landmarks you can see from this spot, including Montara Mountain, Mount Tamalpais, Mount Diablo, Mount Hamilton, Point Reyes, Point San Pedro, and the Farallon Islands.

If you opt for the Sneath Lane paved trail, the trip is simple. The trail begins at a gate at the parking area and slowly winds its way uphill. About two-thirds of the way up, you'll see a yellow line painted on the trail. That's the fog line, which in the 1950s and '60s served as a visual marker for military personnel who serviced the Nike missile site on top of the ridge. Today it's a useful tool for bikers and hikers when visibility is bad.

Once you reach the fog line, the trail enters its steepest stretch, but the views of the peninsula more than compensate. At the top of the ridge, you'll find a major junction of trails. This is where you gain wide westward views to add to your collection of eastern views. Straight ahead is a wooden bench that overlooks the coast. Go left for a few yards to see the Portola monument. Then take the paved ridge trail to the right, which stays level and easy for 0.5 mile, passes a big water tower, and ends at the abandoned buildings of an old Nike missile site, a remnant of the Cold War era.

If you opt for the trail from Skyline College, the trail begins from the back side of Parking Lot B and makes a brief, steep ascent uphill to join an old gravel road. Turn right on the road and enjoy a mellower grade and immediate coastal views. Mount Tamalpais appears to the north. In less than a mile, you'll reach an abandoned military bunker, a reminder of Sweeney Ridge's role in protecting San Francisco from possible military invasion during World War II. Because of the bunker's strategic high point, it has a splendid view of South San Francisco, the South Bay, the Pacific coast, and Mount Diablo to the east.

From the bunker, the trail drops steeply, soon joining a long series of stairsteps leading down into a ravine. If you look to your right, you'll see where the trail is heading—right back up the stairsteps on the far side. It's a mini-workout for your cardiovascular system.

The trail tops out at the abandoned Nike missile site buildings, where the view of coast and bay is appealing enough. But take a stroll along the paved, level ridge trail for 0.5 mile to see the stone monument to Portolà and check out even better views from there.

If you choose to take the route from Pacifica, start at the gate behind Shell Dance Nursery. Take Mori Ridge Trail, an old dirt road, steeply uphill. For almost two miles the trail leads through open grasslands and coastal scrub with nearly nonstop views of Mount Tamalpais, Montara Mountain, and the Pacific Ocean. Occasional Monterey pines present a chance for shade. Where Mori Ridge Trail meets up with Sweeney Ridge Trail (the path from Skyline College), turn right for the last 0.5 mile to the Nike missile site. Continue along the paved trail to the Portolà monument.

Options

If you enjoy the high views from Sweeney Ridge, check out the trails from another ridge above Pacifica, the Golden Gate National Recreation Area's Milagra Ridge. To get there, from Highway 1 in Pacifica take the Sharp Park Road exit and drive east up the hill for 1.5 miles. Turn left at the sign for Milagra Ridge and drive to the end of the road. This grassland-covered ridge top is a favorite of hikers, dog walkers, and kite flyers who relish its sweeping coastal views. Along with nearby Sweeney Ridge, this parkland is one of the last remaining habitat areas for the mission blue butterfly. You can hike a 1.5-mile semi-loop along the ridge. Spring wildflowers are plentiful.

Directions

For the Sneath Lane trailhead: From I-280 in San Bruno, take the Sneath Lane/San Bruno Avenue exit and turn west. At the stoplight, turn left (west) on Sneath Lane. Drive 1.9 miles to the trailhead parking area.

For the Skyline College trailhead: From I-280 in San Bruno, take the

© ANN MARIE BROWN

The Sneath Lane trail to Sweeney Ridge is popular with dog-walkers.

Westborough exit and turn right (west), following the signs for Skyline College. Drive 1.4 miles, then turn left on Skyline Boulevard (Highway 35). Drive 0.7 mile, then turn right on College Drive. Drive 0.5 mile. At the stop sign, turn left, drive 0.25 mile, then turn left at the sign for Parking Lot B (staff lot). The trailhead is located on the left side of the parking lot and several parking spots are signed "Reserved for GGNRA on weekends and holidays."

For the Pacifica trailhead: From Highway 1 in Pacifica, turn east into the driveway for Shell Dance Nursery (north of Reina del Mar Avenue and south of Sharp Park Road). Drive 0.3 mile, past the nursery buildings, to the Sweeney Ridge parking area at the end of the dirt road.

Public transportation: SamTrans Buses #121 and #123 stop at the Skyline College Trailhead. For SamTrans information, phone 800/660-4287 or visit www.samtrans.com.

Information and Contact

There is no fee. Leashed dogs are allowed. Bikes are allowed on all trails except the route from Skyline College. A free map is available by contacting Golden Gate National Recreation Area, Fort Mason, Building 201, San Francisco, CA 94123, 415/561-4700, www.nps.gov/goga. A detailed map of the area is available from Pease Press, 415/387-1437, www.peasepress.com (ask for the *Pacifica* map). For more information, phone the GGNRA Presidio Visitor Center at 415/561-4323.

5 BROOKS FALLS LOOP   BEST (

San Pedro Valley County Park

Level: Easy   **Total Distance:** 2.6 miles round-trip

Hiking Time: 1.5 hours   **Elevation Change:** 500 feet

Summary: In the wet months of the year, a glistening waterfall awaits hikers in San Pedro Valley's sylvan canyon.

The first time you drive to San Pedro Valley County Park you may think you have the wrong directions. You head down Highway 1 into Pacifica, then turn off at a shopping center with a supermarket and a selection of chain restaurants. The place doesn't look much like a nature preserve.

But have patience, because you need only drive another couple of miles before leaving these suburban entrapments behind. In a few minutes on the trail, you'll head up and away from the parking lots, noise, and traffic lights and enter a vastly different world.

If you're hiking in the rainy season, a surprise awaits. By hiking the Brooks Creek Trail in winter or spring, you have a chance to see one of the Bay Area's prettiest waterfalls: Brooks Falls, a tall, narrow cascade of water that plunges 175 feet in three tiers. From a distance, it looks like one of the majestic tropical waterfalls of Hawaii.

Manzanitas dwarf hikers at San Pedro Valley County Park.

© ANN MARIE BROWN

Locate the trailhead for Montara Mountain Trail by the restrooms in San Pedro Valley County Park. A few feet beyond the trailhead, the trail splits: Montara Mountain Trail heads right and Old Trout Farm Trail heads left. Go left and gently uphill through a dense grove of eucalyptus. At trail junctions, small signs direct you "to Waterfall Viewing Area." Bear right at two forks, now following Brooks Creek Trail, and keep heading uphill. The well-graded path soon emerges from the trees to open views of the canyon amid coastal sage scrub, ceanothus, and monkeyflower.

Twenty minutes of well-graded climbing delivers your first glimpse of the waterfall, far off in the canyon on your left. Look for a narrow plume of

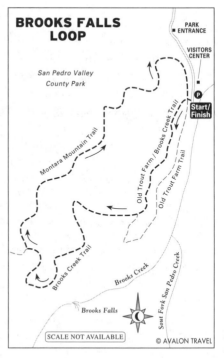

water cascading down the mountainside. Unfortunately, no trails lead to the base of the waterfall; you can only view it from a distance. The best viewpoint is at a conveniently placed bench right along the trail. After a hard rain, you can hear and see the water crashing down the canyon slopes 0.25 mile away. If you want photographs, bring your extra-long telephoto lens.

From the manzanita-lined overlook, continue uphill on Brooks Creek Trail, gaining more views of Brooks Falls. The trail tops out on a ridge with an overlook of Pacifica and the ocean to the west and the Marin Headlands to the north. On the clearest days, even the Farallon Islands show up. Montara Mountain Trail takes off from here; to the left and two miles farther is the summit of Montara Mountain (see *Montara Mountain Summit* listing in this chapter). For a 2.6-mile loop, turn right on Montara Mountain Trail and start to descend. You'll drop 500 feet in elevation through more stands of eucalyptus to reach the trailhead and parking area. If you happen to live in Pacifica, you might be able to pick out your house from the multitude of roofs below.

Keep in mind that Brooks Falls is a seasonal waterfall. This loop trip makes a pleasant hike year-round, but the fall appears only in the rainy season.

Options

To explore more of the park, try a 4.6-mile loop on Hazelnut Trail and Weiler Ranch Road, starting from behind the visitors center. From the group picnic area, take wide and level Weiler Ranch Road up the valley for 1.2 miles, then turn right on Hazelnut Trail. You'll gain 400 feet as you switchback up a ridge through a mixed bouquet of tall chaparral plants—everything from common coyote brush to uncommon chinquapin. From the loop's highest points, you gain surprising views of the Pacific Ocean (even the Farallon Islands on the clearest days) and San Pedro Creek Canyon. The downhill side of the loop is routed through a veritable forest of hazelnut, the trail's namesake.

Directions

From Highway 1 in Pacifica, turn east on Linda Mar Boulevard. Follow Linda Mar Boulevard for two miles until it dead-ends at Oddstad Boulevard. Turn right and drive 50 yards to the park entrance on the left. Park in the upper parking lot (to the right of the visitors center as you drive in). Montara Mountain Trail is located next to the restrooms.

Public transportation: SamTrans Bus #14 stops on Linda Mar Boulevard less than one mile from the park entrance. For SamTrans information, phone 800/660-4287 or visit www.samtrans.com.

Information and Contact

A $5 day-use fee is charged per vehicle. Dogs and bikes are not allowed. Free maps are available at the visitors center, or by free download at www.eparks.net. A detailed map of the area is available from Pease Press, 415/387-1437, www.pease-press.com (ask for the *Pacifica* map). For more information, contact San Pedro Valley County Park, 600 Oddstad Boulevard, Pacifica, CA 94044, 650/355-8289, www.eparks.net.

6 MONTARA MOUNTAIN SUMMIT   BEST (

McNee Ranch State Park/Montara State Beach

Level: Strenuous   **Total Distance:** 7.4 miles round-trip

Hiking Time: 4 hours   **Elevation Change:** 2,200 feet

Summary: On a clear day, this coastal mountain offers sweeping bay-to-ocean views, taking in everything from Mount Diablo to the shoreline from San Francisco to Pescadero.

There are two routes to Montara Mountain's summit: the doggy route and the no-doggy route. Both trails make good hiking and the summit vista is sublime no matter how you get there.

The no-dogs-allowed trail begins in Pacifica's San Pedro Valley County Park and is the preferred choice for hikers who love single-track. You won't encounter any mountain bikers on this path (except in the last 1.1 miles to the summit, where the two trails join), but you can't bring your dog, either. Details on this trail can be found in the *Brooks Falls Loop* listing in this chapter.

The dog-friendly route begins in McNee Ranch, a unit of Montara State Beach on Highway 1 just north of Montara. It's an old paved road that transitions into a dirt fire road as it climbs the mountain, and it is open to hikers, bikers, equestrians, and dogs. The road/trail serves up expansive coastal views as it winds up Montara Mountain's western slope. One advantage of taking this route is that you don't have to hike all the way to the summit to gain a vista; the scenery is good for most of the trip. If you do go all the way, you can take an alternative route back down the mountain, making a nice semi-loop.

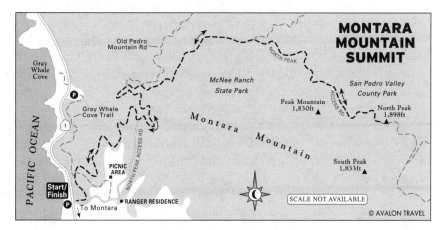

From the Highway 1 trailhead at undeveloped McNee Ranch, begin hiking on the single-track Gray Whale Cove Trail just to the left of the gated road. The first 0.5 mile rises out of a cypress-lined canyon to gain coastal views to the north, including the crashing surf and tall cliffs of Gray Whale Cove. At an unsigned junction, go right and join a crumbling, paved thoroughfare, Old San Pedro Mountain Road, which served as the route from Montara to Pacifica before Highway 1 was built. Head north on this old road. (If you prefer, you can just follow the gated road from the trailhead, then bear left on Old San Pedro Mountain Road by the ranger's residence, but this is a longer, less scenic option.)

The road's broken pavement is being rapidly encroached upon by 10-foot-high pampas grass, coyote brush, and other coastal flora, both native and nonnative. For the next 0.5 mile, you'll lose your coastal views as you traipse through a canyon, but this is the trail's only viewless stretch. Meanwhile, watch for bike riders flying downhill. You'll have plenty of time to see and hear them coming and get out of their way.

The road/trail is extremely well graded. A few benches are in place at strategic resting points. At 1.8 miles, as you pause to catch your breath and admire the ocean views, note a left spur trail signed No Bikes. That's where you'll loop back on your return. Here the panorama opens wide, exposing the crashing surf and tall cliffs of Montara State Beach and Gray Whale Cove.

Here you can pause to consider how often the section of Highway 1 below you—aptly named Devil's Slide—has been closed due to landslides, effectively sealing off the people of Montara and nearby communities from most of the rest of the world and creating traffic nightmares on Highway 92, the Peninsula's only major thoroughfare to the coast. Residents of Montara and neighboring towns will continue to hold their breath until sometime in 2011, when two tunnels through the base of Montara Mountain—each 30 feet wide and 4,200 feet long—will be complete, creating a bypass route for this accident-prone stretch of Highway 1. As this book went to print, construction was nearing completion. When the tunnels are finished and ready for traffic, the bypassed old highway and 70 acres of land surrounding it will be made accessible for public recreation, which should give us all something to cheer about. For updated information on the project and the new recreation area, visit www.dot.ca.gov/dist4/dslide.

One hundred yards past the "no bikes" spur trail, the old pavement veers off to the left; you'll continue uphill to the right on a good dirt road. This is officially Montara Mountain Road; you'll follow it all the way to the summit. Soon the road enters its steepest stretch, which lasts for 0.5 mile. It takes you high up on a ridge, where you can see Pillar Point Harbor and the Half Moon Bay airport on your right and the boxy houses of Pacifica on your left. The road is lined with ceanothus, coffeeberry, and scrub oaks. At 2.6 miles, you'll pass the single-track trail coming in from San Pedro Valley County Park. Both routes share the final 1.1 miles to the summit. Now that you've gained some elevation, the coastal scrub and pampas grass are replaced by chinquapin and manzanita covered with lichen and moss. Tiny ferns grow in crags among the rock. These are a tribute to the amount of fog that Montara Mountain sees.

As you near the top, you'll find the chassis of an old, rusted car, a small sandstone cave, and a spur trail leading west to a slightly lower summit. Straight ahead lie the main peaks of Montara Mountain, littered with microwave towers. Head for the north peak (to your right at the T-junction), the highest peak at 1,898 feet. A spur trail continues past the antennas to the tip-top.

What can you see from the summit? To the east it's the famous sign on U.S. 101 proclaiming "South San Francisco the Industrial City," the Dumbarton Bridge, San Francisco Bay, plus Mount Diablo in the background. To the west it's the wild Pacific coast all the way north to San Francisco and south to Pescadero. The Santa Cruz Mountains rise to the southeast. Mount Tamalpais looms high above the tall skyline of San Francisco. It's a breathtaking panorama.

If you want to get away from the summit's antennas, head for the lower peak to the west that you passed (by the sandstone cave). This bald summit makes a perfect picnic spot, although its views are only to the west.

Your trip back downhill is a treat, with nonstop coastal views in front of you rather than at your back. If you want to skip the long spell on pavement, remember

© ANN MARIE BROWN

coastal views from Montara Mountain

to watch for the alternative return route. When you leave the dirt road and join the old paved road, follow it for 100 yards to the single-track trail on your right. This path has a few extremely steep downhill pitches, so exercise some caution. When the path meets up with Gray Whale Cove Trail paralleling the coast and the highway, take a short side trip—the right fork leads a level 0.25 mile to a viewpoint with two benches. The ocean is so loud here that you can't hear the cars on the highway directly below.

Then backtrack on Gray Whale Cove Trail and follow the edge of the coast all the way back to your starting point.

Options

If Montara Mountain's coastal views have put you in the mood to walk near the ocean, head north through Devil's Slide to one of Pacifica's best attractions: the new, or rather reinvented, trails at Mori Point. Located directly south of Pacifica's Sharp Park Golf Course and just west of Highway 1, two trailheads access the area: one at the west end of Fairway Drive and the other at the south end of Bradford Way. After decades of battles, Mori Point was saved from development and added to the Golden Gate National Recreation Area in 2000, but restoration work didn't really begin until 2008. Much labor has taken place here, including the closure of old, erosion-scarred trails, the construction of environmentally friendly staircases and overlook platforms, and the creation of new frog ponds and a marsh. (As recently as September 2008, the marsh was a repository for hundreds of old tires, which thankfully were removed.) From both trailheads, easy walking paths lead out to extraordinary ocean views.

Directions

From Half Moon Bay, drive north on Highway 1 for 10 miles to Montara. Continue to 0.6 mile north of Montara State Beach and La Costanera Restaurant, just south of Devil's Slide. The trailhead is marked by a yellow metal gate on the east side of the highway. There is parking for about six cars. If this lot is full, you can park farther south at Montara State Beach.

Information and Contact

There is no fee. Leashed dogs and bikes are allowed. A detailed map of the area is available from Pease Press, 415/387-1437, www.peasepress.com (ask for the *Pacifica* map). For more information, contact Montara State Beach at 650/726-8819 or 650/726-8820.

7 TIDEPOOL WALK BEST **(**
Fitzgerald Marine Reserve

Level: Easy **Total Distance:** Up to 5.0 miles round-trip

Hiking Time: 1-2 hours **Elevation Change:** Negligible

Summary: On a small but scenic stretch of the San Mateo coast, explore tidepools teeming with life and the white sands of Seal Cove.

There is no trail on the beach at Fitzgerald Marine Reserve. When you visit, you may hike a few miles or only a few yards. But no matter how much or how little distance you cover, it's probably going to be the slowest walk of your life.

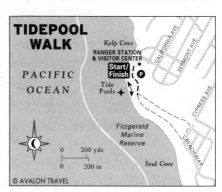

Fitzgerald Marine Reserve is hands-down the best place in the San Francisco Bay Area for exploring tidepools. You'll walk at a snail's pace along the rocky reefs, moving inch by inch and keeping a careful eye out for slippery rocks and sneaking waves. With your head bent down, you'll discover colorful sea creatures that are revealed by the departing tide. You may see mussels, crabs, abalones, barnacles, starfish, anemones, snails, and limpets. If you're lucky, you might spot an octopus or a nudibranch.

Fitzgerald Marine Reserve is part of the Monterey Bay National Marine Sanctuary, the largest marine sanctuary in the United States, which runs along the coast from Marin County to San Simeon. This entire area is federally protected from activities such as oil drilling that would irreparably harm the ecosystem. Within this sanctuary lies a broad, rocky, intertidal reef that runs from Point Montara to Pillar Point. It's one of the largest intertidal reefs in California, and that's the raison d'être for the Fitzgerald Marine Reserve.

During the lowest tides of the year, which occur most often in late fall and winter, as much as 30 acres of tidepools are revealed at Fitzgerald Marine Reserve. More than 200 species of marine animals and 150 species of plants are available for observation. This means that nobody walks away disappointed; it's virtually impossible not to ogle an urchin or stare down a starfish. The reserve is a huge hit with children; they love to watch tiny sea creatures scurrying along the bottoms of clear pools. All kids want to be the first in their family to spot a limpet or a sculpin

Time your trip carefully to get the most out of a visit to Fitzgerald Marine Reserve.

or to find the prettiest periwinkle. If you have children with you, remember to tell them they may look at and gently touch the creatures, but they may not pick them up or take them out of their environment. Because this is a marine reserve, every rock, plant, shell, and marine animal is protected by law.

To optimize your trip, you must take one step: Check the tide chart in the newspaper so that you plan your visit during a low tide, or even better, during a minus tide. With proper planning, you can walk the farthest and see the most.

From the parking lot, a wide trail parallels an ocean-bound creek down to the rocky beach. Head to your left toward Pillar Point in Half Moon Bay, 2.5 miles distant. When the tide is out, you could conceivably cover this distance—if you don't get too distracted in the first few hundred feet.

As you walk, watch for the four central zones of a tidepool area. The first is the low intertidal zone, which is underwater 90 percent of the time, so you get to see its inhabitants only during the lowest tides of the year. This is where the most interesting creatures are: eels, octopuses, sea hares, brittle stars, giant keyhole limpets, sculpins, and bat stars. The second area is the middle intertidal zone, which is underwater only 50 percent of the time, so it's in between the low and high tide line. This area has the creatures we usually associate with tidepools: sea stars or starfish, purple sea urchins, sea anemones, gooseneck barnacles, red algae, and mussels. In the high intertidal zone (underwater only 10 percent of the time), you'll see common acorn barnacles, shore crabs, black tegulas, and hermit crabs. These creatures can live out of water for long periods of time. The final tidepool region is the splash zone, where you'll find rough limpets, snails, and periwinkles.

Armed with all this knowledge, wander as you wish among the rocks and pools. Or, if you'd prefer to go with a pro, sign up for one of the free nighttime tidepool tours at the reserve. Rangers hold these tours just after dark during fall and winter, when tides are extremely low and you can easily observe nighttime activity on the reefs.

Options

A great way to extend this trip, or make a loop out of it during low tides, is to combine the tidepool walk with a walk on the blufftop trail above the marine reserve. Access the unsigned trail, known simply as the Bluff Trail, across from the restrooms at the trailhead parking lot (on the south side of North Lake Street at its junction with California Street). The path climbs uphill and leads through a hauntingly beautiful cypress forest with openings that provide delightful ocean views. A half-mile farther, at a park sign, follow a set of stairsteps (built in 2010) down to the white-sand beach at Seal Cove. From there, at low tide, you simply walk to your right across the reefs to make a two-mile loop. At high tide, you'll have to turn around and head back on the high trail.

Directions

From Half Moon Bay, drive north on Highway 1 for six miles to Moss Beach. Turn left (west) on California Avenue at the sign for Marine Life Refuge. Drive 0.3 mile, then turn right on North Lake Street. The parking lot is on your right.

Information and Contact

There is no fee. Dogs and bikes are not allowed. A free map is available by download at www.eparks.net. For more information, contact Fitzgerald Marine Reserve, P.O. Box 451, Moss Beach, CA 94038, 650/728-3584, www.eparks.net.

8 PURISIMA GRAND LOOP   BEST [

Purisima Creek Redwoods Open Space Preserve

Level: Strenuous   **Total Distance:** 10.0 miles round-trip

Hiking Time: 5.5 hours   **Elevation Change:** 1,600 feet

Summary: One of the most scenic loop trails in the northern Santa Cruz Mountains travels amid the redwoods of Purisima Canyon.

Purisima Creek Redwoods Open Space Preserve is a hiker's heaven. With breathtaking ocean views, towering redwood and fir trees, a year-round creek, and plentiful wildlife and wildflowers, the preserve shows off some of the best features of the Santa Cruz Mountains. Purisima delivers on its Spanish name: It's pristine.

You can access the 3,200-acre preserve from two trailheads on Skyline Boulevard or one on Higgins Purisima Road in Half Moon Bay. Purisima's trails traverse the slopes between Skyline Ridge and the coast, a 1,600-foot elevation change. Choose any path and you'll have to go up and then down, or down and then up.

This 10-mile loop begins at the preserve's northern entrance on Skyline Boulevard, a mere half-hour drive from San Francisco. This is an "upside-down" hike, in which you'll go downhill first, then uphill on your return. Even though it's a relatively mellow ascent, bring plenty of water and snacks to sustain you in the

Purisima's canyon is criss-crossed with fallen redwood trunks.

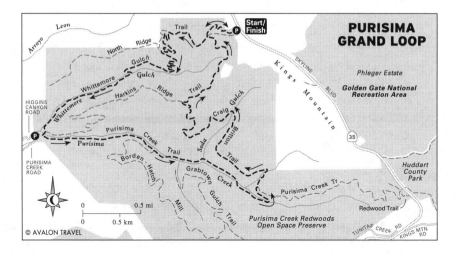

final miles. (If you want to hike the uphill leg first, you could begin the loop at the Higgins Purisima Road trailhead in Half Moon Bay.)

From the Skyline trailhead, follow the single-track, hikers-only trail to the right of the wide fire road. Switchback your way down the trail, enjoying the shade of Douglas firs, tan oaks, and madrones. February–June, the woodland understory is littered with dense clusters of light blue forget-me-nots. Look down at your feet; it appears as if you are walking amid blue and white clouds.

The narrow trail ends 0.5 mile out. Turn right on North Ridge Trail, a fir tree–lined fire road, and follow it for 0.5 mile. A left turn on Whittemore Gulch Trail puts you back on single-track. You'll pass through a seasonal gate used for blocking equestrians and mountain bikers from the trail during the wet season, then begin a series of long switchbacks downhill. The path opens out to chaparral-covered slopes with views of Half Moon Bay and the San Mateo coast. A short spur trail leads to an overlook with a railing to lean on; the coast vista is widest from here.

Continue descending and meet up with Whittemore Gulch, a seasonal tributary to Purisima Creek. Whittemore Gulch Trail follows the gulch downhill; the path bottoms out in a picturesque redwood and Douglas fir forest. Big-leaf maples grow in the understory of the conifers; their leaves turn bright yellow in the fall. You may want to linger in this delightful creekside woodland.

At 3.8 miles from the trailhead, you reach the trail's end and two junctions. Bypass Harkins Ridge Trail on the left and continue across the bridge over Purisima Creek to join Purisima Creek Trail. (The Higgins Canyon/Purisima Creek Road trailhead is located 100 feet west.)

Wide, redwood-lined Purisima Creek Trail climbs practically imperceptibly alongside Purisima Creek, gaining only 400 feet in 2.3 miles. Large redwood stumps are interspersed among the young redwoods, giving you a hint of what this forest looked like before it was logged in the late 1800s. Purisima's first-growth trees were used to build Half Moon Bay and San Francisco after the Gold Rush. The trail itself is an old logging road; seven lumber mills once operated along the banks of Purisima Creek. Today the stream canyon is home to a variety of ferns and a multitude of banana slugs. Its middle reaches are lined with impressive redwood deadfall.

Two miles from its start, Purisima Creek Trail makes a long switchback and heads northward to join with Craig Britton Trail (previously called Soda Gulch Trail). Bear left on this hikers-only pathway, a section of the Bay Area Ridge Trail, which makes a wide curve around the steep slopes of Soda Gulch. You'll traverse both sides of the canyon, crossing several smaller ravines on footbridges. Some of the tallest redwoods found in the preserve grow in the fertile soil around Soda Gulch. Most hikers agree that this 2.6-mile stretch on Craig Britton/Soda Gulch Trail is the most enchanting part of this loop.

As the trail gains elevation, the redwood canopy gives way to mixed hardwoods and chaparral-covered slopes. Craig Britton Trail's last mile offers occasional inspiring views of the Santa Cruz Mountains and distant Pacific Ocean. At a junction with Harkins Ridge Trail, turn right and hike the final 1.4 miles back to the trailhead. In the last 0.5 mile, you can turn right on North Ridge Trail or cross North Ridge and follow the single-track trail on which you began this trip.

Options

Two miles south on Skyline Boulevard is another trailhead for Purisima Creek. From here, the 0.6-mile Redwood Trail, a wheelchair- and stroller-accessible path, winds through dense redwoods. Connect to Purisima Creek Trail for a longer out-and-back hike.

Or, cross Skyline Boulevard and walk 100 feet south to enter the back door to Huddart Park. A downhill jaunt on Summit Springs Road, Crystal Springs Trail, and Dean Trail reveals dense redwoods, ferns, and huckleberry. Stop at redwood-lined McGarvey Flat for a picnic, then zigzag uphill on Chinquapin Trail to make a four-mile loop.

Directions

From San Francisco, drive south on I-280 for 19 miles to the Highway 92 west exit. Go west on Highway 92 for 2.7 miles, then turn left (south) on Highway

35 (Skyline Boulevard). Drive 4.5 miles to the Purisima Creek Redwoods Open Space Preserve parking area on the right.

Information and Contact

There is no fee. Dogs are not allowed. Bikes are allowed on some trails. Free trail maps are available at the trailhead or by download at www.openspace.org. For more information, contact the Midpeninsula Regional Open Space District, 330 Distel Circle, Los Altos, CA 94022, 650/691-1200, www.openspace.org.

9 TAFONI AND FIR TRAIL LOOP

El Corte de Madera Creek Open Space Preserve

Level: Easy/Moderate   **Total Distance:** 6.0 miles round-trip

Hiking Time: 3 hours   **Elevation Change:** 600 feet

Summary: Hidden amid a dense forest of redwoods and Douglas firs are the unique sandstone formations of El Corte de Madera Creek Preserve.

The monolithic sandstone formations at the end of the Tafoni Trail are the main attraction of the 2,800-acre El Corte de Madera Creek Open Space Preserve. Though similar in appearance to the rock outcrops at nearby Castle Rock State Park (see *Saratoga Gap and Ridge Trail Loop* listing in this chapter), the sandstone at El Corte de Madera Creek is composed of a softer, more fragile substance. You won't find any rock climbers here.

The formations stand completely alone in the forest; they're unlike anything else along the trail. The rest of the preserve is primarily trees and more trees, including some magnificent old Douglas firs and younger redwoods. You hike through acres of dense woodland, then suddenly they appear—huge sandstone beasts looming 50 feet high. Just as suddenly, there are no more of them, only trees, trees, and more trees. It's as if Mother Nature told the delivery company to drop the sandstone off at the wrong location.

The preserve has several access points along Skyline Boulevard; unfortunately, most of them don't have ample parking. The two best parking areas are at the

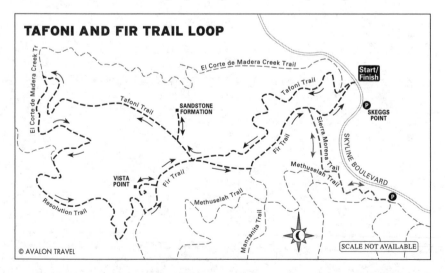

TAFONI AND FIR TRAIL LOOP

El Corte de Madera Creek Tr

El Corte de Madera Creek Trail

Tafoni Trail

Start/Finish

P SKEGGS POINT

Tafoni Trail

SANDSTONE FORMATION

Sierra Morena Trail

Fir Trail

SKYLINE BOULEVARD

VISTA POINT

Fir Trail

Methuselah Trail

P

Resolution Trail

Methuselah Trail

Manzanita Trail

SCALE NOT AVAILABLE

© AVALON TRAVEL

Caltrans Skeggs Vista Point, where there is a paved lot on the east side of the road, and 0.5 mile farther south, where there is parking for about 10 cars on the west side of the road. The latter trailhead has immediate access to the preserve's Sierra Morena Trail. From Skeggs Point, you must walk north along Skyline Boulevard for about 50 yards, then cross the road to access Tafoni Trail at a gated dirt road.

This six-mile figure-eight loop combines stints on Tafoni Trail, El Corte de Madera Creek Trail, Resolution Trail, and Fir Trail. The following description starts on Tafoni Trail; if you are beginning from the southern trailhead, take Sierra Morena Trail north (right) to Fir Trail, then turn right and join the start of Tafoni Trail. This will add 1.2 miles to your round-trip.

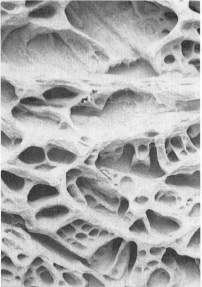

© KEVIN GONG

The intricacies of wind-sculpted sandstone can be seen on the Tafoni Trail.

Hike on a gentle uphill grade through big Douglas firs for the first 1.2 miles on Tafoni Trail. At a four-way junction, turn sharply right to head to the sandstone formations. In just a few hundred yards, you'll reach a sign announcing the tafoni ahead. Turn right on a single-track path (this is the only trail in the preserve that is reserved for hikers only) and descend to the 50-foot-high outcrops. An observation deck provides a good vantage point for gazing in awe at the tafoni.

Although it sounds like an Italian dessert, tafoni is a type of sandstone that is formed by years of weathering. (It was named for an Italian geologist.) A unique combination of coastal fog, tectonic upthrust, and sandstone cliffs provide the right ingredients for tafoni. The glue that holds the sandstone's individual sand grains together eventually erodes away, leaving honeycomb-patterned, lacelike crevices and holes in the smooth rock.

After visiting the outcrops, retrace your steps back uphill to Tafoni Trail and continue northwest. The old logging road continues for another mile in oak and fir forest to El Corte de Madera Creek Trail. Turn left and head mostly downhill for 0.9 mile, paralleling a seasonal creek in the final stretch. Turn left on Resolution Trail and follow it for just over a mile, climbing gradually among some good-sized redwoods. Among the second-growth trees, you'll see burned-out stumps left from logging days.

After you've gained a few hundred feet in elevation, you'll emerge from the forest into chaparral. At a sizable clearing, Resolution Trail meets up with Fir Trail; turn left and then left again on the spur path signed for Vista Point. This ridge-top site has a partially obscured view of the coast and a level, open area for picnicking; it's an abrupt contrast to the dense woods you've been hiking in.

When you rejoin the main Fir Trail, it's only 1.1 miles farther to the Tafoni trailhead or 0.9 mile to the turnoff for Sierra Morena Trail and the southern parking area.

Options

Plenty of hikers visit El Corte de Madera Creek and miss out on a spectacular sight right across the road from its southern parking area, 0.4 mile south of Skeggs Vista Point. A 100-yard stroll from Skyline Boulevard leads to the Methusaleh redwood, which is 14 feet in diameter and more than 1,800 years old. It's worth a visit every time you're on Skyline.

For a more ambitious hike, try the nine-mile Gordon Mill and Lawrence Creek Loop, which follows an old logging road through a sturdy second-growth forest of redwoods and firs. Lawrence Creek is laden with clear pools and mossy rocks. Start hiking at the preserve's CM03 gate, which is 2.9 miles north of Highway 84 on Skyline. Park in the pullout just north of the gate.

Directions

From San Francisco, drive south on I-280 for 19 miles to the Highway 92 west exit. Go west on Highway 92 for 2.7 miles, then turn left (south) on Highway 35 (Skyline Boulevard). Drive 8.5 miles to the Skeggs Vista Point parking area on your left. (It's 1.6 miles south of the intersection with Kings Mountain Road and 3.8 miles north of Skylonda.) You can't turn left into the parking area; you must drive farther south and find a safe place to make a U-turn. After parking, walk 50 yards north on Skyline Boulevard and cross the road to access Tafoni Trail. Or continue 0.4 mile south on Skyline Boulevard from Skeggs Vista Point to the small parking area on the west side of the road. From there, begin hiking on Sierra Morena Trail.

Information and Contact

There is no fee. Dogs are not allowed. Bikes are allowed on most trails in the preserve. Free trail maps are available at both trailheads, or by download at www.openspace.org. For more information, contact the Midpeninsula Regional Open Space District, 330 Distel Circle, Los Altos, CA 94022, 650/691-1200, www.openspace.org.

🔟 BEAR GULCH AND ALAMBIQUE LOOP
Wunderlich County Park

Level: Easy/Moderate **Total Distance:** 5.4 miles round-trip

Hiking Time: 2.5 hours **Elevation Change:** 600 feet

Summary: Located just a few miles off I-280, the woodsy trails of Wunderlich are a pleasant place to spend an afternoon.

Wunderlich is wonderful in the springtime. This San Mateo County park is a mix of redwoods, Douglas firs, creeks, meadows, wildflowers, and winding trails, ideally suited for either short walks or longer day hikes. Located just a few minutes from the tony community of Woodside and I-280, Wunderlich Park is an easy getaway for anyone living or working on the Peninsula.

The park's German name comes from its last private owner, a contractor named Martin Wunderlich, who deeded the land to San Mateo County in 1974. Prior to Wunderlich's ownership, the land belonged to the James A. Folger family, of coffee fame.

Wunderlich is especially popular with runners, who appreciate the smooth, easy grades of its trails. It's also popular with birders; the park's dense woodlands often produce an interesting variety of bird sightings. Pileated woodpeckers, the largest of the woodpecker family, are seen fairly often, as are the more common

Wunderlich Park contains a handful of dense redwood groves.

© KEVIN GONG

nuttall's, acorn, and hairy woodpeckers. Equestrians also share the paths, so you may have to step carefully to avoid horse droppings. Dogs and bikes are not allowed, however.

The following loop tour circles the eastern half of the park. Start your trip on the wide dirt road to the left of the stables, signed as Bear Gulch Trail. A passel of easy switchbacks on Bear Gulch Trail leads you uphill through a mixed forest of black oaks, bay laurel, madrones, Douglas fir, and shrublike California hazelnut. At 0.5 mile from the trailhead, the trail enters a second-growth redwood forest and soon reaches Redwood Flat, near the park border and Bear Gulch Road.

Follow Bear Gulch Trail for another 0.8 mile to The Meadows, elevation 1,430 feet, the high point on this loop. The Meadows is a pleasant, sunny clearing where you could easily while away an afternoon with a blanket and a book. Contrary to its name, this isn't an area of grasslands. Ceanothus, coyote brush, and Scotch broom have taken over.

From The Meadows, continue on Bear Gulch Trail, now starting to descend. Where Bear Gulch Trail joins Alambique Trail at Alambique Flat, watch for a spur trail on the right. The spur leads 50 feet to an enchanting redwood grove along Alambique Creek. This is the most tranquil and inviting spot yet. Stay a while and savor the sound of the creek and the peace of the big trees.

Returning to the junction of Alambique and Bear Gulch Trails, follow wide Alambique Trail downhill. In less than 0.5 mile, you'll pass by a huge virgin redwood alongside the dirt road on your left. It's at least 12 feet in diameter.

While you consider why the loggers chose to spare this particular tree, continue downhill, now coming closer to the steep canyon of Alambique Creek. At a junction with Meadow Trail, an old ranch road, turn left.

Follow this wide road through a eucalyptus grove to Redwood Trail. Not surprisingly, the forest changes to redwoods. Where the trail reaches Salamander Flat, a dense grove of big trees, you'll find an old reservoir remaining from this land's ranching days. Why is it called Salamander Flat? The reservoir now serves as a major breeding ground for California newts every winter.

Bear right on level Madrone Trail to return to Bear Gulch Trail, the path you started on. Then backtrack downhill on those numerous switchbacks all the way to your car.

If you suddenly remembered an important appointment, you could finish out your loop on Alambique Trail instead of turning left on Meadow Trail. This will bring you back to the trailhead in less time (it's a mile shorter). The trail presents some nice views of the South Bay, including the obvious landmark of Hoover

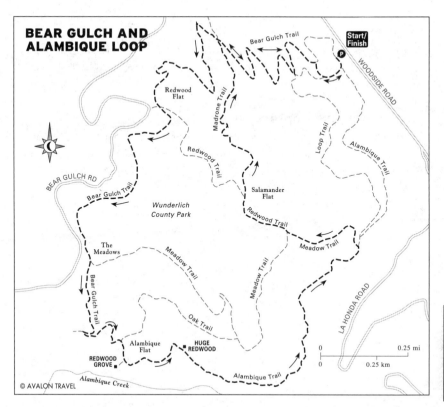

Tower at Stanford University, but it suffers from too much car noise from nearby La Honda and Woodside Roads.

Options

Nearby Huddart Park has plentiful hiking trails, the best of which lead into the neighboring Golden Gate National Recreation Area's Phleger Estate. Start at Huddart's main day-use parking area at Zwierlein Picnic Area. (From Wunderlich Park, go east one mile on Highway 84/Woodside Road. Turn left on Kings Mountain Road and drive 1.5 miles to the park.) In the first 0.5 mile from the picnic area, negotiate a series of junctions, taking Crystal Springs Trail, Dean Trail, and Richards Road to Miramontes Trail and the entrance to Phleger Estate. Now following the clear waters of West Union Creek, stay on Miramontes Trail for 1.4 miles, then take either side of the Mount Redondo and Raymundo Trail loop to join Lonely Trail on the far side. As you climb up toward Skyline Boulevard, you'll swing back on Crystal Springs Trail for an 8.6-mile loop. Make this trip in winter or spring, when the trailside redwoods are looking their best and the forks of West Union Creek are flowing strong.

Directions

From I-280 at Woodside, take the Highway 84 west exit. Drive west for 2.5 miles, through Woodside, to the park entrance on the right. (The sign is small and easy to miss.)

Information and Contact

There is no fee. Dogs and bikes are not allowed. A free trail map is available at the trailhead or by free download at www.eparks.net. For more information, contact Wunderlich Park, 4040 Woodside Road, Woodside, CA 94062, 650/851-1210, www.eparks.net.

11 WINDY HILL LOOP
Windy Hill Open Space Preserve

Level: Moderate

Hiking Time: 4 hours

Total Distance: 8.0 miles round-trip

Elevation Change: 1,100 feet

Summary: An easy "walk in the park" to the view-filled summit of Windy Hill is followed by a more strenuous loop to the quieter regions of the preserve.

Windy Hill Open Space Preserve is best known to two kinds of people: those who love easy-to-reach, panoramic views, and those who fly kites. The former includes dog walkers and sunset-watchers who set out on the 0.75-mile Anniversary Trail for an easy stroll with sweeping views of the Peninsula and South Bay. The latter includes hang gliders, paragliders, remote-control airplane fliers, and children with five-dollar kites, all of whom are drawn to the near-constant updrafts on Windy Hill.

The Anniversary Trail and the high, grassy summit of Windy Hill are well worth a visit on any clear day. But after you walk the short path and admire the 360-degree view from the top of Windy Hill (which includes the Pacific Ocean and even San Francisco on high visibility days), you'll be primed for further exploration in the preserve. The eight-mile Windy Hill Loop is just the ticket.

The loop trail provides some of the same wide vistas of the Peninsula as the short Anniversary Trail, but also includes long stints through fir and oak forests on a narrow, winding path. Windy Hill Loop is best hiked in a clockwise direction,

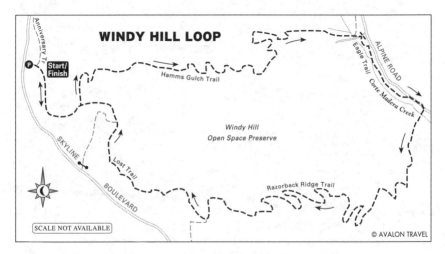

WINDY HILL LOOP

Anniversary Tr.

P Start/ Finish

Hamms Gulch Trail

Windy Hill
Open Space Preserve

Eagle Trail

ALPINE ROAD

Corte Madera Creek

SKYLINE

Lost Trail

BOULEVARD

Razorback Ridge Trail

SCALE NOT AVAILABLE

© AVALON TRAVEL

following the trails in this order: Hamms Gulch Trail, Eagle Trail, Razorback Ridge Trail, Lost Trail. Note that dogs are allowed on Hamms Gulch Trail, Eagle Trail, and the short Anniversary Trail, but not on the other legs of the loop.

Starting at the picnic area, follow the connector trail to the right (the Anniversary Trail leads left). The path roughly parallels Skyline Boulevard as it travels through chaparral for just under 0.5 mile. A well-placed bench affords wide views of the valley.

At the first trail junction, turn left on Hamms Gulch Trail and bid farewell to road noise and other signs of civilization. Hamms Gulch Trail, an old road, travels through open grasslands and a forest of tan oaks, firs, and madrones as it heads gently downhill, losing 1,100 feet in 2.6 miles.

The trail bottoms out near Corte Madera Creek and the gated entrance to Rancho Corte Madera, a private inholding within the preserve. Cross its driveway and bridge and pick up Eagle Trail, which runs in between Corte Madera Creek and Alpine Road. This 0.6-mile stretch is the least appealing leg of the loop, due to the proximity of the road and several private homes. Corte Madera Creek is a pleasant distraction in the wet season.

After a short stint on Alpine Road and then a bridge crossing on a dirt road, you're back on Razorback Ridge Trail. Head into a well-graded climb through numerous switchbacks, shaded by a high forest canopy of oaks and madrones. This 2.3-mile stretch gains nearly 1,000 feet, but the gradient is so mellow that you hardly notice you're climbing. Where the trail nears Skyline Boulevard, turn

Dense forest covers the slopes of Hamms Gulch.

right on Lost Trail, still gently ascending through the forest. The immense Douglas fir trees shading the trail are a sight to behold: Some are as large as eight feet in diameter. A few branches are big enough to be individual trees. In spring, the woodland understory is lined with trillium, hounds-tongue, and milkmaids. In between the trees you gain peekaboo views of the valley below.

Where Lost Trail joins with Hamms Gulch Trail at the start of your loop, continue straight on the connector trail back to Windy Hill's parking lot.

Options

Get permission from the Midpeninsula Regional Open Space District to hike at nearby La Honda Creek Open Space Preserve. Hikers must obtain a permit in advance or join a docent-led group. This secluded preserve features a three-mile hike that shows off ancient trees, unique geological formations, and a panoramic view—all without hordes of other hikers, since access is restricted. The trailhead is 1.7 miles west of Skyline Boulevard, off Bear Gulch and Allen Roads, but you can't park your car there without displaying a permit. Phone 650/691-1200 for permit information.

Directions

From I-280 at Woodside, take Highway 84 west for 6.5 miles to its junction with Highway 35 (Skyline Boulevard). Turn left (south) on Skyline Boulevard and drive 2.2 miles to the main Windy Hill Open Space entrance on the left. (There are picnic tables at the trailhead.)

Or, from I-280 in Palo Alto, take the Page Mill Road exit west. Drive 8.9 winding miles to Skyline Boulevard (Highway 35). Turn right (north) on Skyline Boulevard and drive 4.9 miles to the main Windy Hill Open Space entrance on the right. (There are picnic tables at the trailhead.)

Information and Contact

There is no fee. Dogs are allowed on some trails, but not on the entire Windy Hill Loop. Bikes are not allowed. Free trail maps are available at the trailhead or by download at www.openspace.org. For more information, contact the Midpeninsula Regional Open Space District, 330 Distel Circle, Los Altos, CA 94022, 650/691-1200, www.openspace.org.

12 RUSSIAN RIDGE LOOP   BEST 🌙
Russian Ridge Open Space Preserve

🚶 🚴 🐕 👨‍👩‍👧

Level: Easy/Moderate   **Total Distance:** 4.4 miles round-trip

Hiking Time: 2 hours   **Elevation Change:** 550 feet

Summary: Wildflowers abound in the spring and sweeping views are available year-round on this scenic trail in the hills above Palo Alto.

Russian Ridge Open Space Preserve comprises more than 1,500 acres of wind-swept ridge-top paradise. We're talking location, location, location, as in directly off Skyline Boulevard (Highway 35), near the well-to-do town of Portola Valley. The weather may be foggy on the coast, but the sun is usually shining brightly on Skyline. From the preserve's 2,300-foot elevation, you can look out and above the layer of fog blanketing the ocean. What a pleasure it is to appreciate its cotton-candy appearance without being stuck in the thick of it.

In spring, Russian Ridge will charm you with colorful wildflowers and verdant grasslands. In summer and fall, the hillsides turn gold and the grasses sway in unison to the ridge-top winds. On the rare days of winter when snow dusts this ridge, you can pull out your cross-country skis and glide along the slopes! On a clear day in any season, you'll be wowed by the vistas from 2,572-foot Borel Hill, the highest named point in San Mateo County.

Although many people visit this preserve for the views, Russian Ridge doles out much more. Its acreage combines several plant environments, including lush grass-lands, creeks, springs, and oak-shaded canyons. It is home to substantial wildlife, including a variety of raptors, coyotes, and mountain lions. Most impressive are the

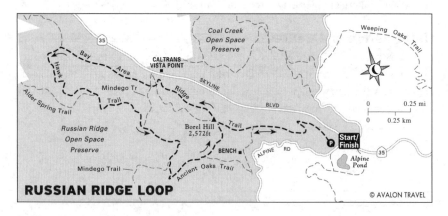

RUSSIAN RIDGE LOOP   © AVALON TRAVEL

spring wildflowers. Every April and May, the grasslands explode in a fireworks display of colorful mule's ears, poppies, lupine, goldfields, Johnny-jump-ups, and blue-eyed grass. Russian Ridge is considered to be one of the best places in the Bay Area to see wildflowers.

This 4.4-mile loop circles the preserve. Take the Bay Area Ridge Trail uphill from the parking lot, heading for the top of grassy Borel Hill in less than a mile. (Stay right at two junctions.) The 2,572-foot summit of Borel Hill is just high enough to serve up a 360-degree view of the South Bay, Skyline Ridge, and all the way west to the Pacific Ocean. Mount Diablo looms in the eastern horizon and Mount Tamalpais guards the north. This has to be one of the most inspiring lookouts on the Peninsula.

Blue-eyed grass is one of the more common flowers that blooms at Russian Ridge.

From the summit, descend gently for 0.5 mile to a major junction of trails near Skyline Boulevard. Bear left on Mindego Ridge Trail, then shortly turn right on Bay Area Ridge Trail. Ridge Trail narrows, curving around grassy knolls and producing more views of the coast and the bay. To the southwest you can see Mindego Hill, an ancient volcanic formation that may be the source of this ridge's scattered rock outcrops.

At a junction with Hawk Trail, turn left to head southeast and start your loop back. Stay straight at the next two junctions and descend to the junction of Mindego Ridge Trail and Ancient Oaks Trail, then follow Ancient Oaks Trail. This short trail leads through a remarkable forest of gnarled, moss-covered oak trees interspersed with equally gnarled Douglas firs, plus some madrones and ferns. You may want to linger a while in this strange, enchanted woodland, at least long enough to climb a few trees. Then turn left at the next junction and cruise back out into the sunlight to rejoin Bay Area Ridge Trail. Or, stay on Ancient Oaks Trail for another 0.3 mile and turn left at a second junction to reach a wooden bench that is nearly overwhelmed by bright orange California poppies in spring. A plaque on its side reads: "There is great peace in this natural beauty. We must all help to preserve it."

Options

The Caltrans Vista Point on Skyline Boulevard, 1.1 mile north of the main Russian Ridge entrance at Alpine Road, is the trailhead for the easy 2.5-mile Clouds Rest and Meadow Loop in Coal Creek Open Space Preserve. The trail's highlight is a walk around flower-dotted Coal Creek Meadow, which provides memorable views of the Peninsula and South Bay. From the Vista Point parking area, walk 50 yards north on Skyline to Clouds Rest Road. Turn right and walk 0.3 mile to the trailhead. Where the path splits, take the right fork to head straight for the scenic meadow.

Directions

From I-280 in Palo Alto, take the Page Mill Road exit west. Drive 8.9 winding miles to Skyline Boulevard (Highway 35). Cross Skyline Boulevard to Alpine Road. Drive 200 feet on Alpine Road and turn right into the Russian Ridge entrance.

Or, from the junction of Highways 35 and 9 at Saratoga Gap, drive seven miles north on Highway 35 (Skyline Boulevard). Turn left on Alpine Road and then right into the preserve entrance.

Information and Contact

There is no fee. Dogs are not allowed. Bikes are allowed. Free trail maps are available at the trailhead or by download at www.openspace.org. For more information, contact the Midpeninsula Regional Open Space District, 330 Distel Circle, Los Altos, CA 94022, 650/691-1200, www.openspace.org.

13 BLACK MOUNTAIN AND STEVENS CREEK LOOP

BEST

Monte Bello Open Space Preserve

Level: Moderate

Total Distance: 6.0 miles round-trip

Hiking Time: 3 hours

Elevation Change: 1,300 feet

Summary: Immerse yourself in Skyline Ridge's natural beauty on this meandering loop to the summit of 2,800-foot Black Mountain.

People who live on the Peninsula are well acquainted with 2,800-foot Black Mountain, the peak that forms a rounded green backdrop for the communities around Palo Alto. The town of Mountain View was named for its vista of the verdant peak. It's always there, anchoring the background in the lives of thousands.

Black Mountain doesn't have a singular peaked summit; rather it's the highest point on long and narrow Monte Bello Ridge. It's also the most prominent feature of Monte Bello Open Space Preserve, a preserve comprised of a varied mix of grasslands, conifers, and chaparral. This six-mile loop trip tours Monte Bello and pays a visit to the summit of Black Mountain.

Begin your hike at the preserve's main entrance on Stevens Creek Nature Trail. The path leads a level few hundred feet to a stone bench and overlook. There you gaze at the source of Stevens Creek, which follows the San Andreas fault zone. Mount Umunhum and Shotgun Valley appear far in the distance.

© ANN MARIE BROWN

rocky outcrops on Black Mountain's summit

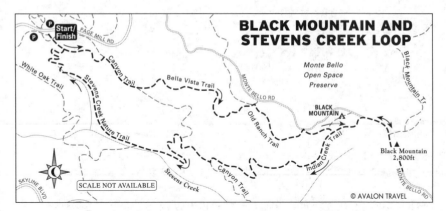

Take the left fork in the nature trail, heading to Canyon Trail in 0.3 mile. Turn right on wide Canyon Trail, walk 0.2 mile, then leave that road for the mountain bikers and bear left on Bella Vista Trail. A wide single-track trail, Bella Vista Trail climbs steadily but moderately and bestows lovely views of the Stevens Creek canyon. Contouring along grassy slopes, the trail provides many opportunities for spotting wildlife. We watched a coyote gallop across the grasslands while two curious deer watched us. During the autumn mating season, large herds of deer are often seen in this preserve.

After almost a mile of climbing, you've nearly reached the ridge top. Bear right on Old Ranch Trail and in 0.5 mile you come to Black Mountain Backpack Camp, the only campground in the Midpeninsula Regional Open Space District. Four family campsites and one group campsite are available for backpackers who have obtained a permit from the district office. You must pack in your own water and camp stove; no fires are permitted. Oddly, the camp has one "civilized" amenity: a pay telephone, just in case your cell phone doesn't work.

Walk around the camp and join Monte Bello Road in a few hundred feet. It's only 0.25 mile to the microwave tower–covered summit of Black Mountain, elevation 2,800 feet even. Black Mountain Trail intersects with Monte Bello Road at the summit. This popular trail is for hikers and equestrians only. Starting from the Duveneck Windmill Pasture Area of Rancho San Antonio Open Space Preserve, it's an eight-mile round-trip to the summit with a 2,300-foot elevation gain.

From Black Mountain's summit, you have a wide view of the Peninsula and Santa Clara Valley. But the lovelier view is just to the west of the summit. To see it, follow Monte Bello Road for another 150 feet, then exit the trail on the right near an odd marker: a 15-mile-per-hour speed limit sign. Here, at a fascinating outcrop of scattered rocks, is the best picnic site and finest view of the day. Stevens Creek canyon lies below you. Untrammeled grassland hills spread to the north and south along Skyline Ridge. In springtime, blue-eyed grass, checkerbloom, farewell-to-spring, and California poppies bloom in the hilltop grasses. It's time to throw down your pack and have lunch.

After admiring the view, backtrack to just before the camp and bear left on Indian Creek Trail. You'll face a steep downhill on the ranch road with views of Indian Creek canyon. (Be sure to take the short spur trail on the left to see more of the densely forested canyon.) Hiking through chaparral, toyon, and lichen-covered oaks, descend 1.2 miles to Canyon Trail. Bear right, walk 0.25 mile, then turn left on Stevens Creek Nature Trail.

Soon you'll cross a footbridge over Stevens Creek and travel alongside the stream. Ferns, Douglas firs, and oaks line the banks of Stevens Creek. This lush riparian area is in extreme contrast to the open grasslands of Black Mountain. After crossing two more footbridges, bear right to stay on Stevens Creek Nature Trail, now on single-track.

The final 1.2 miles of the trip are an easy, streamside ascent with plenty of shade and switchbacks. You'll climb out of the stream canyon, head back into the grasslands, and wind up right back at the stone bench and overlook where you began the hike. Turn left to walk back to your car.

Options

Pay a visit to the San Andreas Fault, one of the world's longest and most active earthquake faults, at Los Trancos Open Space Preserve, directly across Page Mill Road from Monte Bello Open Space Preserve. A trail brochure interprets visible fault signs along the 1.5-mile San Andreas Fault Trail. If you want to hike longer, you can connect to two outer loops on Franciscan and Lost Creek Trails (total mileage is three miles). The trails lead through a shady bay and oak forest along Los Trancos Creek and a flower-filled stretch of grasslands.

Directions

From I-280 in Palo Alto, take the Page Mill Road exit west. Drive 7.2 winding miles on Page Mill Road to the signed preserve entrance on the left.

Or, from the junction of Highways 35 and 9 at Saratoga Gap, drive seven miles north on Highway 35 (Skyline Boulevard). Turn right on Page Mill Road and drive 1.7 miles to the preserve entrance on the right.

Information and Contact

There is no fee. Dogs are not allowed. Bikes are allowed on most sections of this loop. Free trail maps are available at the trailhead, or by download at www.openspace.org. For more information, contact the Midpeninsula Regional Open Space District, 330 Distel Circle, Los Altos, CA 94022, 650/691-1200, www.openspace.org.

14 PETERS CREEK AND LONG RIDGE LOOP
Long Ridge Open Space Preserve

Level: Easy/Moderate

Total Distance: 4.6 miles round-trip

Hiking Time: 2 hours

Elevation Change: 400 feet

Summary: Easy trails follow the path of burbling Peters Creek and lace through meadows and forest on scenic Skyline Ridge.

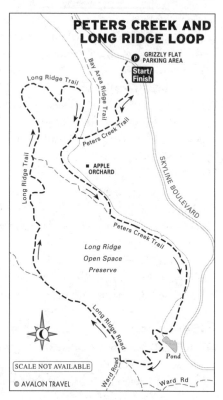

Long Ridge Open Space is a peaceful 2,000-acre preserve along Skyline Boulevard near Saratoga Gap. Its hiking, biking, and equestrian trails are perfect in all seasons—warm and windy in summer, crisp and golden in autumn, fern-laden and mossy in winter, and gilded with wildflowers in spring.

From the Grizzly Flat trailhead, only one pathway enters Long Ridge. It's the start of Peters Creek Trail, which soon connects with the Bay Area Ridge Trail. The latter makes a tight switchback and heads north; you'll continue straight on Peters Creek Trail. Once you get moving, the sight and sound of Skyline Boulevard quickly disappear as the trail drops below the road and into a pristine canyon of grasslands and forest. Fields of wildflowers and rolling grasses in the foreground are framed by a forest of Douglas firs and oaks ahead. Some people walk only as far as this first open meadow, spread out a picnic, then head home.

At a junction with Long Ridge Trail, turn left to stay on Peters Creek Trail and begin a gentle ascent through oaks, firs, and bay laurel. Babbling Peters Creek, a major tributary of Pescadero Creek, meanders along at your side. Ferns and moss-covered boulders line the stream. Woodland wildflowers include tiny two-eyed violets (heart-shaped leaves with white and purple flowers) and purple shooting stars.

The trail wanders in and out of meadows and forest, passing an old apple orchard and ranch site. The trees still bear delicious apples in autumn; in winter, their bare branches are lined with a shaggy gray-green lichen. At 1.6 miles, you'll reach a small pond with huge reeds and a sea of horsetails growing around its edges. Watch for pond turtles sunning themselves. On the far side of the pond is private property belonging to the Jikoji Buddhist retreat center.

The spring flower show continues as you hike. Look for brodiaea, columbine, wild roses, blue-eyed grass, white irises, poppies, lupine, and huge ceanothus bushes with sprays of blue flowers. The variety of species is remarkable.

A few switchbacks lead you to the top of the ridge, where you meet up with Long Ridge Road. At this 2,500-foot elevation, expansive views are yours for the taking. Turn right on Long Ridge Road and traipse along, oohing and aahing at the panorama of neighboring Butano Ridge and the forests of the Pescadero Creek watershed. Be sure to pause at the bench commemorating Pulitzer prize–winning author Wallace Stegner, who lived in this area and aided in the conservation of Long Ridge.

After this sunny, view-filled stint, take Long Ridge Trail back into the forest to finish out the loop. The path makes a wide circle around to the north and then east through a dense forest of leafy oaks, then reconnects with the start of Peters Creek Trail.

Long Ridge's trails are multiuse; you may share your trip with mountain bikers or equestrians. If that concerns you, wait until the rainy season to visit, when

© ANN MARIE BROWN

A loop hike in Long Ridge alternates between shady forest and sunny, exposed slopes.

the Open Space District closes the trails to everyone but hikers. The preserve is at its best then anyway; the ideal time to visit is on a clear winter day soon after a rainstorm.

Options

From neighboring Skyline Ridge Open Space Preserve, you can take the scenic Ridge Trail route to Daniels Nature Center at Alpine Pond for a natural history lesson (the center is open weekends only, April–November, 12–5 P.M.). The 3.2-mile round-trip displays a wealth of wildflowers in the spring. Or, for a shorter walk, meander on the one-mile loop around Horseshoe Lake, a tranquil spring-fed reservoir that's prime for bird-watching. The trailhead for both hikes is located on the west side of Skyline Boulevard, one mile south of Page Mill Road.

Directions

From I-280 in Palo Alto, take the Page Mill Road exit west. Drive 8.9 winding miles to Skyline Boulevard (Highway 35). Turn left on Skyline Boulevard and drive 3.1 miles to the Long Ridge/Grizzly Flat parking area on the left. The trail is located across the road.

Or, from Saratoga, take Highway 9 west to its junction with Skyline Boulevard. Turn right on Skyline Boulevard and drive 3.2 miles to the Long Ridge/Grizzly Flat parking area on the right. The trail is located across the road.

Information and Contact

There is no fee. Dogs are not allowed. Bikes are allowed. Free trail maps are available at the trailhead, or by download at www.openspace.org. For more information, contact Midpeninsula Regional Open Space District, 330 Distel Circle, Los Altos, CA 94022, 650/691-1200, www.openspace.org.

15 HERITAGE GROVE AND HIKER'S HUT LOOP

Sam McDonald County Park

BEST ◖

🔭

Level: Easy/Moderate

Total Distance: 5.0 miles round-trip

Hiking Time: 2.5 hours

Elevation Change: 600 feet

Summary: Witness the majesty of the Heritage Grove redwoods and visit the Sierra Club's Hiker's Hut on scenic Towne Ridge.

If you've ever taken the tortuous drive on Alpine Road between Portola State Park Road and La Honda, you've seen some of the marvelous first-growth redwoods of the Heritage Grove. The big trees are so enchanting that it makes the snaking, serpentine road a pleasure. After all, you don't want to drive fast through these giants.

To see these redwoods at an even slower pace, take this five-mile loop hike at Sam McDonald County Park. From the main parking lot, take the Big Tree Trail across from the ranger station. The path leads through tall redwoods and across Pescadero Road (use caution in crossing). After merging with and then departing from Towne Fire Road, Big Tree Trail begins a gentle uphill with many switchbacks and wooden stairsteps, passing the well-named Big Tree. It then curves around to the west to join Heritage Grove Trail. (Don't miss this turnoff or you'll loop right back to Pescadero Road).

Take Heritage Grove Trail east for 1.2 miles to the Heritage Grove turnoff. The path leads through a forest of mostly Douglas firs with a few redwoods among

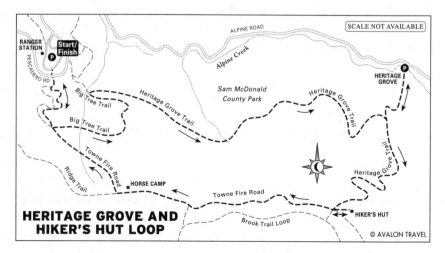

HERITAGE GROVE AND HIKER'S HUT LOOP

© AVALON TRAVEL

them. On clear days, sunlight filters through the trees and cascades down the hillside. On rainy days, you'll have the pleasure of staying nearly dry underneath the dense forest canopy.

Follow the trail to the left all the way downhill to near Alpine Road and wander among the big trees growing along Alpine Creek. These 37 acres of virgin redwoods were scheduled to be logged in the early 1970s, but were saved by a group of citizen activists who raised funds to purchase the grove. After admiring the giant trees, backtrack uphill and take the opposite fork of Heritage Grove Trail.

The trail tops out at a big open meadow and Towne Fire Road. Look for the single-track spur trail on your left signed for Hiker's Hut, only 150 yards away. Amid huge Douglas firs and ridge-top chaparral and grasslands, you'll find the Hiker's Hut. Run by the Loma Prieta Chapter of the Sierra Club, this inviting A-frame building is open to the public and available for rent. It holds up to 14 people at the low cost of $18–25 per adult per night, or a few bucks less for Sierra Club members. The Hiker's Hut has a full kitchen, electricity, a wood stove, a big deck with a picnic table out front, and best of all, a view of the Pescadero Creek canyon and the coast from its backyard on Towne Ridge.

Retrace your steps on the spur trail to Towne Fire Road, then head west (right). In less than a mile, you'll pass an equestrian camp. Turn right just beyond it and follow Towne Fire Road downhill. It leads all the way back to Pescadero Road, but a more scenic option is to take Towne Fire Road to its junction with Big Tree Trail and then take either fork of the Big Tree Trail back to the ranger station.

Options

Visit more redwood groves from a less known trailhead: Follow Pescadero Road east to its junction with Alpine Road, then take Alpine Road east three miles, past the Heritage Grove, to its junction with Camp Pomponio Road. Turn right and drive one mile to the Tarwater Trailhead in Pescadero Creek County Park, near the county jail. Start on the west side of the Tarwater Loop (across the road from the trailhead) and follow the three-mile trail. You'll travel first through meadows and oak forest, then dense redwood groves, while skirting Tarwater Creek, Wally's Creek, and Shingle Mill Creek. (Where the trail meets Camp Pomponio Road at the far end of the loop, go left for 70 yards to regain the trail.)

Directions

From I-280 at Woodside, take Highway 84 west for 13 winding miles to La Honda. Turn left (southeast) on Pescadero Road and drive 1.8 miles to Sam McDonald County Park on the right. (Bear right after the first mile to stay on Pescadero Road.) The trail begins across the parking lot from the ranger station.

Sierra Club Hiker's Hut in Sam McDonald County Park

Information and Contact

A $5 day-use fee is charged per vehicle. Dogs and bikes are not allowed. A park map is available at the ranger station, or by free download at www.eparks.net. For more information, contact Sam McDonald County Park, 13435 Pescadero Creek Road, Loma Mar, CA 94021, 650/879-0238, www.eparks.net.

To reserve the Hiker's Hut, phone 650/390-8411 or visit www.lomaprieta.sierraclub.org. If you don't have at least six people in your party, you may have to share the hut with others on Friday and Saturday nights in summer and fall. The rest of the year, the place is all yours no matter how small your group.

16 PETERS CREEK GROVE   BEST ☾

Portola Redwoods State Park

Level: Strenuous   **Total Distance:** 13.0 miles round-trip

Hiking Time: 7 hours   **Elevation Change:** 1,400 feet

Summary: Plan on a long, rewarding day to hike through some of the most remote lands of San Mateo County and visit the big trees of Peters Creek.

Old-growth redwood trees are indisputably majestic. Even when a highway or a paved trail runs right alongside them, or when they are hemmed in by fences and signs, the big trees retain their profound dignity and grace. While gazing at the ancient redwoods, humans can't help but feel humbled.

But seeing a grove of old-growth redwoods that isn't easily accessible makes the experience even more compelling. That's why a trip to the Peters Creek Grove in Portola Redwoods State Park may be the most awe-inspiring hike in the Bay Area. Simply put, the sanctity of this grove will move you.

The trip is long and on the strenuous side, mostly because of the steep descent required to reach the grove. You'll need most of a day to complete the 13-mile round-trip, plus plenty of water and food. Because Portola Redwoods State Park is a long, circuitous drive from just about everywhere, you should get an early

morning start from your house if you aren't camping at the park. (Portola's car campground is booked in advance almost every weekend in summer. If you want to camp, be sure to make reservations.) In addition, make sure your car has plenty of gas and that you've packed along plenty to eat and drink. There are no stores or services anywhere near the park.

Those who would rather turn the 13-miler into a backpacking trip can stay at Slate Creek Trail Camp, located halfway along the route. Reservations are necessary here, too, but you shouldn't have a problem obtaining a site. You will need to pack in your own water.

That said, the trip is entirely doable

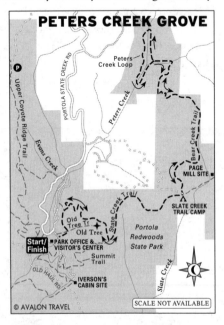

The redwoods in Peters Creek Grove have grown to enormous size.

as a day hike for most people. The trail is well graded and the total elevation change is only 1,400 feet. Because most of the route is shaded, it never gets too hot. And when it's all over, you'll likely agree: Visiting the Peters Creek Grove is worth every step.

Start your trip on either Summit Trail or Slate Creek Trail. The ascent on Slate Creek Trail is slightly more gradual; the two trails meet up after a 600-foot gain and about 1.5 miles. From their junction, head north on the continuation of Slate Creek Trail, following a mellower grade through redwoods, Douglas firs, and huckleberries for 1.5 miles to Slate Creek Trail Camp. If it isn't occupied, the camp makes a good rest stop; you're three miles out and almost halfway to the grove. There are six campsites, picnic tables, and a pit toilet.

From the trail junction near the camp, take the north fork on Bear Creek Trail, an old jeep road. (This is the old Page Mill Road.) You'll climb for another mile up a ridge cloaked in a mixed forest of Douglas firs, oaks, and bay laurel. The jeep trail ends and a narrower, steeper footpath leads into high chaparral country. The manzanita and pines are a surprising contrast to the dense forest you've been traveling in. Ascend a bit more along this dry ridge before beginning a one-mile, 750-foot descent into the canyon of Bear Creek and Peters Creek. The forest returns to a mix of bay laurel and Douglas firs as you make your way steeply downhill. (This may seem like it's going to be a nightmare climb out on the way back, but it's not as bad as it looks.)

Where the trail crosses Bear Creek, 5.8 miles from the start, you're about to enter the big trees. Parallel Bear Creek down to its confluence with Peters Creek, then meet up with Peters Creek Loop Trail. Take either fork to circle the grove, following both banks of Peters Creek. The return route simply retraces your steps.

Acquired by the Save-the-Redwoods League, the Peters Creek Grove is filled with ancient redwoods, many of which are more than 12 feet in diameter and 200 feet tall. Most are at least 1,000 years old. No one is quite sure why these redwoods weren't logged along with other groves in the area. Probably the canyon was too steep to make it feasible to haul out the lumber. A highlight of the grove

© JOHN KLEINFELTER

is the huge Matriarch of the Forest, the largest redwood at Peters Creek. But what makes this place magical is not any one single tree but the sacred ambiance created by the sum total. Isolated from the civilized world, the Peters Creek Grove is one of the most pristine, unspoiled places in the Bay Area.

Options

Another ambitious trek in Portola Redwoods State Park, perfect for hikers who like to climb, is the Butano Ridge Trail Loop. Follow the park road past the visitors center and campground entrance; it turns into a service road. This road ascends to join Old Haul Road, a dirt logging road, in 0.5 mile. Directly across Old Haul Road is Portola Trail, which you follow uphill for one mile to join Butano Ridge Trail Loop. Turn right here, and consider heading back now if you are losing steam, completing a 3.3-mile loop. If you are feeling strong, climb much more steeply for another mile to Butano Ridge at 2,000 feet in elevation. Now the work is mostly over; you just wander along the ridge-top for two miles, then drop back down to Old Haul Road and turn right to finish out a 9.5-mile loop.

Directions

From the junction of Highways 35 and 9 at Saratoga Gap, drive seven miles north on Highway 35 (Skyline Boulevard). Turn left (west) on Alpine Road, drive 3.2 miles and turn left on Portola State Park Road. Drive 3.3 miles to park headquarters.

Or, from I-280 in Palo Alto, take the Page Mill Road exit. Turn west and drive 8.9 miles to Highway 35 (Skyline Boulevard). Cross Highway 35 and continue on Alpine Road as described.

Information and Contact

A $10 day-use fee is charged. Dogs and bikes are not allowed. A park map is available at the visitors center for $2. For more information, contact Portola Redwoods State Park, 9000 Portola State Park Road, Building F, La Honda, CA 94020, 650/948-9098, www.parks.ca.gov or www.santacruzstateparks.org.

17 SARATOGA GAP AND RIDGE TRAIL LOOP

BEST 🌙

Castle Rock State Park

Level: Easy/Moderate

Total Distance: 5.2 miles round-trip

Hiking Time: 2.5 hours

Elevation Change: 600 feet

Summary: Visit Castle Rock's mammoth sandstone formations and watch rock climbers strut their stuff on this popular loop at one of the South Bay's best parks.

Hello, hikers, and welcome to Swiss Cheese State Park. Oops, that's Castle Rock State Park, of course, but all those holey sandstone rocks look more like *fromage* than chateaus. Call it what you like, Castle Rock is one of the most surprising parks in the entire Bay Area. In five miles of hiking, you can visit a 50-foot waterfall in winter and spring, gaze at great expanses of Santa Cruz Mountains wildlands, and explore several large sandstone formations, including the local rock climbers' favorite, Goat Rock.

In recent years, Castle Rock has also become one of the most popular parks in the Bay Area. The park is used by rock climbers as well as hikers, so weekends can be very crowded. For the best experience, plan your trip for a weekday, or get an early morning start on weekends.

Take Saratoga Gap Trail from the far side of Castle Rock's parking lot, heading right. (The trail is signed To Campground.) The pleasure begins immediately as you travel downhill, walking along rocky, fern-lined Kings Creek through a mixed forest of Douglas firs, black oaks, and madrones. The seasonal stream

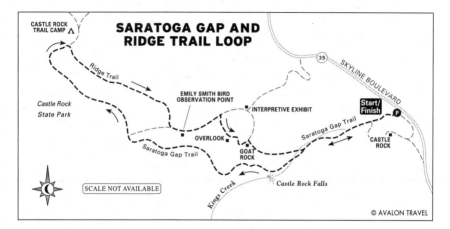

climbing on Castle Rock's holey sandstone

begins as a trickle at the parking lot, then picks up flow and intensity as it heads downhill alongside the trail.

It's a mere 0.8 mile to Castle Rock Falls, which flows with vigor in the wet season. After 15 minutes on the trail, you find yourself standing on a large wooden viewing deck, perched on top of the waterfall. Because you're at its brink, the fall is a bit difficult to see. You'll be torn between searching for the best view of its 50-foot drop and admiring the miles of uninhabited Santa Cruz Mountains wildlands. It's hard to say whether this deck was built for viewing the waterfall or the canyon vista. Both are incredible.

From the viewing deck, continue on Saratoga Gap Trail for another 1.8 miles. The terrain changes quickly from a shady mixed woodland to a sunny, exposed slope with views all the way out to Monterey Bay and the Pacific Ocean. Spring and summer bring forth colorful blooms on bush monkeyflower and other sun-loving chaparral plants. As you progress, you'll notice an ever-increasing number of sandstone outcrops that have been hollowed and sculpted by wind erosion. In some places, the sandstone becomes the trail surface. You'll have to scramble over a few small boulders to continue on your way.

At 2.5 miles from its start, Saratoga Gap Trail junctions with Ridge Trail and the spur to Castle Rock Trail Camp. Pay a visit to the pleasant, forested campsites if you wish (water and picnic tables are available), or just turn sharply right on Ridge Trail, beginning the return leg of your loop. After a 0.5-mile uphill hike through a dense madrone forest, the trail emerges on an open ridge. (Ridge Trail roughly parallels Saratoga Gap Trail, but at a higher elevation.)

Another 0.5 mile of gentle ascent takes you past a connector trail to Saratoga Gap Trail. Just beyond is a short spur to the Emily Smith Bird Observation Point. This forested knoll is a good spot to look for raptors, although views are severely limited by the leafy black oaks.

Nearly four miles into the loop is the spur trail for Goat Rock. Turn right and follow it for 0.25 mile. (The left fork leads to a fascinating interpretive exhibit on the park's geology; you can also loop around to Goat Rock from there.)

You're likely to see rock climbers on the steep south side of Goat Rock, but the north side is easily accessible on two feet. Signs along the path encourage hikers to visit a neighboring overlook area instead of climbing on the 100-foot-high rock, due to its steep and potentially dangerous drop-offs. Weigh the risk for yourself and take your pick. The overlook offers a great view of the Santa Cruz Mountains parading down to the Pacific Ocean, and often more solitude than Goat Rock. If you're sure-footed and cautious, the smooth back side of Goat Rock is a great place to examine the sandstone close-up, as well as enjoy more high views.

Beyond Goat Rock, Ridge Trail continues eastward until it reconnects with Saratoga Gap Trail just above Castle Rock Falls. Turn left and make a 0.5-mile climb back up the creek canyon to the trailhead.

Options

Don't leave the park without walking the 0.7-mile loop trail to Castle Rock, the park's namesake rock formation. A marked spur trail leads off Saratoga Gap Trail on the right, just before you return to the parking lot on the hike outlined earlier.

And in spring, the park's Summit Meadows Trail should not be missed. The trailhead is at Sempervirens Point, a drive-up overlook on the south side of Highway 9, 1.9 miles west of Skyline Boulevard. If the view of the Santa Cruz Mountains from the overlook inspires you, you'll love this two-mile flower-filled walk from the point's north end through Summit Meadows.

Directions

From Saratoga, take Highway 9 west to its junction with Skyline Boulevard (Highway 35). Turn left (south) on Skyline Boulevard and drive 2.5 miles to the Castle Rock State Park parking area on the right. The trailhead is on the west side of the parking lot, opposite the entrance.

Or, from I-280 in Palo Alto, take Page Mill Road west for 8.9 miles to Skyline

Boulevard (Highway 35). Turn left (south) on Skyline Boulevard and drive 13 miles, past Highway 9, to the Castle Rock State Park parking area on the right.

Information and Contact

An $8 day-use fee is charged per vehicle. Dogs and bikes are not allowed. A park map is available for $1 at the entrance kiosk, or by free download at www.parks. ca.gov. For more information, contact Castle Rock State Park, 15000 Skyline Boulevard, Los Gatos, CA 95033, 408/867-2952, www.parks.ca.gov.

18 BERRY CREEK, SILVER, AND GOLDEN FALLS

BEST (

Big Basin Redwoods State Park

Level: Strenuous

Total Distance: 10.4-12.0 miles round-trip

Hiking Time: 5-6 hours

Elevation Change: 1,900 feet

Summary: Ancient redwoods and three glistening waterfalls await hikers on this sylvan hike.

Big Basin Redwoods was established in 1902 as California's first state park. It was well loved a century ago and is equally loved today. Featuring an incredible diversity of terrain, some of the Bay Area's loveliest waterfalls, a freshwater marsh at the ocean's edge, 1,500-year-old redwood trees, and 80 miles of well-built trails, the park leaves little to be desired.

Given its many natural wonders and proximity to San Jose, it's not surprising that Big Basin is heavily visited. But on weekdays in winter and early spring (or early in the morning on weekends) precious solitude can still be found among the redwoods and the waterfalls. Time your trip carefully and don't be afraid to visit on a gray or rainy day. Nothing is more vibrant than a redwood forest in a light rain.

This 12-mile loop is the park's premier hike, beginning at park headquarters and passing three waterfalls: Berry Creek, Silver, and Golden. Although you can also access these falls by following the Skyline-to-the-Sea Trail from Highway 1 near Davenport, that route is shared with mountain bikers and equestrians. The path

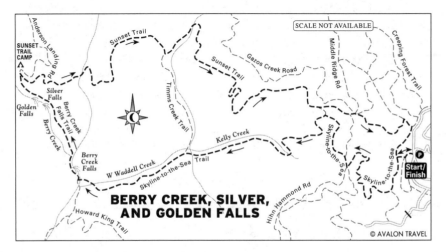

BERRY CREEK, SILVER, AND GOLDEN FALLS

© AVALON TRAVEL

described here is luscious single-track for nearly its entire length and open only to hikers. If you get tired along the way, the trail length can be reduced by a couple of miles by skipping the loop return and instead just hiking out and back.

Begin at the large parking lot by park headquarters. Take the connector trail from the west side of the lot, Redwood Nature Trail, past the campfire circle. After crossing Opal Creek, you'll turn left on Skyline-to-the-Sea Trail.

From its start, the trail meanders among virgin redwoods, some larger than 12 feet in diameter. After climbing 250 feet to gain a ridge in the first mile, the path angles to the right across Middle Ridge Fire Road, then drops down the other side. After a pleasant descent

Berry Creek Falls flows year-round in Big Basin Redwoods State Park.

through more huge redwoods, Skyline-to-the-Sea Trail parallels Kelly Creek and then West Waddell Creek. While you hike, keep an eye out for huge yellow banana slugs slowly crossing the trail and, in the wet season, California newts that always seem to be right under your boots.

At 4.2 miles, just before Skyline-to-the-Sea Trail meets up with Berry Creek Falls Trail, you are rewarded with your first glimpse of Berry Creek Falls through the redwood branches. It's enough to make you quicken your pace. Turn right on Berry Creek Falls Trail and in moments you'll be standing on the overlook platform in front of this breathtaking, 65-foot-tall cataract. Berry Creek Falls tumbles gracefully over a fern-lined, black cliff framed by redwoods.

Many hikers go no farther than this spot. A picnic lunch on the wooden platform and a turnaround here makes a nine-mile round-trip. But since you've come this far, it would be a pity not to hike the rest of the loop. The next two waterfalls are surprisingly different and the remaining scenery is far from anticlimactic.

Follow the trail up the left side of Berry Creek Falls, gaining an interesting perspective looking down over its lip. You'll leave Berry Creek and join West Berry Creek, a narrower and more channeled stream. Another 20 minutes of gentle climbing brings you to the base of Silver Falls. The 70-foot freefall spills over sandstone and limestone tinted in hues of tan, gold, and orange. In summer, you can walk right up to Silver Falls' flow and stick your head under the water. Several redwoods have fallen around the waterfall's base, making good viewing benches.

You'll spot more orange sandstone glowing underneath white water as you climb the wooden steps alongside Silver Falls. The path takes you to the brink of the falls, where it ascends rocky sandstone steps. Steel cables are in place along the trail. During periods of high water, it's wise to keep your hands on the cables.

In short order, you arrive at the lower tumble of Golden Falls cascade, a long drop of slippery orange sandstone. In contrast to Berry Creek and Silver Falls, Golden Falls is nearly horizontal, like a water slide for sea otters. The color of the rock is so striking, and the shape of this waterfall so unusual, that it's hard to believe you're less than a mile from the classic cataract at Berry Creek Falls. Completely different geologic forces seem to have been at work here.

Some hikers make Golden Falls Cascade their turnaround point for a 10.4-mile out-and-back trip. Backpackers can continue for an easy 0.25 mile to Sunset Trail Camp, a coveted overnight spot near West Berry Creek. Hikers opting for the 12-mile loop continue to the trail camp turnoff, then bear right on Sunset Trail. The path soon enters a vastly different—and drier—world, filled with knobcone pines, chinquapin, live oak, and madrone. A brief stretch on an exposed sandstone ridge may prompt you to put on your sunglasses for the first time all day.

Soon enough you head back into the forest canopy. Tan oaks and young redwoods border the steeply descending trail. After crossing West Waddell Creek, Sunset Trail climbs again, touring grassland slopes and mixed forests. Spring wildflowers are often plentiful in this area.

When the trail meets up with Middle Ridge Fire Road, cross it and descend again. Turn right on Dool Trail, then right again on Skyline-to-the-Sea Trail. A left turn puts you back on Redwood Nature Trail to finish out the loop back at the parking lot. When it's all over, you'll be able to count this as one of the finest days you've ever spent.

Options

For a shorter excursion in Big Basin Redwoods, take the Pine Mountain Trail from Blooms Creek Campground and head uphill to Buzzard's Roost, elevation 2,150 feet. The "roost" is a tall knob of rock on top of a large slab of sandstone that offers a great view of the park's surrounding peaks and ridges. From the campground, start by following Blooms Creek Trail southwest for a short distance, then turn left on Pine Mountain Trail. The trail switchbacks up a moderate grade. With the increasing elevation, the trailside vegetation changes to drought-tolerant chaparral plants and knobcone pines. At the top is the rocky summit where views extend in almost every direction except to the west—because Pine

Mountain is in the way. Bring a park map to identify all the landmarks and a picnic to enjoy in this sunny, view-filled spot. The 4.6-mile round-trip includes a 1,100-foot elevation gain.

Directions

From the junction of Highways 35 and 9 at Saratoga Gap, drive six miles west on Highway 9 to Highway 236. Turn west on Highway 236 and drive 8.4 winding miles to Big Basin Redwoods State Park Headquarters. Park in the lot across from park headquarters, then begin hiking from the west side of the lot on a signed connector trail to the Skyline-to-the-Sea Trail.

Information and Contact

A $10 day-use fee is charged per vehicle. Dogs and bikes are not allowed. A park map is available for $1 at the entrance station. A more detailed trail map is available for $8 at the park store or from www.mountainparks.org. For more information, contact Big Basin Redwoods State Park, 21600 Big Basin Way, Boulder Creek, CA 95006, 831/338-8860, www.bigbasin.org or www.parks.ca.gov.

19 SEQUOIA AUDUBON TRAIL   BEST ◖
Pescadero Marsh Natural Preserve

🦌 ✈ 🌸 🛶 🚻

Level: Easy   **Total Distance:** 2.4 miles round-trip

Hiking Time: 1 hour   **Elevation Change:** Negligible

Summary: Wildlife abounds on this easy exploration of Pescadero Marsh, at the meeting place of Pescadero and Butano Creeks and the Pacific Ocean.

Pescadero Marsh Natural Preserve is a 500-acre coastal marsh that backs the scenic San Mateo Coast along Highway 1. Considered to be one of the largest and most important freshwater and brackish marshes in California, Pescadero Marsh serves the important function of water filtration, water storage, and groundwater recharge for Pescadero and Butano Creeks. In addition, the marsh is critical habitat for a diverse assemblage of wildlife, including thousands of migratory birds traveling on the Pacific Flyway.

But what most people notice about Pescadero Marsh is that it's beautiful. Despite being bordered by Highway 1 to the west, the preserve is a peaceful oasis that is marked by the deep, rich blues and greens of plentiful water and foliage. Plein air painters are often seen at the preserve, pulling out their brushes and canvases to try to capture the marsh's voluptuous hues.

The preserve has three trails, which unfortunately are not contiguous. The southern trail along Butano Creek, called Butano Trail, is accessed from a trailhead on Pescadero Road, just 75 yards from its junction with Highway 1. The

© ANN MARIE BROWN

A great egret fishes in the brackish waters at Pescadero Marsh.

preserve's North Pond Trail is accessed by parking at the northernmost Pescadero State Beach parking lot. (Walk across the highway, then follow the trail as it curves around the east side of Pescadero Marsh's freshwater pond.) Sequoia Audubon Trail is the longest of the three trails, and it is accessed by parking in the state beach lot just south of the highway bridge over Pescadero Creek.

Most hikers prefer Sequoia Audubon Trail because of its length and diversity. The trail travels alongside Pescadero Creek for 1.2 miles, providing prime opportunities for wildlife-watching. It begins on the soft sand of the beach, then travels underneath the highway bridge and heads inland, soon providing solid earth beneath your shoes. You'll notice that the ground heats up as you get away from the coastal wind and move into dense vegetation. Spring and summer wildflowers bloom along the trail, including coastal paintbrush, monkeyflower, yellow bush lupine, and nonnative purple and yellow ice plant. A couple of gnarled, low-lying eucalyptus trees grow along the path.

A veritable jungle of wetlands and coastal foliage, the marsh attracts more than 200 species of birds (more than 60 species nest here), as well as numerous mammals and amphibians. Almost everyone who comes to Pescadero Marsh gets rewarded with wildlife sightings. On one trip, we saw two deer wading up to their knees through the marsh waters, half a dozen frogs under a footbridge by the creek, one large turtle, scads of minnows and water bugs, and birds galore—ducks, great egrets, red-winged blackbirds, swallows, godwits, and four great blue herons doing a little fishing. Herons nest in the eucalyptus trees above the marsh.

In late winter, you might get the chance to see steelhead trout swimming up Pescadero Creek to spawn. Or watch for the endangered San Francisco garter snake slithering along the trail.

The far end of Sequoia Audubon Trail climbs above the marsh to a viewing area where a bench affords a vista of the entire wetlands and the ocean beyond. An interpretive sign identifies different birds of prey you may see soaring above you. Hawks, kites, and owls are most common.

If bird-watching is your thing, the best birding times at Pescadero Marsh are late fall and early spring. But there's one prerequisite for a spring hike in the marsh—make sure you wear long pants and long sleeves. Pescadero Marsh might just be the tick capital of the world, and also one of California's greatest natural greenhouses for poison oak. If the trail hasn't been cleared recently, you may think the stuff is grown commercially here. Proceed with caution, or have that bottle of Tecnu ready when you get home.

Options

One of the best ways to see Pescadero Marsh is on a guided hike with a

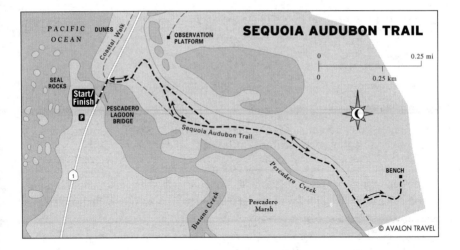

knowledgeable naturalist. Two-hour tours are scheduled on the first Sunday of the month at 10 A.M. and the third Sunday of the month at 1 P.M. No reservations are necessary; simply meet the tour leader at the middle parking lot for Pescadero State Beach on Highway 1 (just south of the bridge, on the ocean side of the highway). For more information, contact the San Mateo Coast Natural History Association (www.sanmateocoastnha.org).

If you'd rather wander on your own, a side trip that's a must is a coastal walk along Pescadero's rocky beaches, starting from the lot where you parked your car. The coastline features long sandy stretches, dramatic rock outcrops, treasure-filled tidepools, and harbor seals lounging around on the rocks.

Directions

From Highway 1 in Half Moon Bay, drive south for 17 miles to just north of Pescadero Road, near Pescadero State Beach. Park in the state beach parking lot south of the highway bridge over Pescadero Creek, on the west side of the highway. Walk to the north side of the bridge (use the pedestrian walkway on the west side), take the stairs to the sand, then follow the trail underneath the bridge and up the canyon.

Information and Contact

There is no fee at this parking lot, but there is an $8 fee per vehicle at nearby lots for Pescadero State Beach. Dogs and bikes are not allowed. A map of San Mateo Coast State Parks and Beaches, which includes Pescadero Marsh, is available for $1 from the Half Moon Bay State Beach ranger station at 95 Kelly Avenue, Half Moon Bay, 650/726-8820. For more information, contact Pescadero State Beach, 650/879-2170, www.parks.ca.gov.

20 BUTANO GRAND LOOP
Butano State Park

BEST ☕

Level: Strenuous

Total Distance: 11.0 miles round-trip

Hiking Time: 6 hours

Elevation Change: 1,300 feet

Summary: This long and varied loop through Butano State Park provides the chance to enjoy some solitude in the Pescadero "backcountry."

There's a forested canyon along the Half Moon Bay coast that looks much the same as it did a century ago. Filled with redwoods, Douglas firs, calypso orchids, and ferns, the canyon is found in 3,200-acre Butano State Park, just outside the coastal town of Pescadero. It's far enough away from the Bay Area's major population centers that its trails are rarely crowded. An 11-mile loop trip through the park is about as close as you can get to a true wilderness experience on a day hike in the Bay Area.

At time of publication, Butano was on a "seasonal closure" schedule, courtesy of the California governor, which means that it is technically closed from November to April. However, even though the park road is gated at the entrance station during those months, hikers are still permitted to walk in and access the park's lovely trails. And you don't have to pay the entrance fee if the park is "closed."

You can hike this loop in either direction—the gradient doesn't change much no matter which way you go. (The route described here saves the best grove of redwoods for the end.) However, before you start, you might want to practice pronouncing the park's name. It's BYOO-tin-oh, with the accent on the first syllable. Almost nobody gets this right on their first visit.

Park by the entrance kiosk and begin your exploration on Año Nuevo Trail.

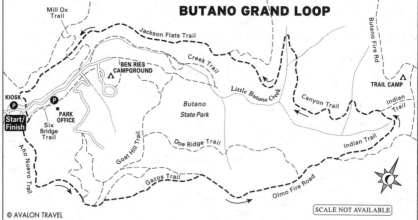

BUTANO GRAND LOOP

Mill Ox Trail · Jackson Flats Trail · Creek Trail · Butano Fire Rd · BEN RIES CAMPGROUND · Little Butano Creek · Canyon Trail · TRAIL CAMP · Indian Trail · KIOSK · PARK OFFICE · Six Bridge Trail · Butano State Park · Goat Hill Trail · Doe Ridge Trail · Indian Trail · Start/Finish · Año Nuevo Trail · Gazos Trail · Olmo Fire Road

SCALE NOT AVAILABLE

© AVALON TRAVEL

© KEVIN GONG

Butano State Park still looks much the same as it did 100 years ago.

The narrow path switchbacks up and up through dense vegetation—primarily thimbleberry, huckleberry, and poison oak vines. The ascent will get your heart pumping immediately. Soon you've climbed high enough to claim a vista through the lichen-covered branches of Douglas firs. The panorama includes the coast and the forested canyon inland; hawks soar over the grassy hills. Take the right spur to a bench 20 feet off the trail. A second bench, a little farther up the trail, has more obstructed views. At one time it had a clear view of Año Nuevo Island, giving this trail its name.

Año Nuevo Trail drops downhill and joins Olmo Fire Road. Follow it for 0.25 mile to the right turnoff for single-track Gazos Trail, which roughly parallels the fire road. Views of the coast are yours for the taking as you cruise up and down along the ridge top. This high ridge is composed of light-colored shale and sandstone—proof that the entire area was once undersea. Manzanita, chinquapin, and knobcone pines line the exposed, gravely slopes.

At Gazos Trail's end, it's worth stopping to admire the long-distance view of the coast before rejoining Olmo Fire Road and continuing to climb. A highlight along the wide dirt road is the 25-foot-tall root ball of a huge fallen Douglas fir. On one visit, it was covered with bright yellow banana slugs, busy doing the important business of decomposition.

Just before the road intersects with narrow Indian Trail (on the left), it becomes noticeably steeper. Where the vegetation opens up, you can clearly see the ridge's sandy shale soil. If you can withstand another 100 feet of climbing, follow the road a short distance past Indian Trail to a high overlook just off the trail. This sunny spot is probably the best potential picnic site of the day.

Follow Indian Trail into a dense oak and madrone forest, curving around the steep slopes of Little Butano Creek canyon to begin the loop's return leg. Where Indian Trail forks right 0.5 mile from its start, the path leads to Trail Camp. A half-dozen, no-frills backpacking sites are hidden in the forest; a pit toilet is the only amenity. (These sites are first-come, first-served, but you must register with the park to camp.) At the turnoff, bear left on chaparral-lined Canyon Trail. You'll have a few more glimpses of the coast through the ceanothus and occasional Douglas firs.

Canyon Trail connects with Jackson Flats Trail, the final leg of this loop. The last 2.8 miles on Jackson Flats Trail are an easy cruise through the park's loveliest stretch of forest. The woodland features fern gardens, many big and small redwoods, and moss-covered Douglas firs growing in some interesting configurations, with trunks and limbs extending every which way. Watch for banana slugs and California newts; the redwood duff is their home and you don't want to step on them. In the early spring (February–April), keep your eyes trained to the forest floor in search of the rare calypso orchid, a small and delicate purple flower.

Options

For Butano campers, or day hikers looking for a shorter hike, a pleasant three-mile loop can be made by starting on Año Nuevo Trail to Olmo Fire Road (as described), followed by an immediate left on Goat Hill Trail. This trail drops down to the service road beyond Ben Ries Campground; turn right and follow it to its end, where Creek Trail begins. Finish out the loop on Creek Trail and Six Bridges Trail. Even though the last leg follows the park access road, it leads through a handsome fern-filled redwood forest along the banks of Little Butano Creek.

Directions

From Highway 1 in Half Moon Bay, drive south for 17 miles to the Pescadero Road turnoff. Turn left (east) and drive 2.5 miles to Cloverdale Road. Turn right on Cloverdale Road and drive 4.2 miles to the park entrance. Turn left and drive 0.75 mile to the entrance kiosk; park in the small lot just beyond it.

Information and Contact

A $10 day-use fee is charged per vehicle. Dogs are not allowed. Bikes are allowed only on fire roads. A park map is available at the entrance kiosk or by free download at www.parks.ca.gov. A detailed map is also available by download at www.virtualparks.org ($1 fee). For more information, contact Butano State Park, 1500 Cloverdale Road, Pescadero, CA 94060, 650/879-2040, www.parks.ca.gov.

21 AÑO NUEVO POINT TRAIL
Año Nuevo State Reserve

BEST

Level: Easy

Total Distance: 3.0 miles round-trip

Hiking Time: 2 hours

Elevation Change: Negligible

Summary: A trip to Año Nuevo in the winter months provides a wildlife show you'll never forget.

When was the last time you saw thousands of animals in one spot? Those kinds of numbers don't happen often for wildlife-watchers, but they occur regularly at Año Nuevo State Reserve. Every year December–March, Año Nuevo Island is the breeding ground for more than 3,000 elephant seals.

It's not just the number of animals that's impressive; it's their immense size. Elephant seals are the kings of the pinniped family (all species of aquatic mammals with fins). The males can grow longer than 18 feet and weigh more than two tons. The females reach as long as 12 feet and weigh more than one ton. Baby elephant seals increase their weight from 60 pounds to 200 pounds in only four weeks after birth. Aside from its huge size, the elephant seal's most elephantine characteristic is its snout. Particularly on the male elephant seal, the snout resembles a short version of an elephant's trunk. It is used primarily for vocalization—to amplify the animal's strange roars.

You can show up any time of year and see pinnipeds at Año Nuevo State Reserve. The mainland beaches, as well as the shores of Año Nuevo Island, are popular with California sea lions and harbor seals year-round. Mid-May–mid-August, stellar sea lions breed on an isolated reef surrounding the island.

But in the winter months, it's the northern elephant seals that steal the show. The huge males arrive in late November to claim the best spots on the beaches; the pregnant females come to shore 2–3 weeks later to give birth and breed. In a

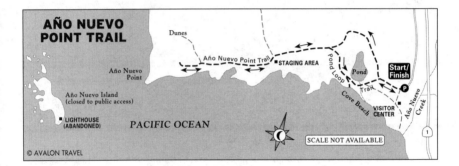

AÑO NUEVO POINT TRAIL

Dunes

Año Nuevo Point Trail

STAGING AREA

Año Nuevo Point

Pond Loop

Pond

Start/Finish

P

Año Nuevo Island (closed to public access)

Cove Beach

Pond Loop Trail

VISITOR CENTER

Año Nuevo Creek

LIGHTHOUSE (ABANDONED)

PACIFIC OCEAN

SCALE NOT AVAILABLE

1

© AVALON TRAVEL

few months, the adults and their young all disappear back into the ocean and are usually not seen again until the following winter.

Given all this, the Año Nuevo Point Trail at Año Nuevo State Reserve is a basic requirement on the resume of any Bay Area nature lover. The trail is an easy three miles round-trip, most of which is nearly level. In addition to the elephant seal show, the path leads to a gorgeous stretch of sand called Cove Beach, where you could easily while away an entire day.

The rules at Año Nuevo are as follows: You may visit the preserve and hike on your own April–November (although you must obtain a free permit at the reserve entrance to do so). During the first two weeks of December, the reserve is completely closed to the public. Mid-December–March, entry is by guided walks only and prior reservations are recommended. It's unwise to drive all the way to the park if you don't have reservations. January, when the baby elephant seals are born, is usually the busiest month.

Those who can't plan more than a day in advance should wait until the end of March, then call the park to find out exactly what day the guided-entry-only period ends. If you show up soon thereafter, plenty of elephant seals will still be hanging around.

The trail to reach the elephant seals is a pleasant walk over densely vegetated coastal bluffs. From the parking lot, you set out through the coastal scrub and soon reach a fork with Pond Loop Trail. Bear right to loop around the high side of a small pond, gaining views of its blue waters and the ocean beyond. Coastal wetlands and ponds such as this one provide critical habitat for the endangered

A guided walk at Año Nuevo brings you up-close and personal with the elephant seals.

San Francisco garter snake and also for its prey, the endangered California red-legged frog. The San Francisco garter snake was once a common sight around Skyline Boulevard and the coast, but is now found at only a few undeveloped areas in San Mateo County. With its striking sky-blue underside and continuous line of black and orange stripes, the snake is considered by many to be the most beautiful North American reptile.

Three-quarters of a mile from the trailhead is a kiosk and staging area for the Wildlife Protection Area. The kiosk features interesting displays on the pinnipeds that call Año Nuevo home. From here you continue west on the trail toward Año Nuevo Point, where you gain a view of the multitudes of elephant seals on Año Nuevo Island and the mainland beaches. An abandoned lighthouse, built in 1890 to warn mariners away from the rock-strewn coastline, has since been claimed by seals and sea lions. When the light was still in use, the lighthouse keeper and his family had to constantly battle the pinnipeds, who took over the island and even forced their way into the keeper's house. In 1948, the lighthouse was replaced by an automatic buoy and the building was left to the animals.

As you near Año Nuevo Point, the cacophony of barking and snorting is tremendous. From your vantage point about 25 feet from the seals, you are close enough to see them brawling with each other and can observe their strange, jerking movements as they go from sand to sea and back.

While staring at the giant creatures, consider that their presence here is a remarkable testament to the healing power of nature. By the year 1900, less than 100 elephant seals were left in the world; the rest had been killed for the oil contained in their blubber. Miraculously, one small surviving group of seals located on an island west of Baja California slowly began to multiply. By the 1920s, elephant seals were occasionally seen off the coast of Southern California, and in 1955 they returned to Año Nuevo Island, one of their traditional breeding grounds.

On your return hike, be sure to walk the south leg of the loop around the pond, then take the short cutoff trail to Cove Beach. It's a great spot for a picnic or a long walk on the sand. And don't miss a visit to the terrific visitors center at Año Nuevo.

Options

Año Nuevo offers several other short trails (not at the main elephant seal area) which are worth exploring. From the main entrance, drive 2.7 miles north on Highway 1 and park in the dirt lot west of the Rossi Road turnoff. A trail leads across the bluffs to a tidepool area, or you can follow it north or south along the edge of the bluffs. Or, continue north 1.4 miles from Rossi Road to the Gazos Creek Beach access. Hike south along the beach to Franklin Point, where the fogbound clipper ship *Sir John Franklin* wrecked in 1865. At the point, you must walk within the cable lines to protect fragile dune vegetation. From the top of the highest dune, the view is inspiring: Pigeon Point Lighthouse anchors the northern coast; Table Rock and Año Nuevo Island rise to the south.

Directions

From Half Moon Bay at the junction of Highway 92 and Highway 1, drive south on Highway 1 for 27 miles to the right turnoff for Año Nuevo State Reserve. (From Santa Cruz, drive 21 miles north on Highway 1.)

Information and Contact

A $10 day-use fee is charged per vehicle. Entry to the elephant seal area is by guided walk only December 15–March 31. Walks are held several times daily and reservations are recommended. The fee is $7 per person (in addition to the $10 per vehicle parking fee). Tickets go on sale up to 56 days in advance. Reservations can be made by phone at 800/444-4445 or at http://anonuevo.reserveamerica.com. Unreserved tickets are sold daily at the park on a first-come, first-served basis. Dogs and bikes are not allowed. A park map is available at the entrance station. For more information, contact Año Nuevo State Reserve, New Years Creek Road, Pescadero, CA 94060, 650/879-2025 or 650/879-0227, www.parks.ca.gov.

22 ANTLER POINT LOOP   BEST ◖

Joseph D. Grant County Park

🏕️ 🦌 ✈️ 🌼

Level: Strenuous   **Total Distance:** 8.8 miles round-trip

Hiking Time: 5 hours   **Elevation Change:** 1,800 feet

Summary: Old ranch roads travel through a grassland and oak savannah in the former Grant Ranch, where wild pigs roam and wildflowers bloom in spring.

Joseph D. Grant County Park is a world apart from the rest of Santa Clara County. Just down the hill lies the hustle and bustle of Silicon Valley, but up at Grant Park, all is tranquil. A few cows graze on the hillsides, ancient oaks and wildflowers dot the grasslands, bluebirds flit among the trees, and golden eagles soar the skies. If you spend a day hiking the park's trails, the biggest excitement you may encounter is the sudden appearance of wild pigs, which scatter and run when they hear you coming.

A few warnings, just so you know what you're in for. Grant County Park, called Grant Ranch by the locals, lies due north of better-known Henry W. Coe State Park, and it shares the same summer weather—hot as Hades. There is very little shade in the park, so plan your trip for autumn, winter, or spring. April and May are the best months to visit, when the grasslands are green and the slopes are gilded with blue-eyed grass, poppies, brodiaea, and lupine.

© KEVIN GONG

From Antler Point, the hustle and bustle of the South Bay seems far, far away.

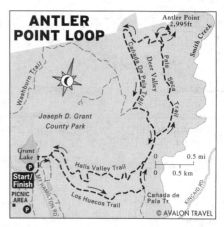

The trails at Grant County Park are predominantly multiuse dirt roads that are very popular with mountain bikers. (If you turn up your nose at anything wider than single-track, you won't be happy here.) The path described in this listing is designed to avoid a good deal of bike traffic, but it won't eliminate it. To reduce your chance of sharing the trails with bikes, plan your visit for a weekday, when the park is usually empty.

This semi-loop trip takes you to the park's highest hill, Antler Point, which tops out at 2,995 feet. The first two miles feature some steep uphill pitches, but the rest of the walk is moderate. Begin your hike at the Grant Lake Trailhead and follow the wide road edging large, shallow Grant Lake. Shoreline fishing for bass and bluegill is popular here. About halfway along the lakeshore, turn right on Halls Valley Trail. After 0.25 mile, turn right on Los Huecos Trail. Because most mountain bikers follow the continuation of Halls Valley Trail uphill, you'll have less company on steep Los Huecos Trail.

The next 1.8 miles are a steady uphill with a few pitches that will leave you gasping for breath. With luck, you're here on a cool day. Expanding vistas of Grant Lake and the park's western ridge are fair compensation for the climb. As you gain elevation, you'll have surprising views of the South Bay's distant shimmering waters.

Bird-watching is exceptional on Los Huecos Trail. Hawks, golden eagles, and other raptors perch on the tall oaks and hunt the grasslands. Songbirds such as western bluebirds and tanagers may be seen in springtime. Black-and-white magpies are present year-round and acorn woodpeckers are frequently heard and seen. These woodpeckers form a social group centered around an acorn granary, a chosen tree in which the birds drill holes, filling each one with an acorn to be eaten later. A single granary may contain thousands of acorns.

Where the trail tops out at Cañada de Pala Trail, turn left and enjoy an easier, more rolling grade. More views of the South Bay are seen to the northwest and Mount Hamilton shows up to the east. Although spring wildflowers are found throughout the park's grasslands, the most abundant displays are found on this high, bald ridge. (I hope you timed your trip for April or May.)

Your destination, Antler Point, is visible straight ahead, the highest hill around. After 0.75 mile, bear right on Pala Seca Trail. Another 1.6 miles through grasslands and past occasional grazing bovines brings you to the spur trail to Antler Point. Turn right and walk the final 0.25 mile uphill to the bald, grassy overlook. This is the day's best view of the South Bay, San Jose, Grant Park's rolling grasslands, and Lick Observatory on top of 4,209-foot Mount Hamilton.

For your return trip, retrace your steps on the spur to Antler Point, then turn right and loop back on Cañada de Pala Trail, enjoying more ridge-top views. Don't miss the right turnoff for Halls Valley Trail for your downhill return to Grant Lake. Mountain bikers are allowed to go uphill only on this trail, so you don't have to worry about being mowed down from behind as you descend.

The sudden appearance of wild pigs, especially in the oak- and laurel-shaded canyon of Halls Valley, may be a surprise to many first-time visitors. More than 500 wild pigs live in the park; rangers keep tabs on their numbers so they don't get out of control. The large animals are descendants of European wild pigs that were brought in by ranchers for sport hunting in the early 20th century. They have thrived and multiplied throughout large areas of California. Most of the pigs in Grant Park are black, although some have bred with domestic pigs and their descendants are multicolored. Pigs seen along the trail will most likely run from you; the bolder ones have taken to rooting around the park's campgrounds.

One more tip to optimize your trip: If you can, time your exit from the park so that you leave right at sunset, just before the gates are locked. Then you'll have the pleasure of driving back down Mount Hamilton Road with an enchanting view of glowing city lights.

Options

If you visit Grant Park during the spring wildflower season, one of the best shows is along the south end of Cañada de Pala Trail, a stretch you'll miss if you travel on the loop described earlier. To head straight for the best blooms, drive 3.5 miles past the Grant Lake parking area to the Twin Gates Trailhead, a small parking lot on the left. Hike out-and-back on Cañada de Pala Trail as far as you wish—the first two miles feature outstanding displays of blue-eyed grass, lupine, Johnny-jump-ups, brodiaea, shooting stars, and goldfields. Another exceptional wildflower route is the Hotel Trail and San Felipe Trail loop, which can be accessed across the road from the Grant Lake parking area.

Directions

From I-680 in San Jose, take the Alum Rock Avenue exit and drive east for 2.2 miles. Turn right on Mount Hamilton Road and drive 7.9 miles to the sign for Joseph D. Grant County Park on the right. Don't turn here; continue for another 100 yards to the Grant Lake parking lot on the left side of the road.

Information and Contact

A $6 day-use fee is charged per vehicle. Dogs are not allowed. Bikes are allowed. A park map is available at the trailhead or by free download at www.parkhere.org. For more information, contact Joseph D. Grant County Park at 408/274-6121; or Santa Clara County Parks and Recreation Department, 298 Garden Hill Drive, Los Gatos, CA 95032, 408/355-2200, www.parkhere.org.

23 COYOTE PEAK LOOP
Santa Teresa County Park, Morgan Hill

Level: Easy

Hiking Time: 2 hours

Total Distance: 4.0 miles round-trip

Elevation Change: 500 feet

Summary: Just a few car honks from U.S. 101, this flower-filled park has pockets of rugged natural beauty and a summit with a view.

Santa Teresa County Park isn't the largest or most wilderness-like park in Santa Clara County. It's better known for its golf course and picnic areas than for its hiking trails. Similarly, the park's high point, Coyote Peak, isn't the tallest summit in the county. But considering its location just off Bernal Road south of San Jose, the park and its 1,155-foot peak are clear winners for an afternoon hike with a stellar South Bay view. A bonus is that Santa Teresa's grasslands

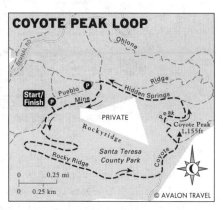

are fertile soil for a bounty of spring wildflowers. Can a park this close to an urban area feel like a nature preserve? Surprisingly, yes.

You drive through a large chunk of this county park to access the trailhead at the far end of the Pueblo Picnic Area. From the parking lot, head west along the wide road by the corral, signed as Mine Trail. Walk a mere 75 yards, then turn left on single-track Rocky Ridge Trail.

Begin a zigzagging climb through the grasslands of Big Oak Valley. The narrow path is open to mountain bikers; you may have to step aside to let them pass. Because you are going uphill, you'll have plenty of time to see bikers coming downhill toward you; bikers going uphill will be traveling at a much slower pace. The trail occasionally passes by ancient, sprawling oaks and lichen-covered serpentine outcrops. Springtime brings bright-colored displays of fiddleneck, poppies, goldfields, and yarrow.

The path meanders gently up and down in a roller-coaster fashion; it seems to have been built with mountain biking in mind. As you ascend the ridge, keep following the trail toward the white building located on a high point. Just below it, Rocky Ridge Trail connects with wide Coyote Peak Trail; turn left. Now it's an easy 0.5 mile to the top of Coyote Peak, elevation 1,155 feet. A bench and

Coyote Peak's summit in Santa Teresa County Park

railing are placed on the flat summit. Views are mainly to the north and east of the Santa Clara Valley. Look for the white dome of Lick Observatory on top of Mount Hamilton, and gaze in wonder at the bustling metropolis the South Bay has become. Less than a century ago, farming and ranching were the main activities in this valley, but now the remaining farms are scattered and few.

After you've observed the wild sprawl of civilization below, backtrack down the summit spur trail to Coyote Peak Trail, then turn right and follow it steeply downhill. The route drops into a canyon lined with bay laurel and oaks. At a junction with Hidden Springs Trail, turn left to head back to the Pueblo Picnic Area in a little more than 0.5 mile. Walk past the various picnic areas to reach the lot where you left your car.

Options

Wildflower lovers, take note: Although much of the park is dotted with spring wildflowers, the best flower show is on the 1.4-mile Stile Ranch Trail. Access it from the trailhead at the junction of Fortini Road and San Vicente Avenue in San Jose. Typical flowers that blossom in this rocky serpentine grassland include goldfields, tidy tips, clarkia, poppies, and gilia. At peak bloom, a dazzling range of colors is splashed over the hillsides.

Directions

From the Santa Clara Valley south of San Jose, take U.S. 101 south to just past the U.S. 101/Hwy. 85 junction. Take the Bernal Road/Hwy. 101 North exit and drive west on Bernal Road for 1.5 miles. After you cross Santa Teresa Boulevard, continue on Bernal Road for another two miles, passing the Santa Teresa Golf Club and climbing into the hills. Turn left at the sign for Pueblo Picnic Area and drive 0.75 mile to the end of the road by the corral, at the far end of the picnic area.

Information and Contact

A $6 day-use fee is charged per vehicle. Leashed dogs and bikes are allowed. A park map is available at the trailhead or by free download at www.parkhere.org. For more information, contact Santa Teresa County Park c/o Hellyer County Park at 408/225-0225; or Santa Clara County Parks and Recreation Department, 298 Garden Hill Drive, Los Gatos, CA 95032, 408/355-2200, www.parkhere.org.

24 FLAT FROG, MIDDLE RIDGE, AND FISH TRAIL LOOP

BEST ☾

Henry W. Coe State Park

Level: Moderate

Total Distance: 7.8 miles round-trip

Hiking Time: 4 hours

Elevation Change: 1,000 feet

Summary: Whet your appetite for the South Bay's most rugged wilderness area on this varied sampler hike in Henry W. Coe State Park.

The closest thing to wilderness in the South Bay is Henry W. Coe State Park. This well-known but not-so-well-traveled state park is the second largest in California (the largest is Anza-Borrego Desert State Park near San Diego). Comprised of tall ridges bisected by deep, steep ravines, Coe Park is notoriously hilly and rugged. Its varied terrain includes grasslands, oaks, chaparral, pines, and mixed hardwoods.

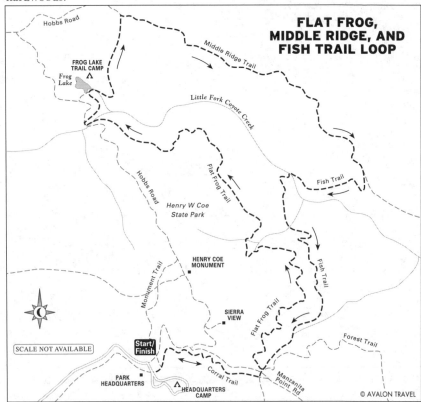

FLAT FROG, MIDDLE RIDGE, AND FISH TRAIL LOOP

Henry Coe is so large—87,000 acres and growing—and its terrain so rugged that to see much of it, you need to take a backpacking trip lasting at least a few days. But day hikers can tour the western part of the park on this nearly eight-mile loop around Middle Ridge.

Two requirements for the trip: First, pick a cool day to hike, ideally in late winter or spring when Coe Park's streams are running. The park is notoriously hot in summer. Second, bring plenty of water, even if the weather is cool.

This loop begins just across the road from the visitors center at park headquarters. It mostly avoids the wide, exposed ranch roads and instead sticks to narrow footpaths. Take the single-track Corral Trail, which parallels Manzanita Point Road. In typical Coe Park fashion, Corral Trail passes through three distinct ecosystems in short order: mixed oak woodland, grasslands, and chaparral. Spring wildflowers are plentiful, especially iris, poppies, buttercups, and popcorn flowers. Watch for the more unusual purple monkeyflowers.

In less than a mile, turn left on Springs Trail to cross Manzanita Point Road, then immediately bear left on Flat Frog Trail to begin a gentle ascent to Frog Lake. This 2.3-mile trail isn't the shortest route to the tiny lake; it's nearly double the length of Hobbs Road to the west. But it's a pleasant, single-track ramble with scenic views of Middle Ridge, traveling through a surprisingly varied woodland. Ponderosa pines are mingled with the black oaks and madrones. In spring, look for giant trillium in the forest understory. Its large, mottled leaves are easy to identify. Bright red columbine, purple shooting stars, and Chinese houses are also common.

Flat Frog Trail connects with Hobbs Road just before Frog Lake; take either trail to the tiny former cattle pond. A backpacking camp is located nearby. One-acre Frog Lake is spring-fed; even in dry years it usually has a little water in it. It supports a few bass and bluegill, but they aren't easy to catch. Frequently the surface of the water is completely covered with green algae, but nonetheless, the pond is a good place for bird-watching. Acorn woodpeckers use the dead snags around the lake as granaries for their acorns. On one April trip, we spotted a pair of colorful western tanagers flitting around the trees bordering the lake. We watched their bright-hued feathers for almost an hour.

Cross Frog Lake's dam and continue uphill to Middle Ridge. The oak-dotted grasslands above Frog Lake support goldfields, lupine, poppies, and even a few dogtooth violets—providing much to pause and admire while you catch your breath on this climb. Once you reach Middle Ridge, look forward to a roller-coaster walk with many lovely views of Coyote Creek canyon. Although the trail initially leads through alternating grassy clearings and groves of pines and black oaks, it later enters a stand of giant, tree-sized manzanitas growing 15 feet tall.

Follow the ridge for just over a mile to the right turnoff for Fish Trail. Enjoy a pleasant descent through two canyons filled with black oaks, bay laurels, and willows. Cross the Little Fork of Coyote Creek. Where the trail parallels Fish Creek, you'll have the good company of this small cascading stream. The final leg of the trail brings you back into grasslands dotted with huge valley oaks. Many bear large clumps of mistletoe growing high in their branches.

Where Fish Trail ends, cross Manzanita Point Road, take Springs Trail to Corral Trail and follow it west for the final stretch back to park headquarters and your car.

Options

A longer hike, but one that is a great adventure in the cool spring months, is the trip out to China Hole, a year-round pool on the Middle Fork of Coyote Creek. Bring along plenty of water and snacks for the 10-mile round-trip, which has many sunny, exposed sections. Follow Corral Trail as outlined, but after crossing Manzanita Point Road, take Forest Trail east, which rejoins Manzanita Point Road shortly before the group campground. Walk through the campground to site 7 and pick up China Hole Trail, which drops 1,200 feet on its way down to the creek. Enjoy the delightful scenery at China Hole, then get ready to climb back uphill. You have a few choices for looping back if you don't want to retrace your steps. Take along a park map.

Henry Coe State Park may be dry and hot in summer, but in winter, the water flows.

Directions

From U.S. 101 in Morgan Hill, take the East Dunne Avenue exit and drive east for 13 miles to Henry W. Coe State Park headquarters.

Information and Contact

An $8 day-use fee is charged per vehicle. Dogs are not allowed. Bikes are allowed on some park trails. Park maps are available at park headquarters or by free download at www.coepark.org. For more information, contact Henry W. Coe State Park, 9000 East Dunne Avenue, Morgan Hill, CA 95037, 408/779-2728, www.coepark.org or www.parks.ca.gov.

25 WATERFALL LOOP TRAIL   BEST (

Uvas Canyon County Park

Level: Easy/Moderate   **Total Distance:** 3.5 miles round-trip

Hiking Time: 2 hours   **Elevation Change:** 700 feet

Summary: Not just one, but a handful of waterfalls can be seen on this family-friendly hike in Uvas Canyon.

Uvas Canyon County Park is a little slice of waterfall heaven on the eastern side of the Santa Cruz Mountains. Although the drive to reach it is a long journey from the freeway through grasslands and oaks, it delivers you to a surprising red-wood forest at the park entrance. From that point onward, you've entered another world—one filled with blissful shade and cascading water.

Uvas Canyon is a small park with camping and picnicking facilities and a short stretch of hiking trails in its 1,200 acres, but it's proof that good things come in small packages. If you're short on time, you can walk the one-mile Waterfall Loop Trail and see Black Rock Falls and several smaller cascades on Swanson Creek. If you're in the mood to stretch your legs, you can make a 2.5-mile loop out to Alec Canyon, then follow the Alec Canyon Trail out and back to Triple Falls, for a total 3.5-mile hike.

The park has enough waterfalls to make any waterfall lover happy. Just make sure you show up in the rainy season, because that's when Uvas Canyon is at its best. Water seems to pour from every crack in the hillsides. By mid-summer, the

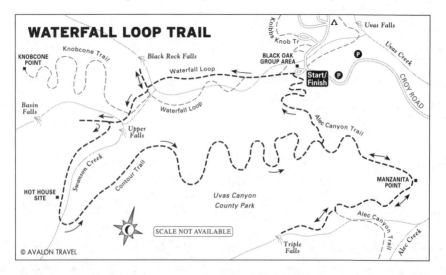

falls are reduced to a mere trickle. The canyon is filled with oaks, laurels, big-leaf maples, and Douglas firs, all thriving in the moist environment around Swanson Creek.

Start your trip either at the Black Oak Group Area on the gated dirt road, or 100 yards farther down the park road, just before the turnoff to the campground. The latter will give you an immediate audience with Granuja Falls, a tiny, five-foot-tall cataract in a very photogenic setting, before leading across a bridge and up a set of stairsteps to join the picnic area trail/road. From Black Oak Group Area, head straight on the road to connect to the Waterfall Loop Trail through the canyon. Cross Swanson Creek on a footbridge, then bear right at the fork and head directly for

An easy walk at Uvas Canyon County Park leads to multiple waterfalls.

Black Rock Falls, 0.25 mile away. You'll find the waterfall on your right, pouring 30 feet down a side canyon over—you guessed it—black rock. Take a few pictures, then continue on the trail, heading for Basin Falls. This waterfall is 20 feet high and surrounded by moss-covered rocks. It makes a shapely S-curve at it carves its way down the canyon. Next you'll reach Upper Falls, a little shorter in height than the other falls, but just as enchanting.

At Upper Falls, it's decision time: Either head back and take the other side of the Waterfall Loop Trail for a short and level one-mile hike, or continue up Swanson Creek and follow the winding Contour Trail to Alec Canyon and Triple Falls. For the longer trip, follow Contour Trail through a dense oak and Douglas fir forest, crossing a few small ravines. Where the trail joins with Alec Canyon Trail, turn right and hike 0.5 mile to Manzanita Point. Here, at an opening in the abundant manzanita bushes, you gain wide views of the South Bay and Diablo Range on clear days.

A short distance farther you enter Alec Canyon's second-growth redwood forest. In the late 1800s, the virgin redwoods in this canyon were cut for lumber to build the nearby mining town of New Almaden. The trail you're following is an old logging road.

Turn right on the short spur trail to Triple Falls. True to its name, Triple Falls is a series of three cascades, totaling 40 feet in height. If you wish, you can find a seat right alongside the cascading fall. Or backtrack to Alec Canyon Trail, turn right, and head for a picnic table right alongside the creek. To finish the loop, follow the road back to Black Oak Group Area, a steep 0.75-mile descent.

Which waterfall at Uvas Park is the best? My favorites are Basin Falls and Triple Falls. Your favorite? Go see them all and decide.

Options

If you didn't time your Uvas Park visit for the winter waterfall season, head for a trail with a radically different demeanor that isn't dependent on the weather: Knibbs Knob Trail. This 3.6-mile out-and-back trip involves a 1,600-foot climb on a rather steep and exposed fire road. It leads to 2,694-foot Knibbs Knob, a forested summit with peekaboo views of the high peaks of the Santa Cruz Mountains, Skyline Ridge, and the mountains and foothills of the Diablo Range. On very rare clear days, the Sierra Nevada can be seen from here. The trail begins at the Upper Bench Youth Camp. Hike 1.5 miles and then turn right on the 0.25-mile spur trail to Knibbs Knob. A picnic table is located at the top.

Directions

From U.S. 101 in Morgan Hill, take the Bernal Road exit west. Turn left on Santa Teresa Boulevard. Travel south three miles and turn right onto Bailey Avenue. Follow Bailey Avenue 2.3 miles to McKean Road. Turn left on McKean Road and drive six miles (McKean Road becomes Uvas Road). Turn right on Croy Road and drive 4.5 miles to the park (continue past Sveadal, a private camp/resort). Park near park headquarters or in one of the picnic area parking lots, then walk down the park road to the trailhead. The trail begins at Black Oak Group Area, or you can access it 100 yards farther down the park road, just before the turnoff to the campground.

Information and Contact

A $6 day-use fee is charged per vehicle. Leashed dogs are allowed. Bikes are not allowed. A park map is available at the entrance station or by free download at www.parkhere.org. For more information, contact Uvas Canyon County Park, 8515 Croy Road, Morgan Hill, CA 95037, 408/779-9232. Or contact Santa Clara County Parks and Recreation Department, 298 Garden Hill Drive, Los Gatos, CA 95032, 408/355-2200, www.parkhere.org.

26 LOCH TRAIL AND HIGHLANDS LOOP
Loch Lomond Recreation Area

Level: Easy/Moderate **Total Distance:** 5.2 miles round-trip

Hiking Time: 3 hours **Elevation Change:** 700 feet

Summary: This surprisingly large reservoir in the Santa Cruz Mountains boasts a bevy of hiking trails and a Sierra-like ambience.

Every summer when I was a kid, my parents took my sisters and me hiking and fishing at a big lake surrounded by a pretty woodland. We'd explore around the lake, learn about the trees and plants that grew there, watch for wildlife, and go fishing in our little motorboat. We'd always take a break at midday, pull up our boat on an island on the lake, sit on a rock, and eat some sandwiches. Then we'd hike in the woods or just sit on the shoreline and admire the scenery.

As an adult, I never thought I'd find any place in urban California to match that lake of my memories. But then I went to Loch Lomond Reservoir, just 10 miles north of Santa Cruz, and found just such a place.

The Loch Trail at Loch Lomond Recreation Area follows the shoreline of a large, deep blue reservoir through a Douglas fir and redwood forest. After a pleasant mile along the water's edge, the trail connects with Highlands Trail, which ascends the

© ANN MARIE BROWN

Docks and picnic tables along the Loch Trail invite anglers and picnickers, as well as hikers, to enjoy the blue waters of Loch Lomond.

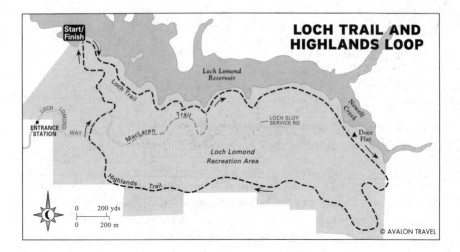

hillside above the lake. With a gentle climb of only a few hundred feet, the trail rises above the treetops for high views of Loch Lomond. The entire loop is only five miles, the perfect length for a morning or afternoon walk.

The key to the trip is to show up in the right season. The 175-acre reservoir and its surrounding land are locked up for six months of the year in order to protect the water supply for the city of Santa Cruz. But each year on March 1, the gates are opened and the public recreation season begins. The park is open daily in spring and summer; from Labor Day through mid-October, it is open weekends only.

As you hike the Loch Trail, you could stop to drop a line in the water (best trout fishing is April–June), or picnic at one of the many shaded tables near the shoreline. Or you might just meander along, admiring the fetching lake. The only thing you can't do is swim; Loch Lomond is a public water supply, so no human contact is allowed. The footpath winds gently around one tree-lined cove after another: Cunningham, MacGregor, Stewart, Fir, and Huckleberry.

At Deer Flat, 1.2 miles out, Loch Trail meets up with Highlands Trail, a wide fire road. Continue on Highlands Trail farther north along the lakeshore and then uphill through the redwoods, climbing 500 feet. The road tops out at a remote weather station where you gain a sweeping view of the lake below and the surrounding forested mountains. Highlands Trail then traverses the ridge southward, now in a more open forest of knobcone pines, chaparral, and nonnative but colorful Scotch broom. Views of the lake and Newell Creek canyon are yours for the taking. Where the trail nears the park road, follow the pavement back downhill to your car.

Options

While at Loch Lomond, don't miss a walk on the one-mile Big Trees Nature Trail. Pick up a free trail guide at the park store; the trail starts at the Glen Corrie Picnic Area and ascends to a ridge, where you'll find the only remaining old-growth redwoods in this watershed. These massive, 500- to 1,000-year-old trees offer a glimpse into the area's pre-logging magnificence. Just around the bend from the giant trees is an area that suffered major storm damage during the 1970s and 1980s from high winds, snowfall, and heavy rainfall. The biggest hit came from a January 1982 storm in which 15 inches of rain fell in a 24-hour period, causing a series of mudslides. As the trail descends through this still-recovering area, observe how some of the trees had their tops knocked off. Remnants of early 20th-century logging activities can also be seen along this short, fascinating trail.

Directions

From I-280 in San Jose, take Highway 17 south for 24 miles to Scotts Valley. Take the Mount Hermon Road exit, turn right, and drive 3.5 miles. Turn left on Graham Hill Road, then turn left immediately on Zayante Road. Drive three miles to Lompico Road. Turn left and drive 1.7 miles to West Drive. Turn left and drive 0.5 mile to Sequoia Road, then enter the park. (The route is clearly signed for Loch Lomond Recreation Area.) Follow the park road to its end near the boat ramp and store. Loch Trail begins by the boat ramp.

Note: Check your calendar before you go: Loch Lomond Recreation Area is open daily March 1–Labor Day, then weekends only until mid-October. It is closed the rest of the year.

Information and Contact

A $4 day-use fee is charged per vehicle. Leashed dogs are allowed ($1 dog fee). Bikes are not allowed. A free trail map is available at the park entrance. For more information, contact Loch Lomond Recreation Area, 100 Loch Lomond Way, Felton, CA 95018, 831/335-7424, www.cityofsantacruz.com.

27 FALL CREEK LOOP
Henry Cowell Redwoods State Park, Fall Creek Unit

Level: Moderate   **Total Distance:** 8.0 miles round-trip

Hiking Time: 4 hours   **Elevation Change:** 1,500 feet

Summary: Visit the quieter side of Henry Cowell Redwoods State Park at Fall Creek, where solitude is in plentiful supply.

Question: Where in the Bay Area can you find a fast running, full flowing stream even in the driest months of summer and fall? Answer: Almost nowhere, except at the Fall Creek Unit of Henry Cowell Redwoods State Park.

The Fall Creek Unit is not the best-known section of Henry Cowell Park. More famous is the northern park unit with its family campgrounds and Roaring Camp steam trains. (See *Observation Deck and Big Rock Hole Loop* listing in this chapter.) But the less-developed Fall Creek Unit is perfectly suited for hikers, with crystal-clear Fall Creek tumbling, cascading, and pooling alongside the park's main trail, even in the dry months of summer and fall.

The Fall Creek Unit isn't huge, so you can make an eight-mile loop around the park and see much of it in one day. In addition to its natural beauty, the park features three 1870s limekilns and other evidence of its history as an important lime producer. The lime was used to make mortar to build the brick buildings of San Francisco and other California cities.

Starting from the Felton Empire Road trailhead just west of Felton, take Bennett Creek Trail gently downhill from the parking lot for 0.25 mile. Immediately you are serenaded by the music of Fall Creek, which quickly drowns out the sound of the nearby road. A left turn on Fall Creek Trail sends you traipsing alongside the

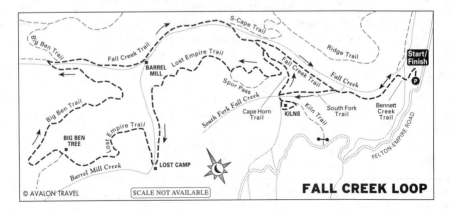

FALL CREEK LOOP

stream, nestled in a cool, shady forest of mixed hardwoods—tan oaks, Douglas firs, big-leaf maples, and bay laurel. (It's worth scheduling a special autumn visit around the colorful big-leaf maples.)

As the trail keeps to the clear, rocky stream, you'll witness a marvelous fern forest, including some huge woodwardia ferns. The park is home to more than 12 fern species. Sorrel and sugar scoop carpet the spaces between them.

Three-quarters of a mile from the trailhead, turn left at the path signed for Lime Kilns. Now following South Fork Trail along South Fork Fall Creek, you'll approach the kiln area in less than 0.5 mile. Evidence of past homesteading is seen along the trail, including spreading purple vinca, English ivy, and low rock walls. About 40 kiln workers and their families lived in this canyon in the late 1800s. The kilns were built by the IXL Lime Company to process limestone from nearby Blue Cliff Quarry. For 30 years, fires as hot as 1,700 degrees burned inside their hollow cores, where today delicate maidenhair ferns have taken hold.

Behind the kilns is the old railroad grade that carried limestone from the quarry. The rock was transported up and down the hill via a gravity cable system.

From the kiln area, head to your right and cross South Fork Fall Creek on Cape Horn Trail. Follow Cape Horn Trail 0.5 mile to Lost Empire Trail, where you turn sharply left and head uphill. Climbing above Fall Creek canyon, you'll face a healthy ascent for almost a mile. The trail levels out for a 0.5-mile stretch to Lost Camp, where Barrel Mill Creek runs through. In the autumn, it's wise to bring your hard hat for this stretch—acorns from the tan oaks come pelting down like raindrops through the forest.

Next comes a second climb on Lost Empire Trail for 0.75 mile to the Big Ben Tree, a virgin redwood and the high point on this loop at 1,800 feet. The tree is clearly marked at the junction of Lost Empire, Big Ben, and Sunlit Trails. After a break to admire Big Ben, head downhill on Big Ben Trail for 1.4 miles through a forest of big, twisted madrones and Douglas firs. Soon you'll descend back into the redwoods along Fall Creek.

Turn right on Fall Creek Trail to finish out the loop. You have only three miles left to return to the trailhead; the majority of this will be spent right alongside splashing Fall Creek. The upstream area, where the canyon is squeezed, exhibits a tremendous amount of deadfall. The redwoods growing on its steep slopes don't always last through the heavy rains of winter. Fall Creek Trail narrows and gets rougher in this section; you'll have to duck under fallen trees and watch your step on the slippery streamside trail. Look for wild ginger and giant trillium growing nearby. In mid-summer, you may get lucky and spot bright orange leopard lilies blooming along the creek's edges.

On the way back to the trailhead, stop at the Barrel Mill site. This water-powered

© ANN MARIE BROWN

lime kilns at Fall Creek Unit in Henry Cowell Redwoods State Park

mill manufactured parts for the barrels that were used to ship the lime. Massive timbers and some abandoned machinery remain at the streamside site.

Options

November–February, it's practically mandatory that nature lovers head to Natural Bridges State Beach to visit the Monarch Butterfly Preserve and hike the easy Monarch Trail. Those who do will be rewarded with the sight of upwards of 100,000 orange-and-black butterflies flitting about a grove of eucalyptus trees—many which have traveled several thousand miles to enjoy the mild winter here. The hike is only 0.5 mile round-trip; the trail ends at a wooden observation platform at the Monarch Resting Area. One caveat: If it's a cool, gray day, the butterflies will not fly; they'll be huddled up on the tree branches with their wings closed.

To get to Natural Bridges from the junction of Highway 9 and Highway 1 in Santa Cruz, take Highway 1 northwest two miles to Swift Street and turn left (west). Follow the signs to Natural Bridges State Beach.

Directions

From I-280 in San Jose, take Highway 17 south for 24 miles to Scotts Valley. Take the Mount Hermon Road exit, turn right, and drive 3.5 miles. Turn right on Graham Hill Road and drive 0.1 mile to Highway 9. Continue straight across Highway 9 onto Felton Empire Road. Drive 0.6 mile on Felton Empire Road to the Fall Creek trailhead on the right. (The main Henry Cowell State Park entrance requires a left turn on Highway 9.)

Or, from Highway 1 in Santa Cruz, take Highway 9 north for 7.5 miles to Felton Empire Road. Turn left and continue as described.

Information and Contact

There is no fee at the Fall Creek Unit parking lot. Dogs and bikes are not allowed. A park map is available at the Henry Cowell Nature Center and/or entrance kiosk at the main state park entrance on Highway 9. A detailed map of the area is available from Pease Press, 415/387-1437, www.peasepress.com (ask for the *Trails of Santa Cruz* map), or by download at www.virtualparks.org ($1 fee). For more information, contact Henry Cowell Redwoods State Park, 101 North Big Trees Park Road, Felton, CA 95018, 831/335-4598 or 831/335-7077 (nature center), www.mountainparks.org.

28 OBSERVATION DECK AND BIG ROCK HOLE LOOP

Henry Cowell Redwoods State Park

Level: Moderate

Total Distance: 6.4 miles round-trip

Hiking Time: 3.5 hours

Elevation Change: 1,000 feet

Summary: Big trees, San Lorenzo River swimming holes, and a high observation deck are the highlights of this ramble.

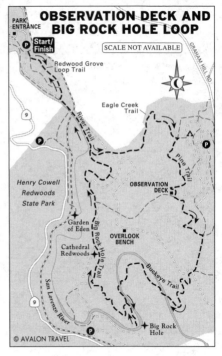

Henry Cowell Redwoods State Park is celebrated for its ancient groves of coast redwoods. It's famous for its Roaring Camp Railroad steam trains, whose whistles blow as they steam around tracks that carve through the center of the park. And the park is well known for the San Lorenzo River, whose rushing waters are home to runs of salmon and steelhead in winter.

But surprisingly, most visitors never hike any farther than the 0.75-mile Redwood Grove Loop Trail that starts by the nature center. Too bad, because miles of footpaths roll gently alongside the river, cruising through dense groves of redwoods, laurels, and Douglas firs, and traversing chaparral-covered slopes. This loop trip tours these areas and visits many of the park's highlights.

Note that the loop described requires two unbridged crossings of the San Lorenzo River. If you're hiking when the river is running too high, you'll have to shorten the loop to bypass the fords. Use good judgment about crossing. Also, carry a park map to help negotiate your way through this loop's many junctions.

Begin your hike by following the short Redwood Grove Loop Trail. This popular path through huge first-growth redwoods is worth seeing; the rest of the park's redwoods are mostly second-growth. Take either leg of the loop into the marvelous virgin grove, then exit the trail at the far end of the loop. Follow the signed path

In the summer months, hikers ford the San Lorenzo River to access the swimming hole at Big Rock Hole.

to paved Pipeline Road, which is popular with dog walkers and bicyclists. Cross the pavement and pick up the hikers-only River Trail, which parallels Pipeline Road and closely follows the east bank of the river. Although the river is only a few inches deep in summer, it can be 20–30 feet deep during winter rains. Its banks are lined with willows, cottonwoods, and sycamores.

In short order, you'll pass under a railroad trestle crossing the San Lorenzo River. Chances are good that at some point during your hike you'll hear the wail of a train screeching around a curve in the canyon. The privately operated Roaring Camp Railroad runs through the park (the ticket office and station are located near the parking lot by the nature center). Some say that the trains sound more like the "Wailing" Camp Railroad.

A quarter-mile beyond the trestle, River Trail and neighboring Pipeline Road meet up with Eagle Creek and its namesake trail. Bear left on Eagle Creek Trail, heading through the redwoods and Douglas firs to begin a moderate ascent into higher, madrone- and manzanita-covered slopes. The trail gets steeper as you go. Small cascades and pools line the stream after winter rains.

Soon after crossing Eagle Creek on a footbridge, turn right on Pine Trail. The earth beneath your feet suddenly gets sandy, and walking becomes more difficult on the sunny, exposed ridge. Follow the signs leading through sun-loving chaparral to the park's observation deck.

This 15-foot-high concrete structure is surrounded by a picnic table, hitching post, and water fountain, plus two surprising kinds of trees: knobcone pines and ponderosa pines. The latter, with its distinctive jigsaw puzzle bark, usually is found at much higher elevations in places like the Sierra Nevada. Here at 800 feet in elevation in the Santa Cruz Mountains, the ponderosa pine grows only in this strange "sand hill chaparral" community. This region's sandy soil is what remains of an ancient ocean floor. Four million years ago, a shallow sea completely covered the area.

Walk up the observation platform's stairs and you'll have a somewhat obstructed view of Monterey Bay. Even if the view is only fair, the sunny platform is a convenient place to sit down and have lunch, or maybe take a catnap.

If the San Lorenzo River was running wide and deep at the start of your trip, now is the time to cut this loop short and follow Ridge Fire Road downhill and back to River Trail. If the river looks safe to cross, continue on Pine Trail to its junction with Powder Mill Fire Road. Follow Powder Mill downhill for 0.5 mile to where it crosses Pipeline Road, then take single-track Buckeye Trail downhill for another 0.5 mile through several switchbacks and across the San Lorenzo River. This is the first of two fords. On the river's far side, Buckeye Trail winds along the riverbank, then crosses it again. Pass an obvious swimming hole on your left, Big Rock Hole, which is lined with granite boulders. If it's summertime, you'll be tempted to take a dip.

After a swim and a rest, you'll be ready to climb again. Follow Big Rock Hole Trail steeply uphill for 0.5 mile to its junction with Rincon Fire Road, where you'll find the Cathedral Redwoods Grove. These trees aren't as large or old as those on the Redwood Loop Trail, but they offer more solitude and a chance to catch your breath after the challenging climb.

Rincon Fire Road continues northward back to a junction with River Trail. The latter will bring you back to the Eagle Creek junction, the railroad trestle, Pipeline Road, Redwood Loop Trail, and finally, the nature center and your car.

Options

Campers at Henry Cowell Redwoods should take a walk on Eagle Creek Trail, which leads 1.5 miles to the park's main redwood grove and nature center (via Eagle Creek Trail and a right turn on River Trail). Or you can take Eagle Creek Trail to visit the observation deck and make a 2.8-mile loop. This lovely trail begins between campsites 82 and 84 and heads gently downhill alongside Eagle Creek to Pipeline Road and River Trail just beyond. Turn left on either of these trails and loop back via Ridge Fire Road to visit the observation deck, then follow Pine Trail back to the campground.

Directions

From I-280 in San Jose, take Highway 17 south for 24 miles to Scotts Valley. Take the Mount Hermon Road exit, turn right, and drive 3.5 miles. Turn right on Graham Hill Road and drive 0.1 mile to Highway 9. Turn left on Highway 9 and drive 0.6 mile to Henry Cowell Redwoods State Park on the left. Continue past the entrance kiosk to the visitors center and main parking lot. Follow the signs to the Redwood Grove and Redwood Loop Trail.

Or, from Highway 1 in Santa Cruz, take Highway 9 north for six miles to the right turnoff for the park.

Information and Contact

A $10 day-use fee is charged per vehicle. Leashed dogs are allowed only on paved Pipeline Road. Bikes are allowed on some trails. A park map is available at the entrance kiosk and/or nature center for $2. A detailed map of the area is available from Pease Press, 415/387-1437, www.peasepress.com (ask for the *Trails of Santa Cruz* map). For more information, contact Henry Cowell Redwoods State Park, 101 North Big Trees Park Road, Felton, CA 95018, 831/335-4598 or 831/335-7077 (nature center), www.mountainparks.org.

29 OLD LANDING COVE TRAIL

Wilder Ranch State Park

BEST C

Level: Easy

Total Distance: 2.5 miles round-trip

Hiking Time: 1.5 hours

Elevation Change: Negligible

Summary: The dramatic Davenport shoreline is spread out before you on this easy, inviting walk.

One foggy November afternoon, we tossed off our responsibilities and headed for the coast south of Davenport and Wilder Ranch State Park. Bundled in our fleece jackets to ward off the gloomy weather, we set off on Old Landing Cove Trail.

In our first 10 minutes of walking, we spotted a bobcat as he leapt off the trail and into the surrounding bushes. Moments later we admired the soaring flight of a harrier over the bluffs and pelicans over the sea. A few more footsteps and we peered down on dozens of harbor seals hauled out on rocks just off the coast. Leaving the bluff-top trail for the sands of Fern Grotto Beach, I marveled at two remarkably divergent creatures that had washed up onshore: a six-inch-long, bright orange sea sponge and the decaying remains of a 20-foot gray whale.

You never know quite what you'll find at Wilder Ranch State Park. A walk on the park's Old Landing Cove Trail is short and easy, but the rewards are great. Spotting wildlife is nearly a given. But even if you aren't fortunate enough to have a bobcat cross your path, you'll still enjoy the trail's other highlights, including a seal rookery, spectacular jagged bluffs, sandy beaches, and a hidden fern cave.

Many people think of Wilder Ranch as a mountain biker's park, but the reality is that most riders stick to the trails on the inland side of the park, across Highway 1. The few bikers you'll find on the short, level Old Landing Cove Trail are absolute beginners or those who are here only for the scenery. They won't be traveling very fast.

Old Landing Cove Trail starts from the parking lot to the right of the restrooms. Bordered by tall, scented stalks of anise, the trail is a wide ranch road that makes a short and direct path to the edge of the ocean. Soon you'll be walking alongside the park's brussels sprout fields. Wilder Ranch's biggest claim to fame may not be its historic ranch buildings, nor its well-developed trail system, nor its alluring beaches and coastal vistas. It's the fact that 12 percent of our national brussels sprouts production happens right here within the park's boundaries. One question: Who's eating all of them, anyway?

Follow the trail toward the coast, then turn right and head out along the sandstone and mudstone bluffs. The first beach you'll see, Wilder Beach, is a critical habitat area for the endangered snowy plover and is fenced off and protected as a natural preserve. An overlook platform with a bench serves as a viewing spot.

In 200 yards you'll reach the trail's namesake, the old landing cove—a remarkably narrow inlet where small schooners pulled in to anchor and load lumber in the late 1800s. Just off Old Landing Cove is a huge flat rock where harbor seals haul out at low tide. They require sunshine to warm their flippers, the only part of their body that isn't well insulated. Your best view of the harbor seals comes after you pass the cove and look back, or on your return trip.

The trail continues along the bluff tops. A highlight of this hike is the descent to Fern Grotto Beach to see Wilder Ranch's fern cave, the oceanside home of a collection of bracken and sword ferns. They hang from the shallow cave's ceiling just low enough to tickle the top of your head. The fern cave is hidden in the back of a sandy, U-shaped cove; it is accessible from the bluff top via a spur path. Watch for post 8 along the main trail; the spur is found a few yards beyond.

© KEVIN GONG

Some of Santa Cruz's loveliest beaches are found along the Old Landing Cove Trail.

The cave's location in the back of the oval-shaped cove partially protects it from the salty ocean air. An underground spring gives the ferns life and keeps them moist and cool. Water continually drips from the cave's ceiling. The floor is covered in driftwood of all shapes and sizes, which has been collected from the sea by the constant motion of the tide.

After admiring the fern grotto, return to the top of the bluffs and Old Landing Cove Trail. A quarter-mile north lies the next beach cove, Sand Plant Beach. A wider and more visible trail leads down to its perfect crescent-shaped strip of sand—an ideal place to have a picnic lunch or sit and watch the waves come in.

Options

Beyond Sand Plant Beach, the Old Landing Cove Trail changes names to Ohlone Bluff Trail. In the next 2.5 miles, the path passes several more beaches: Strawberry, Needle Rock, Three Mile, and finally Four Mile. Explore as far as you like, but be forewarned: The more remote stretches of sand are famous for their clothing-optional tendencies. Also note that the bluffs inland from Sand Plant Beach are private farming property; most of the year hikers cannot pass through. To access the trail north of Sand Plant Beach, you simply take the spur trail down to the sand, walk to the far side of the cove, then follow another spur trail back up to the bluffs, bypassing the private property.

Directions

From Santa Cruz, drive north on Highway 1 for four miles. Turn left into the entrance to Wilder Ranch State Park, then follow the park road to its end and park in the main parking area. Old Landing Cove Trail starts to the right of the restrooms.

Information and Contact

A $10 day-use fee is charged per vehicle. Dogs are not allowed. Bikes are allowed. A park map is available at the entrance kiosk or by free download at www.parks. ca.gov. A detailed map of the area is available from Pease Press, 415/387-1437, www.peasepress.com (ask for the *Trails of Santa Cruz* map). For more information, contact Wilder Ranch State Park, 1401 Old Coast Road, Santa Cruz, CA 95060, 831/423-9703, www.thatsmypark.org or www.parks.ca.gov.

Public transportation: Santa Cruz Metropolitan Transit District Bus #42 stops at Wilder Ranch State Park. For more information, phone 831/425-8600 or visit www.scmtd.com.

30 LOMA PRIETA GRADE AND BRIDGE CREEK LOOP
The Forest of Nisene Marks State Park

BEST 🄲

🥾 ❀ 🚌

Level: Moderate   **Total Distance:** 7.0 or 9.0 miles round-trip

Hiking Time: 4-5 hours   **Elevation Change:** 600 feet

Summary: With easy access from Aptos, the Forest of Nisene Marks is a popular park that offers shady hiking, a sylvan waterfall, and a wealth of fascinating history.

The Forest of Nisene Marks is a relatively undeveloped state park. It's the kind of park that doesn't have car campgrounds, a visitors center, or even paved parking lots. Sounds good, yes? It just gets better. In terms of scenery, the park is like a young cousin to popular Big Basin Redwoods State Park, filled with second-growth redwoods, more ferns than you can shake a stick at, and banana slugs and newts by the dozen. And just like Big Basin, Nisene Marks even boasts a couple of winsome waterfalls.

Two major forces have shaped the land here: the railroad and unstable geology. Although virgin redwoods remained untouched in this steep and winding canyon for hundreds of years, the Loma Prieta Lumber Company procured the valley in 1881 and teamed up with Southern Pacific Railroad to destroy it—oops, I mean

Aptos Creek Trail crosses Aptos Creek under a canopy of big-leaf maples.

© ANN MARIE BROWN

log it. They built a railroad along Aptos Creek and worked the land with trains, oxen, skid roads, inclines, horses, and as many men as they could recruit, removing 140 million board feet of lumber over the course of 40 years. In 1922, when the loggers finally put down their saws, there were no trees left.

Luckily, Mother Nature has been busy since the logging ceased. Today the canyon is filled with Douglas firs and second-growth redwoods; the higher ridges are lined with oaks and madrones.

Mother Nature was especially busy on October 17, 1989, when the park was the epicenter of the Loma Prieta earthquake, which forcefully shook the entire Bay Area. You can visit the epicenter via a hike on Aptos Creek Trail, but there is little to see except a sign marking the spot.

A more interesting hike is the seven- or nine-mile semi-loop up Loma Prieta Grade to Maple Falls, returning via Bridge Creek Trail. The mileage varies according to where you leave your car. In winter, the park road is usually closed off at Georges Picnic Area, requiring a longer walk. If you can park up the road at Porter Picnic Area, you'll save a couple of miles.

From either trailhead begin hiking on Aptos Creek Road, a wide multiuse trail that travels under a thriving canopy of second-growth redwoods. A quarter-mile past Porter Picnic Area, Loma Prieta Grade takes off on the left. Follow this old railroad grade and leave Aptos Creek Road and the mountain bikers behind. The rest of the loop is open to hikers only.

As soon as you're on single-track, what was good becomes gorgeous. You hike among tall trees and ferns alongside Aptos Creek. Considering the lush green canopy of redwoods and Douglas firs in the canyon, it's hard to imagine the clear-cutting that took place here. At a fork signed for Bridge Creek Historic Site to the right, bear left to stay on Loma Prieta Grade. The right fork will be the return of your loop to Maple Falls.

The worn old railroad grade enters into its prettiest stretch as it climbs gently up the slopes above Bridge Creek. The trail is often quite narrow and eroded, so watch your footing. You'll pass Hoffmans Historic Site, the location of a logging camp that was nicknamed Camp Comfort. It housed 300 workers and was used until 1921. The camp's ruins are slowly rotting away.

Four miles from Porter Picnic Area, Loma Prieta Grade ends at Bridge Creek Historic Site, the location of another former logging camp. From here, you'll make a 0.5-mile stream scramble up Bridge Creek to Maple Falls (there is no formal trail, but the route is obvious). Bridge Creek's canyon walls squeeze tighter as you travel upstream, providing close-up looks at the millions of ferns and mini-waterfalls dropping among the rocks and crevices. When Bridge Creek is running strong, you'll have to walk in the creek bed and cross the stream a dozen or more times, so wear your waterproof boots. In summer, the canyon scramble is much easier, but the waterfall is less impressive.

Keep going until you reach the back of the canyon, where its walls pinch together and 30-foot Maple Falls pours over a sandstone wall, blocking any further progress. A few big-leaf maple trees frame the falls. After paying homage to the charming cataract, retrace your steps down the canyon to Bridge Creek Historic Site and take the left fork on Bridge Creek Trail. As you hike through the redwood-lined canyon, look carefully for fossils embedded in the soft sandstone lining the stream. You'll cross Bridge Creek one more time, then rejoin Loma Prieta Grade where you started your loop. Retrace your steps back to the parking area.

Options

Those seeking a more adventurous trip might want to head out in search of Aptos Creek Falls, also called Five Finger Falls. The hike is 12 miles roundtrip, and can be accomplished only when the water level in Aptos Creek is low enough so that you can ford. (As you near the falls, you will have to cross Aptos Creek on foot; there is no bridge.) Follow the main Aptos Creek Road 2.5 miles to the "Bottom of the Incline," just before the old railroad grade begins its ascent near the earthquake epicenter, then cut off on Aptos Creek Trail and cross the creek. Follow Aptos Creek Trail for 2.5 miles to the

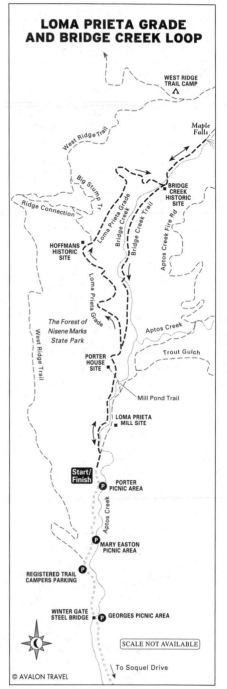

LOMA PRIETA GRADE AND BRIDGE CREEK LOOP

© AVALON TRAVEL

Big Slide Trail junction; one mile farther lies the waterfall, gracefully lined with five-finger ferns.

Directions

From Santa Cruz, drive south on Highway 1 for six miles to the Aptos/State Park Drive exit. Bear left at the exit, cross over the highway, then turn right on Soquel Drive and drive 0.5 mile. Turn left on Aptos Creek Road. Stop at the park entrance kiosk, then continue up the road to Georges Picnic Area or Porter Picnic Area. (Parking at Porter Picnic Area will cut two miles off your round-trip, but the park road is closed beyond Georges Picnic Area in winter.)

Public transportation: Santa Cruz Metropolitan Transit District Bus #54 stops on Soquel Drive 0.5 mile from the park entrance. For more information, phone 831/425-8600 or visit www.scmtd.com.

Information and Contact

An $8 day-use fee is charged per vehicle. Dogs are not allowed. Bikes are allowed only on fire roads. A park map is available at the entrance kiosk or by download at www.virtualparks.org ($1 fee). A detailed map of the area is available from Pease Press, 415/387-1437, www.peasepress.com (ask for the *Trails of Santa Cruz* map). For more information, contact the Forest of Nisene Marks State Park, Aptos Creek Road, Aptos, CA 95001, 831/763-7062, www.thatsmypark.org or www.parks.ca.gov.

RESOURCES

NAPA AND SONOMA PARK AGENCIES

Annadel State Park
6201 Channel Drive
Santa Rosa, CA 95409
707/539-3911
www.parks.sonoma.net or
www.parks.ca.gov

Bothe-Napa Valley State Park & Robert Louis Stevenson State Park
3801 St. Helena Highway North
Calistoga, CA 94515
707/942-4575
www.parks.ca.gov

Jack London State Historic Park
2400 London Ranch Road
Glen Ellen, CA 95442
707/938-5216
www.jacklondonpark.com or
www.parks.ca.gov

Knoxville Wildlife Area
Fish and Game Bay Delta
Regional Office
7329 Silverado Trail
Napa, CA 94599
707/944-5531 or 707/944-5537
www.dfg.ca.gov

Rush Ranch
Solano Land Trust
1001 Texas Street
Fairfield, CA 94533
707/432-0150
www.solanolandtrust.org

Skyline Wilderness Park
2201 Imola Avenue
Napa, CA 94510
707/252-0481
www.skylinepark.org

Sonoma Coast State Park
3095 Highway 1
Bodega Bay, CA 94923
707/875-3483 or 707/865-2391
www.parks.sonoma.net or
www.parks.ca.gov

Sonoma County Regional Parks
2300 County Circle Drive
Santa Rosa, CA 95403
707/565-2041
www.sonoma-county.org or
www.parks.sonoma.net

Sugarloaf Ridge State Park
2605 Adobe Canyon Road
Kenwood, CA 95452
707/833-5712
www.parks.sonoma.net or
www.parks.ca.gov

MARIN PARK AGENCIES

Angel Island State Park
P.O. Box 318
Tiburon, CA 94920
415/435-1915 or 415/435-5390
www.angelisland.org or
www.parks.ca.gov

Audubon Canyon Ranch
4900 Highway 1
Stinson Beach, CA 94970

415/868-9244
www.egret.org

China Camp State Park
101 Peacock Gap Trail
San Rafael, CA 94901
415/456-0766
www.parks.ca.gov

Marin County Open Space District
3501 Civic Center Drive, Room 415
San Rafael, CA 94903
415/499-6387
www.marinopenspace.org

Marin Headlands/Golden Gate National Recreation Area
Fort Barry, Building 948
Sausalito, CA 94965
415/331-1540
www.nps.gov/goga

Marin Municipal Water District
220 Nellen Avenue
Corte Madera, CA 94925
415/945-1438
www.marinwater.org

Mount Tamalpais State Park
801 Panoramic Highway
Mill Valley, CA 94941
415/388-2070
www.mttam.net or
www.parks.ca.gov

Muir Woods National Monument
Mill Valley, CA 94941
415/388-2595
www.nps.gov/muwo

Olompali State Historic Park
P.O. Box 1016
Novato, CA 94948
415/892-3383
www.parks.ca.gov

Point Reyes National Seashore
Point Reyes, CA 94956
415/464-5100
www.nps.gov/pore

Samuel P. Taylor State Park
P.O. Box 251
Lagunitas, CA 94938
415/488-9897
www.parks.ca.gov

Tomales Bay State Park
1208 Pierce Point Road
Inverness, CA 94937
415/669-1140
www.parks.ca.gov

EAST BAY PARK AGENCIES
East Bay Regional Park District
2950 Peralta Oaks Court
P.O. Box 5381
Oakland, CA 94605
888/327-2757
www.ebparks.org

Mount Diablo State Park
96 Mitchell Canyon Road
Clayton, CA 94517
925/837-2525 or 925/837-0904
www.mdia.org or
www.parks.ca.gov

PENINSULA AND SOUTH BAY PARK AGENCIES

Año Nuevo State Reserve
New Years Creek Road
Pescadero, CA 94060
650/879-2025 or 650/879-0227
www.parks.ca.gov

Big Basin Redwoods State Park
21600 Big Basin Way
Boulder Creek, CA 95006
831/338-8860
www.bigbasin.org

Butano State Park
1500 Cloverdale Road
Pescadero, CA 94060
650/879-2040
www.parks.ca.gov

Castle Rock State Park
15000 Skyline Boulevard
Los Gatos, CA 95020
408/867-2952
www.parks.ca.gov

Fitzgerald Marine Reserve
P.O. Box 451
Moss Beach, CA 94038
650/728-3584
www.eparks.net

The Forest of Nisene Marks State Park
Aptos Creek Road
Aptos, CA 95001
831/763-7062
www.thatsmypark.org or
www.parks.ca.gov

Golden Gate National Recreation Area
Fort Mason, Building 201
San Francisco, CA 94123
415/561-4700 or 415/561-4323
www.nps.gov/goga

Henry Cowell Redwoods State Park
101 North Big Trees Park Road
Felton, CA 95018
831/335-4598 or 831/335-7077
www.mountainparks.org

Henry W. Coe State Park
9000 East Dunne Avenue
Morgan Hill, CA 95038
408/779-2728
www.coepark.org

Loch Lomond Recreation Area
100 Loch Lomond Way
Felton, CA 95018
831/335-7424
www.cityofsantacruz.com

Midpeninsula Regional Open Space District
330 Distel Circle
Los Altos, CA 94022
650/691-1200
www.openspace.org

Portola Redwoods State Park
9000 Portola State Park Road,
Building F
La Honda, CA 94020
650/948-9098
www.parks.ca.gov or
www.santacruzstateparks.org

Sam McDonald County Park
13435 Pescadero Creek Road
Loma Mar, CA 94021
650/879-0238
www.eparks.net

San Bruno Mountain State and County Park
555 Guadalupe Canyon Parkway
Brisbane, CA 94005
650/992-6770
www.eparks.net

San Mateo County Parks and Recreation
455 County Center, Fourth Floor
Redwood City, CA 94063
650/363-4020
www.eparks.net

San Pedro Valley County Park
600 Oddstad Boulevard
Pacifica, CA 94044
650/355-8289
www.eparks.net

Santa Clara County Parks and Recreation Department
298 Garden Hill Drive
Los Gatos, CA 95032
408/355-2200
www.parkhere.org

Wilder Ranch State Park
1401 Old Coast Road
Santa Cruz, CA 95060
831/423-9703

www.thatsmypark.org or www.parks.ca.gov

Wunderlich Park
4040 Woodside Road
Woodside, CA 94062
650/851-1210
www.eparks.net

MAP SOURCES
Always obtain a detailed map of the area in which you will be hiking. Particularly helpful are maps that include trails, streams, peaks, and topographic lines. Following are some excellent map sources.

Map Link
30 South La Patera Lane, Unit 5
Santa Barbara, CA 93117
805/692-6777 or 800/962-1394
www.maplink.com

Pease Press
1717 Cabrillo Street
San Francisco, CA 94121
415/387-1437
www.peasepress.com

Tom Harrison Maps
2 Falmouth Cove
San Rafael, CA 94901
415/456-7940
www.tomharrisonmaps.com

U.S. Geological Survey Branch of Information Services
P.O. Box 25286
Federal Center
Denver, CO 80225
303/202-4700 or 888/ASK-USGS
(888/275-8747)
www.usgs.gov

INTERNET RESOURCES

San Francisco Bay Area Hiking Clubs

Looking for some friends to hike with? Check out these Bay Area hiking clubs:

Bay Area Jewish Singles Hiking Club
www.bajshc.org

Bay Area Orienteering Club
www.baoc.org

Berkeley Hiking Club
www.berkeleyhikingclub.pair.com

California Alpine Club
www.calalpineclub.com

Contra Costa Hills Club
www.contracostahills.org

East Bay Barefoot Hikers
www.unshod.org/ebbfhike

East Bay Casual Hiking Group
http://hiking.bondon.com

Hayward Hiking Club
www.haywardhikers.weebly.com

Mary and Martin Hikes
www.maryandmartinhikes.com

North Bay Christian Hikers
www.northbaychristianhikers.com

North Bay Hiking Group
www.northbayhikes.com

Orinda Hiking Club
www.orindahiking.org

San Francisco Hiking Club
www.sfhiking.com

Sierra Club Loma Prieta Chapter
(Peninsula and South Bay)
www.lomaprieta.sierraclub.org

Sierra Club San Francisco Bay Chapter
(Marin, San Francisco, and East Bay)
www.sanfranciscobay.sierraclub.org

South Bay Ramblers
www.southbayramblers.com

Walk California
www.walkcalifornia.com

Wildflower Information

California Academy of Sciences
www.research.calacademy.org/botany

California Native Plant Society
www.cnps.org

Friends of the Regional Parks Botanic Garden
www.nativeplants.org

A Photo Album of Coe Park Wildflowers
www.coepark.org/wildflowers/
flower-album.html

Wildflower Hotline
www.theodorepayne.org/hotline/
hotlinelinks.html

Yerba Buena Nursery
www.yerbabuenanursery.com

Other Sources for Bay Area Outdoor Information

High/Low Tide Schedules
Tidelines
www.tidelines.com

Hiking Expertise and Gear Reviews
Adventure 16 Outdoor &
Travel Outfitters
www.adventure16.com

Backpacker Magazine
www.backpacker.com

Gear Junkie
www.gearjunkie.com

REI
www.rei.com

Trailspace
www.trailspace.com

Hiking Gear for Your Dog
Ruff Wear: For Dogs on the Go
www.ruffwear.com

Your Active Pet: Adventure Gear
for Your Dog
www.youractivepet.com

Weather Information
National Weather Service
Regional Western Headquarters
www.wrh.noaa.gov

San Francisco Chronicle
www.sfgate.com/weather

The Weather Channel
www.weather.com

Index

www.moon.com

DESTINATIONS | ACTIVITIES | BLOGS | MAPS | BOOKS

MOON.COM is ready to help plan your next trip! Filled with fresh trip ideas and strategies, author interviews, informative travel blogs, a detailed map library, and descriptions of all the Moon guidebooks, Moon.com is all you need to get out and explore the world—or even places in your own backyard. While at Moon.com, sign up for our monthly e-newsletter for updates on new releases, travel tips, and expert advice from our on-the-go Moon authors. As always, when you travel with Moon, expect an experience that is uncommon and truly unique.

MOON IS ON FACEBOOK—BECOME A FAN!
JOIN THE MOON PHOTO GROUP ON FLICKR